The Land and the Book

You are holding a reproduction of an original work that is in the public domain in the United States of America, and possibly other countries. You may freely copy and distribute this work as no entity (individual or corporate) has a copyright on the body of the work. This book may contain prior copyright references, and library stamps (as most of these works were scanned from library copies). These have been scanned and retained as part of the historical artifact.

This book may have occasional imperfections such as missing or blurred pages, poor pictures, errant marks, etc. that were either part of the original artifact, or were introduced by the scanning process. We believe this work is culturally important, and despite the imperfections, have elected to bring it back into print as part of our continuing commitment to the preservation of printed works worldwide. We appreciate your understanding of the imperfections in the preservation process, and hope you enjoy this valuable book.

JERUSALEM FROM THE MOUNT OF OLIVES.

THE LAND AND THE BOOK;

OR,

BIBLICAL ILLUSTRATIONS DRAWN FROM THE MANNERS AND CUSTOMS, THE SCENES AND SCENERY OF

THE HOLY LAND.

By W. M. THOMSON, D.D.,

TWENTY-FIVE YEARS A MISSIONARY OF THE A.B.C.F.M. IN SYRIA AND PALESTINE.

Maps, Engravings, &c.

IN TWO VOLUMES.

VOL. II.

NEW YORK:
HARPER & BROTHERS, PUBLISHERS,
FRANKLIN SQUARE.
1860.

Entered, according to Act of Congress, in the year one thousand eight hundred and fifty-eight, by

HARPER & BROTHERS,

In the Clerk's Office of the District Court for the Southern District of New York.

LIST OF ENGRAVINGS IN VOL. II.

	PAGE
Jerusalem from the Mount of Olives	Frontispiece.
View of an Arab House	6
Lodge at Butaiha	11
Teraphim	25
Ruins of Gadara	61
Shooting the Rapids (of the Jordan)	64
Lake of Tiberias, from the Baths	67
Tiberias and Lake looking to the Northeast	73
Centipede	95
Wild Mustard	100
Syrian Locust	103
Mejdel and the Plain of Gennesaret	109
Assault of Robbers (at Irbid)	114
Kulaet Ibn M'an, Wady Hamam	115
Kefr Kenna	119
The Vale of Nazareth	127
Sefûrieh—Plain of Buttauf	133
Tabor	137
Khan et Tejjar—Arab Fair	153
Nain and Little Hermon	159
Beisan (Bethshan)	172
Colocynth	179
Jezreel	181
Painted Eye	184
Meel and Mûkhûly	184
Jenin	187
Samaria	195
Entrance to Nablûs	201
Jacob's Well, Shechem	207
Foundations of Samaritan Temple on Gerizim	213
Plan of Theatre	237
Mole of the Harbor of Cæsarea	241
Crocodile	245
Ancient Harbor of Cæsarea	253
Water-spout	256
Flying-fish	258
Stone Pine (Tree)	265
Cone of the Pine	266
Pinus Orientalis	267

Vol. II.—A

LIST OF ENGRAVINGS.

	PAGE
Jaffa from the North	271
Na'ura—Persian Water-wheel	276
Shadûf	277
The Na'ura, or Water-wheel at Hamath	279
The Potter and Wheel	282
Fountain in Jaffa	285
Lydd	291
Church of St. George (at Lydd)	292
Women grinding at a Mill	294
View of Ramleh	297
Well near Emmaus	305
Mowrej (Threshing Instrument)	314
Egyptian Mowrej	315
Usdûd (Ashdod)	317
Ruins of Askelon	325
Serpent at Gaza	332
Gaza	334
Shield and Spear	344
Dancing-girls	345
Beit Jibrin	359
Swords, Khanjars, and Daggers	371
Syrian Bear	373
Arab Camp	377
Water-jars and Bottles	379
Mandrake Leaf, Flower, and Root	380
Hebron	389
Pomegranates	393
Egyptian Donkeys	407
Lentils ('Adis)	409
Lower Pool of Hebron	410
Rock of Masada	417
Wild Goats	421
Ground-plan of Solomon's Pools	422
Tekoa—Fureidis	425
Valley of Etam (Urtas)	429
Convent of Santa Saba	433
Juniper	437
Plain of Jericho—North End of Dead Sea	441
Dead Sea from the North	447
View around North End of Dead Sea from Akabet ed Deir	459
Dead Sea from Top of Olivet	465
Wall at Southeast Corner of Temple Area	472
Golden Gate, Interior View	473
Tower of David	475
Tombs in the Valley of Jehoshaphat	479
Absalom's Tomb (restored)	482
The Mount of Olives, Church of the Virgin, &c.	485
Tombs of the Kings	487

LIST OF ENGRAVINGS.

	PAGE
Tombs of the Judges, Front View	489
Lower Pool of Gihon	495
Rachel's Tomb	502
View of Bethlehem	504
Cave of the Nativity	506
Interior of the Church of the Nativity	514
Pool of Hezekiah	522
Pool of Siloam	524
Gibeon from Mizpeh	543
Anathoth (Anata)	549
Church of the Holy Sepulchre (Front View)	558
View of the Holy Sepulchre	561
House of a Christian Family in Jerusalem	568
Specimen of Tesselated Pavement	570
Specimen of Wood Panel-work	571
Kanûn	576
Kanûn, and Mode of playing it	577
Kamanjeh, and Performer on it	578
Mode of playing the 'Ood	578
Deff, Tambourine, and Castanets	579
Derbekkeh	580
Mosque of Omar and Temple Area	581
Vaults under El Aksa	585
Jews' Wailing-place	587
Spring of the great Arch	589
Bethany	598

tiful polish." Jub Yusuf—Well of Joseph—where Moslem

THE LAND AND THE BOOK.

XXV. TABIGA—KERSEH.

Thursday, March 23d.

I PROMISE you a most interesting ride to-day, and, while the loads go directly along the shore to the entrance of the Jordan, we will ascend toward the northeast for half an hour, to visit the site of Chorazin. This triangular part of Naphtali, between the northwestern corner of the lake and Jisr Benat Yacobe, has ever been a wild, semi-deserted region, destitute of water, of trees, and of human habitations, and, of course, there are no *ruins* of importance upon it. It is, however, a fine pasture-field for the flocks of the Arabs, and I found it covered, in mid-winter, with camels and cattle from the cold Jaulan. Those parts adjacent to the shore have neither snow nor frost, and are clothed with grass and flowers in January, but the ascent is very great, not less than two thousand feet at the highest part of the road, and much higher west of it toward Safed, where the hills are often buried under deep snow. The flocks and their shepherds can therefore pass from winter to summer in an hour, and for several months can graduate their range so as to enjoy just the temperature which is most agreeable to their tastes. In May, however, the pasturage dries up, water fails, and the heat sends the flocks and herds to the higher and colder regions east of the Jordan. It is a ride of four hours from Khan Minyeh to the bridge, most of the distance over rough black basalt, interspersed in a few places with a white marble, intensely hard, and sufficiently compact to take a beautiful polish. Jub Yusuf—Well of Joseph—where Moslem tradition locates the pit in which that unfortunate lad was cast by his envious brethren, is midway between the lake and the bridge. The *khan* there is like this of Minyeh, but not so dilapidated, though equally deserted. Indeed, there is not an inhabited house in the entire region. The land, however, is fertile, and in some coming day of peace and prosperity it will be a picturesque, fruitful, and most healthy province.

Before we pass entirely away from this vicinity, I wish to inquire whether there is any thing in the construction of modern Arab houses to explain the manner in which the man sick of the palsy was placed at the feet of Jesus. I have never been able to understand it.

AN ARAB HOUSE.

The record in Mark ii. 1-12 and Luke v. 18-26 states that there was such a dense crowd around our Lord that the four men could not force their way through it, and therefore they went to the roof of the house, broke up part of it, and let down the sick man from above. The following considerations may make this act intelligible. We must banish from our minds every form of European or American houses. Those of Capernaum, as is evident from the ruins, were, like those of modern villages in this same region, low, *very low*, with flat roofs, reached by a stairway from the yard or court. Jesus probably stood in the open *lewan*, and the crowd were around and in front of him. Those who carried the paralytic not being able "to come at him for the press," ascended to the roof, removed so much of it as was necessary, and let down their patient through the aperture. Examine one of these houses, and you see at once that the thing is natural, and easy to be accomplished. The roof is only a few feet high, and by stooping down, and holding the corners of the couch—merely a thickly-padded quilt, as at present in this region—they could let down the sick man without any apparatus of ropes or cords to assist them. And thus, I suppose, they did. The whole affair was the extemporaneous device of plain peasants, accustomed to open their roofs, and let down grain, straw, and other articles, as they still do in this country.

The only difficulty in this explanation is to understand how they could break up the roof without sending down such a shower of dust as to incommode our Lord and those around him. I have often seen it done, and have done it myself to houses in Lebanon, but there is always more dust made than is agreeable. The materials now employed are beams about three feet apart, across which short sticks are arranged close together, and covered with the thickly-matted thorn-bush called *bellan*. Over this is spread a coat of stiff mortar, and then comes the marl or earth which makes the roof. Now it is easy to remove any part of this without injuring the rest. No objection, therefore, would be made on this score by the owners of the house. They had merely to scrape back the earth from a portion of the roof over the *lewan*, take up the thorns and short sticks, and let down the couch between the beams at the very feet of Jesus. The end achieved, they could speedily restore the roof as it was before. I have the impression, however, that the covering, at least of the *lewan*, was not made of earth, but of materials more easily taken up. It may have been merely of coarse matting, like the walls and roofs of Turkman huts, or it may have been made of boards, or even stone slabs (and such I have seen), that could be quickly removed. All that is necessary, however, for us to know is, that the roof was flat, low, easily reached, and easily opened, so as to let down the couch of the sick man; and all these points are rendered intelligible by an acquaintance with modern houses in the villages of Palestine.

But we must now make our way more to the east, across this Wady Nashif, as I hear it called by the Bedawîn. It runs directly down to the lake on the east side of Tell Hûm, and Khorazy lies over against us in that side valley which joins Wady Nashif directly below us. We may as well walk over these basaltic boulders, and each one take care of himself and horse as best he can. And here we are among the shapeless heaps of Chorazin, which attest most impressively the fulfillment of that prophetic curse of the Son of God. I have scarcely a doubt about the correctness of the identification, although Dr. Robinson rejects it, almost with contempt. But the name, Khorazy, is nearly the Arabic for Chorazin; the situation—two miles north of Tell Hûm—is just where we might expect to find it; the ruins are quite adequate to answer the demands of history; *and there is no rival site.* I am utterly at a loss, therefore, to discover any other reason for rejecting it, but that its location at this point might seem to favor the claims of Tell Hûm to be Capernaum. To me, however, this is an additional evidence of the correctness of the identification in both cases. But we must leave the discussion of such questions to those who have leisure and learning, and turn down to the southeast over this vast field of black basalt, to visit the equally prostrate Bethsaida. Both fell beneath the same woe, and both have long been lost to the student and traveler. I am still in doubt as to the actual site of Bethsaida. The name is now generally affixed, in maps, to a *Tell* a short distance up the Jordan, on the east side; but the only ruins of importance are below, along the foot of the hills bordering the vale of the Jordan, and at its debouchure on the west side. When I was here in 1855, the Bedawîn in the Butaiha applied the name Bethsaida to a bank on the shore of the lake which is distinguished by a few palm-trees, and in some modern maps this site is called Misadiyeh, a derivative from the same root as Bethsaida, both having reference to *fishing*. Mesady, however, is the name of a site on the rocky hill *west* of the Jordan, and higher up the gorge. Doubtless the city of Andrew and Peter derived its name from this act and occupation of fishing, and, therefore, it is nearly certain that it was located on the shore, and not several miles from it, at the *Tell* to which the name is now affixed. Josephus also says that it was at the entrance of the Jordan into the lake.

I call your attention, in passing, to these remains of ancient buildings on the *west* side of the river, because we shall have occasion to refer to them hereafter. They mark that part of Bethsaida which was, as I suppose, on the *west* bank of the Jordan, and, of course, in Galilee, while those on the east belong to that part which Philip repaired and called Julias. We shall come among them after crossing the river, which we might do on the sand-bar along the margin of the lake; but I prefer the ford above, where the bottom is less marshy.

Again we meet the mire-loving buffaloes, and they seem as fond of the mud as the very swine.

They are, and when they can not find a marsh they bathe in pure water. I once ascended Olympus above Brusa, and near the very top, buffaloes were lying in a pool of ice-water, collected from the surrounding snow-banks, and they appeared to enjoy this cold bath as much as these do this black mud. By the way, it was just here that Josephus fought the Romans under Sylla; concerning which battle he says, with his usual vanity, "I would have performed great things that day if a certain fate had not been my hinderance; for the horse on which I rode, and upon whose back I fought, fell into a quagmire, and threw me on the ground, and I was bruised on my wrist, and was carried into a certain village called Caphernome or Capernaum."[1] This paragraph is not only curious in itself, but it confirms the idea that Capernaum was at Tell Hûm, and that it was then only a village. But turn up to the margin of this marsh along the foot of the hill, or you will encounter that certain fate which hindered Josephus from doing great exploits against Sylla. These black spongy places are treacherous to the last degree, as David appears to have found by sad experience; for he speaks of sinking in deep mire to which there was no bottom. It is a curious fact that dry, rocky, and mountainous as this country is, yet it abounds in bogs and quagmires to an extraordinary extent. The rivers of Damascus all subside into vast swamps: the Orontes creeps through them from Ribla to Antioch. The Jordan does the same from Dan to Tiberias. The Kishon and the Naamany find their way to the Bay of Acre through bottomless marshes, and so does the Zerka or Crocodile River at Cesarea, the Abu Zabûra, the Kanah, the Falej, and the Aujeh, between that city and Jaffa. David was therefore perfectly familiar with these deceitful and dangerous pits, and could speak of them from painful personal experience.

Here we are at the ford, and though the water is not deep, the bottom is rocky, and there down goes the mule, with all our bedding and wardrobe, into the river. This "certain fate," however, is less painful than that of Josephus, and, as the day is clear and warm, we shall be able to sun and dry every thing before night. And now we have the flowery but rather muddy Butaiha through which to saunter for two hours. Dr. Robinson says correctly that it resembles Gennesaret—the one on the northwest, and the other along the northeast shore of the lake, both well watered and extremely fertile, and also both very unhealthy. The Butaiha has the largest and most permanent brooks, Gennesaret the most numerous and largest fountains. I can confirm the statement of Burkhardt that the Arabs of Butaiha have the earliest cucumbers and melons in all this region. I once visited it in early spring with a guide from Safed,

[1] *Life, 72d paragraph.*

who came, according to custom, to load his mules with these vegetables for the market in that town. The vines are already up and spreading rapidly, and there comes the gardener with a basket of cucumbers to sell, which, of course, we will purchase for our salad in the evening.

LODGE AT BUTAIHA.

And that is the lodge, I suppose, which Isaiah speaks of; just such a frail, temporary thing suggested that sad complaint of the prophet, The daughter of Zion is left as a cottage in a vineyard, as a lodge in a garden of cucumbers.[1]

No doubt; but the true point of the comparison will not appear until the crop is over, and the lodge forsaken by the keeper. Then the poles fall down, or lean every which way, and those green boughs with which it is shaded will have been scattered by the wind, leaving only a ragged, sprawling wreck, a most affecting type of utter desolation—"as Sodom, and like unto Gomorrah."

If this is the Julias which Philip built, and named in honor of the daughter of Cæsar, it was certainly no great compliment.

And yet Josephus says he advanced it to the dignity of a city, both by the number of inhabitants it contained and its other grandeur,[2] of which grandeur nothing now remains but these heaps of unmeaning rubbish. The fact is that the Jewish historian is not to be trusted in such matters. I have visited all the cities which Philip is said to have built, and there neither is, nor could have been, much of royal magnificence about them. This is a fair specimen;

[1] Isaiah i. 8.   [2] Ant. xviii. 2, 1.

and, though Sogana and Seleucia were somewhat larger, they could never have been any thing more than agricultural villages. I suppose Philip repaired and enlarged this part of Bethsaida in order to detach it from Galilee, and to secure to himself this rich plain of Butaiha which appertained to it.

As we have leisure enough while sauntering down this flowery plain, I should like to hear some account of this Jaulan above us. It is the Golan of the Hebrews, the Gaulanitis of the Greeks, and yet is almost an utter blank on our maps and in books of travel.

I have repeatedly explored parts of it, and once rode through it lengthwise from Hermon to the Jermuk. With a pleasant party of friends I started from Banias on the morning of February 28th, to visit first the ruins at Seid Yehuda. After examining these interesting remains of antiquity, we ascended the basaltic hills eastward for more than an hour to Sujan, the Sogana of Philip. The surrounding country was once well cultivated, as appears evident from the broken terraces along the sides of the mountain; but at present it is absolutely deserted by all except lawless Bedawîn. The view from Sujan over the Hûleh and the surrounding regions is magnificent, and I imagine that one great attraction of the place was its cool and healthy atmosphere. From Sujan we wandered upward and eastward over vast fields of lava, without road, or even path, for more than an hour, to Skaik, probably the Sacaca mentioned by Ptolemy. It is one of the largest ruins in Gaulanitis, and was better built than most cities of this region. My aneroid marked 2670 feet for the elevation of this site, and we found the air clear, cold, and bracing. Skaik was inhabited until modern times, and celebrated as the general rendezvous and point of departure for caravans to the east and south; and the existing remains of vast cisterns and caravanserais show that ample provision had been made for the accommodation of these large trading companies.

Half an hour south by west from Skaik is a large and very ancient ruin, called Summakah. This word seems to

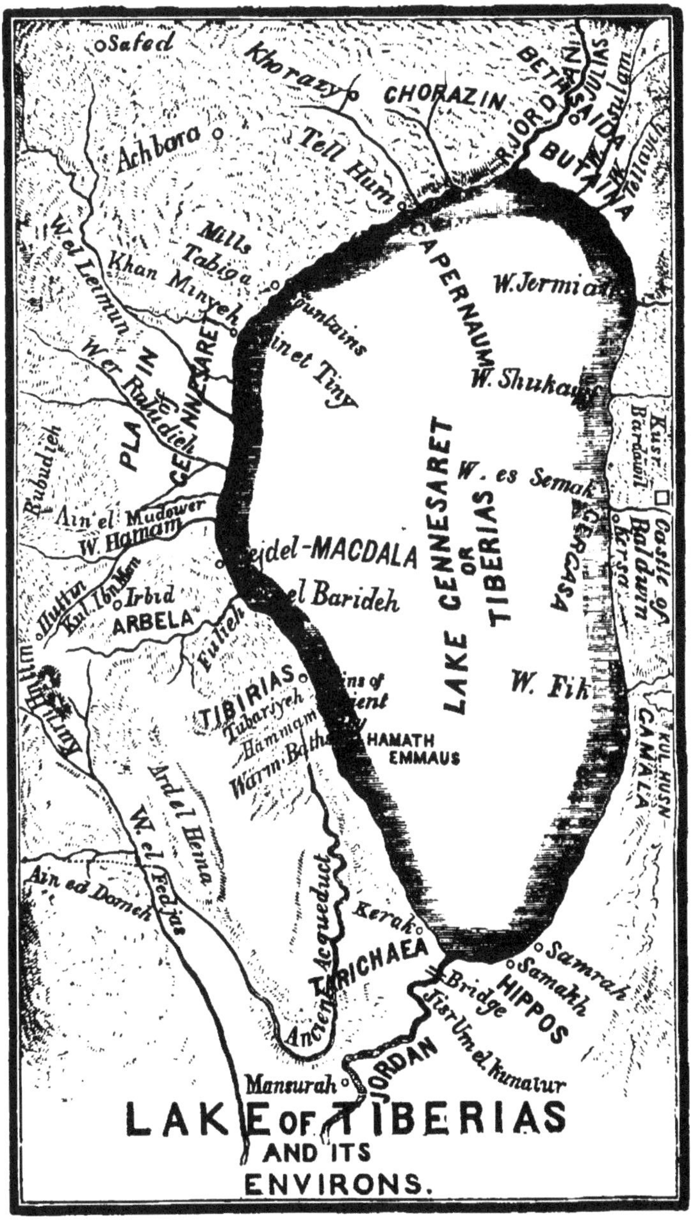

LAKE OF TIBERIAS AND ITS ENVIRONS.

contain the elements of Samachonitis, the Greek name for the Hûleh. It is, however, pronounced as though written with a *koff* (*guttural k*) instead of *kaf*, and in that case it is the name for the bush sŭmmāk, the sumach of the tanner. Whatever be the origin and relations of the name, the position is beautiful, and it is supplied with a fine spring of water, flowing out from the base of the hill. Half an hour farther south are ruins called Joaiza, and there we encamped for the night, near the tent of the Emeer Hussein el Fŭdle—the supreme chief of all the Arabs in that part of the Jaulan. He is a young man of quiet manners and modest deportment, of few words, but sincere and truthful—all remarkable exceptions in his race and station. He traces his pedigree back directly to Mohammed, and the highest sheikhs and emeers of the Jaulan kiss his hand in acknowledgment of his superior rank. We were received with great respect; fresh coffee was roasted, and a sheep brought up, slaughtered, and quickly cooked before our tent, and the extemporaneous feast spread for us in presence of the emeer. Though he did not literally run to the herd and bring it himself, others did at his bidding, and the whole affair brought the patriarch Abraham most vividly to mind. Like our emeer, he dwelt in tents, and his dependents were encamped about him with their flocks and herds.

There were not more than thirty tents at this encampment, and, upon inquiry, I found, to my surprise, that the people were nearly all the slaves of the emeer. They and their ancestors have belonged to his family for so many generations that all trace of their real origin is lost. Their complexion also has softened into the bronze of the genuine Arab, and the negro features are almost obliterated. The true Bedawîn, however, never intermarry with them, though the villagers and artisans who settle among them occasionally do. They are the property of the emeer in a restricted sense, and so are the flocks and herds which they are permitted to hold, and he does not hesitate to take what he wants, nor can they refuse his demands, whatever they may be. But then custom, or law, or both, utterly forbids him to sell them. I inquired into all these matters the next day as we rode through the country under the protection and guidance of his head-servant, who reminded me constantly of "Eliezur of Damascus." In answer to my question, he exclaimed, in indignant surprise, "Sell us! *istugfar Allah*—God forbid!" They are, in fact, the home-born servants of the very ancient *house* of el Fŭdle, and, like the three hundred and eighteen in Abraham's family, they are his warriors in times of need, which, in one way or another, happens almost daily. They seem to be attached to the emeer, or rather, perhaps, to his family name, rank, power, and honor. Their own honor, safety, and influence all depend upon him. I was almost startled to find that the emeer was entirely governed by one of his own slaves. He does nothing of himself; and this modern Eliezur not only disposes of his master's goods, but manages the affairs of government very much as he pleases. All the Arabs of the Hûleh and Jaulan greatly fear and court this chief servant. He is shrewd, efficient, and sometimes cruel; nor is any man's life safe if its owner becomes obnoxious to Master Dauk. But a truce to him and his master. Other matters about this encampment of genuine Ishmaelites were equally interesting.

In the evening the flocks began to concentrate around this Joaiza from every part of the surrounding desert. It was a noisy, lively, and really beautiful scene. The young donkeys, calves, kids, and lambs that had been kept up during the day, now let out from the folds, rushed bleating and braying every which way, seeking their parents. They were finally shut in, and every thing in the camp became quiet except the dogs. These kept up an incessant and angry barking all night long; and I understood that there were supposed to be robbers lurking about, who, but for these watchful sentinels, would carry off lambs, and even camels, from the outskirts of the encampment.

These dogs of the Bedawîn are extremely fierce, and it is not a little dangerous, as I have repeatedly experienced, to come upon an encampment in the night. They are an indispensable part of the shepherd's equipage, and appear to have been so even in the time of Job. And, by the way, this Jaulan was Job's country. His flocks and herds roamed over these same wild "walks," and were exposed to the very same dangers that now task the courage of these Arab shepherds. In these inaccessible ravines were the lion's den, the tiger's lair, and pits for bears and wolves; and across these vast plateaus the flying bands of Sabean robbers roved in search of plunder. The country, the people, the manners and customs, remain unchanged from remote antiquity. Job was a great emeer of the Hauran; and if he were there now, he might find the same kind of enemies to plunder and kill, and even natural phenomena very similar to the great fire that burnt up the sheep, and the mighty wind from the wilderness that overturned the houses of his children. Destructive fires often sweep over the desert, and angry hurricanes hurl to the ground the habitations of man. I would not, however, be understood to bring down the patient man of Uz to a level with the modern emeers of Arabia. He was an agriculturist as well as shepherd; an honest man, and not a robber; one that feared God and eschewed evil, and not a fanatical follower of the false prophet.

The night air at Joaiza was keen and cold; indeed, there was a sharp frost, and ice appeared on all the little pools about the camp. Jacob had experience of such alternations between blazing sun and biting frost. In the day the draught consumed me, and the frost by night, and my sleep departed from me, was the indignant reply to his avaricious father-in-law.[1] In the present case the cold was owing mainly to the great elevation of the Jaulan—not less, on an average, than two thousand five hundred feet above the sea. It is a grand volcanic plateau, comparatively level, but with a line of singular *tells* running from Hermon southward to the Jermuk. The first is Tell Ahmar, south of Lake Phiala. Three miles south of this is Tell Sheikha, then Tell Bŭrm, next the great double Tell Aramein—the north peak called Aram, and the south Abu Nidy. About four

[1] Gen. xxxi. 40.

miles farther south is Tell Yusuf, and next it Tell el Khanzîr. Tell el Farus is the last and the loftiest of the list. Few persons, I presume, ever ride over the hills of Galilee without admiring these tall, sugar-loaf landmarks on the eastern side of the Jordan, and wishing to know their names and character. To such, at least, the above list will be satisfactory; and the only additional statement I have to make in regard to them is that, though seen at such a great distance they appear small, they are, in reality, rough volcanic *mounts*, and some of them very respectable *mountains*. Beyond them, eastward and southward, stretch the vast and fertile plains of the Hauran, now and always the granary of Central Syria and Northern Arabia. The Jaulan, however, is entirely given up to pasturage, and, from the nature of the soil and climate, it will continue to be so, although there are places which might be cultivated with any kind of grain, and orchards would flourish every where. It is exceedingly well watered in all parts, except the region between the Lakes Phiala and Tiberias. There the fountains and streams dry up early in spring, and the weary traveler must carry his water-bottle with him if he would not be "consumed with drought."

We started early next morning with a letter and guide from the emeer to Sheikh Fareij, whose camp was *somewhere*, about a day's journey in the desert southward of Joaiza. In that general direction our guide led us across endless fields of lava, and most of the time without any road that I could see, or my horse either. We crossed many tracks, however, which led down to the Hûleh, to Jisr Benat Yacobe, and to this Butaiha, and encountered numerous wadies, some shallow, others deep and ugly, which descend to the Jordan and the lakes. For the first hour we were surrounded by the droves and flocks of the emeer, and I noticed a shepherd kindly carrying in his '*aba* a new-born lamb, and a woman sedulously teaching a young calf what its mouth was made for, and how to manage its spasmodic legs. Such acts not only remind one of the patriarchs who dwelt in tents and tended cattle, but also of that Good Shepherd from whose bosom no enemy shall ever be able to pluck even the weakest lambkin of the flock.

Two miles from Joaiza I took "bearings" from an elevated site called Sindiana, and a mile farther south is the pretty Tell Delwa, with a ruin upon, and a wady descending from it toward the Jordan. Three miles farther we came to Thûban and Kefr Neffakh, both very large ruins, but particularly the last, which exhibits an enormous mass of prostrate houses. After this we wandered about over broken ground for an hour in search of a Turkman sheikh, and found his camp hid away in Wady Ghadarîyeh, which joins, lower down, the far greater one of Ruzzanîyeh. This wady has many tributaries and much water, and here, where it enters the Butaiha, is called Em el 'Ajaj, and also Wady Sulam, incorrectly written Sunam on maps. Having procured a guide, we reached Selukia—the Seleucia of Philip—in half an hour. The ruins of this place are extensive, but the position does not accord very well with the statements of Josephus. He, however, had never visited it, and spoke at random, as he often does in regard to matters with which he was not personally acquainted. Directly south is a place called 'Ain Selukia, from a collection of fountains whose water flows west, and unites with Wady Ruzzanîyeh. We had some difficulty in crossing another deep wady, about a mile farther south, named Tellaiya, from a number of low *tells*, a few miles east of our line of march. This Tellaiya may be the same that enters the Butaiha to the east of us, and is called Dalia by Dr. Robinson. It has cut a deep channel through the hard lava, and a fine stream of water rattles over its rocky bed.

Down to this Wady Tellaiya the country had been more or less wooded; though the oaks that cover the hills south of Banias and 'Ainfît gradually become more and more rare, smaller also, and more *scraggy*, still they are found, solitary or in groups, quite to the wady, but south of it they disppear altogether, and the country is naked and cheerless. So, also, the flocks became more rare; indeed, for many miles we saw none, although the pasturage is equally good, and water even more abundant than farther north. Lively little brooks crossed our track every five minutes; but I suppose this deserted region is a sort of neutral territory between the northern and southern tribes, who are not always on such terms as renders it safe to be caught too far away from their friends.

We were obliged to make a long detour to the east, in order to get round the impracticable gorge of the Jermaiah—that wady which comes down to the lake near the southeastern corner of the Butaiha. It is the largest and most savage of all the ravines into which we looked during our ride of nine hours, and is said to be the chosen resort of leopards, wolves, hyenas, boars, and other wild animals. In fact, the whole Gaulanitis abounds in game. We saw many gazelles, and another species of deer, called *waal*, considerably larger and more like our American deer; partridges also, and grouse, ducks, geese, cranes, and pelicans delight in these solitudes, which their grand enemy, man, rarely invades, or if he does, has too many causes of solicitude to admit of delay, or to make it safe to have the crack of his musket heard.

After heading Wady Jermaiah we turned nearly west down a gentle declivity for half an hour, and then came to a large ruin called Kunaitera; not that of the same name on the road to Damascus from Jisr Benat Yacobe, but one more ancient, and much larger than that ever was. *Sehm* Jaulan is the name of a well-known ruin to the east of this, and I suppose it marks the site of the Biblical Golan, from which this province takes its name. There is also a Khurbet Saida some distance to the east of our track, but no Beit Saida. From Kunaitera to Khurbet Arba'in—*ruin of forty*—is half an hour. This city was originally well built for a place where no stone but basalt is found, and it must have been inhabited until a comparatively recent period. Crossing a smooth and fertile plain for some two miles, we plunged abruptly into the gorge of Wady Shukaiyif by an almost perpendicular path, down which our animals slid rather than walked, greatly to their annoyance and our amusement; and here we found Sheikh Fareij, with his large camp, hid away so perfectly that it could not be seen until one is directly above it. Our nine hours' ride had made us all weary, and we gladly pitched our tent near that of the sheikh. He was not then at home, but a brother supplied his place, with a boisterous and rather ostentatious welcome. He berated our guide for bringing guests at an hour so late that it was impossible to give them such a reception and feast as were becoming. The sheep were all at a distance, and none could be got to sacrifice in honor of the occasion, and the parties, until morning, etc., etc. I assured him that we had all necessary provision for ourselves, and needed only provender for the horses. This was speedily brought, and every thing arranged to our mutual satisfaction.

Just after our arrival a knot of Arabs gathered round the sheikh's tent, in earnest and angry discussion, and I felt rather anxious to know whether or not we were the subject of controversy. Upon inquiry, it appeared that some of the sheikh's men had fallen in with a party of robbers that morning, who were driving off the cattle of these poor peasants who cultivate this Butaiha, and, after a skirmish with them, succeeded in rescuing the stolen cattle, and brought them into their camp. The owners had come to claim their property, and the rescuers demanded four hundred piastres before they would give them up. The case was brought before the sheikh, who ordered them to be restored without ransom; and, of course, there was grumbling on one side, and loud thanks on the other.

I noticed at all the encampments which we passed that the sheikh's tent was distinguished from the rest by a tall spear stuck upright in the ground in front of it; and it is the custom, when a party is out on an excursion for robbery or for war, that when they halt to rest, the spot where the chief reclines or sleeps is thus designated. So Saul, when he lay sleeping, had his spear stuck in the ground at his bolster, and Abner and the people lay round about him.[1] The whole of that scene is eminently Oriental and perfectly natural, even to the deep sleep into which all had fallen, so

[1] 1 Sam. xxvi. 7.

that David and Abishai could walk among them in safety. The Arabs sleep heavily, especially when fatigued. Often, when traveling, my muleteers and servants have resolved to watch by turns in places thought to be dangerous, but in every instance I soon found them fast asleep, and generally their slumbers were so profound that I could not only walk among them without their waking, but might have stolen the very *'aba* with which they were covered. Then the cruse of water at Saul's head is in exact accordance with the customs of the people at this day. No one ventures to travel over these deserts without his cruse of water, and it is very common to place one at the "bolster," so that the owner can reach it during the night. The Arabs eat their dinner in the evening, and it is generally of such a nature as to create thirst, and the quantity of water which they drink is enormous. The *cruse* is, therefore, in perpetual demand. Saul and his party lay in a shady valley, steeped in heavy sleep, after the fatigues of a hot day. The camp-ground of Sheikh Fareij, in Wady Shukaiyif, is adapted in all respects to be the scene of the adventure. David, from above, marks the spot where the king slumbers, creeps cautiously down, and stands over his unconscious persecutor. Abishai asks permission to smite him once, only once, and promises not to smite a second time; but David forbade him, and, taking the spear and cruse of water, ascended to the top of the hill afar off, and cried aloud to Abner: Art not thou a valiant man? and who is like to thee in Israel? * * * As the Lord liveth, ye are worthy to die, because ye have not kept your master, the Lord's anointed. And now see where the king's spear is, and the cruse of water that was at his bolster.[1] What a strange sensation must have run through the camp as David's voice rang out these cutting taunts from the top of the hill! But David was perfectly safe, and there are thousands of ravines where the whole scene could be enacted, every word be heard, and yet the speaker be quite beyond the reach of his enemies.

Among the incidents of that memorable ride was the fol-

[1] 1 Sam. xxvi. 15.

lowing: A hardy little girl, about twelve years old, accompanied us on foot. She was the daughter of our guide, and he was bringing her to her husband, at this camp of Fareij, who had purchased her for a thousand piastres (*forty dollars*). She had no companion or friend of any kind, except a young donkey, as little and as lively as herself. This she drove before her with infinite trouble. It was constantly running hither and thither, and she after it, over sharp rocks and through tangled thorns; but still she never seemed to grow weary. I became quite interested in the brave girl, and from my heart hoped and prayed that she might find, in her hitherto unseen husband, a kind companion. When we arrived at the camp of Fareij, she was taken immediately into the harem of the sheikh, and I saw her no more. She carried nothing in the shape of outfit except the little donkey. I noticed that when she left her mother's tent at Joaiza she had on a pair of high red leather boots. These, however, she quickly drew off, and, tucking them under her sash or girdle, raced over the rocks after her pet in bare feet, and this she did from early morning until after sunset. Our girls don't do such things on their wedding day.

Sheikh Fareij spent the evening in our tent, and greatly interested us by his dignified manners and intelligence, and by a certain air of sadness that pervaded his whole conversation and deportment. He complained bitterly of the course pursued by government, whose tax-gatherers robbed and plundered the Arabs without mercy, and he maintained that they were compelled to plunder in turn. This was by way of apology for the admission which he seemed somewhat ashamed to make that robbing was their trade, and that he and his men were engaged in it daily, either as aggressors or defenders. He farther lamented that the ancient, generous customs of the Bedawîn were being corrupted by Turkish oppression. They now robbed one another, and even murder is often added to plunder. "I myself," said he, "live day by day by the life of this good sword," striking his hand fiercely upon the formidable tool at his side. He admitted that, without my guide from the emeer, I could not have reached his tent in safety, and that, without similar assistance from himself, I should not be able to proceed on the morrow round the eastern shore of the lake. Of the truth of this I had certain and rather startling evidence next morning, for I found myself suddenly confronted by a troop of the most savage Bedawîn I ever encountered; and they made no secret of the fact that they were restrained from plundering us solely by the guard from Sheikh Fareij. What significance do such incidents impart to a thousand allusions to robbers in the Bible, particularly in the history of David, and in his Psalms!

Your wanderings over the Jaulan must have led you near the track that Jacob followed on his return from Mesopotamia. Could you hear any thing about that Mizpeh where Laban overtook him?

Mizpeh must have been to the east of our track; but I have never been able to identify any of the places mentioned in that remarkable narrative. The entire scene is eminently rich in allusions to Oriental manners and customs. The behavior of Laban is true to life, and every expression is familiar to my ear "as household words." Laban says: The God of your father spake unto me yesternight, saying, Take thou heed that thou speak not to Jacob either good or bad.[1] Now we should think that Laban was uttering his own condemnation, and it appears strange that Jacob did not retort upon him by asking, Why, then, have you followed me? You have disobeyed the command of God, according to your own admission. Jacob, however, knew very well that such a plea would avail nothing. Laban believed that he fulfilled the intent of the divine command merely by refraining to injure Jacob, and so the latter understood it. The terms of the order were most comprehensive and stringent; but the real intention was to forbid violence, and this sort of construction must be applied to Oriental language in a thousand cases, or we shall push simple narratives into absurdities, and make men, and even the God of Truth, contradict himself.

[1] Gen. xxxi. 29.

If Jacob gave as a reason for his departure from Mesopotamia that he "sore longed after his father's house," he appears to have stretched the truth to find a motive. It is one of the most mysterious parts of his conduct that, even after he entered Palestine, and was within a short distance of the aged, widowed, and blind Isaac, he allowed a number of years to pass (so far as appears from history) before visiting him. He resided first at Succoth, then at Sychem, and then at Bethel. Two things may throw light upon this singular delay. Jacob was never a favorite with his father, and his fond and partial mother was dead. The home of his youth, therefore, had but few attractions for him. Then, again, it is highly probable that he had good reason to fear his elder brother, especially after their meeting at Mahanaim. One thing is certain, that Jacob had some strong motive to avoid his father, or he was a colder and more selfish son than even his history would indicate.

The charge of stealing Laban's *teraphim* greatly provoked the idol-hating Jacob, and he very likely thought it a mere device to conceal some evil purpose. But the thing is interesting to us as the earliest distinct notice we have of the existence and worship of these images. They are frequently mentioned in after times, but here we first find them in this patriarchal family. They must have been so small as to be easily concealed under the *saddle* of Rachel; and, by the way, it is still very common for Arabs to hide stolen property under the padding of their saddles. They probably resembled the small images of saints which are now carried about by Oriental Christians, and may have been honored and consulted in much the same way. Some of those saints are celebrated for assistance given to women afflicted with Rachel's sorrow; and perhaps she herself had been driven to this sort of idolatry in her agony to become a mother. It would be Orientally feminine in an eminent degree if this were the cause of her *stealing* her father's gods. Nor does this act of stealing a god to worship strike these people about us as monstrous or absurd. I have known many such thefts of modern teraphim (pictures and images), and by women too. And why not? It is surely not absurd to *steal the god* whose aid you invoke to assist you to steal other things. It is well known that Greek pirates are most devout worshipers of the saints; and, what is even more monstrous, the Moslems, who claim to worship only the one true God, yet pray to this very being for success even in their lowest intrigues and vilest lusts, and constantly mention his holy name in their lewd songs, blasphemously blessing him for success in their deeds of darkness. In this respect, as in most others, the "Thousand Nights" do but reflect the actual manners of the present generation of Arabs.

Another Oriental trait comes out very offensively in the conduct of Laban, and afterward in that of Jacob —a most undisguised and grievous *favoritism.* Laban searches all before he visits Rachel's tent, because she was the pet of his own and of Jacob's family; and so, when Jacob prepared for the worst in the immediate prospect of a hostile visit from Esau, he placed the handmaids and his sons by them foremost, Leah and her children next, and Rachel and her son last; that, as he said about the cattle, if Esau come to the one company and smite it, then the other company shall escape. Nor was there the least attempt to disguise this offensive and injurious favoritism, even in this hard extremity. There is nothing generous in the whole matter; nothing like saying, "These are all my children; I can not choose between them; come life, come death, it shall come upon us all together." Far, far from this noble spirit. He in effect says, "You handmaids and your children go first; if any are to be killed, let it be you. And Leah, go you and your sons

TERAPHIM.

VOL. II.—B

next." (Would she not in her heart of hearts say, "He never loved me, and is willing now to sacrifice me and my sons, if by doing so he can make an additional opportunity for his beloved Rachel and Joseph to escape?") Such is the unmistakable English of this whole manœuvre, and, no doubt, those concerned understood and remembered it long after that dreadful day of trial. This story needs two remarks to set certain matters in their proper light. The *first* is, that Jacob, in this affair, is no more than a type of every Arab emeer in the country, and, indeed, of nearly every Oriental household. Such favoritism is, and always has been, the prevailing custom of the East. He therefore did nothing but what the laws and domestic regulations of his day and generation sanctioned. The *second* remark is, that we have in this conduct of the father an explanation of the intense hatred to Joseph—I had almost said, a sort of palliation for it.

But to return to the meeting at Mizpeh. The terms with which Laban and Jacob reproved and berated each other are in admirable keeping with the parties and the story, and abound in allusions to Oriental customs, especially of a pastoral people. Twenty years long, cries Jacob, have I served thee. The ewes of thy flock have not cast their young. Evidence of most careful and successful treatment. The *rams* of thy flock have I not eaten. Implying that then, as now, the males of the flocks alone were used for food, or sold to the butcher. Then, as now, wild beasts tore some of the flock; but Jacob the shepherd, not Laban the landlord, bore the loss. Then, too, as at this day, thieves prowled about; but Jacob made good whatever was stolen. Of course, he had to watch by day and night, in winter's storms and summer's burning suns. It was, therefore, no mere figure of speech that the drought consumed him by day and the frost by night. Thus do the hardy shepherds suffer in the same regions at the present time. But it is a dog's life, in spite of all the eclogues and pastorals of love-sick poets. *Real* shepherds on the plains of Syria never wrote hymns in praise of their hard vocation.

We must not pass from these scenes in Jacob's history without noticing the admirable tact with which he appeased his justly-offended brother. He sends an embassy to him from a long distance. This itself was a compliment, and, no doubt, the embassadors were the most respectable he could command. Then the *terms* of the message were the best possible to flatter and to conciliate an Oriental. He calls Esau his *lord*, himself his servant—or *slave*, as it might be rendered—and he thus tacitly, and without alluding to the old trick by which he cheated him of his birthright, acknowledges him to be the elder brother, and his superior. At the same time, by the large presents, and the exhibition of great wealth, Esau is led to infer that he is not returning a needy adventurer to claim a double portion of the paternal estate, and it would not be unoriental if there was intended to be conveyed by all this a sly intimation that Jacob was neither to be despised nor lightly meddled with. There was subtle flattery, mingled with profound humility, but backed all the while by the quiet allusion to the substantial position and character of one whom *God had greatly blessed and prospered.* All this, however, failed, and the enraged brother set out to meet him with an army. Jacob was terribly alarmed; but, with his usual skill and presence of mind, he made another effort to appease Esau. The presents were well selected, admirably arranged, and sent forward one after another, and the drivers were directed to address Esau in the most respectful and humble terms: "They be thy *servant* Jacob's, a present unto my *lord* Esau; and be sure to say, Behold, thy *servant* Jacob is behind us; for he said, I will appease him with the present that goeth before me, and afterward I will see his face." Jacob did not miscalculate the influence of his princely offerings, and I verily believe there is not an emeer or sheikh in all Gilead at this day who would not be appeased by such presents; and, from my personal knowledge of Orientals, I should say that Jacob need not have been in such mortal terror, following in their rear. Far less will now "make room," as Solomon says, for any offender, however atrocious, and bring him before great men with acceptance.[1]

Esau was mollified, and, when near enough to see the lowly prostrations of his trembling brother, forgot every thing but that he was Jacob, the son of his mother, the companion of his childhood. He *ran* to meet him, and embraced him, and fell on his neck, and kissed him; *and they wept.* All this is beautiful, natural, Oriental, and so is their subsequent discourse, but we can not dwell upon it. Throughout the entire scene Esau behaves nobly, and, in apparent magnanimity, fairly eclipses the wary Jacob. The latter had good reason, perhaps, to doubt the permanence of his brother's affection; at any rate, he wanted nothing so much as to get safely rid of him and his as quickly and quietly as possible. He refuses every offer of assistance, but insists upon the reception of his own presents, carries his point, and thus brings the stringent law of custom in such matters to bind his brother to be at peace with him; and, finally, he induces him to take back all his followers, with the promise to lead on softly until he came to him in Seir. This promise Jacob did not intend to fulfill; or, at least, *he led on so very gently* that he died before accomplishing it. In fact, he turned down westward, and made for a place where he would be safe from Esau's resentment. It is, therefore, highly probable that the reason why Jacob did not go directly on to Isaac was the fear of again meeting Esau, whom he had distrusted and deceived in the very hour of reconciliation. It is commonly the case that the offender is much slower to forget and *confide* than he who has been injured. Whatever may have been the motives which governed Jacob in all these transactions with his brother, it is certain that on this occasion Esau carries off the palm for generosity and kindness of heart. It is not in contests like this that Jacob was calculated to shine. Indeed, he *could not* meet Esau but on very disadvantageous terms. He had injured him deeply, and beyond the possibility of reparation. And, still more to the point, it was obviously the purpose of God to bring

[1] Prov. xviii. 16.

his chosen servant into these terrible trials, in order to work the deeper conviction of his former sin, and the more thorough repentance and reformation. And *here it is* that Jacob appears as a guide and model to all mankind. In his utmost distress and alarm, he holds fast his hope and trust in God, wrestles with Him in mighty supplication, and as a prince prevails. I will not let thee go except thou bless me. And he said, What is thy name? And he said, Jacob. And he said, Thy name shall be called no more Jacob, but Israel; for as a prince hast thou power with God, and with men, and hast prevailed.[1]

Our long ride through the Jaulan has whiled away the time and the road quite to the end of this Butaiha, and this bold headland marks the spot, according to my topography, where the five thousand were fed with five barley-loaves and two small fishes.[2] From the four narratives of this stupendous miracle, we gather, 1st, that the place belonged to Bethsaida; 2d, that it was a desert place; 3d, that it was near the shore of the lake, for they came to it by boat; 4th, that there was a mountain close at hand; 5th, that it was a smooth, grassy spot, capable of seating many thousand people. Now all these requisites are found in this exact locality, and nowhere else, so far as I can discover. This Butaiha belonged to Bethsaida. At this extreme southeast corner of it, the mountain shuts down upon the lake bleak and barren. It was, doubtless, desert then as now, for it is not capable of cultivation. In this little cove the ships (boats) were anchored. On this beautiful sward at the base of the rocky hill the people were seated to receive from the hands of the Son of God the miraculous bread, emblematic of his body, which is the true bread from heaven. When all had eaten, and the fragments were gathered up, they departed in haste, for the day was far spent.

A vast amount of learning and critical research has been expended in efforts to reconcile the different directions given (or supposed to be given) to the disciples by our Lord, and to make the entire narratives accord with the topog-

[1] Gen. xxxii. 24, 27, 28.   [2] Matt. xiv. 15; John vi. 9.

raphy of this region. According to John,[1] the disciples went over the sea toward Capernaum, while Mark says that Jesus constrained them to get into the ship, and to go to the other side before unto Bethsaida. Looking back from this point at the southeastern extremity of the Butaiha, I see no difficulty in these statements. The case was this, I suppose: As the evening was coming on, Jesus commanded the disciples to return home to Capernaum, while he sent the people away. They were reluctant to go and leave him alone in that desert place; probably remonstrated against his exposing himself to the coming storm and the cold night air, and reminded him that he would have many miles to walk round the head of the lake, and must cross the Jordan at Bethsaida before he could reach home. To quiet their minds, he may have then told them to go on before toward Bethsaida, while he dismissed the crowd, promising to join them in the night, which he intended to do, and actually did, though in a manner very different from what they expected. Still, they were reluctant to leave him, and had to be *constrained* to set sail. In this state of anxiety, they endeavored to keep near the shore between this and Bethsaida, hoping, no doubt, to take in their beloved Master at some point along the coast. But a violent wind beat off the boat, so that they were not able to make Bethsaida, nor even Capernaum, but were driven past both; and when near the plain of Gennesaret, at the northwest corner of the lake, Jesus came unto them walking upon the sea. All this is topographically natural; and easily to be understood on the supposition that the miracle took place on this spot; that Bethsaida was at the mouth of the Jordan, and Capernaum at Tell Hûm. Nor is there need even of the marginal rendering in our Bible: "Over against Bethsaida." The disciples would naturally sail *toward* Bethsaida in order to reach Tell Hûm. Neither is there any thing inconsistent with the statement of John,[2] that the people took ship the next day and came to Capernaum, seeking Jesus. They came from the southeast, where the miracle had been

[1] John vi. 17.   [2] John vi. 24.

wrought, and would naturally seek him in Capernaum, for that was his home; but it seems that they did not find him there, for John immediately adds that when they had found him *on the other side of the sea*—a very singular mode of expression if they found him in Capernaum itself, but perfectly natural on the supposition that they had *to go on* to the plain of Gennesaret, where he had landed. They would probably find him somewhere about 'Ain et Tîny, near which, I presume, the party reached the shore from their wonderful sail. But if it should appear to any one more probable that the people actually found Jesus in Capernaum, this might easily be, for Capernaum was not more than one hour's walk from the corner of Gennesaret, and he could easily have returned home, for they reached the shore very early in the morning. I, however, have very little doubt but that the people had to pass on from Tell Hûm to 'Ain et Tîny to find him whom they sought.

It follows, of course, from this explanation, that Capernaum was *itself not in Gennesaret;* and I must add that neither Matthew, Mark, Luke, nor John locate it in that plain; nor does Josephus, nor any other ancient author. It is carried thither and anchored there by a modern theory, which, I think, is a mistake.

I am of opinion, also, that the *invention* of a second Bethsaida is wholly unnecessary. Reland, who first started the idea, confesses that he has no authority for it, but merely resorts to it as an *ultimum refugium*, a last resort, to solve an otherwise invincible topographical difficulty. But I do not believe that another instance can be found of two cities of the *same* name close together on the same part of a small lake; and such hypothetical cities should not be created without absolute necessity, and no such necessity exists in this case. All admit that there was a Bethsaida at the entrance of the Jordan into the lake. The greater part of it, certainly that part which Philip repaired, lay on the east bank of the river, and therefore, it is maintained, must have belonged to Gaulanitis, and not to Galilee; and as the Bethsaida of Andrew, Peter, and Philip was a city of Galilee,[1] it is thought that we must have a second town of this name. But I think this unnecessary. Any city built at the mouth of the Jordan would almost necessarily have part of its houses on the west bank of the stream, and this would be literally and geographically within the territory of Galilee. Peter, Andrew, and Philip were born there, and would be mentioned as Galileans. And, farther, I think it highly probable that the whole city on both banks of the river was ordinarily attached to Galilee, and that one object which Philip the Tetrarch had in rebuilding the part on the east side, and changing its name, was to detach it entirely from its former relations, and establish his own right over it. I believe, therefore, that there was but *one* Bethsaida at the head of the lake, and that it was at the mouth of the Jordan; and thus we settle the sites of all the places in this neighborhood which are intimately related to the history of our blessed Lord and his disciples.

My experience in this region enables me to sympathize with the disciples in their long night's contest with the wind. I spent a night in that Wady Shukaiyif, some three miles up it, to the left of us. The sun had scarcely set when the wind began to rush down toward the lake, and it continued all night long with constantly increasing violence, so that when we reached the shore next morning the face of the lake was like a huge boiling caldron. The wind howled down every wady from the northeast and east with such fury that no efforts of rowers could have brought a boat to shore at any point along that coast. In a wind like that, the disciples *must* have been driven quite across to Gennesaret, as we know they were. To understand the causes of these sudden and violent tempests, we must remember that the lake lies low—six hundred feet lower than the ocean; that the vast and naked plateaus of the Jaulan rise to a great height, spreading backward to the wilds of the Hauran, and upward to snowy Hermon; that the water-courses have cut out profound ravines and wild gorges, converging to the head of this lake, and that these act like gigantic *fun-*

[1] John xii. 21.

nels to draw down the cold winds from the mountains. On the occasion referred to we subsequently pitched our tents at the shore, and remained for three days and nights exposed to this tremendous wind. We had to double pin all the tent-ropes, and frequently were obliged to hang with our whole weights upon them to keep the quivering tabernacle from being carried up bodily into the air. No wonder the disciples toiled and rowed hard all that night; and how natural their amazement and terror at the sight of Jesus walking on the waves! The faith of Peter in desiring and *daring* to set foot on such a sea is most striking and impressive; more so, indeed, than its failure after he made the attempt. The whole lake, as we had it, was lashed into fury; the waves repeatedly rolled up to our tent door, tumbling over the ropes with such violence as to carry away the tent-pins. And, moreover, those winds are not only violent, but they come down suddenly, and often when the sky is perfectly clear. I once went in to swim near the hot baths, and, before I was aware, a wind came rushing over the cliffs with such force that it was with great difficulty I could regain the shore. Some such sudden wind it was, I suppose, that filled the ship with waves "so that it was now full," while Jesus was asleep on a pillow in the hinder part of the ship; nor is it strange that the disciples aroused him with the cry of Master! Master! carest thou not that we perish? And he arose and rebuked the wind, and said unto the sea, Peace, be still; and the wind ceased, and there was a great calm. And the disciples feared exceedingly, and said one to another, What manner of man is this, that even the wind and the sea obey him?[1]

Salîm reminds me that we are to encamp early, in order to dry our bedding and clothes, and thinks that this Wady Semak is the best place for the purpose that we are likely to find. While the men pitch the tents, we will stroll up the valley for exercise in part, and partly that I may show you the remains of antiquity that are still to be found in it. Some four miles higher up are the broken walls of Kusr

[1] Mark iv. 38–41.

Bardawîl, as the castle of Baldwin, the famous Crusader, is called by the Arabs. We can not go there, nor is there any thing worth the trouble at it. Here, however, is something of great interest to me, and I think, will be to you before we are done with it. The name of this prostrate town is *Kerza* or *Gersa*, as my Bedawîn guide shouted it in my ear the first time I visited it, on that windy day we have been describing. It was a small place, but the walls can be traced all round, and there seem to have been considerable suburbs. I identify these ruins with the long-lost site of Gergesa, where our Lord healed the two men possessed with devils, and suffered those malignant spirits to enter into the herd of swine. If this be correct, it is a discovery of some importance. From Origen down to the last critic who has tried his skill upon the Greek text of the New Testament, the conflicting and contradictory readings of manuscripts in regard to the place where the miracle was performed have furnished a fruitful source of discussion. Matthew locates it at Gergesa;[1] Mark[2] and Luke[3] at Gadara. A few various readings give Geresa. The Vulgate, Arabic, and others that follow the Vulgate, read Gergesa in all the evangelists; nor are these all the discrepancies in regard to the name of this place. Only one of these readings can be correct. Which shall we select? This is the question to be settled. Our inquiries will, of course, be confined to the topographical indications which may have a bearing upon the problem.

Our first point is that the miracle *could not have occurred at Gadara*. It is certain, from all the accounts we have of it, that the place was near the shore of the lake. Mark says that when he came out of the ship *immediately* there met him a man, etc. With this precise statement the tenor of all the narratives coincides, and therefore we *must* find a locality directly on the shore, and every place must be rejected that is not consistent with this ascertained fact. *Again*, the *city* itself, as well as the *country* of the Gergesenes, was at the shore of the lake. All the accounts imply this fact. *Lastly*,

[1] Matt. viii. 28.   [2] Mark v. 1.   [3] Luke viii. 26.

there was a steep mountain so near at hand that the herd of swine, rushing down it, were precipitated into the lake. Now Gadara does not meet any one of these necessary conditions. I take for granted, what I believe to be true, that Um Keîs marks the site of Gadara; and it was, therefore, about three hours to the south of the extreme shore of the lake in that direction. There is first a broad plain from Khurbet Samra to the Jermuk; then the vast gorge of this river, and after it an ascent for an hour and a half to Um Keîs. No one, I think, will maintain that this meets the requirements of the sacred narratives, but is in irreconcilable contradiction to them. It is true that a celebrated traveler, from his lofty stand-point at Um Keîs, overlooks all intervening obstacles, and makes the swine rush headlong into the lake from beneath his very feet. But to do this in fact (and the evangelists deal only in plain facts), they must have run down the mountain for an hour and a half, forded the deep Jermuk, quite as formidable as the Jordan itself, ascended its northern bank, and raced across a level plain several miles before they could reach the nearest margin of the lake, a feat which no herd of swine would be likely to achieve, even though they were "possessed." The site of the miracle, therefore, *was not at Gadara*. This is an important result. Nor was it in the *country* of the Gadarenes, because that country lay south of the great river Jermuk; and, besides, if the territory of that city did at any time reach to the south end of the lake, there is no mountain there above it adapted to the conditions of the miracle; and, farther, the *city itself where it was wrought was evidently on the shore*. There we must find it, whatever be its name. And in this Gersa or Chersa we have a position which fulfills every requirement of the narratives, and with a name so near that in Matthew as to be in itself a strong corroboration of the truth of this identification. It is within a few rods of the shore, and an immense mountain rises directly above it, in which are ancient tombs, out of some of which the two men possessed of the devils may have issued to meet Jesus. The lake is so near the base of the mountain that the swine, rushing madly down it, could not stop, but would be hurried on into the water and drowned. The place is one which our Lord would be likely to visit, having Capernaum in full view to the north, and Galilee "over against it," as Luke says it was.[1] The *name*, however, pronounced by Bedawîn Arabs is so similar to Gergesa, that, to all my inquiries for this place, they invariably said it was at Chersa, and they insisted that they were identical, and I agree with them in this opinion.

In studying the details of the miracle, I was obliged to modify one opinion or impression which had grown up with me from childhood. *There is no bold cliff overhanging the lake* on the eastern side, nor, indeed, on any other, except just north of Tiberias. Every where along the northeastern and eastern shores a smooth beach declines gently down to the water. There is no "*jumping-off place*," nor, indeed, is any required. Take your stand a little south of this Chersa. A great herd of swine, we will suppose, is feeding on this mountain that towers above it. They are seized with a sudden panic, rush madly down the almost perpendicular declivity, those behind tumbling over and thrusting forward those before, and, as there is neither time nor space to recover on the narrow shelf between the base and the lake, they are crowded headlong into the water, and perish. All is perfectly natural just at this point, and here, I suppose, it did actually occur. Farther south the plain becomes so broad that the herd might have recovered and recoiled from the lake, whose domain they would not willingly invade.

How do you suppose these discrepancies in the name of this place crept into the text?

We must leave that question to professed critics. I have an abiding conviction, however, that Matthew wrote the name correctly. He was from this region, and personally knew the localities. His Gospel, also, was written first of all, and mainly circulated, in the beginning, in these Oriental regions. John does not mention the miracle, and Mark and Luke

[1] Luke viii. 26.

were strangers to this part of the country, and may possibly have intended, by mentioning the *country* of the *Gadarenes*, to point out to their distant Greek and Roman readers the mere vicinity of the place where the miracle was wrought. Gergesa, or Gerasa, or Chersa, however pronounced, was small and unknown, while Gadara was a Greek city celebrated for its temples and theatres, and for the warm baths on the Hieromax just below it. They *may*, therefore, have written "*country* of the Gadarenes;" but I think it far more probable that intermeddling scholiasts made the change from Gergesa to Gadara, in order to indicate to the unlearned the spot where the wonder took place. There is a certain resemblance between the names, and, when once introduced into a leading manuscript, the basis for the controversy would be fairly laid down. Learned annotators would be misled by the very extent of their geographical knowledge, which, however, would not be sufficiently exact to prove to them that the miracle *could not* have taken place at Gadara. Origen, who, I believe, first attempted to correct the text in those passages, seems to have been acquainted with this very site we are upon, and this might well have been the case, since he resided at Cæsarea; still, his notice of it is confused, and his criticisms had no valuable result. The mistake spread and became permanent. But, leaving to others more competent to decide how much weight should be allowed to accurate topographical research in settling the reading of a controverted *name* in manuscripts, we may certainly inquire, without presumption, whether it is safe to correct the text of Matthew by that of Luke (as some modern critics have done), and thus locate an important transaction in the life of our Saviour at a place where it could not possibly have occurred. One thing, I fear, is certain: if the light shed upon this question by careful topographical examinations can not settle it, then must it remain forever unsettled. Let any one examine the "various readings" of these passages as collected in Alford and Tregelles, and he will despair of ever arriving at even a safe probability from mere manuscript authority.

And now, by way of relief, let me draw your attention to the fact that this Wady Semak is every where *plowed* up by wild hogs in search of the esculent roots upon which they live at this season of the year. Whether there is any lineal connection between them and the herd that was feeding on this mountain, I leave you and every one else to decide according to his particular fancy. It is *fact*, however, that these creatures still abound at this place, and in a state as wild and fierce as though they were still "possessed."

XXVI. KERSÀ TO TIBERIAS.

March 24th.

A long ride and much to see promise a busy and a very pleasant day. We are to make the circuit of the entire southern half of the lake, and encamp among the ruins of that famous city from which it derives its present name. Here on the shore are warm sulphurous springs, which emit steam with an odor intolerably offensive. The place is called Mizferah, and is probably what Burckhardt heard of as a ruined town at the mouth of Wady Semak, which he calls Medjeifera. There is no such *ruin*, and the names are very similar.

You observe that the plain (if so narrow a margin along the shore deserve such a name) is smooth, hard, and quite barren. A Roman road, or at least one well made, once ran along the shore quite to Kersa, whence it appears to have ascended to the Jaulan. We have now an excellent opportunity to study the grand geological characteristics of this region. The lower strata on our left are limestone, but all above is basaltic; and this formation is of vast thickness. The descent, through Wady Shukaiyif, from the lofty plateau of the Jaulan is full two thousand feet before the trap gives place to calcareous rock. This immense volcanic field consists every where of irregular heaps of amorphous lava and disintegrating scoriæ, with gigantic mounds of globular basalt, which in a few localities shows a tendency to separate into rudely-shaped columns; but I have seen no genuine columnar basalt in the Jaulan. Were it not for the countless springs of water in the southern part, this whole province would be a black and barren wilderness, incapable of sustaining even the goats which now rejoice in its wild ravines.

Our Arab neighbors behaved very respectfully last night, and to-day I see no reason to apprehend any interruption to our researches.

A rare chance, and owing to political combinations in Tiberias, which render all parties particularly anxious to obtain or retain the good-will of the European consuls. This is especially true of 'Akil 'Aga, who now controls all these lawless tribes. We may well congratulate ourselves, for this is just the most dangerous part of the country to traverse. When passing this way from Banias, I took the precaution to get a letter from Sheikh Fareij to Sheikh Mahmood, then at the head of a large tribe encamped a little south of Kŭl'aet Hŭsn. With this, and three of his horsemen as guide and guard, we passed safely; but it was well we had them, for just at that little wady ahead of us we were suddenly confronted by a troop of Bedawîn robbers on their fleet horses, and armed with their tremendous spears. Our guard galloped up to them, and explained that we were under the protection of Sheikh Fareij, and must be allowed to pass. They grumbled a good deal, and looked viciously at our loaded mules, but did not dare to lay hands on any thing belonging to our party. They acknowledged without a blush, however, that they had come up from the Ghor (Valley of the Jordan) on an expedition for plunder; and when leaving us, said they intended to visit the Butaiha that very night. Alas for the poor peasants! Such visits, constantly repeated, desolate the country, and drive the farmers farther and farther inland, to find a place where these lawless villains dare not follow them. When such a *raid* breaks into a village, they compel the people to feed both themselves and their horses, and in the morning they march off with every valuable article they can find. Here is the true explanation of the widespread desolations of this beautiful country; and, unless some stronger government than the Turkish shall come in to repress these intolerable robbers, the farmers will be driven in toward the sea-board, until the whole interior is abandoned, and changed to frightful deserts.

The marauding party that met us belonged to a tribe called Diab, which interpreted means *Wolves*, a most significant and appropriate name. I visited their camp, and after reading my letter, and making some private inquiries of the guard, the sheikh was very gracious, though the reception at first was austere enough, and somewhat alarming. He was surrounded by a troop of most villainous-looking cutthroats. One aged warrior, in particular, might have sat for Rob Roy, or any other of Scott's wild Highland robbers. Indeed, there are many points of resemblance between these Arab *tribes* and the Highland *clans* of former days. Perhaps the Arab is the more poetic, if not the most respectable character. The sheikh of these Diab urged me to spend the night with him; but, finding me resolved to pass on, he rose and left the tent, saying that I must not go until he returned. After some time he came out of the *hareem*, or female department, with some fresh-baked bread, and a plate of *dibs* (a kind of grape molasses), and, taking his seat by my side, he broke off a bit of bread, dipped it in the *dibs*, and gave it to me to eat; and in like manner he required all my companions to partake, and even had the muleteers called in to eat of it. After this, all those about the tent tasted of it. This was the ceremony, and he explained its significance somewhat in this fashion: "We are now brethren. *There is bread and salt between us;* we are *brothers* and *allies*. You are at liberty to travel among us wherever you please, and, so far as my power extends, I am to aid, befriend, and succor you, *even to the loss of my own life*." The eating of this bread was the sign and seal of the covenant of *Brotherhood* (*Khûwy*, as they term it); and they tell us that this bread will *never* leave the heart of a true and loyal Bedawy; and, of course, the covenant, of which it is the symbol, can never be forgotten or renounced. They often upbraid the civilized Frank because he does not keep *bread and salt*—is not faithful to the covenant of brotherhood; and I have even heard them assert bluntly that we *have no bread and salt*.

They tell us that this custom has come down to them from the remotest antiquity; and, in reflecting upon this very striking incident, I have thought it not impossible that the apostles, who were plain fishermen, born and bred on this very shore, had been familiar with this custom, and fully appreciated its significance; and that our blessed Lord appropriated, expanded, and infinitely ennobled it in the bread of the Eucharistic Supper. The points of resemblance are many, extremely significant, and impressive. In both, the *element* and the *act* are almost identical; the bread, in both, is the symbol of a *covenant;* the act of eating is the seal of the covenant. In both it is a covenant of *brotherhood*, introducing the participants into that near and sacred relationship. The covenant is *perpetual;* the *bread* never leaves the loyal heart. In both it supposes the tenderest affection, and guarantees protection and succor *even unto death*. These are not all the points of resemblance, but they are sufficient, I think, to rescue the idea of connection between them from the charge of irreverence. If our Lord did actually base the Eucharistic Supper upon a custom well known to his disciples, and deeply significant, this would be in pleasing unison with other similar institutions. When he would enter into covenant with the earth that it should not be again destroyed by a deluge, he selected the beautiful and familiar bow that gilds the retiring storm-cloud to be the sign and seal of the covenant. When, too, he made a covenant with Abraham, it is more than doubted by the learned whether the remarkable seal of that covenant was an act then performed for the first time. And, however this controversy may be settled, it is certain that *baptism*, which has taken the place of *circumcision*, was known and extensively practiced long before our Lord appropriated and sanctified it to its present important office in his Church. I see no objection, therefore, to the idea that we have in this bread of the *Khûwy* an original and primitive custom, upon which our Saviour ingrafted the precious institution of the Supper; and the thought throws around this Arab institution an inexpressible charm.

It certainly does; and may we not find traces of a custom somewhat similar to this among those Bedawîn in early Bible history? Abraham, and Isaac, and Jacob, to mention no others, appear to have *sealed* their covenants on various occasions by *eating*. At first it may have been merely a friendly repast; but having been associated for some time with the making and the ratification of solemn contracts, it came to be regarded as a necessary finale and seal of the transaction, and then to be the principal formula of the covenant itself.

Such a transition would be natural, and is in itself highly probable; but we must leave these speculations for the student and the commentator. They are rather abstruse for a discussion on horseback.

Be it so; but, before we get on to some topic altogether foreign, I want to make an inquiry which the Arab proverb about *bread and salt* suggested. Our Lord, in the Sermon on the Mount, says, Ye are the salt of the earth; but if the salt have lost its savor, wherewith shall it be salted? It is thenceforth good for nothing but to be cast out and trodden under foot of men.[1] To what fact in experience does he allude?

It is plainly implied that salt, under certain conditions so generally known as to permit him to found his instruction upon them, did actually lose its saltness; and our only business is to discover these conditions, not to question their existence. Nor is this difficult. I have often seen just such salt, and the identical disposition of it that our Lord has mentioned. A merchant of Sidon having farmed of the government the revenue from the importation of salt, brought over an immense quantity from the marshes of Cyprus—enough, in fact, to supply the whole province for at least twenty years. This he had transferred to the mountains, to cheat the government out of some small percentage. Sixty-five houses in Jûne—Lady Stanhope's village—were rented and filled with salt. These houses have merely earthen floors, and the salt next the ground, in a few years, entirely spoiled. I saw large quantities of it literally thrown into the street, to be trodden under foot of men and beasts. It was "good for nothing." Similar magazines are common in this country, and have been from remote ages, as we learn from history both sacred and profane; and the sweeping out of the spoiled salt and casting it into the street are actions familiar to all men.

It should be stated in this connection that the salt used in this country is not manufactured by boiling clean salt wa-

[1] Matt. v. 13.

ter, nor quarried from mines, but is obtained from marshes along the sea-shore, as in Cyprus, or from salt lakes in the interior, which dry up in summer, as the one in the desert north of Palmyra, and the great lake of Jebbûl, southeast of Aleppo. The salt of our Sidon merchant was from the vast marshes near Larnaca. I have seen these marshes covered with a thick crust of salt, and have also visited them when it had been gathered into heaps like hay-cocks in a meadow. The large winter lake southeast of Aleppo I found dried up by the last of August, and the entire basin, farther than the eye could reach, was white as snow with an incrustation of coarse salt. Hundreds of people were out gathering and carrying it to Jebbûl, where the government stores were kept.

Maundrell, who visited the lake at Jebbûl, tells us that he found salt there which had entirely "lost its savor," and the same abounds among the debris at Usdum, and in other localities of rock salt at the south end of the Dead Sea. Indeed, it is a well-known fact that the salt of *this country*, when in contact with the ground, or exposed to rain and sun, does become insipid and useless. From the manner in which it is gathered, much earth and other impurities are necessarily collected with it. Not a little of it is so impure that it can not be used at all, and such salt soon effloresces and turns to dust—not to fruitful soil, however. It is not only good for nothing itself, but it actually destroys all fertility wherever it is thrown; and this is the reason why it is cast into the street. There is a sort of verbal verisimilitude in the manner in which our Lord alludes to the act: "it is cast out" and "trodden under foot;" so troublesome is this corrupted salt, that it is carefully swept up, carried forth, and thrown into the street. There is no place about the house, yard, or garden where it can be tolerated. No man will allow it to be thrown on to his field, and the only place for it is the street, and there it is cast to be trodden under foot of men.

But we must return to the tent of our new brother Mahmood. It would be an intolerable insult to depart without a courteous and somewhat ceremonious adieu. The sheikh accompanied us down to the road, and then sent two of his followers to guide us, as he said, to Semak, but, in reality, to guard us from some stray "brother," who might not be disposed to act in exact accordance with the claims of our extemporaneous relationship. One of these horsemen was very talkative, and, among other matters, stated, without the least reserve, that he wanted to have accompanied the marauding expedition which we encountered in the morning, but his sheikh would not permit him to go. "Well," said I, "if you had met me, would you have assisted to plunder me?" "Certainly, if you had not been protected by Sheikh Fareij." "What! rob your *brother?*" "Oh, you would not have been my brother then." Strange customs, and most singular people! It was something novel to be riding gayly along this solitary shore with professed robbers, and these bushy ravines swarming with their comrades, prowling about like beasts of prey. He lieth in wait secretly as a lion in his den; he lieth in wait to catch the poor.[1] My talkative "brother" gloried in the title of robber; and when I asked him why they did not cultivate the rich valley of the Jordan, he curled his lip in disdain, and exclaimed, "What! a Bedawy drive the plow? *istugfar Allah*—God forbid! We are robbers. *This is our trade,* and by this we will live, or, *wallah!* by this we will die," striking his terrible spear fiercely into the ground. This fellow (as usual) was not satisfied with his present, and when I told him he might take or leave it, just as he pleased, he went away, muttering to the servant that we should meet him again in Wady Mandhour, "and then," said he, "*inshallah*—if God please—I will *take* whatever I want." We remained encamped on the shore of the lake at Samakh three days, and I know he watched us like a lynx, and if we had attempted to enter Wady Mandhour he would have made his threat good. Such insolence is intolerable, and I long for the day when a strong government will take these wild Arabs in hand. They might easily be tamed. Their ostentatious courage would utterly fail before even a small force of Eu-

[1] Ps. x. 9.

ropean soldiers. They are great boasters, and, like all such, great poltroons.

I am amazed to find sensible and highly-cultivated gentlemen the defenders and eulogists of the Bedawîn. Burckhardt was both a learned man, and an unsophisticated, straightforward writer, and yet he seems to have been captivated with the character and customs of these wild Arabs. But, according to his own account (which, so far as it goes, I can confirm), they are a nation of universal liars, thieves, and robbers, with all the vices which *must* ever attend such a course of life. They are also cowardly and mean. Rarely, indeed, will they venture to attack even a very inferior party, if armed and prepared to resist; but wherever and whenever they overtake a poor defenseless stranger, they pounce upon him like hungry wolves. Even helpless women and children are robbed and stripped without mercy or remorse. True, Burckhardt says that *some* of them turn their backs while the *women are made to strip*, and are then so generous as to toss back a few of the rags which they do not want. Wonderful generosity! In accordance with their whole character, they tyrannize over the women, who are, in fact, their slaves, made to do all the degrading and severe drudgery incident to their mode of life. The men lounge idly and lazily about the tent, smoke, drink coffee, and play at games of hazard, of which they have a considerable variety. They are execrably filthy and foul-mouthed, totally uneducated, and supremely proud. Their very virtues are vices, or are contaminated by an odious selfishness. Such is their one boasted virtue of hospitality. It is a mere social regulation, and without something of the kind these troops of *land-pirates* could not carry on their detestable vocation —could not even exist. Away, then, with all this mawkish complacency in the brutal character and habits of these insolent barbarians! They would reduce Paradise itself to a howling wilderness in five years, and no civilized government could or would tolerate them for a day. This they well know, and hence they have an extreme dread and jealousy of this constant increase of European influence in the country. They do not hesitate to say that, whenever this influence becomes dominant, *they* must decamp forever. So it certainly will be, and I should rejoice to witness the realization of their worst apprehensions. Not till then can this fair and fertile land be regenerated.

But yonder is the *hump* of the *camel* which constituted the citadel, and gave name to the famous fortress of *Gamala;* for this is the Oriental word for camel, and it was appropriated to this isolated promontory from its resemblance to the back of that animal. By my aneroid it is eleven hundred and seventy feet above the lake, and we must leave our horses at its base, and climb on foot to its giddy summit as best we may. And now, within its mighty ramparts, let us sit down on one of these broken columns, and read Josephus until sufficiently rested to take a survey of this strongest of Jewish fortifications; for Jewish it is, and no mistake, whatever may be said of other castles. It was the last that was sacked by Vespasian and Titus before the siege of Jerusalem, and it has remained to this day just as they left it. It has not been repaired, and the materials have never been wanted for any other place. He who would study the architecture and mode of fortification at the time of Christ, should visit this Kŭl'aet Hŭsn, as Gamala is now called. No other ruin in this country has remained so intact and perfect.

Josephus informs us that, even after the taking of Jotapata and all other places in these regions, the people of Gamala refused to surrender to the Romans. "They relied upon the difficulty of the place, which was greater than that of Jotapata, for it was situated upon a rough ridge of a high mountain, with a kind of neck in the middle. Where it begins to ascend it lengthens itself, and declines as much downward before as behind, insomuch that it is like a camel in figure, from whence it is so named." He goes on to speak, in his accustomed style of exaggeration, of deep valleys all around it, and frightful precipices, which made every approach to it quite impossible. These were rendered still more impregnable by walls and towers above, and deep ditches below. This is sufficiently graphic, and *almost* accurate, for it is naturally one of the very strongest positions I have ever examined. But, notwithstanding this, it was doomed to utter destruction. On the last of September, in the year *sixty-nine* of our era, the invincible legions of Rome closed around it, never to leave while a living man remained in Gamala. The *Fifteenth* fortified their camp on that ridge over against us to the east; the *Fifth* did the same farther round toward the north, as I read Josephus; and the *Tenth* filled up the ditches on the southeastern part, along that narrow *neck* which connects this citadel with the main mountain on the south. Strong detachments also watched and hemmed in the devoted city on all sides, so that escape was impossible.

When the ditches were filled, and the way leveled up to a part of the wall that protected the lower city (there on the *neck*, I suppose), the battering-rams were made to play upon it in three places with such fury that it soon gave way and fell. Through the gap rushed the iron-clad legions, with "mighty sound of trumpets, and noise of armor and shout of soldiers." But despair and phrensy nerved the hearts and arms of the Jews. They threw themselves madly upon their enemies, beat them back by main force, and overwhelmed them from above with darts, stones, and any thing within reach. The Romans, hard pressed, rushed into the houses (that hung one over another along that steep declivity) in such numbers that the foundations gave way, and those above falling on those below, carried all away in their headlong descent, house upon house, in horrible confusion, burying up and crushing to death whole ranks in a moment. Thus it happened that "a great number were ground to powder by those ruins, and a great many of those that got from under them lost some of their limbs, but a still greater number were suffocated by the dust that arose from those ruins." Josephus was then a prisoner in the Roman camp, and witnessed the awful scene from a high point on this overhanging mountain. His description is therefore very minute and graphic; true also, I suppose, for there was no particular temptation to exaggerate or falsify. He says that the houses which fell with the Romans were low and not firm, and an inspection of the place shows that none but very low houses could have stood there at all, for the face of the mountain is nearly perpendicular. After immense confusion and wild disorder, in which Vespasian himself was in extreme danger of perishing, the Romans retreated to their camps, and the Gamalites celebrated their unexpected victory with the most extravagant rejoicings.

Brief was their triumph. Vespasian comforted and encouraged his army in a set speech. Titus came back from Syria with re-enforcements; a high tower on the wall was undermined, and fell with prodigious noise; the soldiers rushed in again, led on by Titus himself; every thing gave way, and went down before the tenfold fury of the onset—the outer city first, and then this wonderful citadel itself was taken, and every thing that breathed was put to the sword, even to the women and helpless infants. *Five thousand* of these most miserable people, seeing escape impossible, destroyed themselves; husbands threw their wives over the walls; parents seized their children and leaped madly from the ramparts, and were crushed into hideous masses in those yawning gulfs below. Look over, if your head is steady enough, and see into what awful depths they must have plunged. So fell Gamala on the 23d of October, A.D. 69, after a siege of twenty-nine days. Of the entire population that thronged this city and citadel, only *two women* escaped. The next act in the drama of Israel's destruction opens on the hills around Jerusalem, where the long, bloody tragedy winds up with the total overthrow of the city and the holy temple, amid agonies and carnage never seen before, and never to be repeated while the world stands.

Let us now take a walk around the fortifications of old Gamala. You observe that this "hump of the camel" extends from southeast to northwest. The diameter from the eastern gate to the one at the northwestern extremity is *seven hundred and sixty-five paces*, and a straight and well-defined street ran from gate to gate. The average width was not quite half the length, and the entire shape of the summit approaches an oval. On all sides it is surrounded by deep ravines, except the narrow neck which joins it to the main mountain. This *neck* is much lower than the *hump*, and both are several hundred feet lower than the surrounding heights. Indeed, the *hump* looks as though it had broken away from those gigantic cliffs, pushed out lakewise to the northwest, and *sagged* down some five hundred feet below its original position, having only this narrow ridge to connect it with the parent mountain. Along this ridge, and particularly the eastern side of it, the exterior city was built, and in such fashion that Josephus says it looked as though it would fall down upon itself. The citadel, or *hump*, was entirely surrounded by a strong wall, which was carried along the very brink of the precipices, and in some parts arches had to be thrown from cliff to cliff to secure a practicable foundation. Josephus intimates that he built this wall, which is simply absurd; but the man that could build the walls around the top of Tabor in *forty days*, might possibly construct these of Gamala in some idle moment! The fact is, that in neither case could Josephus have done more than slightly repair works which were already there.

This entire citadel, nearly a mile and a half in circuit, was covered with heavy buildings, and as the material was indestructible basalt, they remain very much as the Romans left them. This *tower* in the centre appears to have been the largest and highest of all. Near it once stood a temple or splendid synagogue, and another to the northeast of it. Is it not marvelous to see the ground hereabouts thickly strewn with granite columns from Egypt? How did they get them up to this giddy perch? There must have been great wealth in the city, and roads, and machinery, of which the Syrians of this day have no conception. The entire wealth and power of the present generation would be exhausted, and fail in the attempt to carry any one of these columns from Tiberias to the top of this *hump* of the camel; and here are at least *thirty* of them in this immediate vicinity, and some of them more than fourteen feet long. On the east of this tower is an immense underground cistern, the vault of which is a fine specimen of the Roman arch. There were also numerous cisterns in every part of the citadel, and necessarily so, because there was no other supply of water. Here are some Corinthian capitals neatly cut in hard black basalt—a curiosity in their way; and these sarcophagi and sepulchral stones are entirely peculiar to this city—at least I have seen nothing like them elsewhere. But what marks it as a genuine Hebrew city is the total absence of inscriptions. There is not a solitary letter in any language.

Josephus incidentally mentions a phenomenon which I happened to verify in my own experience. Speaking of the last assault upon the citadel, when Vespasian brought the whole army to support his son Titus, he says, "Now this upper part of the city was very rocky, and difficult of ascent, and elevated to a vast altitude, and very full of people on all sides, and encompassed with precipices, whereby the Jews cut off those that came up to them," etc. "However, there arose such a *divine storm* against them as was instrumental in their destruction. This carried the Roman darts upon them, and made those which they threw return back, and drove them obliquely away from them. Nor could the Jews, indeed, *stand upon their precipices* by reason of the violence of the wind," etc., etc. Without supposing there was any thing specially *divine* in the wind which blew down these ravines and over these ruins on my first visit, yet it was so vehement that I could not stand upon the ramparts for half a minute. Indeed, the depths below are so profound, in many parts, that no one can look into them without a shudder even in the calmest weather. It occurred to me at the time that this incidental notice by a contemporary of a furious wind rushing down toward and upon the lake is a happy corroboration of the evangelical narratives, in which similar phenomena are repeatedly mentioned. To say the least, it is in beautiful correspondence with them.

With the single exception of Jerusalem, Gamala furnishes the most remarkable fulfillment on record of those terrible predictions of our Saviour concerning the destruction of the Jews, and in its haggard desolation and utter solitude it is at this day a much more impressive monument of divine judgment than even the Holy City itself.

We may now return, and thus relieve the real or pretended fears of our guide, who has been impatient of our long ramble. He says that this is a chosen resort of robbers, which, by the way, I do not believe. They rarely frequent such a place as this unless it be in search of hid treasure. When I descended from here to the camp of Mahmood they were extremely suspicious of the purpose of my visit, and no explanations, reasonings, or protestations had the slightest effect in removing their belief that I had gone there to search for gold. When I appealed to the fact that some of their own men were with me, they replied that all I did then was to take a copy of the localities where the treasure was, so that I might come back in the night and carry it away. When asked why they did not take it themselves, they gave two reasons: first, that they had no *daleel*, or guide to the exact spot; and, secondly, that they had no *charm* of sufficient potency to subdue the spirits (jin) that keep guard over the treasure. The Bedawîn universally believe in the existence of such guards, and of charms or *names* which will subdue them. There is no tale on this subject in the "Thousand Nights," however extravagant, but what is to them credible and real. A large part of their conversation is made up of preposterous stories of this kind. They enter into the most minute details of the localities, the caves, rooms, closed doors, slabs with iron rings, etc., etc., ending always with some obstinate door which none of their *charms* could open; or, if they broke it open by main force, they were beaten back, thrown to the ground, blinded, suffocated with fumes of sulphur, or in some other miraculous way compelled by the guardian spirits to abandon the attempt. Of these creatures, also, they give the most outlandish descriptions, and appear firmly to believe their own stories. Several of the wildest of these romances have their locality in these very ruins of Gamala.

This amazing superstition is not only a source of constant annoyance to the traveler, but in these out-of-the-way parts of the country greatly increases the difficulties and the dangers of exploration. I am not sure but that my talkative guide from Sheikh Mahmood was induced to watch us so strictly under the idea that we either had or were intending to carry away their coveted treasure, and this absurd superstition might have cost us our lives if we had fallen into their hands in Wady Mendhour. Doubtless, too, it is this apprehension that induces Arabs often to conceal interesting localities from the traveler, or to refuse to accompany him to them; and, indeed, they have been known to mislead by false directions. This is one reason of the ridiculous blunders and topographical errors of certain tourists. Only this last year the British consul of Damascus (who had more influence over the Arabs of this country than any other man), in furnishing me with letters of protection to a large number of sheikhs in these mountains east of the Jordan, informed me that I must not take any instruments with me, nor be seen to take drawings, for it would certainly endanger my life, in spite of all the protection which the British government could throw around me. These remarks, of course, apply chiefly to the remoter parts of the land—to routes and sites entirely under the control of the Bedawîn. Other places can be visited with but little annoyance from this cause, and yet, even in the most civilized districts, the people are provokingly pertinacious in ascribing our visits to old ruins to this, the only intelligible motive to their minds. The idea of coming far, toiling hard, and *spending money* merely to examine historic sites is to them absurd and ridiculous.

Before we bid a final adieu to these mournful ruins, let us take a glance at their neighbors, some of which are not wanting in historic interest. That fortified rock on the north is called Nkeib, and the ruins upon it are evidently of the same age as these of Gamala. That sharp pinnacle farther north, which resembles a church steeple, is Kureîn el Jerady. East of us about two miles is Fîk, a considerable village on the top of the mountain, occupying the site of the ancient Aphek, the city to which Benhadad fled after one hundred thousand of his soldiers had been slain in battle by Ahab. The city, however, proved almost as destructive as the army of Israel, for a wall fell upon twenty and seven thousand of the men that were left.[1] This tremendous destruction was caused, as I suppose, by an earthquake; and after having seen the effects of the earthquake in Safed and Tiberias, I can easily understand and readily credit this narrative. We are not required to limit the catastrophe to the falling of a single wall, or, if this be insisted upon, we have only to suppose that it was the wall of the city, and a little consideration will convince any one familiar with Oriental fortifications that it might overwhelm a whole army. Those ramparts were very lofty and massive. An open space was always left along their base, and this would be packed full and tight, from end to end, by the remnants of Benhadad's mighty host, and escape from the falling towers would be impossible. The peculiar character of the site would render the destruction only the more extensive and inevitable. I have not visited it, but Burckhardt passed through it in 1812, and he informs us that the town is built around the base of a hill in the shape of a crescent, not unlike the topography of Safed, and it was this circumstance which rendered the overthrow of that place so destructive. The Fîk of our day is a mere village, containing about two hundred families, dwelling in huts built out of the rubbish of the ancient city.

Burckhardt seems to have visited Kŭl'aet Hŭsn, or, at least, he heard of it, and supposed that it marked the site of Argob, the capital of the kingdom of Og. This is not very probable; indeed, it is not certain, from the various notices of Argob, that it was a city at all. In Deut. iii. 13, 14, we read of the *region* of Argob, and of *all the country* of Argob, and the same in first Kings iv. 13; but nothing is said of a *city* of that name, nor can I hear of any such ancient site. It is worthy of note, however, that the Bedawîn familiarly speak of this whole district as Arkoob or Argoob. Thus they call the mountain on which Um Keîs stands Argoob

[1] 1 Kings xx. 26–30.

Um Keîs, and this mountain above us Argoob Hŭsn; and although this word is applied to any rough, mountainous country, I have nowhere else heard it thus used in common conversation; and since the kingdom or district of Argob was in this immediate neighborhood, I think it nearly certain that we have the identical name still preserved among these primitive inhabitants. And as this province is very wild and broken, may not its own proper name have been transferred, as an adjective, to all similar districts?

Burckhardt speaks of a plain which extends from Fîk far into the interior of the Jaulan, and I myself passed over a portion of it, and thought it beautiful and very fertile. Josephus, in his account of the defeat of Benhadad, says he pitched his camp *in the great plain*,[1] a phrase often applied to Esdraelon, the valley of the Jordan, and other places. In the present case he probably means this very plain north of Fîk, since the remnants of his army fled into this city.

Directly south of el Hŭsn, on the mountain, is an inhabited village called Kefr Hârib, and below it are the ruins of a castle, said to have belonged to it in olden times. The plain, between the shore and the mountain, you observe, widens as we advance, and becomes more fertile. The thickness of the superincumbent trap also decreases, and yellow calcareous rock crops out nearer and nearer the surface, until, at the valley of the Jermuk, the former ceases altogether, and cretaceous limestone takes its place. The scenery becomes less savage and more picturesque, the soil richer, the pastures more luxuriant, and noble forests of oak, terebinth, and other trees adorn the hills and valleys. All tourists agree in representing this as one of the most charming regions of the East, and we draw the same conclusion from the incidental references to it in Bible history. I long to explore Gilead and Bashan, and hope to do it on some future occasion, but at present we must continue the even tenor of our way round the southern shore of this lake. Here are traces of an old village called Dueir Ban, and a little farther south is Khurbet Samra. A long low ridge di-

[1] Ant. viii. 14, 4.

vides the plain of the Ghor quite down to the Jermuk. It is called Tell et Tâlib, and also Kusr el Kelb, from an old castle of that name. Khan 'Agaba, mentioned by Burckhardt, is on the side of it. He says that this Khurbet Samra was inhabited when he passed this way in 1812, but, to judge from present appearances, he must have been mistaken, for it seems to have been an utter ruin for generations. It *may* have been occupied by a few Arab huts, and certainly there could have been nothing here forty years ago of a more substantial character. We should not be too positive, however, because the peasants in all this region build very ephemeral habitations with small stones and mud, which, if deserted, soon fall and melt away like summer snow on the mountains. It is surprising to see how quickly houses which no man inhabiteth become heaps, as Job has it,[1] and Solomon noticed the same thing. By much slothfulness the building decayeth, and through idleness of the hands the house droppeth through.[2] The roof of any of these huts, forsaken or neglected through idleness, will "drop through" in a single winter, and then the unprotected walls *wash down* by the rain, and speedily become mere shapeless "heaps." The cause is easily explained. The roof is made by heaping a thick stratum of earth over the brush, thorns, and cane which are laid on the beams to receive it. This earth, if not constantly *rolled*, or carefully plastered so as to shed the rain, absorbs it, until the weight breaks the beams, and then the whole mass drops through, bursting out the feeble walls, which now have nothing to bind them together. The mortar used is without lime, and, when thoroughly saturated by the rain, becomes as slippery as soap, and thus the whole fabric tumbles into a dismal ruin. Indeed, such frail houses often fall suddenly during great storms, and crush the inhabitants to death. This is particularly the case where there is much snow, and the people can not properly roll their terraces.

It was such facts as these, perhaps, that suggested to Ezekiel the terms of that terrible rebuke to the prophets of Is-

[1] Job xv. 28.   [2] Eccl. x. 18.

rael: Because, even because they have seduced my people, saying Peace, and there was no peace; and one built a wall, and lo, others daubed it with untempered mortar. Say unto them that daub it with untempered mortar *that it shall fall.* There shall be an overflowing shower, and ye, O great hailstones, shall fall, and a stormy wind shall rend it.[1]

Yes, these are the very agencies by which the Lord now overthrows in a night whole villages thus built with untempered mortar. "So will I break down the wall that ye have daubed with untempered mortar, and bring it down to the ground, so that the foundations thereof shall be discovered, and it shall fall, *and ye shall be consumed in the midst thereof.*" A calamity, this, of very frequent occurrence. I have known many such during my residence in this land, and this whole passage is so graphic and true to experience, that the prophet, beyond a doubt, drew the picture from scenes with which he was personally familiar. This Samakh which we are approaching is a striking specimen of walls built and daubed with such mortar, and not a few of the houses threaten to crush their inhabitants beneath their ruins. It is at present the only inhabited village in this fertile delta formed by the lake, the Jordan, and the Jermuk, and it probably marks the site of the ancient Hippos. One or two of the houses, and the *menzûl* for strangers, are partly built of cut stone which belonged to the old city, but the remainder are made of small *cobble-stones* from the shore and *untempered* mortar, loosely laid up, and daubed on the outside with the same.

The plain is some twenty feet above the lake, quite level, but declines rapidly to the junction of the Jordan and the Jermuk, some six miles to the south. It is a mere mud deposit, and indicates that the level of the lake has been, at some former period, much higher than it is now. The people of the village informed me that in very rainy years the water rises several feet above its present low mark, and should any thing dam up the narrow exit of the Jordan, it would, of course, rise at once to the level of the plain.

[1] Ezek. xiii. 10–16.

I once spent several days encamped on the pebbly beach below Samakh, and had ample time to explore the entire southern shore of the lake, as well as the outgoings of the Jordan. The shore is covered with pebbles of flint, jasper, chalcedony, and agate, mixed with several kinds of freshwater shells. The largest is a variety of the *unio*. The exit of the Jordan is correctly laid down by Captain Lynch, but by no other author that I have seen. The ruins of an ancient bridge partly choke up the exit, and narrow it to about one hundred feet in width at low water, and even then it was not more than four feet deep; the current, however, is very swift. The shore and the river I found crowded with ducks, crane, and other water-fowl in the latter part of February, and, were it safe, it would be a delightful spot for the sportsman and the lover of fish and game. Samakh has about two hundred wretched huts, packed in together in the most uncomfortable manner possible. The inhabitants are all Moslems, and of course, or of necessity, confederates in robbery with their neighbors, those *Diabs—wolves*—whose tents we saw along the base of Tell Tâlib. No wonder the Bedawîn prefer the open country and the canvas cover to such a congregation of dust, filth, vermin, and every other abomination which men and brutes can make. Nothing would induce me to dwell in such a village. And yet it is situated on the shore of this sweet and beautiful lake, with the most interesting scenery in the world around it. Alas! it is a splendid jewel in a swine's snout.[1]

The regular path leads directly to the ford below the broken bridge, Em el Kŭnâtur, but we will follow the shore to the exit of the Jordan. We have now a good view of the entire lake, and can see at a glance that it narrows rapidly on both sides, until it is not more than three miles wide at this extremity of it. The Jordan leaves it near the southwest corner, and its exit was commanded by those fortified tells on the north side, now called Tells of Kerak. The triangular plat north of them is the site of the ancient Taricea or Tarichea, so famous in the wars of the Jews. A branch

[1] Prov. xi. 22.

of the river once came down on the west side, and, of course, made the site of the city an island; nor would it be difficult to make that again the main outlet of the river, as it probably was in former times. This Kerak was the great naval station of the Jews in the time of the Roman war. Josephus collected *two hundred and thirty ships* at this place to attack Tiberias, and here occurred the only sea-fight between the Jews and Romans. The ships probably lay at anchor within and around the exit of the Jordan, protected by towers upon these tells. The situation is admirable for the purpose, and there is no other safe harbor on the whole lake. It must, therefore, have been a place of great importance, so long as there were ships to need a refuge from the wild winds which often sweep over it. I have seen it lashed into fury for thirty consecutive hours by a tempest that would have wrecked a hundred fleets such as those of Josephus, had they been exposed to its violence.

How different the condition of these shores now from the time when Josephus could gather at this point more than two hundred ships in a single day! There is not at this hour a boat of any kind upon the lake, and I never but once saw a single sail unfurled upon its deserted bosom. Josephus, however, who lived, and sailed, and fought on it in the time of the apostles, abundantly corroborates their accounts of the ships that then sailed over it, and my own experience confirms all the other phenomena mentioned by them. Small as the lake is, and placid, in general, as a molten mirror, I have repeatedly seen it quiver, and leap, and boil like a caldron, when driven by fierce winds from the eastern mountains, and the waves ran high—high enough to fill or "cover" the ships, as Matthew has it.[1] In the midst of such a gale "calmly slept the Son of God," in the hinder part of the ship, until awakened by the terrified disciples.

Gadara, with her prostrate temples and theatres, is seated on the top of the mountain south of the great gorge of the Jermuk, and the celebrated hot baths of another Hamath are below on the bank of the river. The fountains are of

[1] Matt. viii. 24.

immense size, and the entire locality extremely interesting and wild. Until quite recently the Christians of Nazareth held a grand fair at those baths, and they still speak in raptures of the happy times they used to enjoy there, and curse these Arab wolves who now prowl about, and render it utterly impossible to hold their joyous festa.

The great highway from the west, into Perea, Decapolis, and the distant east passed the Jordan at this bridge to which we are coming, now called Jisr el Kŭnâtur, in reference to the many high arches on which it rested. They appear to have been ten, but are all so broken and choked up with rubbish that one can not be quite certain as to the number. The ford below it would be excellent were it not for the fragments of the bridge which strew the bottom. The river is about three hundred feet broad, and it is not more than three feet deep except in early spring. The only bridge still in repair is Jisr el Mŭjamia, about seven miles below the lake. I spent a night and day there last spring with 'Akil 'Aga, and then followed the west bank of the Jordan to this point. The junction of the Jermuk is in a rough, rocky channel, about a mile north of the Mŭjamia, and it is also spanned by a strong stone bridge. Farther up the river is a ruined site called Dalhamia or Dalmamia. One could make Dalmanutha out of this word, if the geography of the New Testament would admit the location here of that place, to which our Lord came on his return from Cæsarea Philippi (Banias) through the midst of the coasts of Decapolis.[1] This journey of our Saviour appears to have been unusually extended and very circuitous. Departing from Tyre and Sidon, he came to this lake, not by the direct route, but, going first to Banias, he then made a circuit through the region of Decapolis, on the east of the lake and the Jordan. Now, if he visited Jerash, Pella, Gadara, and Hippos, he might return by this Dalhamia on his way home, or might come hither by boat, as Mark states. It must be remembered, however, that Matthew says Jesus came into the coasts of *Magdala*[2] after the very same miracle mention-

[1] Mark vii. 31.   [2] Matt. xv. 39.

RUINS OF GADARA.

ed by Mark, just before he came to Dalmanutha; and this want of correspondence (for it is not a contradiction) between the two records my geographical knowledge does not yet enable me to clear up. It is generally supposed that the name in Mark is an error, and ought to be corrected into Magdala. This solution I do not accept. It is certain that but a *very few* points in this long journey are mentioned by any of the evangelists, and Jesus may well have gone to both Magdala and Dalmanutha; and since he must have passed very near to this Dalhamia (as it is now called), it is not unlikely that he visited it. At any rate, there is abundant room in the country, and in the narratives, for *a* Dalmanutha, and I see no good reason for supposing that Mark has fallen into a geographical error. If this Dalhamia is not it, I confidently expect that some other more fortunate explorer will ere long reveal the true site. Let us wait patiently. Every extension of our knowledge in this department lessens the number of topographical obscurities, and in time all will be cleared away.

How strangely the Jordan winds about, as if reluctant to leave its mother for the hard, downward race to the Sea of Death! On coming out of the lake it first runs northward, then west, southwest, and finally south, and all within a mile. Here at the bridge its course is south, but it soon departs from this western side of the plain and makes a long detour to the east, and thus it continues meandering about in the most eccentric fashion, often darting along rocky rapids, or leaping down noisy cataracts as if in sport, and then stealing silently away in some new direction, beneath overhanging willows and thick sycamores. On the whole, one is very much amused with its behavior, and quite satisfied that the Jordan should be as peculiar in its character as it is unique in its history. Its manifold windings and doublings, with all the green islets inclosed, are accurately laid down in Captain Lynch's map, so far as I have followed the course of the river. There must have been far more water when he passed down it than there is now, or it would have been impossible to get the boats through the rocks in safety. To judge from the pictures we have of that expedition, the act of shooting these rapids must have been sufficiently perilous, even under the most favorable circumstances.

SHOOTING THE RAPIDS.

About three miles lower down is a large village, on a singular tell near the river. It is called Abadîyeh, and the surrounding lands are well cultivated. South of that the entire valley of the Jordan is abandoned to the Bedawîn, and there is not an inhabited village until you reach Jericho. Beyond those nearest hills on our left is a deep wady called

Fedjâs, which runs far up to the northwest. In it is a copious fountain, the water of which was anciently carried along the declivity of the valley in an aqueduct which bent round the end of the ridge northward, and was taken to the old city of Tiberias. You can see the remains of that great work here above us on the side of the mountain. Those who built it seem not to have been acquainted with the *arch*, for the canal was frequently led into the heart of the hill in order to get round some narrow ravine. I have not seen this curious old work noticed by any traveler, and I myself passed this way repeatedly without seeing it. The chief design of it, I suppose, was to *irrigate* the orchards and gardens of Tarichea, Emmaus, and Tiberias, because the water of Fedjâs is not particularly good to drink, and the inhabitants on this shore desire no better water than that of the lake itself. There are ruins of a building on the hill side, now called Tâhûn es Sŭkkar — that is, sugar-mill, and it seems to have been driven by water from the canal. It is not impossible that sugar-cane was once grown on this part of the Jordan valley (as it certainly was about Jericho), and that this canal was made to serve the double purpose of irrigating the sugar plantations and of driving the mills to crush the cane. This double use of aqueducts is every where made, where the condition of the adjacent land will admit it. Of course this supposition implies that the canal has been in use in comparatively modern times.

We have now an easy ride of an hour along the shore to the celebrated hot baths of Tiberias. A castle once crowned this eminence on the left, and this old wall ran from its base across the ancient bed of that branch of the Jordan which ran on the west side of Tarichea. This wall and castle would entirely command the road along the shore, so that it would be impossible to pass without permission. The *wall* may also have served as a causeway to the city when the delta on which it stood was surrounded by water.

This place on our left is now called Shŭgshab, but it must mark the site of Sennabris according to Josephus, for the Roman army encamped at it was in full view of Tiberias, and it is only at this spot (half an hour down the lake from the baths) that this could have been true. There are traces of old buildings hereabouts, and the name is sufficiently outlandish to have come down from the dark ages.

There has been a smart shower here, while at Samakh the ground was baked hard, and the grain drooping sadly. The same was true on a former occasion when I came up the Jordan valley. The ground in the Ghor was like a parched desert. There had not been sufficient rain to bring up the grain, and "the seed sown had rotted under the clod," while here at Tiberias the whole country was a paradise of herbs and flowers. And thus it was in former times. The Lord caused it to rain upon one city, says Amos, and caused it not to rain upon another city. One piece was rained upon, and the piece whereupon it rained not withered.[1] It was literally so about Samakh and 'Abadîyeh, while their nearest neighbors were rejoicing in abundant showers. There are other interesting allusions to matters in agricultural experience in this passage of Amos. "I have withdrawn, says God, the rain from you when there were yet three months to the harvest." This is utterly ruinous to the hopes of the farmer. A little earlier or a little later would not be so fatal, but drouth *three months before harvest* is entirely destructive. In the 8th verse we read, "So two or three cities wandered unto one city to drink water, but they were not satisfied"—a fact often repeated in this country. No longer ago than last autumn it had its exemplification complete in Belad Besharah, the ancient inheritance of Naphtali.

Here are the far-famed baths. They are often mentioned by Josephus, who says they were a *little distance* from Tiberias, in a village called Emmaus.[2] I am inclined to think that this was the Hammath given to Naphtali; and if so, then Rakkath, mentioned in connection with it, may have been the ancestor of Kerak at the outgoing of the Jordan. There is a certain similarity in the names either in sound or in signification. Kerak and Rakkath ring on the Arab ear alike; and Emmaus and Hammath are but different

---

[1] Amos iv. 7, 8.   [2] Ant. xviii. 2, 3.

LAKE OF TIBERIAS, FROM THE BATHS.

modifications of the word from which Hammam, the name for warm baths, is derived. Tiberias itself *may* occupy the site of Chinneroth, from which the lake derived its primitive name, as it now gets that of Tiberias from its successor. We throw out these suppositions without vouching for their truth, or attempting to establish it. I can not doubt, however, but that there was a city near Tiberias far older and more splendid than that built by Herod. The granite columns mingled among the now visible ruins must have an antiquity much higher than the first century of our era. I suppose the city of Herod occupied the same situation as the present town, for it is plainly implied in many notices by Josephus that it was at a considerable distance from the hot baths, while these ancient remains extend quite down to them. They can not, therefore, be the ruins of Herod's city, but of one still older than it. Emmaus (alias Hammath) lay chiefly south of the baths, and its walls can be traced out without any doubt or difficulty. But this is quite enough of topography for once.

The water of these springs has a sulphurous and most disagreeable smell, and is so nauseous that it can not be drunk, and is not used internally. The baths, however, have a great medicinal reputation, and their sanitary virtues are believed by the ignorant to be almost adequate to remove all the ills to which frail flesh is heir. The accommodations for bathing are every thing but satisfactory, and the entire establishment is filthy and offensive in the extreme, and yet it is always crowded with the lame, the halt, the withered, and the leprous—a disgusting rabble of greasy Jews and scurvy Arabs. There is but one common bathing cistern, where the water is hot enough to cook an egg, and it is always crowded with naked patients seething and steaming like slaughtered swine in a scalding vat. What healthy person would dare to bathe in such a cistern, and with such company! How they can endure the water at from 130° to 140° of Fahrenheit is a mystery. I once had the bath cleared, and made the experiment, but should have fainted in a very short time if I had not made my escape from it.

Little by little, however, they get used to it, and some delight to roll about in it by the hour, happy as a hippopotamus in the Nile.

The temperature of the fountains varies in different years, and at different seasons of the same year. According to my thermometers, it has ranged, within the last twenty years, from 136° to 144°. I was here in 1833, when Ibrahim Pasha was erecting these buildings, and they appeared quite pretty. The earthquake which destroyed Tiberias in 1837 did no injury to the baths, although the fountains were greatly disturbed, and threw out more water than usual, and of a much higher temperature. This disturbance, however, was only temporary, for when I came here about a month after the earthquake they had settled down into their ordinary condition.

Are these hot springs ever mentioned in the Bible?

The name of the place perhaps is, but the baths themselves are not alluded to either in the Old or the New Testament. There is a curious passage in Gen. xxxvi. 24, which I suspect refers to warm mineral springs and their medicinal virtues. In our translation it reads thus: This was that Anah that found *the mules* in the wilderness as he fed the asses of Zibeon his father. The Hebrew word *yamim*, here translated *mules*, means *waters;* and the Vulgate and Arabic translations render it *warm waters*, which rendering Jerome and others among the ancients favor, and not a few modern critics agree with them. Of one thing I am well satisfied, that Anah did not find *mules*, whatever may be the true meaning of *yamim*. And since such hot fountains exist, not only here, but in Wady Mendhour, below Gadara, and at Callirrhoe, east of the Dead Sea, it is quite possible that Moses may have become acquainted with them when in that region, and also with the fact that Anah had first discovered them, or at least had found out their medicinal virtues, and brought them into public notice. Perhaps some remarkable cures upon Jews of distinction rendered it still farther appropriate for Moses to commemorate the discovery and the discoverer.

XXVII. TIBERIAS.

March 25th.

You should have been out with me on the promontory which overhangs the lake, to see the day break along the eastern mountains. At first it was intensely dark, but by-and-by it began to soften low down and far to the north. Then suddenly the note of a lark rang out, silvery and joyous, as if from the very midst of the stars. In rapid succession, bird after bird rose up, hymning their early matin, until the whole "marble vault of heaven" was vocal with invisible choristers. One by one the stars faded out before the growing day, and every moment the scene shifted and changed from bright to brighter—from glory to glory, throwing down dark shadows from the eastern cliffs upon the broad bosom of Gennesaret. At length the first rays of the sun gleamed on the snowy head of Hermon, revealing deep wrinkles, which the storms of a thousand generations have drawn across his stern cold brow. It was the very perfection of this style of beauty, nor do I understand how any one can call it tame. Doubtless time and season, pleasant company, good health, and cheerful spirits add immensely to the effect of such a scene. In the glare and burning heat of midsummer, a weary traveler, with eyes inflamed, might see nothing to admire, but I have never thus visited it. To me Gennesaret and its surroundings are ever fair, and always invested with unparalleled interest. Here our blessed Lord dwelt with men, and taught the way of life. Here he preached in a ship, slept in the storm, walked on the waves, rebuked the winds, and calmed the sea. Here is Magdala, Capernaum, Chorazin, and Bethsaida, with its desert place, where five thousand hungry souls were fed with miraculous bread; and Gergesa, where devils went from men to swine, and both together into the sea. Here he opened his mouth, and taught, with authority, that divine sermon on the mount; and on one of these solitary summits Moses and Elias, in shining robes, came down from heaven to converse with him in the glory of his transfiguration. And not least, from this shore he selected those wonderful men who were to erect his kingdom, and carry his Gospel to the ends of the earth. Is there another spot on the globe that can compare with this?

John is the only evangelist who mentions Tiberias; but he not only speaks of the city, but calls the lake by this name more than once.[1] May we not find in this an incidental corroboration of the opinion that his gospel was written last of all, and toward the close of the first century, and for those who by that time had come to know the lake most familiarly by the name of Tiberias?

This supposition becomes the more probable when we remember that it was quite a modern town when our Lord frequented this region, having been built and named by Herod about the time of his advent. Seventy years afterward, Josephus found it an important city, and no other in Galilee is so often mentioned by him. Almost every other city was destroyed by Vespasian and Titus, but this was spared, and rewarded for its adherence to the Romans by being made the capital of the province. John, writing many years after these events, would naturally mention both the city and the lake, and call the latter by its then most familiar name, Tiberias. But the other apostles wrote before these events had taken place, and therefore do not speak of Tiberias at all.

Is it not somewhat strange that our Saviour never entered Tiberias?

This is not quite certain, for he undoubtedly visited many places which are not mentioned by any of the evangelists; and if the tradition respecting the site of the present old church has any foundation in fact, he did actually enter it, and even after his resurrection. It is my opinion, however, that he never came to Tiberias, and for several reasons, which, by the aid of Josephus, we are able to discover. He tells us that Herod, in order to people his new city, brought many strangers, and people called Galileans, and many not even freemen, but slaves.[2] In short, Herod gathered up all classes, and compelled them to settle in Tiberias. This was

---

[1] John vi. 1; xxi. 1; vi. 23.   [2] Ant. xviii. 2, 3.

TIBERIAS AND LAKE, LOOKING TO THE NORTHEAST.

not a population with which our Lord and his disciples would choose to associate. Josephus farther states that to make this place habitable was to transgress the ancient laws of the Jews, because "many sepulchres were here to be taken away in order to make room for the city of Tiberias, whereas our law pronounces that such persons are unclean for seven days." Jesus, therefore, *could not enter* this city without becoming ceremonially unclean, and we know that both he and his disciples scrupulously avoided any such violation of the law of Moses. He *never visited Tiberias*, and thus the silence of the evangelists in regard to it is explained.

This piece of history suggests one or two other remarks. It is nearly certain that Tiberias was built, in part at least, upon the cemetery of a neighboring city then in ruins, for without such a city whence came the many sepulchres spoken of? And that this city was ancient, and long since deserted, is evident from the fact that these sepulchres had no owners to be outraged by their demolition. The people who once used that cemetery had totally disappeared from the vicinity before Tiberias was erected. We may also determine with certainty that this *former* city was *south* of the present one, for there is no place for it on the north, or in any other direction but south. This confirms the idea that the ruins between Tiberias and the baths are the remains of a city more ancient than that built by Herod. The remark of Josephus about the sepulchres also shows that the present town occupies the site of Herod's city. The face of the hill on which the northern part of it stands is covered with a very peculiar kind of tombs, and apparently as old as the rock itself. Many of them were wholly destroyed when the wall was built, for they extend under it, and into the city itself, while the whole hill side north and northwest of it is crowded with them—the forsaken graves of an extinct city and race. What was the name of this more ancient city must ever remain a matter of mere conjecture. It was many times larger than the modern town, for it covered the plain and side of the mountain quite down to the baths, and was a city of palaces, and temples, and splendid edifices, as the remains abundantly show. Perhaps it was Hammath itself, named from the hot baths, great and rich, from their celebrity in olden time. Perhaps it was Chinneroth, from which the lake took its most ancient, as it has derived its modern name from its successor. Perhaps—but it is idle to multiply suppositions of this kind.

It would be tedious to enter minutely into the history of this city and its varied fortunes; nor is this necessary. Reland, and Burckhardt, and Robinson, and Wilson, and Kitto have done this at large. Ever since the destruction of Jerusalem, it has been chiefly celebrated in connection with the Jews, and was for a long time the chief seat of rabbinical learning. It is still one of their four holy cities. Among the Christians it also early rose to distinction, and the old church, built upon the spot where our Lord gave his last charge to Peter, is a choice bit of ecclesiastical antiquity. Though we need not accept this age or origin, still I am not so sure as Dr. Robinson is that, because the arch of its vault is slightly *pointed*, its "antiquity must necessarily be limited to the time of the Crusades at the earliest." If not greatly mistaken, I have seen *such arches* far older than the twelfth century. But the entire subject of the *arch* is yet to be properly developed, and until this is done the unlearned must not be too positive. Let that pass. The present city is situated on the shore, at the northeast corner of this small plain. The walls inclose an irregular parallelogram, about one hundred rods from north to south, and in breadth not more than forty. They were strengthened by ten round towers on the west, five on the north, and eight on the south. There were also two or three towers along the shore to protect the city from attack by sea. Not much more than one half of this small area is occupied by buildings of any kind, and the north end, which is a rocky hill, has nothing but the ruins of the old palace. The earthquake of 1837 prostrated a large part of the walls, and they have not yet been repaired, and perhaps never will be. There is no town in Syria so utterly filthy as Tiberias, or so little to be desired as a residence. Being *six hundred* feet below the

HIGH TEMPERATURE—SIZE OF THE LAKE. 77

level of the ocean, and overhung on the west by a high mountain, which effectually shuts off the Mediterranean breezes, it is fearfully hot in summer. The last time I was encamped at the Baths the thermometer stood at 100° *at midnight*, and a steam went up from the surface of the lake as from some huge smouldering volcano. Of course it swarms with all sorts of vermin. What can induce human beings to settle down in such a place? And yet some two thousand of our race make it their chosen abode. They are chiefly Jews, attracted hither either to cleanse their leprous bodies in her baths, or to purify their unclean spirits by contact with her traditionary and ceremonial holiness.

The lake itself is too well known to need much description. It is an irregular *oval*, with the large end to the north. I can not make it more than fourteen miles long, and nine wide from Mejdel to Wady Semak. It is about *six hundred* feet lower than the Mediterranean, and this great depression accounts for some of its remarkable phenomena. Seen from any point of the surrounding heights it is a fine sheet of water—a burnished mirror set in a frame-work of rounded hills and rugged mountains, which rise and roll backward and upward to where hoary Hermon hangs the picture against the blue vault of heaven.

This profound basin owes its origin, I suppose, to volcanic agency at some remote epoch in geological chronology, but it is not necessary to maintain that the whole of it was once an active crater. Perhaps no part of it was, though it is surrounded by vast regions of trap rock. It *may*, therefore, have been a gigantic crater, with waves of burning lava instead of water. The lake is fed mainly by the Jordan, but, besides this, there are the great fountains of Fûlîyeh, el Mudowera, 'Ain et Tiny, and Tabiga, and in winter the streams from wadies Hamam, er Rŭbŭdîyeh, 'Amûd, and Leimûn from the west and northwest; and Sulam, Tellaiyeh, Jermaiah, Shŭkaiyif, and Semak on the east. During the rainy season these streams pour an immense amount of water into the lake, and raise its level several feet above its present mark. The effect is seen particularly along the southern end, and at the outlet of the Jordan. The old story, told by Tacitus and others, that the Jordan flows directly through the centre without mingling with the lake, has no other foundation than the fancy of those who repeat it. The water is sweet and wholesome, and the fish abundant and of an excellent quality. They are, however, but little troubled by either hook, net, or spear.

By the way, this reminds me that in all our rambles around this most Biblical of lakes, I have constantly missed two pictures with which it has ever been associated on fancy's tablet—the little ships and the fishermen. The absence of the former is easily explained. The few semi-savage Arabs who now frequent this shore have no occasion for ships. But why are there no fishers about Gennesaret? There are fish enough in these waters, as we have frequently seen.

The Arabs, particularly the Bedawîn and the peasant, have an invincible dread and repugnance to the sea, nor can they be tempted to trust themselves upon its treacherous bosom. Some of their favorite proverbs are intended to express this national aversion. If the lake was covered with boats, they would travel all round its shores on the slow-paced camel rather than sail directly across to our city. As there is no demand for boats, the very art of building them is lost. You could not find a carpenter on this whole coast who has either the materials, the tools, or the skill to construct one, or even to mend it if broken. They have no more use for boats than for well-made roads; both disappeared together when the Arabians conquered the country, and both will reappear together as soon as a more civilized race rises to power.

The cause for the absence of fishermen is likewise found in the character and habits of these Arabs. You could never persuade a genuine son of the desert to sit or stand all day holding a rod over the water with a string and hook at the end of it. If you put it into his hands all ready baited, you would soon hear "Yŭkta 'amrû" as he flung the whole apparatus into the lake. Those who dwell in the cities and villages along the coast of the Mediterranean have partially departed from these primitive habits, and learned from Greeks and Franks the piscatory art, but even they have no enthusiasm for it. Out here it is held in utter contempt.

How do you account for the fact that so many of the apostles were chosen from this class of fishermen? It could not have been accidental.

Nothing in the kingdom of Christ is accidental or the result of caprice, least of all the vital matter of its first teachers and founders. There was, no doubt, an adaptation, a fitness in the occupation of these men to develop just those attributes of character most needed in the apostolic office. There are various modes of fishing, and each calculated to cultivate and strengthen some particular moral quality of great importance in their mission. Thus angling requires *patience*, and great perseverance and caution. The line must be fine; the hook carefully concealed by the bait; and this, too, must be such as is suited to the capacity and taste of the fish you seek to catch. A mistake in any of these things defeats the object. If the hook is too big or not well covered—the bait too large or not adapted to the taste—of course you take nothing, or bring up a useless crab. There may be deceptive nibbles, but nothing more. So, also, the line must not alarm them, nor will it do to dash the hook in impatiently. And the man must not put *himself* forward; *he should not be seen at all.*

Then there is fishing with the hand-net. This is beautiful and picturesque. You see it to best advantage along the coast from Beirût to Sidon. The net is in shape like the top of a tent, with a long cord fastened to the apex. This is tied to his arm, and the net so folded that, when it is thrown, it expands to its utmost circumference, around which are strung beads of lead to make it drop suddenly to the bottom. Now see the actor: half bent, and more than half naked, he keenly watches the playful surf, and there he spies his game tumbling in carelessly toward him. Forward he leaps to meet it. Away goes the net, expanding as it flies, and its leaded circumference strikes the bottom ere the silly fish is aware that its meshes have closed around him. By the aid of his cord the fisherman leisurely draws up the net and the fish with it. This requires a keen eye, an active frame, and great skill in throwing the net. He, too, must be patient, watchful, wide awake, and prompt to seize the exact moment to throw.

Then there is the great drag-net, the working of which teaches the value of united effort. Some must row the boat, some cast out the net, some on the shore pull the rope with all their strength, others throw stones and beat the water round the ends, to frighten the fish from escaping there; and as it approaches the shore, every one is active in holding up the edges, drawing it to land, and seizing the fish. This is that net which gathered of every kind, and, when drawn to the shore, the fishermen sit down and collect the good into vessels, but cast the bad away.[1] I have watched this operation throughout a hundred times along the shore of the Mediterranean.

Again, there is the bag-net and basket-net, of various kinds, which are so constructed and worked as to inclose the fish out in deep water. I have seen them of almost every conceivable size and pattern. It was with some one of this sort, I suppose, that Simon had toiled all night without catching any thing, but which, when let down at the command of Jesus, inclosed so great a multitude that the net brake, and they filled two ships with the fish until they began to sink.[2] Peter here speaks of toiling all night, and there are certain kinds of fishing always carried on at night. It is a beautiful sight. With blazing torch, the boat glides over the flashing sea, and the men stand gazing keenly into it until their prey is sighted, when, quick as lightning, they fling their net or fly their spear; and often you see the tired firshermen come sullenly into harbor in the morning, having toiled all night in vain. Indeed, every kind of fishing is uncertain. A dozen times the angler jerks out a naked hook; the hand-net closes down on nothing; the drag-net brings in only weeds; the bag comes up empty. And

[1] Matt. xiii. 47, 48.   [2] Luke v. 4-9.

then, again, every throw is successful—every net is full; and frequently without any other apparent reason than that of throwing it on the right side of the ship instead of the left, as it happened to the disciples here at Tiberias.[1]

It is wholly unnecessary to apply these things to the business of fishing for men in the great seas of sin. *That* we may leave to the commentator and the preacher. No one occupation of humble life, not even that of the shepherd, calls into exercise and develops so many of the elements necessary for the office of a religious teacher as this of fishing.

Are we to understand from John xxi. 7 that Peter was actually naked?

Not necessarily so. Here in this hot climate, however, it is common to fish with nothing but a sort of shawl or napkin tied round the waist. The fisher's coat which he girt about him was the short *'abáyeh* which they now wear, and which they very often lay aside while fishing. They can doff and don it in a moment. When worn, it is girt tight about the loins with the zunnar, and Peter did this when hastening to meet the Lord.

As to "ships," they have all disappeared, and there is but one small boat on the lake, and this is generally out of repair. The owner has been here, and told the servant that he will take us for a short sail this evening. We will go to Mejdel, and then you will have completed the entire circuit of this "sacred sea."

26th. What a charming sail on Gennesaret we had last night! I would not have missed it for any consideration.

It was indeed delightful, especially the row back after sunset, while twilight was fading into the solemn mysteries of night; and how prettily the stars came out, twinkling so sociably at us like old friends! These very stars thus gazed with their loving eyes upon Him who made them when he sailed over this same lake eighteen hundred years ago. Mystery of mysteries! The God-man, the Divine Logos, by whom all things were made which are in heaven and which are on earth, did actually sail over this identical sea

[1] John xxi. 6.

in a boat, and by night, as we have done; and not stars only, but angels also beheld and wondered, and still do gaze, and ever will, "desiring earnestly to look into those things." This is not fancy, but fact; and shadowy indeed must be his faith in whose breast these sacred shores awaken no holier emotions than such as spring from common earth and ordinary lakes. He must be of those who have eyes but see not, ears but hear not, and hearts that can not comprehend. Shame on us all, that we can frequent the haunts and the home of Him who came from heaven to die for our redemption with little reverence and less love. We would not plead for apocryphal relics or fabulous caverns. It is wise and well to refuse all homage to such cunning fabrications. But surely it is unnatural, if not impious, to withhold or restrain those emotions which the scenes we are contemplating are calculated to awaken, which they *will* inspire in every mind having faith enough to invest the Gospel narratives with reality and life. Depend upon it, the eye that looks unmoved on these shores is in the head of a practical infidel.

I have always supposed that the Gospel narratives would be more interesting and better understood, and that the instructions of our divine Teacher would fall with more power upon the heart in the places where they were first delivered, than when read or heard on the other side of the world; and to a limited extent I find this to be true. Still, there is a sense of vagueness which I can not dissipate. I regret this the more, because it is so different from what I anticipated. It is a favorite theory of mine that every true book has a birth-day and a home; so has every prophet and religious teacher; and we not only have a right to subject their recorded history and instructions to the test of time and place to ascertain their authenticity and truthfulness, but, if they are genuine, such scrutiny will greatly illustrate and emphasize their meaning. Nor is it irreverent to apply these tests to the life and teachings of Him who spoke as man never spoke—as one having authority, and not as the scribes. Can we not do something toward gathering

THE TEACHINGS OF JESUS. 83

and concentrating the scattered rays of light which these wanderings about the home of our Lord have struck out?

Perhaps; at any rate, we can *try*, and without the slightest apprehension that the record may prove a forgery. Every thing will be found in most perfect agreement with all ascertained facts of chronology, topography, and history. The references to *time* are not very numerous or significant, but they agree most beautifully with the assumed age of our Lord's advent. When there is occasion to allude to matters in which this idea is involved, it is done with the utmost simplicity and naturalness. As an example—one of many equally pertinent—take the demand about the tribute-money, and the answer of Jesus, Render unto Cæsar the things that are Cæsar's. We have examined the "image and superscription" of this Roman *penny* on the very spot where the tax-gatherer sat, and with the evidences scattered all around us that these lordly Romans were actually here. History, the treasured coin, and these prostrate ruins, unite in proving that the teacher Jesus, the caviling Pharisees, and the tax-gathering Romans were all here, and the entire incident is admirably illustrated and confirmed.

The references to topography are very numerous and entirely satisfactory. We need only mention Nazareth, and Cana, and Capernaum, and Chorazin, and Bethsaida, and the regions around this lake. Every thing is natural, and in accordance with ascertained facts, even to the omission of this city of Tiberias in the list of places visited by our Lord. There is also a sort of verbal accuracy at times which is always pleasant to meet. Thus Jesus is said to *go down* from Cana to Capernaum, and we now know that the latter place is not only the lowest, but actually six hundred feet lower than the Mediterranean Sea. And so, also, in the appeal to "a city set on a hill:" if he pointed to Safed, as he probably did, nothing could be more emphatic. This town is seen from an immense distance, and can not be hid. And if not Safed, there are many other towns all about the region where the remark was made, and a reference to any one of them was perfectly natural and emphatic.

The allusions to manners and customs are still more numerous than those to the topography of the land, and they agree most perfectly with the supposed age of the world and character of the people. It is implied in almost countless ways that those with whom our Lord associated on these shores were accustomed to out-door life. They meet on the mountain to hear him preach; they follow him into a desert place of Bethsaida to be fed; they spend whole days there without any apparent provision for either shelter, sleep, or food; they are found in the open court of houses or on the shore of the lake at all times, etc., etc. Now all the specifications are here, just as they should be—the mountain, the desert place, the shore, the open court, the climate so warm as to lead the people into the open air, the present habits of the people—*every thing* in exact accord with the Gospel narratives. The inhabitants not only go forth into the country as represented in the New Testament, but they remain there, and sleep in the open air, if occasion require, without the slightest inconvenience. Again, the incidental mention of *women* and *children* in the great assemblies gathered around Jesus is true to Oriental life, strange as it may appear to those who read so much about *female seclusion in the East*. In the great gatherings of this day, at funerals, weddings, festas, and fairs, women and children often constitute the largest portion of the assemblies. I have seen hundreds of these gatherings in the open air; and should a prophet now arise with a tithe of the celebrity of Jesus of Nazareth, there would quickly be immense assemblies about him "from Galilee, and from Decapolis, and from Jerusalem, and from Judæa, and from beyond Jordan." Bad, and stupid, and ignorant, and worldly as the people are, their attention would be instantly arrested by the voice of a prophet, and they would flock from all parts to see, hear, and be healed. There is an irresistible bias in Orientals of all religions to run after the mere shadow of a prophet or a miracle-worker. A grand fraud was enacted in Lebanon a few years ago, in order to raise the wind to build a church. The water that burst out while the workmen were digging the foundation, it was published abroad, would restore the blind to sight, and quickly multitudes of these unfortunate people, from all parts of Palestine and Syria, and even ship-loads from Egypt, hastened to the spot, to bathe their sore or sightless balls in the wonder-working water. I myself saw long files of *blind leading the blind*, marching slowly and painfully on toward the blessed stream, and it was not until great suffering and loss that the insane multitude could be restrained from making the worse than useless pilgrimage. Such are Orientals of this day; and to know what was the character, in these respects, of those to whom Christ preached, we need only study that of the people around us. In nothing does the East of this day throw more light upon New Testament history than just on this point, and it is certainly one of much importance.

Instructions addressed to such a people, assembled in the open country or on the sea-side, would naturally, almost necessarily, abound in illustrations drawn from country life and from surrounding objects. No others would so seize upon their attention, be so readily comprehended, or so tenaciously remembered. Accordingly, we hear the divine Teacher exclaim at Shechem, "Lift up your eyes to the fields, already white to the harvest. Pray ye the Lord of the harvest to *send forth* laborers into the fields." Thus, too, He speaks of the vineyards; of the good branches *purged;* of the dry ones gathered *for the fire;* of the penny-a-day laborers *standing in the market waiting to be hired*, and of their receiving their wages at the close of each day. Such things as these we now see constantly, daily, and to the minutest shade of verbal accuracy. Again, the sparrows that chatter on every man's house teach lessons of filial trust in the providential care of our heavenly Father, and lilies more gloriously arrayed than Solomon rebuke undue solicitude as to wherewithal we shall be clothed. Then we have the leaven and its lesson; the mustard-seed, with its prophetic promise to the Church; the sower's four sorts of soil, and their diverse results; the good seed, and the tares of the enemy; the fig-tree, with its promise of spring, and its threatenings to the fruitless. Or, descending from the land to the lake, we have the fishermen, their ships, their nets, and their occupation, so suggestive to apostles and preachers who must be fishers of men. We need not enlarge this list; every reader of the New Testament can add to it from his own recollection; but it is important to remark that all these allusions are perfectly natural and appropriate to the country, the people, the Teacher, the age, and every other circumstance mentioned or implied in the evangelical narratives. We have the *originals* still before us. The teachings and illustrations of our Lord would have been out of place in any other country except this. *They could not have been uttered any where else.*

There is one aspect of Christ's character, and one class of allusions in his public teaching which deserves special consideration. Our Lord was most emphatically a religious teacher and reformer, and, of course, we expect to find constant reference to the manners and morals, the superstitious and religious ceremonies of the people; and so there is, and with wonderful correspondence to the existing state of things in this same land. Contemplate, then, the man Jesus, the Teacher, the Reformer, as he stood on the shores of this lake eighteen hundred years ago. Who and what was he to the men of that age? He was a Jew. But what was it to be an ordinary Jew of Nazareth in the year *thirty* of our era? In very many respects, just what it is to be one now in this Tiberias or in Safed—to be intensely and most offensively fanatical—to regard one's self as pre-eminently holy, the special favorite of God, and to despise all others—to be amazingly superstitious—to hold obstinately, and defend fiercely an infinite number of silly traditions and puerile fables—to fritter away the whole life and power of religion in a rigid observance of trifling ceremonies. The common Jew of Tiberias is self-righteous, proud, ignorant, rude, quarrelsome, hypocritical, dishonest, selfish, avaricious, immoral, and such, in the main, were his ancestors eighteen centuries ago. We *know* this, not so much from the New Testament as from Josephus, that special pleader and grand apologist for his nation.

Now here is a problem for the skeptic, How comes it that there is *nothing* of this Jew in Jesus? How could "*the* model man"—ay, the *perfect pattern* for all ages and all lands—how, I say, could he grow, develop, and mature in Nazareth? Who taught him the maxims of the sermon on the mount? Whose example of charity, kindness, and compassion did he copy? How did he alone, of all Jews, nay, of all mankind, conceive, propound, and practice perfectly a purely spiritual religion? That he did all this is undeniable, and it is for those who find in Jesus of Nazareth nothing but a common Jew to explain the wonderful phenomenon.

Again, Jesus grew up from his youth to manhood among a people intensely *mercenary*. This vice corrupted and debased every relation of life. Here, again, Josephus not only agrees with the writers of the New Testament, but goes far beyond them. We can fill up the outlines of his picture from the every-day life and manners of the people about us. Every body trades, speculates, cheats. The shepherd-boy on the mountains talks of *piastres* from morning to night; so does the muleteer on the road, the farmer in the field, the artisan in his shop, the merchant in his magazine, the pasha in his palace, the kady in the hall of judgment, the mullah in the mosque, the monk, the priest, the bishop —money, money, money! the desire of every heart, the theme of every discourse, the end of every aim. Every thing, too, is bought and sold. Each prayer has its price, every sin its tariff. Nothing for nothing, but every thing for money—at the counter of the merchant, the divan of the judge, the gate of the palace, the altar of the priest. Now our Lord was an *Oriental*, and grew up among just such a people; but who can or dare say that there is the faintest shadow of this mercenary spirit in his character? With uncontrolled power to possess all, he owned nothing. He had no place to be born in but another man's stable, no closet to pray in but the wilderness, no place to die but on the cross of an enemy, and no grave but one lent by a friend. At his death he had absolutely nothing to bequeath to his mother. He was as free from the mercenary spirit as though he belonged to a world where the very idea of property was unknown. And this total abstinence from all ownership was not of necessity, but of choice; and I say there is nothing like it, nothing that approaches it in the history of universal man. It stands out perfectly and divinely original.

And, finally, Jesus was the founder of a new religion; and the desire and effort of all merely human minds would be to secure its acceptance by connecting discipleship with personal pleasure or temporal advantage. Milton makes the Devil say to Jesus, "If at great things thou wouldst arrive, get riches first; get wealth, and treasure heap." And this temptation no man under such circumstances ever did or could resist. But Christ, from the first, took this position above the human race, and to the end retained it without an effort. He divorces his Gospel from any alloy of earth. Money, property, and all they represent and control, have nothing to do with membership in his society, with citizenship in his kingdom. The very conception of the idea was divine. Not only is it not human, but it is every whit contrary to what is human. He could not have borrowed it, for he was surrounded by those who were not able to comprehend the idea—no, not even the apostles, until after the day of Pentecost. As to the multitude, they sought Jesus, not because they saw the miracles and were convinced, but because they ate and were filled. And so it always has been, and is now in this same country. In this matter our missionary experience is most painful, and I hope *somewhat* peculiar. It would not be charitable—possibly not just— to say to every applicant, You seek us, not because you have examined our doctrines and believe them, but for the loaves and fishes of some worldly advantage which you hope to obtain; and yet it is difficult for me at this moment to recall a single instance in which this was not the *first* moving motive. Nor does this apply to converts to Protestantism merely, but to all sects, and to all religious changes among the people. Religion is, in fact, a species of property, valued, not for its truth, but for its available price in the market. And thus it was in the time of our Saviour, and he knew it. He *knew* that the multitude followed him for the loaves and fishes; that they sought to make him king, that they might revel in ease, luxury, and power; that they crowded about him to be healed as people now do around our physicians; that one called him *master* to obtain a decision in his favor against his brother in regard to the estate, as many join the missionaries, the better to press their claims in court. The determination to make religion, or the *profession* of it, a meritorious act, deserving temporal remuneration or personal favor, is almost universal. It was so in the time of Christ. According to the parable, some will even claim admittance into heaven because they had eaten and drunk in his presence, and, still more absurd, because he had *taught in their streets*. Now, however ridiculous such pretensions may appear to men in the Western World, I have had applications for *money* in this country, urged earnestly, and even angrily, for precisely the same reasons. Our Lord founded the parable, *even to its external drapery and costume*, not on fancy, but on unexaggerated fact.

How utterly loathsome must have been such a spirit to the unworldly heart of Jesus, and yet it was ever manifesting itself even in his chosen apostles. Here, again, Christ is our divine example. Hateful as was this earthly, groveling spirit, yet how patiently he bears with it! It is related of Dr. Chalmers that a certain man visited him several times as a religious inquirer, and when he imagined that he had awakened sufficient interest in his behalf, he cautiously let out the fact that he *was in want of money;* but no sooner was his object apparent than the wrath of the good doctor burst out in a furious tempest, and he almost kicked the mercenary wretch out of his house. Without stopping to inquire whether or not in this he imitated the gentleness and forbearance of his Master under similar provocation, I will only say, that if the doctor had been a missionary in this country, and had adopted the same summary mode with those who sought his presence from precisely the same motives, he might just as well have remained at home in his mother's nursery for all the good he would have effected here. But Christ did not thus dispose of the matter. He treated it as one, and only one of the radical corruptions of religion which it was his mission to reform, and in attempting it he manifested the same divine wisdom and forbearance which characterize his whole course. He had to deal with it even to the day of his death, in his chosen friends. They were constantly thinking of the temporal kingdom, and of seats of honor and power in his royal divan. Nor need we start and stare in amazement, as at some rare and monstrous development of selfishness. There are not half a dozen men in Syria who do not believe, or at least *feel*, that the assumption of the evangelical costume, for example, does, *ipso facto*, entitle the person to share the temporalities of those by whom they have been discipled. This is neither slander nor exaggeration, and in numberless cases where this claim was denied even in the kindest possible manner, they have been offended, and forsook at once both the teacher and the Gospel.

I have sought earnestly and painfully for the cause of this odious element in the religious character of Orientals. Customs so deeply rooted, and so general, and yet so manifestly base, must have their origin in powerful influences, acting steadily and universally upon society. Close observation and long reflection lead me to the conclusion that there are, and have been from remote ages, several causes, all tending to connect religion indissolubly with man's selfish interests and his temporal affairs. They may all be traced, perhaps, to the *constitution of civil society*. There are two conditions in which men must seek and find some other security for property, liberty, and life, than what can be derived from government—*under absolute despotism* and in *lawless anarchy*. Where either of these prevails, man instinctively resorts to religion (or superstition) for an asylum, and not in vain. Rarely is a tyrant so daring as to trample under foot the sanctions and safeguards of firmly-rooted religious rights, and when any one has been mad enough to attempt such a violation, it has generally cost him his life. Even unbridled and ferocious anarchy is held in restraint, and ultimately subdued by the sanctities and sanctions of religion. Now the East has very generally been cursed with one or other, or with both of these tyrannies, and is at this hour. Hence the people have resorted and do resort to religion for assistance and safety, and have designedly made her spread her protecting robes over the entire interests of society, temporal as well as spiritual. They have at length come to regard it mainly as a means to obtain and maintain the safety of person and property, and that religion which secures to its followers the greatest amount of relief and prosperity is the best. Hence they are ready to embrace a new faith for a few piastres, for relief from a trifling tax, or for any other earthly advantage, and, naturally enough, they change back again with equal facility if disappointed, or if better prospects and promises solicit them. In this they are merely making that use of religion which they understand and think most valuable, nor do they feel ashamed of thus dealing with it. It is a legitimate use of the precious commodity. To us, who have always lived under a form of government where our temporal rights and privileges have been guarded by law, this is a monstrous perversion, and we can not adequately appreciate the pressure which has crowded these people into such mercenary ways.

It is a fact that to this hour religion is made to throw her shelter around the separate existence and the temporal rights of the various classes and tribes that dwell in this country. They depend upon it, and employ it without scruple on all occasions. Even European influence in their behalf is mainly based upon it, and, to a certain extent, increases the evil. One nation protects the Maronites *because* they are papists; another the Greeks *as such;* a third the Greek Catholics; a fourth the Druses, etc., through the whole list. True it is that in thus dealing with those tribes they do but avail themselves of customs inwrought into the very constitution of society and from remote antiquity. I know not when to date their beginning. The divinely established economy of the Hebrews contained this element largely developed. The Hebrew commonwealth (or Church) was a religious corporation which guaranteed to every faithful member of it extensive worldly advantages. The *letter* of its promises is almost wholly temporal; and if we glance back at the history of this land from Abraham to this day, we shall find that religion has been inseparably interwoven with the secular affairs of the people. This important fact accounts, in a great measure, for the present phenomena in regard to it. By a process short, natural, and certain to be adopted by corrupt human nature, religion has been made the servant of man's mercenary desires and evil passions.

This miserable and fatal perversion Jesus of Nazareth alone, of all religious teachers, earnestly and honestly attempted to thoroughly correct. He laid the axe to the root of this old and corrupt tree. He revealed a pure spiritual religion, and established a kingdom not of this world; but, alas! his followers either could not or would not maintain it. They slid quickly down from his high position into bondage to the beggarly elements of this world, and nothing, apparently, but a second revelation of the same divine power can lift the Gospel once more out of the mire of this pit into which it has fallen. He who is *Truth*—who came into the world to bear witness to the *truth*, divinely accomplished his mission. With the world and all its solicitations and comprehensive entanglements beneath his feet, he tolerated nothing in his kingdom but *truth*. This cut up by the roots the vast systems of *clannish* and *state religions*, founded on fables, and upheld by falsehood, force, and hypocrisy. He spurned with indignation the traditions of priests and the cunning adjustments of politicians. He would have nothing but truth for doctrine, nothing but honest faith in the disciple. To understand how vast the number of superstitions, lying vanities, idle fancies, vain ceremonies, abominable deceptions, and foul corruptions which had overgrown religion in his day, it is only necessary to examine that which claims to be religion in this same country at the present moment. And should this divine Truth again visit the land, with fan in hand, he would scatter to the four winds, from the great threshing-floor of his indignation, the mountains of chaff which have gathered there for ages, and he would hurl the thunderbolts of his wrath against a thousand hypocritical deceivers of mankind. Oh how radical, profound, and far-reaching are the simplest laws of Christ, and how prodigious the revolution they contemplate and require! "Swear not at all." Why, the whole Arab race must quit talking altogether. They *can not* say simply Yea, yea, nay, nay. "Lie not one to another." Impossible! every thing within, without, and about you is a lie. "Do to others as ye would that they should do to you." This precept seems to want a *not* somewhere or other. "Salute no man by the way." Absurd! we *must* manufacture compliments as fast as possible, and utter them with grace and gravity to friend and foe alike. But why multiply any farther comparisons and contrasts? The subject is inexhaustible, and enough has been said or hinted to prove that Jesus did not borrow the lessons he taught. They are not from man, of man, nor by man, *but they are of God*.

Shut to the tent door, and put the candle outside, or we shall be overwhelmed by a deluge of gnats. This is one of the plagues of this filthy city. Once, when encamped on this very spot, they came in such incredible swarms as literally to cover up and extinguish the candle. In five minutes their dead carcasses accumulated on the top so as to put it out. It seemed to me at the time that Tiberias might be rendered absolutely uninhabitable by this insignificant, almost invisible enemy. Has it never occurred to you that the writers of the Bible were very indifferent to those sources of annoyance which travelers now dwell upon with such vehement and pathetic lamentation? Gnats, for example, are only mentioned once, and then not as an annoyance, but to introduce and give point to a severe rebuke upon pharisaical scrupulosity: Ye blind guides, which strain at (or *out*) a gnat and swallow a camel.[1] And certainly no comparison could better express the absurdity and hypocrisy of their conduct.

As another instance of this indifference to small annoy-

[1] Matt. xxiii. 24.

ances, I can not but think just now of the *flea*. These most troublesome creatures are only mentioned by David in his complaint to Saul: After whom dost thou pursue—after a dead dog, after a flea? For the King of Israel is come out to seek a flea, as when one doth hunt a partridge in the mountains.[1]

True; but the reference is very emphatic. There are at this moment myriads of men, women, and children chasing these nimble creatures through all the mysteries and hiding-places of their manifold garments. Still, it is remarkable that such an omnipresent source of vexation should not be more frequently mentioned, and the more so, as in this matter the Bible differs entirely from all Oriental writings. The Arabs, in their poetry, fables, stories, and general literature, not only mention the flea, but with every possible term of dislike and malediction. The Bedawîn, though filthy to a proverb, and patient, *ad nauseam*, of other vermin, have the greatest dread of the flea, and whenever they appear in their camp they break up and remove to another. Indeed, it is quite in the power of fleas to compel an evacuation. I have seen places where Arabs had been encamped literally swarming with them, as though the very dust had turned to fleas. One could not stand a moment on such a spot without having his legs quite black with them; and, beyond a doubt, if a person were bound and left there, he would soon be worried to death. An Arab proverb informs us that the king of the fleas holds his court in Tiberias. It is fortunate that etiquette does not oblige us to frequent it.

I was somewhat startled to find myself this morning in close proximity to a more formidable species of vermin than either gnats or fleas. While seated on a dilapidated sepulchre, an immense centipede crawled out cautiously, and made directly for my hand, which I quickly gave, and with it a smart stone, to add emphasis to the salutation. Are these ugly creatures really dangerous?

I am surprised to find them stirring so early in the spring, though Tiberias is hot enough for them or for any thing

[1] 1 Sam. xxiv. 14, and xxvi. 20.

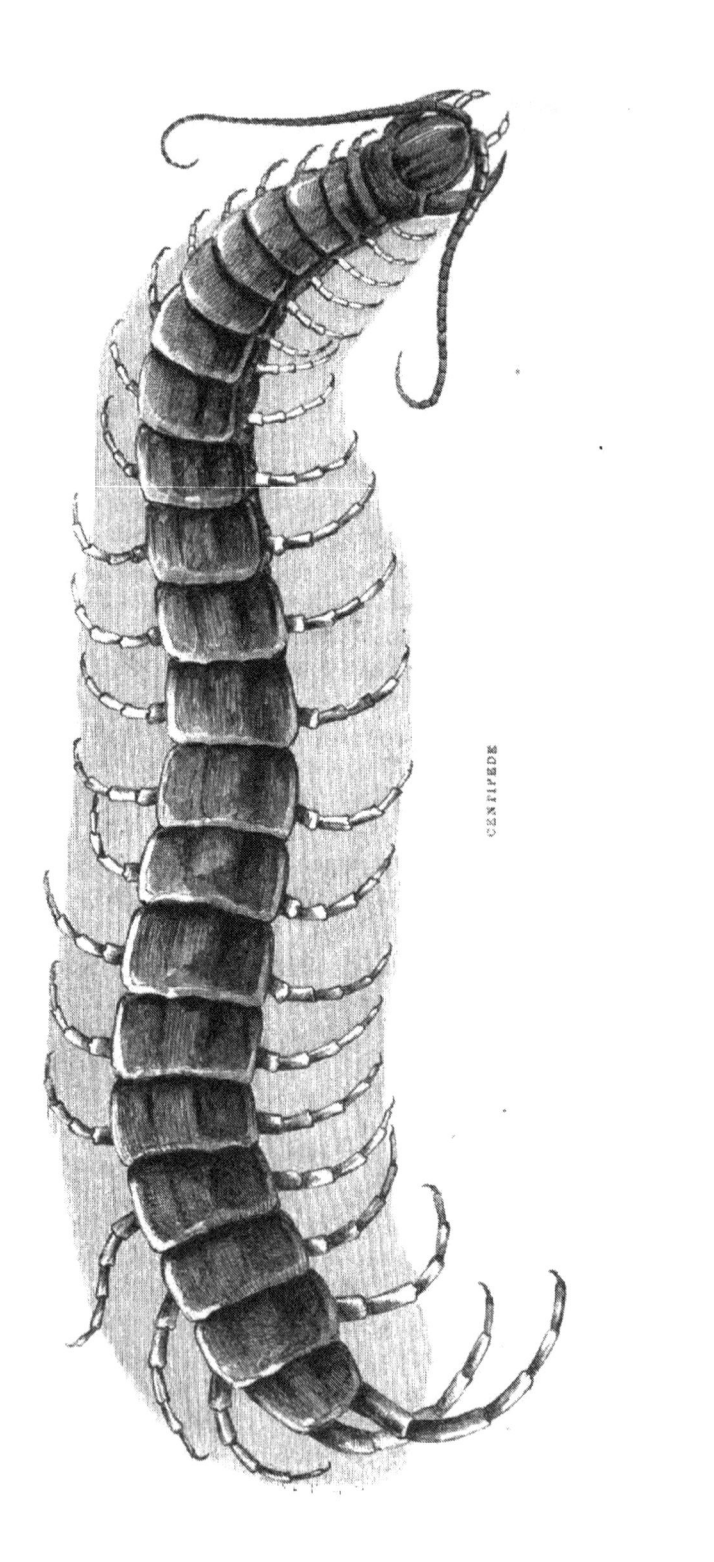

CENTIPEDE

else. The bite of the centipede is not fatal, but is said to be extremely painful, and very slow to heal. The Arabs say that it strikes its fore claws into the flesh, and there they break off and remain, thus rendering the wound more troublesome. I never saw a person bitten by them, but their mere appearance makes one's flesh creep. While the locusts were passing through Abeîh, they started up a very large centipede near my house, and I was greatly amused with its behavior. As the living stream rolled over it without cessation for a moment, it became perfectly furious; bit on the right hand and the left, writhed, and squirmed, and floundered in impotent wrath, and was finally worried to death. During this extraordinary battle its look was almost satanic.

How sweetly the day draws to a close around this warm and delightful lake! and there come the droves of cattle and donkeys down from the green hills where they pasture! I have seen no place where there are so many, or at least where they are brought home *together*, and in such crowds. Last night the thought struck me as they were entering the gate, and away I hurried after them, to see whether these Tiberian donkeys were as wise as those Isaiah mentions. True to life, no sooner had we got within the walls, than the drove began to disperse. Every ox knew perfectly well his owner, his house, and the way to it, nor did he get bewildered for a moment in the mazes of these narrow and crooked alleys. As for the asses, they walked straight to the door, and up to their master's "crib," without turning to bid good-night to their companions of the field. I followed one company clear into their habitation, and saw each take his appropriate manger, and begin his evening meal of dry *tibn*. Isaiah says in all this they were wiser than their owners, who neither knew nor considered, but forsook the Lord, and provoked the Holy One of Israel.[1] These "cribs" of Isaiah are, I suppose, the "mangers" of the New Testament, in one of which the infant Redeemer was laid? It is so understood by the Arabs, so translated in their

[1] Isa. i. 3, 4.

Bible, and I doubt not correctly. It is common to find two sides of the one room where the native farmer resides with his cattle fitted up with these mangers, and the remainder elevated about two feet higher for the accommodation of the family. The mangers are built of small stones and mortar, in the shape of a box, or, rather, of a kneading-trough, and, when cleaned up and whitewashed, as they often are in summer, they do very well to lay little babes in. Indeed, our own children have slept in them in our rude summer retreats on the mountains.

As to the donkey, he is a slandered and much-abused animal. He is poorly fed, hard worked, overloaded, and beaten without reason or mercy. Their saddles are so ill-shaped, so hard, and so ragged, that they wound the back and shoulders; and the rough ropes which bind on the burdens lacerate the flesh wherever they come in contact with it. No wonder, therefore, that he has a gaunt frame, a tottering gait, ears which slouch heavily round his head, and a stupid and woe-begone stare out of hopeless eyes. But when young and unbroken, they are as lively and playful as kittens; and when well fed, the male is, without exception, the most pugnacious brute on earth. Dogs full of fire and fight as Dandy Dinmont's varieties of pepper will yet sometimes be at peace, but two fat male donkeys can never be brought together, night or day, in summer or in winter, without instant war.

XXVIII. TIBERIAS TO NAZARETH.

March 28th.

It is six hours to Nazareth, but as there is nothing of special interest along the direct route by Lubieh, we will turn northward over this rocky shore to Mejdel. The path commands one of the finest views of the lake and surrounding scenery, and when the water was covered with boats and ships, and the land adorned with villas, orchards, and groves, the *tout ensemble* must have been beautiful, and even magnificent. But now, how solitary and sad! There is something oppressive in this unbroken silence; the very ducks on the lake are "shockingly tame," and the stupid fish gather in crowds, and stare up into one's face without the least alarm. Let us stop and look at them congregated around these copious tepid and nauseous fountains of Fûlîyeh. Travelers call them 'Ain el Barideh—*Cold* Fountains; but I have not heard that name applied to them by the Arabs, and there is no propriety in it, for they are decidedly *warm*. Dr. Robinson says that the great road from the south comes down to the shore at this point, along this Wady 'Ammas; but, if this was formerly the case, it is nearly deserted now, and the main road descends Wady Hamâm. I myself have always ascended by that ravine, nor have I ever seen any one pass up this wady of Abu el Ammâs.

These circular structures about Fûlîyeh have puzzled all travelers who have noticed them. They are ancient, and some think they are ruined baths, but there are no traces of any of the necessary accessories to such establishments, and without these they could not have been used for bathing. They do not appear to have been vaulted over, and the probability is that they were erected, like those at Ras el 'Ain, near Tyre, and at Kabery, to elevate the water of the fountains to irrigate this little vale of Fûlîyeh and to drive the mills of Mejdel. An inexhaustible mill-stream must always have been of immense importance to the inhabitants of this neighborhood.

Is this wild mustard that is growing so luxuriantly and blossoming so fragrantly along our path?

WILD MUSTARD.

It is; and I have always found it here in spring, and, a little later than this, the whole surface of the vale will be *gilded over* with its yellow flowers. I have seen this plant on the rich plain of Akkâr as tall as the horse and his rider. It has occurred to me on former visits that the mustard-tree of the parable probably grew at this spot, or possibly at Tabiga, near Capernaum, for the water in both is somewhat similar, and so are the vegetable productions. To furnish an adequate basis for the proverb, it is necessary to suppose that a variety of it was cultivated in the time of our Saviour, which grew to an enormous size, and shot forth large branches, so that the fowls of the air could lodge in the branches of it.[1] It may have been perennial, and have grown to a considerable tree, and there are traditions in the country of such so large that a man could climb into them; and after having seen *red pepper* bushes grow on, year after year, into tall shrubs, and the *castor bean* line the brooks about Damascus like the willows and the poplars, I can readily credit the existence of mustard-trees large enough to meet all the demands of our Lord's parable.

Irby and Mangles, going from the south end of the Dead Sea to Kerak, found a tree in great abundance, which had a berry growing in clusters like currants, and with the color of a plum. The taste was pleasant, though strongly aromatic, and closely resembled that of mustard, and, if taken in considerable quantity, it had precisely the same effects as mustard. The leaves had the same pungent flavor as the seed, although not so strong. They think this is the tree of the parable, and it may be so. They give no name to this remarkable plant, but it well deserves a more careful and scientific examination. At any rate, I should not be surprised to find in some such locality a *mustard plant*, which, when grown, "is the greatest among herbs, and becometh a tree, so that the birds of the air come and lodge in the branches thereof." I once discovered a veritable *cabbage-tree* on the cliffs of Dog River, and many curious vegetable anomalies doubtless remain to be detected and described.

We are not to suppose that the mustard-seed is the least of all seeds *in the world*, but it was the smallest which the husbandman was accustomed to *sow*, and the "tree," when full grown, was larger than the other herbs in his garden. To press the *literal* meaning of the terms any farther would be a violation of one of the plainest canons of interpretation. This ample size, with branches shooting out in all directions, yet springing from the very smallest beginnings, contains, as I suppose, the special meaning and intention of the parable. It is in this sense only that the kingdom of heaven is like a grain of mustard-seed. Our Saviour did not select it because of any inherent qualities, medicinal or

[1] Matt. xiii. 31, 32; Mark iv. 30–32; Luke xiii. 18, 19.

otherwise, which belonged to it. True, it is *pungent*, and *penetrating*, and *fiery*, and *searching*, and must be *bruised* or *crushed* before it will give out its special virtues; and one might go on enumerating such qualities, and multiplying analogies between these properties of mustard and certain attributes of true religion, or of the Church, or of the individual Christian, but they are foreign to any object that Jesus had in view, and must therefore be altogether fanciful. Such exposition dilutes the sense, and dissipates the force and point of his sayings, and should not be encouraged.

Here, on the side of this mountain, above Fûlîyeh, I had my first introduction, some twenty years ago, to the far-famed locusts of the East. Noticing something peculiar on the hill side, I rode up to examine it, when, to my amazement, *the whole surface became agitated, and began to roll down the declivity.* My horse was so terrified that I was obliged to dismount. The locusts were very young, not yet able *even to jump;* they had the shape, however, of minute grasshoppers. Their numbers seemed infinite, and in their haste to get out of my way they literally rolled over and over, like semi-fluid mortar an inch or two in thickness. Many years after this I became better acquainted with these extraordinary creatures in Abeîh on Lebanon.

Early in the spring of 1845, these insects appeared in considerable numbers along the sea-coast and on the lower spurs of the mountains. They did no great injury at the time, and, having laid their eggs, immediately disappeared. The people, familiar with their habits, looked with anxiety to the time when these eggs would be hatched, nor were their fears groundless or exaggerated. For several days previous to the first of June we had heard that millions of young locusts were on their march up the valley toward our village, and at length I was told that they had reached the lower part of it. Summoning all the people I could collect, we went to meet and attack them, hoping to stop their progress altogether, or at least to turn aside the line of their march. Never shall I lose the impression produced by the

SYRIAN LOCUST.

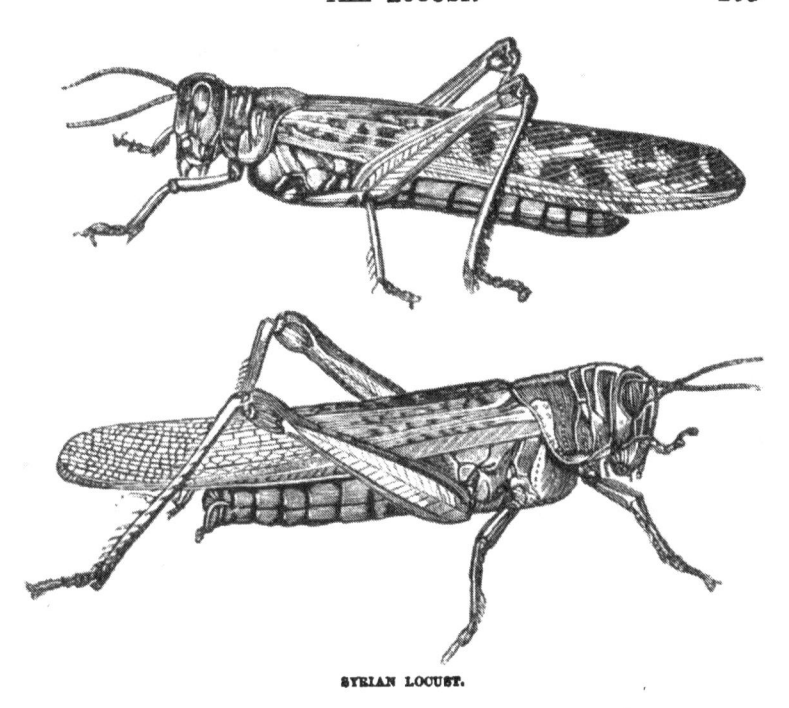

first view of them. I had often passed through clouds of *flying* locusts, and they always struck my imagination with a sort of vague terror; but these we now confronted were without wings, and about the size of full-grown grasshoppers, which they closely resembled in appearance and behavior. But their number was astounding; the whole face of the mountain was black with them. On they came like a living deluge. We dug trenches, and kindled fires, and beat, and burned to death "heaps upon heaps," but the effort was utterly useless. Wave after wave *rolled up* the mountain side, and poured over rocks, walls, ditches, and hedges, those behind covering up and bridging over the masses already killed. After a long and fatiguing contest, I descended the mountain to examine the *depth* of the column, but I could not see to the end of it. Wearied with my hard walk over this living deluge, I returned, and gave over the vain effort to stop its progress.

By the next morning the head of the column had reached my garden, and, hiring eight or ten people, I resolved to rescue at least my vegetables and flowers. During this day we succeeded, by fire, and by beating them off the walls with brushes and branches, in keeping our little garden tolerably clear of them; but it was perfectly appalling to watch this animated river as it flowed *up* the road and ascended the hill above my house. At length, worn out with incessant skirmishing, I gave up the battle. Carrying the pots into the parlor, and covering up what else I could, I surrendered the remainder to the conquerors. For four days they continued to pass on toward the east, and finally only a few stragglers of the mighty hosts were left behind.

In every stage of their existence these locusts give a most impressive view of the power of God to punish a wicked world. Look at the pioneers of the host, those flying squadrons that appear in early spring. Watch the furious impulse for the propagation of their devouring progeny. No power of man can interrupt it; millions upon millions, with most fatal industry, deposit their innumerable eggs in the field, the plain, and the desert. This done, they vanish like morning mist. But in six or eight weeks the very dust seems to waken into life, and, moulded into maggots, begins to creep. Soon this animated earth becomes minute grasshoppers, and, creeping and jumping *all in the same general direction*, they begin their destructive march. After a few days their voracious appetite palls; they become sluggish, and *fast*, like the silk-worms, for a short time. Like the silk-worms, too, they repeat this fasting *four* times before they have completed their transmutations and are accommodated with wings. I do not remember to have seen this fact in their history noticed by any naturalist. In their march they devour every green thing, and with wonderful expedition. A large vineyard and garden adjoining mine was green as a meadow in the morning, but long before night it was naked and bare as a newly-plowed field or dusty road. The noise made in marching and foraging was like that of a heavy shower on a distant forest.

The references to the habits and behavior of locusts in the Bible are very striking and accurate. Joel says, He hath laid my vine waste, and barked my fig-tree: he hath made it clean bare, and cast it away; the branches thereof are made white.[1] These locusts at once strip the vines of every leaf and cluster of grapes, and of every green twig. I also saw many large fig orchards "clean bare," not a leaf remaining; and as the bark of the fig-tree is of a silvery whiteness, the whole orchards, thus rifled of their green veils, spread abroad their branches "made white" in melancholy nakedness to the burning sun.

In view of the utter destruction which they effect, the prophet exclaims, Alas for the day! for the day of the Lord is at hand, and as a destruction from the Almighty shall it come. Is not the meat cut off before our eyes?[2] This is most emphatically true. I saw under my own eye not only a large vineyard loaded with young grapes, but whole fields of corn disappear as if by magic, and the hope of the husbandman vanish like smoke.

Again, How do the beasts groan! the herds of cattle are perplexed because they have no pasture; yea, the flocks of sheep are made desolate.[3] This is poetic, but true. A field over which this flood of desolation has rolled shows not a blade for even a goat to nip. The land is as the garden of Eden before them, and behind them a desolate wilderness; yea and *nothing shall escape them*. Before their face the people shall be much pained: how emphatically true! all faces gather blackness. They shall run like mighty men; they shall climb the wall like men of war, and they shall march every one on his ways, and they shall not break their ranks.[4] When the head of the mighty column came in contact with the palace of the Emeer Asaad in Abeîh, they did not take the trouble to wheel round the corners, but climbed the wall like men of war, and marched over the top of it; so, when they reached the house of Dr. Van Dyck, in spite of all his efforts to prevent it, a living stream rolled right over the roof. They shall run to and fro in the

[1] Joel i. 7. [2] Joel i. 15, 16. [3] Joel i. 18. [4] Joel ii. 3, 6, 7.

city; they shall run upon the wall; they shall climb up upon the houses; they shall enter in at the windows like a thief.[1] Every touch in the picture is true to the life. If not carefully watched, they would have devoured the flowers which were carried into the inner rooms in pots.

The Prophet Nahum says that the locusts camp in the hedges in the cold day; but when the sun ariseth they flee away, and the place is not known where they are.[2] Paxton and others have remarked that there is much difficulty in this passage, but to any one who has attentively watched the habits of the locust, it is not only plain, but very striking. In the evenings, as soon as the air became cool, at Abeïh they literally camped in the hedges and loose stone walls, covering them over like a swarm of bees settled on a bush. There they remained until the next day's sun waxed warm, when they again commenced their march. One of the days on which they were passing was quite cool, and the locusts scarcely moved at all from their *camps*, and multitudes remained actually stationary until the next morning. Those that did march crept along very heavily, as if cramped and stiff; but in a hot day they hurried forward in a very earnest, lively manner. It is an aggravation of the calamity if the weather continues cool, for then they prolong their stay and do far more damage. When the hot sun beats powerfully upon them, they literally *flee* away, and the place is not known where they are. This is true even in regard to those which have not wings. One wonders where they have all gone to. Yesterday the whole earth seemed to be creeping and jumping, to-day you see not a locust. And the disappearance of the clouds of flying locusts is still more sudden and complete.

David complains that he was tossed up and down as the locusts.[3] This reference is to the flying locust. I have had frequent opportunities to notice how these squadrons are tossed up and down, and whirled round and round by the ever-varying currents of the mountain winds.

Solomon says, The locusts have no king, yet go they

[1] Joel ii. 9.   [2] Nahum iii. 17.   [3] Ps. cix. 23.

forth all of them by bands.[1] Nothing in their habits is more striking than the pertinacity with which they all pursue the same line of march, like a disciplined army. As they have no king, they must be influenced by some common instinct.

I am not surprised that Pharaoh's servants remonstrated against his folly and madness when they heard the plague of locusts announced. Let the men go, said they to their proud master, that they may serve the Lord their God. Knowest thou not yet *that Egypt is destroyed?* And when they came they were *very grievous*, for they covered the face of the whole earth, so that the land was darkened, and they ate every herb of the land, and all the fruit of the trees, and there remained not any green thing in the trees, nor in the herbs of the field. Moses declared that they should cover the face of the earth so that one can not be able to see the ground.[2] I have this dreadful picture indelibly fixed on my mind. For several nights after they came to Abeîh, as soon as I closed my eyes the whole earth seemed to be creeping and jumping, nor could I banish the ugly image from my brain.

The coming of locusts is a sore judgment from God. If I command the locusts to devour the land, says the Lord to Solomon.[3] Yes, it is the command of God that brings these insects to scourge a land for the wickedness of the inhabitants thereof.

Do you suppose that the meat of John the Baptist was literally locusts and wild honey?[4]

Why not? by the Arabs they are eaten to this day. The perfectly trustworthy Burckhardt thus speaks on this subject: "*All* the Bedawîns of Arabia, and the inhabitants of towns in Nejd and Hedjaz are accustomed to eat locusts." "I have seen at Medina and Tayf *locust shops* where these animals were sold by *measure*. In Egypt and Nubia they are only eaten by the poorest beggars." "The Arabs, in preparing locusts as an article of food, throw them alive into boiling water with which a good deal of salt has been

[1] Prov. xxx. 27.
[2] Ex. x. 4–14.
[3] 2 Chron. vii. 13.
[4] Matt. iii. 4.

mixed. After a few minutes they are taken out and dried in the sun; the head, feet, and wings are then torn off; the bodies are cleansed from the salt and perfectly dried, after which process whole sacks are filled with them by the Bedawîn. They are sometimes eaten boiled in butter, and they often contribute materials for a breakfast when spread over unleavened bread mixed with butter." Thus far Burckhardt. Locusts are not eaten in Syria by any but the Bedawîn on the extreme frontiers, and it is always spoken of as a very inferior article of food, and regarded by most with disgust and loathing—tolerated only by the very poorest people. John the Baptist, however, was of this class, either from necessity or election. He also dwelt in the desert, where such food was and is still used, and therefore the text states the simple truth. His ordinary "meat" was dried locusts; probably fried in butter and mixed with honey, as is still frequently done. This honey, too, was the article made by *bees*, and not *dibs* from grapes, nor dates from the palm, nor any thing else which ingenious commentators have invented. Wild honey is still gathered in large quantities from trees in the wilderness, and from rocks in the wadies, just where the Baptist sojourned, and where he came preaching the baptism of repentance.

Nor did John transgress the law of Moses by thus eating locusts. Disgusting and nauseous as this food appears to us, the Hebrews in the wilderness—probably in Egypt also—were accustomed to use it, and in Levit. xi. 22 it is declared to be clean in all its varieties, one of which is wrongly called *beetle* in our translation. No people ever eat any of the *beetle* tribe so far as I can discover, and there can be no reasonable doubt but that *sal'am*, rendered *beetle*, and *khargal, grasshopper*, are both varieties of the locust.

Here is Mejdel, seated on the southern margin of Gennesaret. It is a wretched hamlet of a dozen low huts huddled into one, and the whole ready to tumble into a dismal heap of black basaltic rubbish. This is the city of Mary Magdalene, out of whom went seven devils, and it seems to be in very significant keeping with the only incident that

MEJDEL AND THE PLAIN OF GENNESARET.

has given it a history. Evil spirits of some sort must possess the inhabitants, for they are about the worst specimen in the country; and yet they dwell on the shore of this silvery lake, and cultivate this plain of Gennesaret, which Josephus calls the "ambition of nature."

And so it well may be called, to judge from this large expanse of luxuriant barley and wheat. The whole plain is one waving field of grain, without hedge, ditch, or fence of any kind to break the even continuity.

Turn westward here, along the base of the mountain, and in half an hour we shall enter the great gorge of Wady Hamâm. Let me call your attention to these "tares" which are growing among the barley. The grain is just in the proper stage of development to illustrate the parable. In those parts where the grain has *headed out*, they have done the same, and *there* a child can not mistake them for wheat or barley; but where both are less developed, the closest scrutiny will often fail to detect them. I can not do it at all with any confidence. Even the farmers, who in this country generally *weed* their fields, do not attempt to separate the one from the other. They would not only mistake good grain for them, but very commonly the roots of the two are so intertwined that it is impossible to separate them without plucking up both. Both, therefore, must be left to *grow together* until the time of harvest.[1]

TARES OF PALESTINE.

[1] Matt. xiii. 29, 30.

The common Arabic name for the tare is *zowan*, and this, I presume, is the root of the Greek name *zizanion*. The tare abounds all over the East, and is a great nuisance to the farmer. It resembles the American *cheat*, but the *head* does not droop like cheat, nor does it branch out like oats. The grain, also, is smaller, and is arranged along the upper part of the stalk, which stands perfectly erect. The *taste* is bitter, and when eaten separately, or even when diffused in ordinary bread, it causes dizziness, and often acts as a violent emetic. Barn-door fowls also become dizzy from eating it. In short, it is a strong soporific poison, and must be carefully winnowed, and picked out of the wheat, grain by grain, before grinding, or the flour is not healthy. Of course the farmers are very anxious to exterminate it, but this is nearly impossible. Indeed, grain-growers in this country believe that in very wet seasons, and in marshy ground, the *wheat itself turns to tares*. I have made diligent inquiries on this point, and find this to be their fixed opinion. Nor is this a modern notion, or one confined to the ignorant. It is as old, at least, as the time of our Saviour, and is met with both in heathen writers and in the expositions of the early fathers. Still, I am not at all prepared to admit its truth. If it could be proved, as these old authors assert, that *zizanion* is merely a degenerated wheat or barley, it would be reasonable to allow that such degeneration might occur in a soil and season adapted to cause it, but I do not believe the fundamental fact in the question. *Zowan* differs so essentially from wheat, that it will take the very strongest evidence to establish their original identity. Besides, it does not accord with the general law of degeneracy that it is completed at *once*, and by a single process. Such changes are gradual, and require successive production and reproduction, each adding to the gradual deterioration, before such a radical change can be effected. The farmers, however, stoutly maintain that they "sow good seed in their fields," and in clean ground, and yet that the whole is turned to *tares* in consequence of extraordinary rains during winter—that is, that perfect *wheat* is changed to perfect tares by one single process; and farther, that this change is *permanent*. These extemporaneous tares ever after produce tares, and tares only, nor can you, by any legerdemain, *reverse* the process, and change *tares* back to wheat. *If* this be true, it is a species of original sin in the vegetable kingdom every way surprising.

But how are you to answer a farmer who takes you to a field nearly all tares, and declares that he there sowed clean seed, and that in previous years he always reaped good harvests of pure grain? Whence the present crop of tares? he asks, and so do you. I have repeatedly examined such fields with all the care in my power, and without finding an answer. It would be easy to say, as in the parable, an enemy hath done this; but, though I have read in authors *who never resided in Palestine* that bad men do thus injure their enemies, I have never found a person in the country itself who had either known or heard of such an act. It is certainly remarkable that Arab malice has never adopted this mode of injuring its victims; but the fact must be told, it is altogether unknown at the present day. It must have been done, however, in the time of our Saviour, or He would not have mentioned it in his parable. At all events, the farmers of this day will not admit that their fields have thus been filled with tares, and I believe them. We must, therefore, find some other solution of a phenomenon which occurs so often that I have myself had frequent opportunities to verify it. I suppose that several separate causes conspire to bring about the result. First, very wet weather in winter *drowns* and kills *wheat*, while it is the most favorable of all weather for *tares*. In a good season the wheat overgrows and chokes the tares, but in a wet one the reverse is true. The farmers all admit this, but still they ask, Whence the *seed* of the tares? we sowed "good seed." To this it may be answered, The tare is a very light grain, easily blown about by the wind; that a thousand little birds are ever carrying and dropping it over the fields; that myriads of ants are dragging it in all directions; that moles, and mice, and goats, and sheep, and nearly every other animal, are aiding in this work of dispersion; that much of the tares *shell out* in handling the grain in the field; that a large part of them is thrown out by the wind at the threshing-floor, which is always in the open country; that the heavy rains, which often deluge the country in autumn, carry down to the lower levels this outcast *zowan*, and sow them there; *and these are precisely the spots where the transmutation is said to occur.* It is my belief that in these and in similar ways the *tares* are *actually sown*, without the intervention of an enemy, and their presence is accounted for without having recourse to this incredible doctrine of *transmutation*.

Enough about tares. We are just entering the throat of this tremendous gorge. It is called Hamâm, from the clouds of *pigeons* which "flock to their windows" in these rocks. Look up now to that cliff on the left. It is more than a thousand feet high, and a large part is absolutely perpendicular. It is perforated by a multitude of caverns, holes, and narrow passages, the chosen resort of robbers in former days. The walls and fortifications which united these caverns, and defended them against attack, are still visible. They are now called Kŭlaet Ibn M'an, but anciently they bore the name of Arbela, from a village on the top, a little back from the precipice, the ruins of which are now named Irbid. Josephus has a graphic description of the capture of these caves by Herod the Great. After various expedients to expel them had failed, he let boxes filled with soldiers down the face of the precipice, and landed them at the entrance of the caverns. This was a most daring ex-

ASSAULT OF ROBBERS.

ELIJAH'S FOUNTAIN, WADY KANAH.

ploit, but it succeeded, and by fire and sword the robbers were entirely exterminated. Josephus himself afterward fortified this place in preparation for the Roman war, but he does not appear to have made any use of it.

This is truly a most surprising gorge, and there is nothing in this region which leads the traveler to expect such precipices.

The country above is yet more deceitful, and one is on the very edge of the awful cliffs before he is aware of their existence. I have passed up this ravine many times, and yet can never get through without stopping again and again to gaze, admire, and almost shudder. But we have still a hard ascent to the top, and must no longer loiter here. See these prodigious blocks, each "large as a meeting-house." They have tumbled from those giddy heights, and nearly block up the wady. Some of them have fallen since I last came this road. Dr. Wilson is mistaken as to the size of this brook, but still here is a fountain of delicious water. My first ascent through this stupendous gorge had all the romance of a veritable discovery. I had never heard of it, and was almost wild with excitement.

This is indeed a fatiguing ascent, but now we have gained the summit, what a beautiful plain spreads out to the south and west! and those cone-like hills must be the Horns of Hûttîn.

They are, and that village at their base on the north has the same name. It is half an hour hence, and our path lies through it. Dr. Clark and others have exaggerated the height of these "Horns," and the grandeur of the prospect from them; yet Dr. Robinson, who makes the criticism, scarcely does them justice. Neither the Horns themselves, nor the prospect of plain, and gorge, and lake, and mountain, is to be despised.

Nor are these gigantic hedges of cactus which surround this village to be passed without remark.

They are very large, and you will find the same at Lûbieh, three miles south of us, and at Sejera, between that and Tabor. In fact, the cactus hedges form impenetrable ramparts around many of these villages in Galilee, which neither man nor beast will scale, and which fire can not consume.

There are no antiquities of any significance in this Hŭttîn, and nothing else to detain us except to get a drink of their good water. We shall find none equal to it between this and Nazareth. There is a Moslem *mazar* hid away in this ravine, which comes down from this nearest of the "Horns." It is called Neby Shaiyib, and is celebrated for the cure of insanity. Sheikh Yûsŭf of Abeîh was brought here several years ago, and two of our muleteers were of the party. They are now laughing at the foolish experiment. The poor sheikh derived no advantage from the long journey, hard usage, and silly ceremonies; but that will not deter others from making a similar experiment. Ten thousand failures a thousand times repeated apparently have no tendency to cure the mania for miracles and miracle-working saints and shrines.

Was not the "sermon on the mount" preached upon one of these "Horns," according to ecclesiastical tradition?

When I first passed from Nazareth to Tiberias, I was taken to the very stone upon which the Great Teacher was said to have stood. It lies round on the southeastern slope of the second Horn, but it is needless to say that there is not the slightest evidence in favor of this locality. The same remark applies with even more certainty to the tradition that the feeding of the "five thousand" took place on this mountain; and this in spite of the half dozen "stones of the Christians"—Hajâr en Nusâra—which are still shown to substantiate the fact. These Horns of Hŭttîn, however, will always have a melancholy celebrity in memory of the miserable and utterly ruinous defeat of the Crusaders in A.D. 1187, by the great Saladin. Michaud has given a minute account of this terrible battle in the second volume of his great work, and Dr. Robinson, in the third volume of his Researches, a much better one, which you can consult at your leisure. Nothing so forcibly pictures to my mind the deplorable mismanagement of the Crusaders, or the inca-

KUT KHAN.

pacity of their leaders, as the fact that they allowed them-selves to be hemmed in upon these barren Horns of Hŭttîn, to *die for want of water*, when there was this copious fountain at the base, within a bow-shot of their perishing ranks.

If you wish for an opportunity to cultivate your antiquarian ability, try it on this ancient ruin which we are approaching. It is now called Meskîna, and has evidently been a place of importance, to judge from the rock-tombs, cisterns, and old foundations scattered over the plain; but I do not recall any such name either in the Bible or elsewhere. The same, however, is true of 'Ain Baida, 'Ain Mâhy, Em Jebeîl, and half a dozen other sites along the ridge upon our left, between Lûbieh and Kefr Kenna. That large village ahead of us, and almost concealed among the olive-groves, is called Tûr'an, and from it this long, narrow plain takes its name.

When riding up this road on a former occasion, I pestered every body I could find on the right and the left, farmers, shepherds, Bedawîn, and travelers, with inquiries about the place where the *water was made wine*. With one consent they pointed to Kefr Kenna. Some of them knew of a ruin called Kânâ, on the north side of the great plain of Bŭttauf, but only one had ever heard of the word Jelîl as a part of the name; and, from the hesitancy with which this one admitted it, I was left in doubt whether he did not merely acquiesce in it at my suggestion. It is *certain* that very few even of the Moslems know the full name Kânâ el Jelîl; and yet I think Dr. Robinson has about settled the question in its favor as the true site of the miracle recorded in the second chapter of John. Kefr Kenna, however, is worth looking at for its own sake, and also because it has long borne the honors which are probably due to its neighbor, and *may* possibly have a right to them. It is prettily situated on the side of a shallow vale, has some ruins of ancient buildings, and some tolerably respectable modern ones, and, above all places in this vicinity, abounds in flourishing orchards of pomegranates. Pomegranates have a certain mystical office to perform in native marriages, and no doubt those from Kefr Kenna have special virtue and value. We shall not trouble ourselves to look up the fragments of the six water-pots which were shown to me long ago, nor any other fabulous antiquities of the place. Here, at this well, I always find a troop of bold, but good-looking girls, like those of Nazareth. If this were the Cana of the New Testament, the servants doubtless drew water from this identical fountain, for the village has no other.

As we can not now turn aside to visit the Kânâ on the other side of the Bŭttauf, I will give you an account of my ride thither on a former occasion. We obtained our guide from this village, and, as they are hunters, and familiar with every acre of this region, they are the best that can be procured. Where the vale of Kefr Kenna unites with the plain of Tûr'an is a very ancient ruin, called Jiftah (or Geftah). This, I suspect, is the site of the Gath-hepher, mentioned by Jerome as being two miles east of Sephoris, on the way to Tiberias. A respectable tradition makes this the birth-place of the Prophet Jonah. His *tomb* is now shown by the Moslems of this neighborhood at Meshhed, on a hill a little to the south of it. This Jiftah, with the curious addition of the article *el*, is the name of the important bounding valley, repeatedly mentioned by Joshua,[1] between Zebulon and Asher, and it is the only place that now bears that name. It is situated on the edge of the long valley of Tûr'an, which stretches from above Tiberias westward into the Bŭttauf, and thence southwest, under the name of Nehar el Mĕlĕk, down to the Kishon, at the base of Carmel, and there the boundaries of the two tribes might meet, for both extended to Carmel. I have the impression, therefore, that this is in reality the valley of Jiphthah; and as that part of it which spreads out into the Bŭttauf was doubtless the great plain of Zebulon, a new idea struck me while exploring it as to the proper punctuation (if you choose) of that remarkable prophecy concerning the great light of the Sun of Righteousness that rose on Zebulon and Naphtali. Nazareth, Kefr Kenna, Kânâ, and all the regions adjacent, where our Lord

[1] Josh. xix. 14, 27.

lived, and where he commenced his ministry, and by his miracles "manifested forth his glory," were within the limits of Zebulon; but Capernaum, Chorazin, and Bethsaida were in Naphtali. It was this latter tribe that was "by the way of the sea beyond Jordan, Galilee of the Gentiles."[1] Zebulon did not touch the sea of Galilee at any point, but the territories of these two tribes met at the northeast corner of the Bŭttauf, not far from Kânâ, and within these two tribes thus united our Lord passed nearly the whole of his wonderful life. To others there may not appear to be much in these remarks, and yet the facts, as they came out clear and distinct during my ride round the "plain of Zebulon," seemed to me to add a beautiful corroboration of the ancient prophecy and promise.

But let this pass. Crossing the plain of Tûr'an toward the northwest, we followed the stream which drains off the water into the Bŭttauf. It is called Jerrûban, and was on that day a boisterous brook, in consequence of the heavy rain that, in spite of Mackintoshes and umbrellas, was soaking us to the skin, from head to foot. In an hour from Kefr Kenna we came to Rŭmmaneh, on the very edge of the Bŭttauf. This, no doubt, marks the site of the ancient Rimmon that belonged to Zebulon.[2] Between it and Seffûrieh is a ruin called Rûm—the Ruma, I suppose, mentioned by Josephus as the birth-place of two of his heroes of Jotapata.[3] The hills around the Bŭttauf, east, north, and west, are wild, picturesque, and crowded with ancient ruins, some of them with old columns, as at Em el 'Amûd and at Sûr, west and northwest of Hŭttîn. The day we crossed the Bŭttauf the eastern half of it was a lake, and the path from Rŭmmaneh to Kânâ led through the oozy, spongy end of it. It was the most *nervous* ride I ever made. For two miles the horses waded through mud and water to the knees, along a path less than two feet wide, which had been *tramped down* to a consistency sufficient to arrest the sinking foot for a moment; but if the careless or jaded nag stepped elsewhere, he sank instantly into a quivering quagmire. After several adven-

[1] Matt. iv. 15. [2] 1 Chron. vi. 77. [3] Wars, iii. 7, 21.

tures of this sort, we "came to land" just at the foot of Kânâ.

Leaving our tired animals to rest and crop the grass and shrubs, we ran eagerly up and down the hill on which the village was built. It faces the southeast, and rises boldly from the margin of the Bŭttauf. The hill itself is nearly isolated. Wady Jefât comes down to, and then along the southwestern base of it, and another deep ravine cuts it off from the general range on the north and northeast, and it is thus made to stand out like a huge *tell*.

The houses were built of limestone, cut and laid up after the fashion still common in this region, and some of them may have been inhabited within the last fifty years. There are many ancient cisterns about it, and fragments of water-jars in abundance, and both reminded us of the "beginning of miracles."[1] Some of my companions gathered bits of these water-jars as mementoes—witnesses they could hardly be, for those of the narrative were of *stone*, while these were baked earth.

There is not now a habitable house in the humble village where our blessed Lord sanctioned, by his presence and miraculous assistance, the all-important and world-wide institution of marriage. This is a very curious fact, and might suggest a whole chapter of most instructive reflections. It is a sort of divine law of development to hide away the beginnings of things the most momentous in some almost undiscoverable point. This is an example. Innumerable millions in their happiest hours have had their thoughts and hearts directed to Kânâ. Poor little lonely thing! the proudest cities on earth might envy your lot. Nineveh, and Babylon, and a thousand other names may be forgotten, but not Cana of Galilee. It may even come to pass that Paris, London, and New York will be dropped out of mind, and their very sites be lost; but to the end of time, and to the end of the world, whenever and wherever there shall be the voice of the bride and the bridegroom, then and there will Cana of Galilee be remembered. Some names we

[1] John ii. 1–11.

pronounce with honor, some with shame and sorrow, many with cold indifference, but *Cana* will ever mingle in the song of the happy, to symbolize the peace and purity of domestic happiness—the bliss of wedded love.

Kânâ is not only deserted itself, but, so wild is the immediate neighborhood, that it is the favorite hunting-ground of the Kefr Kennits. Ibrahim, our guide, had shot a large leopard among its broken houses only a week previous to our visit. He had been hunting wild boar in Wady Jefât; and up this wady we next proceeded in search of Jotapata. It took just half an hour to ride from Kânâ to the foot of the rock of Jefât, which Mr. Schultz first identified with the site of that far-famed castle. It is therefore about two miles west of Kânâ. The path is in the bed of Wady Jefât, and is easy enough for a single horseman, but it would be quite impracticable for an army, and this agrees well with the description of Josephus. The sides and lateral ravines, of which there are many, are covered with a thick jungle of oak coppice—the very best haunt for the wild boar, and wild Arabs too. We, however, saw nothing more formidable than a jackal.

From the nature of the place and its surroundings, Jotapata could never have been any thing much more respectable than a retreat for robbers. Whatever appears greater than this in the account must be put down to the imagination or the *necessity* of the historian. The wadies about it are neither deeper nor more savage than scores of other wadies in Galilee, and Gamala was vastly more difficult to attack. The absence of fortifications on the top of Jefât can easily be explained. The original works were ephemeral, extemporized for the emergency, and built of the soft cretaceous rock of the place, and being demolished and deserted, they would crumble into just such rubbish as now covers the extreme edges of the rock. There are a few caves and old cisterns about it, quite sufficient for the story *reduced*, as this, above all others in Josephus, ought to be. He manifestly intended to rest his fame as a warrior upon the defense of Jotapata, and with this idea to stimulate his pen, there is scarcely any conceivable length of exaggeration to which he would not go.[1]

But there lies Nazareth in its pretty vale, and I leave you to walk or ride down these slippery paths as you prefer, and to enjoy in silence your own reflections, which must be far more impressive than any words of mine.

[1] See Wars, iii. 7 and 8.

THE VALE OF MATLOCK.

XXIX. NAZARETH.

March 29th.

"Can there any good thing come out of Nazareth? Come and see," as Philip said to Nathaniel.

Why not? It appeared really charming last night as we came down the mountain from the northeast with the grateful shadows of evening falling softly around it. The vale is small certainly, but then the different *swellings* of the surrounding hills give the idea of repose and protection; and, for my part, I would infinitely prefer to have the home of Mary and her divine Son in such a quiet seclusion, than to be obliged to force my way to it through the dust, and confusion, and hard worldliness of any crowded city.

I most emphatically accord with that opinion, or rather *feeling;* and there is a sort of latent beauty and appropriateness in the arrangement by which He who made all *things out of nothing* should himself come forth to the world *out of a place that had no history*. The idea here tempts one to linger upon it and expatiate, but this would throw us quite off our present track, which is to go "round about" and describe this city of Nazareth and her neighbors.

It is certainly remarkable that this place, dearest to the Christian heart of all on earth except Jerusalem, is not mentioned in the Old Testament, nor even by Josephus, who was himself on every side of it, and names the villages all about it, but seems yet totally ignorant of its existence. It was probably a very small hamlet, hid away in this narrow vale, and of no political importance whatever. And, so far as its subsequent history can be gathered from Eusebius, Jerome, and other ancient records, it never rose to distinction until the time of the Crusades. It was then made the seat of a bishopric, but long after this it was an insignificant village, and remained such through many a dark age of lawless violence. Within the last hundred years, however, it has gradually grown in size and risen into importance, until it has become the chief town of this district. It is now larger and more prosperous than in any former period in its history, and is still enlarging. The present population must exceed three thousand, but it can never become a great city. The position is not favorable, and there is a distressing want of water. Even at this early season there is an incessant contest for a jar of it around this fountain of the "Annunciation," which is the only one in the village. The present growth of Nazareth is mainly owing to the unchecked inroads of the Arabs from beyond Jordan, which has rendered it unsafe to reside in Beisan and on the great plain of Esdraelon. Most of the villages have been recently deserted, and this work of destruction is still going on; and the villagers from the plains are here in Nazareth, at Jennin, and still farther in toward the sea-board. Should a strong government again drive these Arabs over the Jordan, the population and importance of Nazareth would decline at once. It must, however, always be a spot sacred to the whole Christian world, for here our blessed Saviour passed the greater part of his life while on earth. But what a profound silence rests upon those thirty years of mysterious existence! We only know that here the child Jesus grew up from infancy to childhood and youth, increasing in stature as other children do, and in knowledge, and in favor both with God and man, as none ever have done. Here, too, he spent the years of his ripening manhood in humble labors and in sinless communion with God. How natural the desire to lift the veil that shrouds all this period in impenetrable darkness! Hence the spurious gospel of the "Infancy of Christ," stuffed with puerile or profane fables.

Let any one, curious to see what weak, uninspired man makes of the history of Jesus, turn to the First and Second Gospels of the Infancy, or the "Gospel according to Nicodemus," and he will be devoutly thankful to know that they are miserable forgeries, so foolish that they are rejected by all; and, so far from desiring to have the veil which covers the early life of the incomprehensible God-man lifted, he will adore the wisdom and the kindness that has thus concealed what we could not rightly appreciate nor even understand. Infinite wisdom decided that it was not well to encourage such inquiries, and has taken effectual care that they should never be answered. *There remains not one acknowledged anecdote of his life during all these years.* And, farther, I am most happy to believe that there is not a fragment of the ancient Nazareth itself which can be identified. It is nearly certain that every stone of the small hamlet where the Saviour of the world spent so many years has long ago dissolved back into the white marl of the hills from which it was quarried. This kind of rock disintegrates with great rapidity, and, as the place was often almost or quite destroyed and forsaken, the soft stones thus exposed would not last fifty years.

Well, thus I would have it. I like to feel assured that the *church* of the annunciation, the *cave*, the *kitchen* of Mary, the *work-shop* of Joseph, the *dining-table* of our Lord and his apostles, the *synagogue* where he read the Prophet Isaiah, and the *precipice* down which his enraged fellow-villagers were determined to cast him headlong, *as now shown*, are all fabulous, apocryphal, and have no claims to my veneration or even respect. The eye rests on nothing with which our Lord was familiar except his own glorious works. These remain the same. This narrow vale, on the side of which the village is built, climbing up the steep mountain back of it, is very much now what it was then. To this fountain the young Jesus came for water just as these fine healthy children now do with their "pitchers." Shut in on all sides by *fourteen* swelling eminences on the circling mountains, as Dr. Richardson counts them, Nazareth must have been always, as at present, very hot, particularly in the early part of the day. It was also wanting in prospects and distant views. Hence, no doubt, our Saviour would often climb to the top of this western hill, which rises at least five hundred feet above the bottom of the wady. There he could behold the distant sea, and breathe its fresh breeze. From thence, too, his eye would rove delighted over a vast expanse of sacred scenery. We can do the same, and in the doing of it hold converse with his spirit, and enjoy what he enjoyed, without one doubt to trouble, or one fable of meddling monk to disturb. Let this suffice. God does not admit impertinent curiosity behind the veil of his own privacy.

Of places which immediately surround Nazareth little need be said, because few of them are mentioned in the Bible, or have ever risen to any distinction. Tabor, and Debûrieh, and Ksalis, Endor, and Nain, we shall visit hereafter. Yafa here, to the southwest two miles, is the Japhia of Zebulon. Semmûnia, mentioned along with it, is in the same great oak woods two or three miles still farther west. Josephus also mentions Jibbata in the plain south of Semmûnia. Sefûrieh, the Sephoris which figures so largely in Josephus and during the Crusades—the Diocæsaria of the Romans and the fathers—is about five miles to the northwest. The fine fountains south of Sefûrieh, the more valuable for their rarity in this region, have witnessed many a contest between Crusader and Saracen, as it was a favorite camp-ground for both. Though it was an important city for several centuries after the advent of Christ, as appears abundantly from Josephus and Roman authors, and had coins struck with its name, yet it owes its celebrity mostly to the tradition that Joachim and Anna, the supposed parents of the Virgin Mary, resided there. It is now a considerable village, and flourishing for this region. The ruins of a castle, probably built by the Crusaders, may still be seen on the hill above it; and other remains, more ancient, are below on the west side. The latter may have belonged to a church or convent of the Middle Ages. The place is favorably situated, being nearly half way between Acre and Tiberias, with the fat and fertile Büttauf on the north, the long vale of Tur'an east, and the magnificent oak glades for many miles to the south, west, and northwest. The inhabitants are not the most complacent to strangers, and I have never liked to spend the night there.

30*th*. You have been making good use of this bright morning, I suppose, for you left the tent at an early hour?

I went at the call of the bell, and heard the monks say mass in their "Chapel of the Annunciation." The organ and the chant were quite affecting in this strange land and

JERUSALEM—PLAIN OF REPHAIM.

sacred place at early dawn. But I have little satisfaction in looking at shrines in which I have no faith, or in examining the cells of monks for whose institutions and characters I entertain very little respect. The convent appeared to me more like a castle than a house of prayer, but I suppose it is none too strong to keep out Arab robbers. Issuing through its iron gates, I strolled away in search of the precipice of "Precipitation;" and, were it not so far from the village, I should acquiesce in it at once, for it is well adapted to the murderous purpose which animated the townsmen of our Lord. My guide pointed out a small ruin much nearer the precipice, where, he said, the village was originally built; and this, if one could place confidence in the tradition, would relieve the difficulty as to distance. I rather suspect, however, that the bold cliff which overhangs the Esdraelon was selected because of its striking appearance, and the grand prospect which it commands.

On my way back through the upper part of the town I found precipices enough for all the requirements of the narrative in Luke.[1] Most of them, it is true, appear to be partly *artificial*, but doubtless there were some of the same sort in ancient days. I stopped also at the *fountain* of the annunciation, according to the Greek tradition, and, among other things, attempted to purchase one of those singular rolls of old coins which the girls of Nazareth bind around their foreheads and cheeks; but I could not succeed in my negotiation, for they refused to sell at any price. Most travelers speak of the beauty of these girls, and not altogether without reason. To me, however, they appear unusually bold, and their obvious want of modesty greatly depreciates their good looks. I fear that a very intimate acquaintance with the Nazareth of this day might lead me to ask the very question of Nathaniel, and therefore I am ready and quite willing to prosecute our pilgrimage.

The only preliminary is breakfast, and that has been waiting for half an hour. We send the tents to Sulam, and go thither ourselves by way of Tabor.

[1] Luke iv. 29.

TABOR.

March 30th.

It is about five miles nearly due east to the northwestern base of Tabor, whence only it can be ascended on horseback. The road winds over the hills, and down a long wady to the plain, a short distance north of Debûrieh. We, however, shall not follow the valley, but keep round farther north, and come upon the mount from the great oak woods which lie between it and Sejera. On one occasion I went directly up from Debûrieh with my aneroid, and found the ascent from Esdraelon to be thirteen hundred and forty-five feet. I had formerly made the base of the mountain about four hundred feet higher than the Bay of Acre, and the entire elevation, therefore, is not far from eighteen hundred feet. The southern face of Tabor is limestone rock, nearly naked, but the northern is clothed to the top with a forest of oak and terebinth, mingled with the beautiful mock-orange (Syringa). The road (if road it may be called) winds up through them, and, notwithstanding the experience of other travelers, I have always found it difficult, and in certain parts actually dangerous.

The mount is entirely composed of cretaceous limestone, as are the hills west and north of it, but all to the east is volcanic. I have never seen a picture of it that was perfectly satisfactory, although every artist who comes in sight of it is sure to take a sketch. Their views differ widely, owing mainly to the points whence they are taken. Seen from the south or north, Tabor describes nearly an arc of a great circle; from the east it is a broad truncated cone, rounded off at the top; from the west it is wedge-shaped, rising to a moderate height above the neighboring hills. Its true figure is an elongated oval, the longitudinal diameter running nearly east and west. The most impressive view, perhaps, is from the plain between it and Endor.

Esdraelon is seen to the greatest advantage, not from the summit, but from a projecting terrace some four hundred feet above Debûrieh. It appears like one vast carpet thrown

TABOR.

back to the hills of Samaria and the foot of Carmel. In variety of patterns and richness of colors it is not equaled by any thing in this country. Both the Mediterranean and the Lake of Tiberias are visible from a point near the summit, the former to the northwest, and the latter on the northeast. The Dead Sea, however, can not be seen from any part of Tabor, and those who have made the statement were probably deceived by the silvery haze which fills the ghor of the Jordan in that direction. There is often an actual mirage, which would mislead any one who had not previously examined the point on a day unperplexed by these phenomena. And now for this exciting and romantic climb. I will lead the way, and leave you to your own meditations, with the hint to look well to your horse, lest you change romance to tragedy before we get up.

Here we are on the top of Tabor! Let us breathe our tired animals beneath this fine old oak at the entrance into the fortress. You observe that a fosse once protected the wall on all this part of the summit, because it is less precipitous than elsewhere. This narrow plot on the north side, I suppose, was leveled into its present shape by the inhabitants of the ancient city for gardens, or to make a hippodrome and parade-ground. South of this a rocky ridge rises some fifty feet higher, and the entire summit was surrounded by a heavy wall, strengthened with towers at suitable distances, and farther defended by a ditch when needed. These works are obviously of very different ages, and history not only accounts for, but demands them. There was a town here, and no doubt fortified, at or before the time of Joshua. Here Barak and Deborah assembled the thousands of Naphtali to attack Sisera. And Tabor is never lost sight of either by Hebrew historian or poet. It has therefore a story many times too long for us to repeat—Canaanitish, Jewish, Græco-Macedonian, Roman, Christian, Saracenic, Frank, and Turk. Parts of these fortifications are doubtless Jewish, but it is quite impossible to distinguish the various ages of architecture with certainty. Nothing remains now but a confused mass of broken walls, towers, vaults, cisterns, and houses, some of which indicate the sites of the convents and churches erected by the Crusaders. The Greek Church has recently fitted up, with the assistance of Russian gold, two or three vaults here on the left, as a chapel and residence of the solitary priest and keeper—a foreign monk, whose appearance is not over-saintly, nor his cell particularly sweet. Both it and the chapel smelt of *arrack* the last time I was here, and the red eyes and bloated countenance of the priest did not indicate "total abstinence." The Latin monks from Nazareth also celebrate mass here on certain festivals. I once saw a large procession, with drums and cymbals, singing and clapping hands, and the indispensable roar of muskets, set out from that town to keep the feast of the Transfiguration here at these forsaken shrines.

Do you suppose that this is the scene of that stupendous

event? I see it called in question by many modern tourists and critics.

If I hesitate to admit the claims of Tabor to the honor of the Transfiguration, it is not from any thing in the mount itself. No more noble or appropriate theatre for such a glorious manifestation could be found or desired. Nor does the fact that there may have been a village on the top at that time present any difficulty. There are many secluded and densely-wooded terraces on the north and northeast sides admirably adapted to the scenes of the Transfiguration. I have been delighted to wander through some of them, and certainly regretted that my early faith in this site had been disturbed by prying critics; and, after reading all that they have advanced against the current tradition, I am not fully convinced. You can examine this vexed question at your leisure, and have as good a right to form an independent opinion on it as any body else, for all that is known about it is found in Matthew xvii., Mark ix., and Luke ix., which you can see at a glance contain nothing very decisive against the claims of Tabor. The topographical indications are very uncertain and obscure.

But, however we may dispose of this question, Tabor will always be a place of great interest. Its remarkable shape and striking position would attract admiration in any country, and the magnificent prospect from the top will always draw pilgrims and tourists thither. I have climbed to it many times, and shall certainly repeat my visits whenever I pass this way. It is from Tabor that one gets the best general view of central Palestine, and especially of the rise and direction of the different water-courses by which the great plain of Esdraelon is drained. In common with others, I have carefully sought the summit level of this part of the plain, and, until lately, without entire success. In my youthful days I was familiar with old maps which made the Kishon run in a broad, straight canal from the Bay of Acre to the Jordan. Of course, this is absurd in itself, and rendered still more so by the well-ascertained fact that the Jordan east of Tabor is seven or eight hundred feet lower than the Mediterranean. The old tradition, however, is not without a semblance of fact to rest upon. I once went directly across from Debûrieh to Nain, which you see to the southwest of us about four miles, on the slope of Jebel ed Dûhy. Between these two villages the plain is so perfectly level that I could not determine the exact line where the water would flow east and where west, nor could the eye detect the slope either way except at a considerable distance. An immense amount of water descends in winter from these oak-clad hills north and west of Tabor, and enters the plain between Ksalis and Debûrieh. It might well happen, therefore, that this flat space would be so flooded that a part would find its way westward to the Kishon, and another part descend along the base of Tabor into Wady Sherrar, and thence into the Jordan. And this it actually does, as I have clearly proved this winter. Being detained in Nazareth by a very heavy storm, our company set out, during a temporary lull, for a gallop to Endor and Nain. Descending to the plain at Ksalis by the most frightful of all ridable paths, we struck out into Esdraelon direct for Endor, and, of course, the path led diagonally across toward the southeast. It was all flooded with water, and *spongy* enough; but my search ended in palpable certainty. *All the water that came foaming off these hills east of Ksalis ran directly for this Wady Sherrar*, and no mistake, while all west of that village (and there was plenty of it) flowed without hesitation *westward* to the Kishon. So, also, the drainings of Jebel ed Dûhy from about Endor went to the *Sherrar* and the *Jordan*, while those to the west of it joined the Kishon. A line drawn from Ksalis to Endor, therefore, passes directly along the summit-level between the Kishon and the *Sherrar*. The Wady Jalûd, however, on the other side of Jebel ed Dûhy, extends much farther to the west than this, draining the central part of Esdraelon into the valley of Jezreel from about Fûlîeh. These two streams, the Jalûd and the Kishon, therefore, overlap one another for many miles, the arms of the latter, north and south of Jezreel, carrying the waters from the mountains to the Mediterranean, while the Jalûd takes those

SOURCES OF THE KISHON—BATTLE-FIELD OF BARAK. 141

from the centre into the Jordan. The winter torrents, which come down from the regions of Jelbûn east of Jenîn, are the most distant branches of the Kishon; but the most distant perennial *source* of this famous river is the Fountain of Jenîn itself—the En Gannim (Fountain of Gardens) given to Issachar by Joshua.[1] This is re-enforced on its way westward by the waters of Lejjûn, and many other rivulets from the hills of Samaria and wadies of Carmel, and also from springs and marshes in the lower part of the plain itself; but they are not strong enough to keep the river running during the summer and autumn. I have crossed the bed of the Kishon (even after it enters the plain of Acre) in the early part of April, when it was quite dry. The truth is, that the strictly permanent Kishon is one of the shortest rivers in the world. You will find the source in the vast fountains called Sa'adîyeh, not more than three miles east of Haifa. They flow out from the very roots of Carmel, almost on a level with the sea, and the water is brackish. They form a deep, broad stream at once, which creeps sluggishly through an impracticable marsh to the sea; and it is *this* stream which the traveler crosses on the shore. Of course, it is largely swollen during the great rains of winter by the longer river from the interior. It is *then* much easier to find than to get over. I once crossed diagonally through the lower part of Esdraelon from Semmunia to Wady Kŭsab, and had no little trouble with its bottomless mire and tangled grass.

I have described thus minutely this noble plain and "ancient river," partly because I have nowhere met with a good and correct account of them, and partly to prepare the way for an intelligible conversation about some of those Biblical scenes in which they figure most largely. I, of course, refer to the battle of Barak, the sacrifice of Elijah, and the slaughter of Baal's priests at the Kishon.

Is the battle-field of Barak visible from here?

Very distinctly. On the border of the plain to the southwest you can distinguish the bold artificial Tell el Mutsel-

[1] Josh. xxi. 29.

lim, near Lejjûn, the Megiddo of the Bible. Southeast of it is a village called Te'ennûkh, the Taannach of Judges. Below these two, on the plain, the host of Sisera was encamped. Barak, accompanied by the heroic Deborah, was where we now are, with their ten thousand courageous Naphtalites from Kadesh. On the morning of that eventful day, probably long before it was light, Deborah set the little army in motion with the energetic command and animating promise, Up, for this is the day in which the Lord has delivered Sisera into thine hand. Is not the Lord gone out before thee?[1] Rapidly they descend the mountain, cross over by Nain into the valley of Jezreel, then incline to the left to avoid the low and marshy ground, and by the first faint light of the morning they are upon the sleeping host of the Canaanites. This assault, wholly unexpected, threw them into instant and irrecoverable confusion. But half awake, the whole army fled in dismay down the plain, hotly pursued by the victorious Barak. No time was allowed to recover from their panic. God also fought against them: "The earth trembled, the heavens dropped, the clouds also dropped water." Josephus adds that a storm from the east beat furiously in the *faces* of the Canaanites, but only on the *backs* of the Jews. The storm is required by both the narrative of the action and the song of victory. It was to this, I suppose, that Deborah alluded, "Is not the Lord gone out before thee?" and this it certainly was which swelled the Kishon, so that it swept away and drowned the flying host, for it never could do that except during a great rain. The army of Sisera naturally sought to regain the strongly-fortified Harosheth of the Gentiles, from which they had marched up to their camping-ground a short time before. This place is at the lower end of the narrow vale through which the Kishon passes out of Esdraelon into the plain of Acre, and this was their only practicable line of retreat. The victorious enemy was behind them; on their left were the hills of Samaria, in the hand of their enemies; on their right was the swollen river and the marshes of Thora; they had no

---
[1] Judg. iv. 14.

alternative but to make for the narrow pass which led to Harosheth. The space, however, becomes more and more narrow until within the *pass* it is only a few rods wide. There horses, chariots, and men become mixed in horrible confusion, jostling and treading down one another; and the river, here swifter and deeper than above, runs zigzag from side to side of the vale, until, just before it reaches the castle of Harosheth, it dashes sheer up against the perpendicular base of Carmel. There is no longer any possibility of avoiding it. Rank upon rank of the flying host plunge madly in, those behind crushing those before deeper and deeper in the tenacious mud. They stick fast, are overwhelmed, are swept away by thousands. Such are the conditions of this battle and battle-field that we can follow it out to the dire catastrophe. We only need to know where Harosheth is, and that is now easily found and identified. The narrative of the battle leads us to seek it somewhere down the Kishon, for only in that direction would they fly from an attack coming from the northeast. Again, it can not be very far from the camp, for the Hebrews pursued them to it. They had before the battle marched some ten or twelve miles, and we can not suppose that they could pursue an enemy more than eight or ten miles farther. Now, exactly in the line of their necessary retreat, and about eight miles from Megiddo, at the entrance of the pass to Esdraelon from the plain of Acre, is an enormous double mound, called Harothîeh, which is the Arabic form of the Hebrew Harosheth, the signification of the word being the same in both languages. This *Tell* is situated just below the point where the Kishon in one of its turns beats against the rocky base of Carmel, leaving no room even for a footpath. A castle there effectually commands the pass up the vale of the Kishon into Esdraelon, and such a castle there was on this immense double tell of Harothîeh. It is still covered with the remains of old walls and buildings. The village of the same name is now on the other side of the river, a short distance higher up, and, of course, nearer the battle-field. I have not the slightest doubt of this identification.

It was probably called Harosheth of the *gentiles*, or *nations*, because it belonged to those gentiles of Acre and the neighboring plains, which we know from Judges i. 31 the Hebrews could not subdue; and, by the way, I believe that Sisera pitched between Taannach and Megiddo, because, as is stated in the passage from Judges, those towns were still in the hands of the Canaanites.

It may be objected that our supposition makes the authority of Jabin extend very far. It does; but, instead of weakening, this fact is rather confirmatory. Hazor, situated in the centre of the mountains of the present Belad Beshara, we are distinctly informed by Joshua, was the *head of all those nations* who assembled at the waters of Merom. Among them were the kings of Dor, of Taannach, and Megiddo, and very likely of Acre itself. As Hazor was rebuilt, and another King Jabin of the same dynasty now reigned in it, the probabilities are great that he would still be the acknowledged "*head*" of all these Canaanitish cities. Moreover, Jabin could only use his nine hundred chariots of iron on the plains, such as those of Acre and Esdraelon, and no better position for his horses and chariots could be found than just this site of Harosheth, nor a more commanding position taken by his chief captain Sisera.

But if Harosheth is this Harothîeh, how comes it to pass that Jael, the wife of Heber the Kenite, is found so near the battle-field that Sisera could light down from his chariot and flee to her tent? We are told in this very narrative that their home was near Kadesh, which is two days' travel to the northeast of the battle-field.

Even this, when carefully examined, confirms our identification. It is mentioned in the eleventh verse that Heber the Kenite, which was of the children of Hobab, had severed himself from the Kenites, and pitched his tent unto the plain of Zaanaim which is by Kadesh; and I suppose the object of this brief notice thus thrown into the narrative is, in reality, to account for the appearance of Jael on this scene of action. The other Kenites were settled in the hill country of Judah, not far from Hebron. If you ask, Why state that Heber had settled near Kadesh when you want to know how he came to have his tent down at the bottom of Esdraelon? my answer is, that such was the fact. Heber did settle there. And it is because he did that there came to "be peace between Jabin and the Kenites," for Hazor was only a few miles from Kadesh. An incident which happened to myself will explain why Heber was found at the bottom of this plain at the time of the battle. With a guide from Nazareth, I once crossed the lower part of Esdraelon in the winter. It was then full of Arab tents, and at first I felt a little nervous, but my guide assured me there was no danger, for he was well acquainted with these Arabs. Their home was in the mountains north of Nazareth, toward Safet, and they only came down here to pass the cold months of winter. This was the very thing that Heber did, and who knows but that these Arabs are lineal descendants of that heroic Jael. I peered curiously into the faces of the women, but they were all tawny brass or dirty bronze; and I could find none that looked at all heroic, though some of them seemed as if they could drive a nail into the temple of a sleeping enemy. To all this some one might object, that if Heber lived near Kadesh, why not descend to the Hûleh immediately below for the winter, rather than migrate to this distant place? For the simple reason, I answer, that this place was under the government of his ally Jabin, and the other was not. It is interesting to notice how all parts of this narrative, even to its remote and incidental implications, correspond and corroborate each other. In addition to the above, the habits of these tent-dwellers require that the battle should have occurred in the winter, or very early spring, for only then would Heber's tent be found here. Now this is nowhere stated in just so many words, but the song of victory says that the clouds dropped down rain, and it only rains on Esdraelon in the winter. The same thing is necessarily implied by the fact that "the river of Kishon swept them away, that ancient river, the River Kishon," and this it could not do except in winter.

What have you to say with regard to the deed of Jael,

Vol. II.—G

which is highly praised by Deborah? Dr. Kitto, after presenting the whole transaction and the supposed motives of the actor in the most unfavorable light, sums up the whole thus: "It was a most treacherous and cruel murder, wanting all those extenuations which were applicable to the assassination of King Eglon by Ehud." I feel unwilling to accept this explanation. It shocks my ideas altogether to suppose that an inspired prophetess should foretell the deed, and then celebrate it and its author in the highest strains of congratulation and eulogy, if it were a mere treacherous, cold-blooded murder.

Certainly this is the very last conclusion we shall adopt. We need by no means take for granted that because the Kenites were not at war with the tyrannical Jabin, that therefore they were treated with justice by him. In the same neighborhood at the present day, the tribes of settled Arabs (and the Kenites were of this class) are most cruelly oppressed by the sheikhs of the districts where they reside. They are at peace with them, however, through fear, and from inability to throw off the galling yoke, as Heber was with Jabin. Now it is nearly certain that in those lawless times the defenseless Kenites would be oppressed by Jabin, and would sigh for and gladly embrace any opportunity to escape from this intolerable bondage. Their deliverer, therefore, would be esteemed a patriot and hero, not a murderer.

In the second place, if it must be supposed that Jabin was a kind friend and just protector of the Kenites, it does not follow that *Jael* might not have had special reasons to fear and hate *Sisera*. He had the command of the immediate neighborhood where the Kenites were encamped, and, unless he differed from modern commanders of Eastern tyrants, he would most certainly abuse them, and allow them to be insulted without redress by his rude retainers. Jael might have thus been injured in the highest degree, if not by Sisera himself, by some of his lewd captains. Or there may have been a recent blood-feud between the tribe and this man or his family, which not only justified Jael, according to the law of retribution, but rendered it obligatory upon her, and every one of the tribe, to take revenge upon their enemy.

In the third place, we are not to take for granted that certain fantastic laws of the modern Bedawîn in regard to the asylum of the tent were in force among these *settled* Kenites. These notions are carried to such an absurd pitch in some tribes that a man is obliged to protect the murderer of his father if he succeeds in reaching the tent; but the *settled* Arabs know no such *laws*, and I do not believe that the Kenites did.

Again, it may be assumed as nearly certain that Jael would not have ventured upon this daring act unless she knew that her husband and her whole tribe would not only justify, but rejoice in it as a righteous retribution upon their oppressor, and as the means of escape from an intolerable bondage, against which they were watching for an opportunity to revolt.

And yet once more. On the nearly incredible supposition that neither the Kenites as a tribe, nor Jael as an individual, had any cause of complaint against Sisera, we may fairly conclude that they were believers in Israel's God and friends of *his* people. This their whole history confirms. They must therefore have been deeply grieved at the cruel oppression which their brethren in faith and worship suffered from Sisera. In their defenseless condition they had not dared to take sides openly against Jabin, but in heart they were with the oppressed Israelites, and regarded it as a duty to help them to the utmost of their power. The total overthrow of the Canaanites offered the wished-for opportunity, and Jael boldly availed herself of it.

The reason why it is mentioned that the Kenites were neutral in this war was not to give the idea that they were under any obligation to take sides with Sisera or to protect him if defeated, nor even to account for the fact that Sisera fled to Heber's tent. He *may*, and probably *had* little enough reason to claim this protection. But it was necessary to make the statement about the Kenites, as we have before said, in order to account for their being down on Esdraelon at all when the army of Sisera was there. It deserves also to be remembered that if the Kenites had attempted to shield and aid Sisera after his defeat, they would have rendered themselves partisans in the war on the losing side, and might have been treated as enemies by the now victorious Israelites. On the whole, therefore, I conclude, that if all the circumstances and influences which impelled Jael to the daring act, and sustained her in it, were known, we should find that she violated neither the customs of her people, nor the laws of war then in force, nor the abstract and greater laws of righteousness, by thus destroying the enemy of God's people and the oppressor of her own, who from necessity sought in her tent an asylum to which he had no right, and the granting of which might have involved her and her whole family in ruin.

Under these impressions, I can join with Deborah in celebrating the deed and the actor.

Blessed above women shall Jael, the wife of Heber, the Kenite, be; blessed shall she be above women in the tent. He asked water, and she gave him milk; she brought forth butter in a lordly dish. She put her hand to the nail, and her right hand to the workman's hammer, and with the hammer she smote Sisera, she smote off his head when she had pierced and stricken through his temples. At her feet he bowed, he lay down; at her feet he bowed, he fell; where he bowed, he fell down dead. The mother of Sisera looked out at a window, and cried through the lattice, Why is his chariot so long in coming? why tarry the wheels of his chariots? Her wise ladies answered her, yea, she returned answer to herself, Have they not sped? have they not divided the prey, to every man a damsel or two; to Sisera a prey of diverse colors, of diverse colors of needle-work, a prey of diverse colors of needle-work on both sides, meet for the necks of them that take the spoil? So let *all thine enemies perish, O Lord; but let them that love him be as the sun when he goeth forth in his might.*[1] There is nothing, ancient or modern, more beautiful, appropriate, or sublime than this close

[1] Judg. v. 24-30.

of Deborah's triumphal ode. No gloss, paraphrase, or comment can add to its graces.

There are a few allusions, however, in it which may be better understood by brief explanations. The "nail" which Jael used was a *tent-pin*, now, as then, called *wated*, and the "hammer" was the mallet with which it is driven into the ground. It is not necessary to suppose that either of them was of iron, as *nail* and *hammer* would imply. The *wated* was probably a sharp-pointed pin of hard wood, and the hammer was the ordinary mallet used by these tent-dwelling Arabs.

There is a curious use of the word *nail* in Isaiah xxii. 23, 25, which must also refer to those wooden *wateds*, I suppose, for it is the same Hebrew word: I will fasten him with a nail—yutad—in a sure place; and again, in the 25th, this yutad, fastened in a sure place, shall be removed, and *cut down*, and fall. It is not every place that will hold the tent-"nail" securely; it must be driven into suitable ground.

Doubtless a wooden pin or peg is here meant, not an iron nail. It is, however, not a tent-pin, but a peg driven into the *wall*, and used to hang clothes and household utensils upon. There is significance in the statement that it should be made fast in a *sure pláce*, because, in general, these pins are driven into the wall through the plaster, and are every thing but steady and secure. Not one in a score of them but what bend down, or get loose and fall out. There is a reference to the same thing, and the same Hebrew word, in Zech. x. 4: Out of him came forth the corner, out of him the *nail—yutad.* And this, by the way, gives an intelligible idea to this expression of Zechariah. The tent-pin is absolutely essential to the stability and safety of the Arab's habitation.

Again, it is absurd to suppose that Jael brought Sisera *butter* to drink. Neither the ancients nor the modern Orientals make *butter* at all, as we understand the word, and what takes the place of it is never used as a beverage. Butter is the exponent of milk in the other member of the paralellism, showing that sour milk, or *leben*, was meant, and this, properly prepared, makes a most cooling and refreshing drink.

Lastly, the entire soliloquy of Sisera's mother is worked out with admirable skill and truthfulness. When standing on the lofty tell of Harosheth, which commands the view of the pass up the Kishon, and out into Esdraelon toward Megiddo, I could fancy her ladyship sitting at a latticed window, and impatiently looking up the wady. She knew that a battle was to take place, was certain of victory, and longed not so much to see her son as to grasp the spoils. Knowing that these lewd warriors would chiefly value the fair damsels of the Hebrews, she mentions them first, but does not appear to relish this sort of "prey" for her house, and therefore does not give any to Sisera—most mothers can understand and sympathize with her—but she feasted her imagination with the goodly garment of diverse colors which her son was to lay at her feet. She looks at it again and again; turns it over first on this side, then on that, to see and admire the "diverse colors." This is eminently Oriental and feminine; and the childish repetition of "diverse colors" is all the more striking in an ode distinguished for rapid narrative, abrupt exclamation, and the utmost conciseness of style and diction.

This Deborah was certainly a remarkable lady, prophetess, poet, judge, and warrior. It is not a little singular that though her residence was near Jerusalem, between Ramah and Bethel, yet we meet her far north, at Kadesh in Naphtali, with Barak, who was of that city. We find her name also here, at the foot of Tabor, perpetuated in this miserable village of Debûrieh.

As judge and inspired guide to Israel, she probably itinerated a good deal, as did Samuel and other prophets; and her patriotic zeal would lead her wherever she could be of service to her oppressed people. I suppose she dwelt in a tent, like her heroine Jael, under that palm-tree which bore her name near Bethel, in Mount Ephraim. It was called *the palm-tree* of Deborah (see the Hebrew).[1] It seems to me to be a fair inference from such expressions that *trees* were as rare in Palestine, even at that early age, as they are at

[1] Judg. iv. 5.

the present day, or we should not so often read of *the* oak, *the* terebinth, *the* palm-tree, of this or that important place or event. If trees were abundant, such a designation would signify nothing, and would not have been employed.

And one other thought about these remarkable trees. This country abounds in them. We have sacred trees, and trees that are inhabited by *jin*, or evil spirits; and we have single trees all over the land covered with bits of rags from the garments of passing villagers, hung up as acknowledgments, or as deprecatory signals and charms; and we find beautiful clumps of oak-trees sacred to a kind of beings called Jacob's daughters. These are doubtless relics of most ancient superstitions; and in the fact that the old patriarchs and prophets lived, and prophesied, and were buried under such trees, we find, I imagine, the origin of this curious custom and belief.

But it is time to descend and pursue our ride to Sulam, whither our tents have preceded us. There is no path but the one we came up, for on the south and east the declivity is too precipitous for roads. I once attempted to find my way down toward Khan et Tejjar, but did not succeed, and was obliged to return to our present path. The road to the khan leads through this rough oak wood for more than an hour, when the forest and the limestone on which it grows terminate together. Below, and all east to the valley of the Jordan, the country is volcanic and destitute of trees. The wady in which the khans are situated is called Mîdy. It comes from the northwest, drains all that part of the forest, and passes down southeast to the Sherrar and the Jordan. There are two khans: one on a hill about one hundred feet square, and having octagonal towers on the corners. It served the double purpose of castle and caravanserai. The other is in the vale below, and was much larger. It had also a division through the centre, with vaults and magazines on either side of it, and the great advantage of a fountain of water within the walls. It was fitted up with rooms for the protection of merchandise and the accommodation of travelers. The place is now entirely deserted, nor is there an inhabited house in sight. Caravans do not spend the night there for fear of Arabs, who are always prowling about, watching for an opportunity to rob. I have never halted there for half an hour without having some of these rascals pass along, and scrutinize my party closely, to see whether or not it would do to attack us.

On Monday of each week a great fair is held at the khans, when, for a few hours, the scene is very lively and picturesque. These gatherings afford an excellent opportunity to observe Syrian manners, customs, and costumes, and to become acquainted with the character and quality of her productions. Thousands of people assemble from all parts of the country either to sell, trade, or purchase. Cotton is brought in bales from Nablûs; barley, and wheat, and sesamum, and Indian corn from the Hûleh, the Hauran, and Esdraelon. From Gilead and Bashan, and the surrounding districts, come horses and donkeys, cattle and flocks, with cheese, *leben*, *semen*, honey, and similar articles. Then there are miscellaneous matters, such as chickens and eggs, figs, raisins, apples, melons, grapes, and all sorts of fruits and vegetables in their season. The peddlers open their packages of tempting fabrics; the jeweler is there with his trinkets; the tailor with his ready-made garments; the shoemaker with his stock, from rough, hairy sandals to yellow and red morocco boots; the farrier is there with his tools, nails, and flat iron shoes, and drives a prosperous business for a few hours; and so does the saddler, with his coarse sacks and his gayly-trimmed cloths. And thus it is with all the arts and occupations known to this people.

The noise is incessant, and at a distance sounds like that "of many waters." Every man is crying his wares at the top of his voice, chickens cackle and squall, donkeys bray and fight, and the dogs bark. Every living thing adds somewhat to the many-toned and prodigious uproar. It is now a miscellaneous comedy in full operation, where every actor does his best, and is supremely gratified with his own performance.

The people find many reasons for sustaining these anti-

KHAN EL KHALEEL—ARAB FAIR.

quated and very curious gatherings. Every man, woman, and child has inherited the *itch* for trading, and, of course, all classes meet at this grand *bourse* to talk over the state of the markets, from the price of a cucumber to that of cotton, or of a five thousand dollar horse from the Hauran. Again, every Arab is a politician, and groups gather around the outskirts of the crowd to discuss the doings of the "allied powers," the last firman from the sultan, or the new tax demanded by their own petty emeer. Descending to more ordinary matters, these fairs are great places for gossip and scandal. Friends meet friends, and exchange the news of weddings, births, and deaths, and all the multifarious incidents and accidents between those grand extremes of human life. In a word, these fairs supply the places of many of the appliances of more civilized society. They are the daily newspaper, for there is one for every day within a circuit of forty miles. They are the exchange, and the *forwarding office*, and the political caucus, and the family gathering, and the grand festa and gala days, and underlying the whole is the ever-present idea and aim of *making money*.

Thus it is at Khan et Tejjar (the Inn of the Merchants) on Monday morning, but long before sunset not a soul of this busy throng remains on the spot. All return home, or take refuge in some neighboring village. I attended once, and then took my way eastward to the valley of the Jordan, at Jisr el Mujamia, in search of 'Akil 'Aga. The country for the first three miles is a rich, volcanic plain. The path then leads down to a brook, called Sāāra, which descends from the north, past a village of the same name. The water, yellow-green and foul, flows off in a deep gorge to the Sherrar. Half an hour farther is M'ather, with hovels nearly concealed behind hills of manure. The only things at work about the village were the bees, of which there are more hives than there are houses, and the air rings with the hum of these industrious purveyors of honey. Two miles farther east is Hadathy, large and better built, with an enormous chasm, washed out of the surrounding bluffs by fountains which run out from the crumbling banks. This region was thickly inhabited until quite recently; and in little more than a mile from Hadathy is 'Aolam, a large village in ruins. It is probably the Ulama of the ancients. It has excellent water, and very large fig-trees still flourishing, for it was sacked and destroyed by the Arabs only three years ago, as was also the next village, called Seerîn. Having thus ridden for three hours through this depopulated country, I *dived* suddenly into the valley of the Jordan, having the gorge of the Sherrar between me and Kaukab el Howa, the splendidly-situated castle of Belvoir. The descent to the jisr was extremely steep, and greatly surprised me by its depth. It is difficult to remember, or practically realize, that the Jordan is there *eight hundred feet* lower than the ocean. Down, down I walked, until, tired out, I resumed the saddle. The entire ghor presented a most singular appearance. It is far from level, tilted up, in fact, into fantastic hills and shelving bluffs by vast dikes of obtruding lava. Half way down I came upon ruins of a large place, called Yidma, evidently very ancient. The ghor was alive with Arabs, dotted with tents, and clothed with flocks.

I pitched my tent at sunset near that of the aga, and tried in vain to sleep. An intensely hot sirocco had commenced to blow, and this made every man and beast in this large encampment almost as nervous and restless as myself. Early next morning, while sitting in my tent-door smoking an argely, I was startled to see a large panther (nimr) scouring the plain in full chase of a pack of dogs that had attacked him. Making a long circle, they swept around my tent, when the panther left the dogs, leaped over the corner of the tent, tossed my argely to the winds, and then bounded away after the dogs. In another minute he returned, sprang on to the top of the tent, and laid himself down there. I was confounded, but sat still, and he soon jumped from the tent, and crouched down close to my feet. He was out of breath, and panted fearfully. Though not at all pleased to have the fierce brute so near, I kept my eye steadily and sternly fixed on his. He remained quiet until his keeper came from the aga's tent to recapture him. Then he growled fiercely, and was disposed to fight for his liberty; nor was it until they brought some fresh meat that they were able to get hold of him. He was a tame one, so far as *nimrs* can be tamed, brought up by the aga to hunt gazelles. The aga told me that these *nimrs* require seven years to complete their growth, and a constant course of careful training all that time to make them good hunters. He is extremely cunning in his approaches toward his victim; lies flat on his belly, and creeps almost insensibly toward the flock. His color then is so like the surrounding grass and stubble that the aga said he could not keep track of him. He will thus manœuvre for hours, until finally within leaping distance, when he springs with one tremendous bound upon his terrified prey. If he misses it, he gives over for that time, nor will any thing induce him to follow up the chase.

I was glad enough to get clear of my tiger, but, strange to say, I met him again under very different circumstances. Returning from Jaffa to Beirût some months after, when we came to Haifa, I saw a large cage coming in a boat toward the steamer, and there was my quondam acquaintance en route to Paris. The aga had sent him to the emperor through the French consul of Beirût. The poor fellow was miserably sea-sick, which made him perfectly furious. Leaping with all his might against the bars, he broke through, and seized a passenger who was standing near, and it was only by enveloping him in a heavy sail that he was subdued, and forced back into his cage.

I think David must have been acquainted with the hunting habits of the panther. Speaking of the "wicked," he says, He *croucheth* and *humbleth* himself that he may catch the poor.[1] It is true that the Psalmist is speaking in this place of the lion, but the description applies so accurately to the wily manœuvres of this hunting *nimr* that I imagine the royal poet must have also been acquainted with him and his ways.

This is certainly possible; and it is certain that, in his

[1] Psalms x. 10.

early pastoral life, David was familiar with the bear as well as the lion. Both these have disappeared from the hills where the son of Jesse tended his father's flocks, but these nimr still abound there. And now we have reached the foot of Tabor; and this is Debûrieh, so called possibly from Deborah, but if so, this name has been *substituted* for some other one in the catalogue of places given to Zebulon by Joshua, for it is found in chapter xix. 12, though he wrote long *before* the time of the prophetess. These heavy stones may have belonged to the church said to have been erected here in the early ages of our era, or perhaps to some edifice still more ancient. The inhabitants have long borne a bad character, and my own reception among them has not inclined me to defend their reputation. The whole neighborhood, indeed, is unsafe, for the Arabs, from the Jordan and the lawless regions east of it, make frequent inroads up the plain, and plunder all whom they can conquer. We shall pass over to Endor, and then around the eastern slope of "Little Hermon" to Sulam. This mount is now called Jebel ed Dûhy, and that small hamlet on the northwest corner of it is Nain, famous for the restoration of the widow's son to life. It was once a place of considerable extent, but is now little more than a cluster of ruins, among which dwell a few families of fanatical Moslems. It is in keeping with the one historic incident that renders it dear to the Christian, that its only antiquities are tombs. These are situated mainly on the east of the village, and it was in that direction, I presume, that the widow's son was being carried on that memorable occasion.[1] It took me just an hour to ride from the foot of Tabor to Nain, and the path lies near the watershed between the Sherrar and the Kishon. The soil is deep and fertile, as it is along this road to 'Ain dûr, as the home of Saul's far-famed witch is now called.

It is a most wretched-looking place, and yet the position, at the northeast corner of the mountain, facing Tabor, and overlooking the valley between them, is really beautiful. Jerome has said correctly that the distance from Tabor is

[1] Luke vii. 11-15.

RAIN AND LITTLE KERMÖR.

four miles, for it has taken us an hour and ten minutes to ride it. There does not seem to be much to attract attention here, and, as it is growing late, I think we had better move on, and find our tent before these straggling Bedawîn find us.

It is only about an hour to Sulam, and there is just at present no particular danger of being robbed; let us, therefore, before we leave this place of evil notoriety, look into some of its caves. You observe that the declivity of the mountain is every where perforated with them, and most of the habitations are merely walls built around the entrance to these caverns. Observe, too, that the cattle are stalled in them along with their owners; and so it was in the time of Saul. The "witch" doubtless occupied one of these caves, and in its dark recesses she secretly performed her "damnable sorceries." The whole place is in most striking accord with its ancient story; and these old hags grinning at us from the yawning mouths of their blackened habitations, look more like witches than women. Hark, how they curse the *fathers* and *grandfathers* of us Christian dogs, a kind of salutation you now never hear but from the very vilest people in the country. Whether witches or not, they are undoubtedly "possessed," and we may just as well pass on out of their sight. See, here are half a dozen little calves at the mouth of this cave, kept up from their mothers, who are at pasture under the care of the shepherd. I do not mean that there is any thing unusual in this, but merely that just such a calf did the witch kill for Saul on that dismal night when he sought her dwelling.

She must have been extremely expeditious in her kitchen and cookery. A hungry man, as was Saul, would think it hard to wait for supper until a calf was slaughtered and cooked, and fresh bread baked, and all this after midnight.[1]

Such things are common even in our day. With the Bedawîn it is nearly universal to cook the meat immediately after it is butchered, and to bake fresh bread for every meal. Visit 'Akîl 'Aga, for example, whose tent is now in the

[1] 1 Sam. xxviii. 24.

valley below us, and you will experience the entire process. A sheep or calf will be brought and killed before you, thrust instanter into the great caldron which stands ready on the fire to receive it, and, ere you are aware, it will reappear on the great copper tray, with a bushel of *bŭrgŭl* (cracked wheat), or a *hill* of boiled rice and *leben*. In our native Cincinnati, a hog walks into a narrow passage on his own feet, and comes out at the other end bacon, ham, and half a dozen other commodities; at the aga's camp, it is a calf or sheep that walks past you into the caldron, and comes forth a smoking stew for dinner.

It seems that this killing, cooking, and eating in rapid succession is a very old custom. Abraham, and Manoah, and many others besides the witch of Endor, were expert in getting up such impromptu feasts; and our Saviour has given it a proverbial expression in the fatted calf of the "prodigal son."

Not only is this true, but among unsophisticated Arabs the killing of a sheep, calf, or kid, in honor of a visitor, is strictly required by their laws of hospitality, and the neglect of it keenly resented. They have a dozen caustic terms of contempt for the man who neglects to honor his guest with the usual *dŭbbĭhah* (sacrifice), as it is universally called—a name suggestive of the *ancient religious rites* of hospitality, and no less suggestive of the important fact that our own *dŭbbĭhah* is waiting for us. The very idea will quicken our pace over the shoulder of Mount Dûhy to our tent in Sulam.

XXX. SULAM TO JENIN.

March 31st.

This is the very luxury of travel; bright days and joyous, air cool and fragrant, hill-side and vale robed in green and spangled with flowers, bird, and beast, and man himself gay and happy. Yes, give me the tent, the open country, and the clear blue sky, at least while spring lasts. And then these nights, so solemn, almost sad, and yet so very sweet—the bustling activities of the day laid aside, every harsh sound subdued, and the soul called home to rest or *reverize*. It is a sort of bliss merely to lie still and breathe. Thus, half waking and half asleep, hour after hour of last night stole away, while by-gone memories, historic associations, and recent experiences chased each other through all the labyrinths perplexed of Fairy-land. Finally my dreamy meditations arranged themselves into historic sequence, and the wonderful deeds which immortalized this neighborhood in olden times passed in review.

First in order came those sad days when, because of the Midianites, the children of Israel made them dens, which are in the mountains, and caves, and strongholds. And when Israel had sown, the Midianites came up, and the Amalekites, and the children of the East, with their cattle and their tents, and they came as grasshoppers for multitude. Both they and their camels were without number, and they entered the land to destroy it.[1] In precisely the same manner do the Bedawîn Arabs, these modern Midianites, come up this Wady of Jezreel and Wady Sherrar "after the people have sown," and destroy the increase of the earth, and not only destroy the increase of the field, but commit wholesale murder, as those did upon the brethren of Gideon at Tabor. In fact, the sacred historian expressly says that these Midianites were *Ishmaelites*, and we have under our very eyes the descendants of this ancient people committing similar depredations in the very same spot. Both these valleys are now swarming with these children of the East, come over Jordan to consume the land.

[1] Judges vi. 2, 3, 5.

But have you any Gideon to work out deliverance for this oppressed and impoverished country?

Alas! no; and I fear generations will pass away before any adequate liberator can arise; and, by the way, this history of Gideon is very remarkable, and we are in the midst of scenes immortalized by his glorious achievements. Ophra, the city of his inheritance, was on the general range of mountains south of Zer'in, and when he comes into notice the invaders lay along in this valley of Jezreel as *locusts* for multitude. It was harvest, and consequently a little later in the season than this. Gideon, instead of carrying his grain to the ordinary threshing-floor, took it into the midst of his vineyard, to hide both it and himself from the Ishmaelites. These summer threshing-floors are in the open country, and on an elevated position, to catch the wind when winnowing the grain, and of course they would be altogether unsafe at such a time, while the vineyards are hid away in the wadies and out on the wooded hills, and thus adapted for concealment. Indeed, I myself have seen grain thus concealed in this same country during the lawless days of civil war. There, by the wine-press, the angel of the Lord appeared, and said unto him, The Lord is with thee, thou mighty man of valor.[1] After confirming his faith by wonderful miracles, he commissions him to destroy the enemies of Israel. The Lord looked upon him and said, Go in this thy might; have not I sent thee?

This whole narrative reads most life-like and stirring here among the scenes described. The angel, who was no other than Immanuel—the Word-in-flesh assumed for the occasion—came and *sat under an oak*, as you and I would do in one of those mountain vineyards, for the *harvest* sun renders the shade necessary, and the *oak* is the tree you will find near the wine-press. I have seen many such. The sacred narrative reveals the sad religious apostasy of even Gideon's family. His father had a grove and an altar to Baal, the abomination of the Zidonians. This Gideon is commanded to destroy, and from that act he received the name of Jerub-

[1] Judges vi. 12.

Baal, the *tryer* of Baal, to translate according to Arabic, and having performed this daring deed, he blows the trumpet, and assembles about him, out of Manasseh, Asher, Zebulon, and Naphtali, thirty-two thousand men. We are in the centre of these tribes, and can see at a glance from whence he gathered his army. It is worthy of remark that the men of Issachar are not mentioned, and we can from this point readily imagine the reason. The people of Issachar lived here on this great plain, and were, of course, altogether surrounded by and at the mercy of the Midianites, as these villages of Sulam, Shutta, Zer'in, etc., now are in the power of these Bedawîn. They therefore *could not* join the army of Gideon. Of those assembled, twenty-two thousand were afraid, and returned home at the first offer. Ten thousand more were dismissed by divine command at the "water," where "the three hundred" drank "by putting their hand to their mouth," a thing I have often seen done, and not always by heroes either. These three hundred alone were retained, and that very night this small band moved forward to the brow of that steep mountain which overhangs the vale and the fountain of Jezreel. Gideon, with Phua, his servant, let himself cautiously down from rock to rock until he stood among the tents of their enemies. There he overheard "a man telling his fellow" this strange story, Behold, I dreamed a dream, and lo! a cake of barley bread tumbled into the host of Midian, and came unto a tent, and smote it that it fell, and overturned it that it lay along. And his fellow answered and said, This is nothing else save the sword of Gideon, the son of Joash, a man of Israel, for into his hand hath God delivered Midian and all his host.[1] This dispelled every lingering doubt, and he returned to order the attack at once.

What possible analogy can there be between a sword and a cake of barley bread, that could have suggested this idea to the Midianite?

Doubtless there was divine influence in the matter; but even this does not quite cover the whole case, I apprehend.

[1] Judges vii. 13, 14.

Divine wisdom ordinarily works with means adapted to produce the intended effect, and there is no conceivable reason why He should not suggest to this dreaming Midianite something calculated to bring Gideon into view; and so he doubtless did, and in a way best of all calculated to bring about the desired result. As to the line of connection in the mind of the "interpreter," we may remember that *barley* bread is only eaten by the *poor* and the *unfortunate*. Nothing is more common than for these people, at this day, to complain that their oppressors have left them nothing but *barley bread* to eat. I remember that this was the identical lamentation of a wealthy farmer who rode with me last summer from Zer'in to Jenin. This cake of barley bread was therefore naturally supposed to belong to the oppressed Israelites; it came down from the mountain where Gideon was known to be; it overthrew the tent so that it lay along, foreshadowing destruction from some quarter or other. It was a contemptible antagonist, and yet scarcely more so than Gideon in the eyes of the proud Midianites. That the interpreter should hit upon the explanation given is not, therefore, very wonderful; and if the Midianites were accustomed, in their extemporaneous songs, to call Gideon and his band "*eaters of barley bread*," as their successors, these haughty Bedawîn, often do to ridicule their enemies, the application would be all the more natural. At any rate, the interpreter read the riddle right, and reached the true intent of the prodigy.

What a strange stratagem was that of Gideon!

And yet it was well adapted to produce the effect intended; nor was the action, in the manner of it, at all remarkable. I have often seen the small oil lamp of the natives carried in a "pitcher" or earthen vessel at night. Armed with this curious weapon, the three companies took up their stations round the slumbering host. They would, no doubt, leave the road toward the Jordan open for the enemy to take in his flight, and so one band of *lamp-bearers* must have planted themselves along the base of the hill there below Zer'in; another, between that and this Sulam, along the west side of the host; and the *third* band would stand along the brow of this hill, extending down eastward toward Shŭtta. The Midianites, we know, lay in the valley between this and Jezreel. Thus arranged around the slumbering host, at a given signal the *three hundred* pitchers are broken, *three hundred* trumpets bray harsh alarms on every side, and *three hundred lights*, as of so many different bands of assailants, flash upon their blinded eyes. It is not wonderful, therefore, that the Midianites rush in wild dismay and dire confusion one upon another. In the darkness they can not distinguish friend from foe, and thus every man's sword was against his fellow. The very vastness of the army would render the rout more ruinous; and in that horrible slaughter there fell a hundred and twenty thousand men that drew sword.[1]

How was it possible for the men of Manasseh, Asher, and Naphtali to hear the news and join in the pursuit of the Midianites in so short a time, and amid the urgencies of such a day?

This is not difficult to explain. We are here on the very battle-ground, for the host lay in this valley, and, fleeing, they passed this Shŭtta to the east of us. Look around, and you find that we are in the centre of these tribes. The cities given to Manasseh, on the west of Jordan, were along the southern margin of Esdraelon and on the hills above. Asher came up to Carmel, at the bottom of this plain, and a swift runner could reach them in an hour. A portion of Naphtali occupied the western shore of the lake of Tiberias, and could be reached in the same way, and in about the same time. It was possible, therefore, for them to receive the summons and respond to it. Of course, only those who lived adjacent to this scene of action are intended. The attack of Gideon was at night, and, in all probability, just before day. Gideon could not have made his visit, returned, and made all the necessary arrangements before the night was far spent; and, moreover, it is the invariable custom of these *modern* Midianites to select that hour for their assaults. It is pro-

[1] Judges viii. 10.

verbially the darkest, and both men and animals are then buried in deepest sleep. The very watch-dogs become drowsy. Besides, if successful, they want the opening light of day to complete the victory, and secure the plunder; and, if defeated, they need the light to gather up their scattered troops, and make good their retreat. Gideon, therefore, had the entire day, and that in harvest time, to collect the surrounding tribes, and pursue the flying foes.

Is it still the custom for *men* among these Bedawîn "Ishmaelites" to wear gold earrings?

I have often seen them, and among certain of the tribes it is quite the fashion; but these golden earrings belonged, in part, no doubt, to the women. Bedawîn women not only have them in their ears, but also large rings are suspended from the nose. These are the *face* jewels, I suppose, which are mentioned very early in Biblical history. But you interrupt the order of my midnight memories. "A change came over the spirit of my dream." I was back at Endor, and the witch stood within a dismal cavern, working out her wicked sorceries. Samuel arose "out of the earth, an old man covered with a mantle," and God-forsaken Saul fell prostrate before the awful apparition.[1] I heard his voice sepulchral pronounce the dreadful decree, To-morrow shalt thou and thy sons be with me, and the Lord also shall deliver the hosts of Israel into the hand of the Philistines. Poor Saul! doomed to death, and returning in despair to fight and fall with his sons and all Israel before the sword of Philistia. It was a fearful ride that dark night, for the Philistines were encamped in this very village of Shunem, directly between Gilboa and Endor.[2] He probably kept to the east of Jezreel, crossed the valley below 'Ain Jalûd, and thence over the shoulder of this Jebel ed Dûhy to Endor; but it must have been perilous in the extreme, and nothing could have induced Saul to venture thither but the agony of despair.

This Sulam affords an admirable camp-ground for a large army; Jebel ed Dûhy rising abruptly behind, and the top

[1] 1 Sam. xxviii. 13, 14.   [2] 1 Sam. xxviii. 4.

of it commanding a perfect view of the great plain in every direction, so that there could be no surprise, nor could their march be impeded, or their retreat cut off. The fountain, it is true, is not very copious, but there are others toward Fûleh, and in the valley below. On the morning of that disastrous day, the lords of the Philistines passed on by hundreds and by thousands out of this valley of Jezreel, ascended by the city, and joined battle with Israel upon those rough mountains east of it. Israel was beaten and fled, closely pursued by their victorious enemies, and Saul and his sons were surrounded and cut down. "Tell it not in Gath, publish it not in the streets of Askelon. The beauty of Israel slain upon thy high places; how are the mighty fallen! Ye mountains of Gilboa, let there be no dew, neither let there be rain upon you nor fields of offerings, for there the shields of the mighty were vilely cast away." We have the whole theatre of this bloody battle before us, memorable not only in itself and in its results, but as the occasion of that most touching lamentation of David over Saul and Jonathan.[1] The victorious Philistines descended to Bethshan, and there fastened the body of Saul to the wall of the city. Sad, sad day to Israel, and doubly sad to David. O Jonathan! slain in thy high places. I am distressed for thee, my brother Jonathan; very pleasant hast thou been unto me. Thy love to me was wonderful, passing the love of women. How are the mighty fallen, and the weapons of war perished!

When I was young, it was the fashion to speak of Gilboa as still suffering the curse of David, and to this day I think of it as a withered wilderness without dew, or rain, or any green thing to relieve its stern desolation. Of course, there is no foundation for such an idea?

Certainly not. In my own personal experience I have had abundant evidence that both dew and rain descend there as copiously as elsewhere. David's poetic imprecation had no more influence upon the mountain, or on the clouds, than had Job's malediction upon the day of his birth; nor were

[1] 2 Sam. i. 17-27.

either expected to produce any such malign effects. Similar expressions of profound sorrow or of deep displeasure are common in the East, and are found elsewhere in the Bible. Jeremiah says, Cursed be the day when I was born; let not the day wherein my mother bare me be blessed,[1] &c. The *thought* is natural, and who is there that has not indulged it? The *child* vents its displeasure upon its rattle; the *boy* strikes the stone against which he stumbles; the man curses adverse winds, and every senseless thing which annoys him, resists his will, or thwarts his plans.

In regard to these imprecations, and others in the Bible like them, we should remember that they were never intended to act upon the physical and senseless elements of nature; and the same remark applies with equal truth to many of the "burdens" of prophecy. Though announced in figurative terms, which are drawn from natural objects, yet every child knows, or ought to, that such things are not accountable agents. Even the denunciations against cities, such as Tyre, Damascus, Gaza, Askelon, Petra, Babylon, Jerusalem, and many others, must, in general, be restricted to the *inhabitants*, and not to their habitations. God has no controversy with earth, and rocks, and ruins; nor do I believe that this *land* of Palestine now lies under any physical curse, which renders it unfruitful or unhealthy. The rains, early, middle, and latter, are sufficiently abundant, and the dews as copious as ever; the fields, also, yield as generous harvests to the careful cultivator as they ever did, or as do any others in the world.

This is perhaps true, and yet I have a "feeling" that it is not the *whole* truth.

We have not said that it was. It is not the sum total of our own ideas on this subject, and at some other locality we may enlarge upon the matter. Such a place as the vale of Siddim, I suppose, was really burned and blasted by the direct agency of God; and some other spots, once fertile, may now exhibit tokens of the displeasure of the Almighty "for the wickedness of the inhabitants thereof," and as a

[1] Jer. xx. 14.

warning to the world. And there is a sense in which the whole earth has been smitten with a curse, and, in consequence, produces thorns and thistles instead of wholesome fruits. But the desolation and barrenness of this glorious plain, for example, is in no sense the effect of any physical change in the soil or climate, but is owing entirely to the people who dwell here, and to the Bedawîn who destroy it; and the same is true of Gilboa.

This valley of Jezreel seems to expand, and to spread out an immense distance toward the southeast. To which of the tribes did it belong?

Esdraelon and its surrounding hills and vales constituted the portion of Issachar, and yet we learn from the 17th chapter of Joshua that many important cities in and about it were given to Manasseh. Endor, and Bethshan, and Taannach, and Megiddo, and this valley of Jezreel itself, belonged to that tribe, or, rather, were *assigned to* them, for they do not appear to have got possession of these cities. These "children of Joseph" complained that "all the Canaanites who dwell in the land of the valley have chariots of iron, both they of Bethshan and her towns, and they who are of the valley of Jezreel," and therefore they could not drive them out.[1] This is the earliest mention of Jezreel; and it is interesting to find that this famous valley still retains its original characteristics. Chariots of iron have indeed disappeared, but the inhabitants are eminently impracticable and rebellious; and one can readily believe that when the "jumping chariot" raged through the vale of Jezreel, and down the ghor of Beisan, the children of Joseph found it impossible to expel the inhabitants.

In my walk this morning I noticed an immense tell far down toward the Jordan: has it à name?

It is called Hŭsn, and is the centre of those ruins that mark the site of Bethshan—the Scythopolis of the Greeks —the Beisan of the Arabs.

Indeed! it seems much nearer than that city should be, according to my geography; and it must be uncommonly high, and of gigantic proportions every way.

[1] Joshua xvii. 16.

BEISAN.

Though it is full three hours distant, and that much out of our line, still, if it were safe, we would spend the night there instead of Jenin, for it is well worth the ride and the time. But the ghor is said to be swarming with wild Bedawîn from beyond Jordan, and therefore we must abandon the idea of going into it.

Since our friends the Arabs will not allow us that pleasure, the next best thing is for you to describe it.

I once came to Beisan direct from Tiberias in a little more than six hours. The itinerary, in brief, runs thus: half an hour to the Baths; one and a half to Kerak, at the outgoing of the Jordan; two hours to El Mansûrah; two and a half to entrance of the Jermuk into the Jordan; three hours to Jisr el Mujameah; and half an hour more to the camp of 'Akil

'Agâ, near the western hills, on the bank of the Sherrar, and just below Koukab el Howa. At four hours and forty minutes, passed a ruin with a few short columns, called Nusleh, near a large encampment of the Arabs of Rŭbâh. At five hours is the great Wady Osheh (or Ushey), with a large tell of the same name, and in ten minutes farther Wady Mukhŭrkŭsh crosses the plain on its way to the Jordan. The ruined town, called es Soudah, half an hour south of this, has many columns and sarcophagi, and from that onward the remains of the great Bethshan begin to appear, and constantly multiply for nearly an hour before you reach the castle. We rode rapidly, and the distance from Tiberias can not be far from twenty-four miles. I have already led you over the route from Jisr el Mujameah to Tiberias, and need not repeat. From the bridge, on this occasion, we ascended the western side of the ghor to 'Akil's tent under Koukabah, and then kept south along the base of the hills, with the plain of the Jordan on our left. This plain constantly widened by the falling back of the hills, until at es Soudah the great valley of Jezreel, in which Beisan is situated, opens to the west its noble expanse. From the city eastward it is called Ghor Beisan, and it spreads out to the southeast farther than the eye can follow. For the last hour there is a steady ascent, and the aneroid indicates an elevation for the city above the Jordan of more than five hundred feet. Owing to this, the whole plain can be watered by the fountains that send their copious streams across the site of Beisan. In fact, few spots on earth, and none in this country, possess greater agricultural and manufacturing advantages than this ghor, and yet it is utterly desolate.

But to our description. Beisan is naturally one of the strongest places even in this country of strongholds. About half a mile south of the tell you saw is a square tower, constructed in part of large *beveled* blocks of white limestone. Around this are grouped some forty or fifty wretched hovels of trap rock, loosely built, and ready to tumble down upon their inhabitants. These are as sinister a looking gang as can be found, and are, in fact, as great robbers as the Bedawîn themselves. The ancient city consisted of several distinct quarters, or wards, separated by deep ravines, with noisy cascades leaping over ledges of black basalt. I have seen no city except Damascus so abundantly supplied with water. Most of the streams take their rise in large marshes to the southwest of the city, and so high above it as to send their brooks over every part of the area; and it is evident, from the tufaceous deposits in all directions, that the inhabitants made good use of their privileges in this respect.

The largest *wards* of the city appear to have been around the present castle, and on the west of Tell Hŭsn; but there are extensive ruins both to the east and north of it. The great Wady el Jalûd passes down on the north side of the tell, and Wady el L'ab on the south, meeting below, and thus almost surrounding it. The position of the tell is therefore very strong, and it rises about two hundred feet high, with the sides nearly perpendicular. A strong wall was carried round the summit, and the gateway was high up the steep declivity at the northwest angle. In the huge buttresses of this gateway are built fragments of columns, and handsome Corinthian capitals. It was on the wall of this tell, I suppose, that the bodies of Saul and his sons were fastened by the Philistines after the battle on Gilboa; and this supposition enables us to understand how the men of Jabesh Gilead could execute their daring exploit of carrying them away. Jabesh Gilead was on the mountain east of the Jordan, in full view of Bethshan, and these brave men could creep up to the tell, along Wady Jalûd, without being seen, while the deafening roar of the brook would render it impossible for them to be heard. I have often been delighted with this achievement. The people of Jabesh had not a good character among their brethren. None of them came up to the great war against Benjamin[1] in the matter of the Levite and his concubine, and for this neglect they were condemned to utter destruction. In the days of Saul, however, it had again become a considerable city, and had

[1] Judges xxi. 8-12.

acquired a fair reputation.[1] All Israel hastened, with almost incredible dispatch, to rescue it from the cruel doom of Nahash the Ammonite. It was, no doubt, in gratitude for this deliverance, effected wholly through the energy of Saul, that the men of Jabesh hazarded their lives in order to secure his headless body from insult. History should always rejoice to record noble deeds, and most of all those instances of public gratitude which now and then throw a gleam of sunlight over its gloomy chronicles of selfishness and sin.

There is not much more to be said about Beisan. A bridge of extraordinary height spans the Jalûd east of Tell Hüsn. It appears to have led from the south to the north quarter of the city. The *theatre* is in the wady southwest of the tell. It is built entirely of basalt, and much of it is thrown down. The chord of the circle is one hundred and ninety-three feet, and though the seats are nearly gone, the vomitories, with dens for wild beasts on either side, are almost perfect. Some of them are now used for stables. Beisan was a city of temples. They are now entirely destroyed, and most of the materials have long since been carried away for other building. Their number, however, can be ascertained, and their localities traced out, from partial foundations and prostrate columns. Some of these columns were four feet in diameter, mostly of white limestone from the neighboring mountain, or of basalt from the place itself, and only a few are foreign granite. I do not think that the city could have been all embraced within one general wall, for it would have required one at least five miles long. It is more probable that the various wards, separated by deep ravines, had each its independent fortifications.

Whenever a good government shall restore order and security to this region, Beisan will rapidly rise to an important city. Its water privileges and other advantages will not only make it a delightful residence, but render it a great manufacturing centre. All kinds of machinery might be driven with the least possible expense by its abounding brooks; and then this lovely valley of Jezreel above it, ir-

[1] 1 Sam. xi. 1-11.

rigated by the Jalûd, and the Ghor Beisan below, watered in every part by many fertilizing streams, are capable of sustaining a little nation in and of themselves. Besides, Beisan is the natural highway from Bashan and the east to the sea-board at Haifa and Acre, and also to southern Palestine and Egypt. The ghor once teemed with inhabitants, as is evident from ruined sites, and from tells too old for ruins, which are scattered over the plain. I took down their names as now known to the Arabs, but none of them have any historic significance. Of Salim and Enon, which must have been in the ghor at no great distance, I could hear nothing. Succoth is well known under the name of Sakût. Tûbûkat Fahel is in full view over the Jordan, and is, doubtless, the Pella of history. My guide assured me that *Felah* was the true name; and this is their way of pronouncing Pella, for, having no *p* in their language, they sometimes use *b*, and at others *f*, instead ot it. Wady Yabis, at the head of which was Jabesh Gilead, is a little to the south of Tûbûkat Fahel.

Bethshan has figured largely in the history of this country from a very early age. It was given to Manasseh, but, like many other grants, seems never to have been in their possession. At what time it took the name of Scythopolis, and on what account, is uncertain. Some suppose it was so called from a colony of Scythians who got possession of it. This is more probable than that its name was derived from Succoth, a mere village many miles to the southeast of it. Be this as it may, it is thus called in the Apocryphal books of the Old Testament, in Josephus, who often mentions it, and by nearly all profane authors. It early became a Christian city, with a bishop of its own, and was the ecclesiastical metropolis of the Third Palestine. *Beisan* is, of course, merely the Arabic form of the original name Bethshan, given to it by these barbarians, whose mission is destruction, and under their sway it soon fell into decay and obscurity, and thus it must remain until they are driven over the Jordan into their native desert.

But it is time for us to prosecute our journey. How sad

to know that even this pretty home of the Shunamite, with its orchards and gardens, will soon be deserted and destroyed, unless these accursed Bedawîn be driven back by the government! See! what a large encampment stretches down toward Zer'in, and their black tabernacles dot the plain in all directions far as the eye can reach.

We are now on ground poetically, or, rather, prophetically illustrious. In this immediate neighborhood, the Tishbite, and his scarcely less wonderful disciple Elisha, performed their amazing miracles. Here, in this very village, dwelt that good Shunamite, who built a little chamber (an ullîyeh, upper room) on the wall for the "holy man of God," and put there a table, and a bed, and a stool, and a candlestick.[1] In some part of these fields, which slope down southward into Jezreel, her only son, given in reward for her hospitality to Elisha, received a stroke of the sun while looking at the reapers, and I know by experience that this valley glows like a furnace in harvest-time. The poor lad cries out to his father, My head! my head![2] and, being carried home, he sat on his mother's knee till noon, and then died. Elisha was on Carmel—probably near the altar of Elijah—at El Makhrakah, ten or twelve miles off. The mother saddled an ass, and said to her servant, Drive and go forward, slack not thy riding for me except I bid thee; and away she flew past Fuliyeh, and westward down the plain to the foot of Carmel. The man of God sees her coming in such haste, fears some calamity, and sends Gehazi to meet her with these three inquiries, Is it well with thee? is it well with thy husband? is it well with the lad?[3] She answered, It is well; but, at the same time, she rushes up the "hill," and seizes the prophet by his feet. This scene is natural, and very graphic. If you ask after a person whom you know to be sick, the reply at first will invariably be, *Well, thank* God, even when the very next sentence is to inform you that he is dying. Then the falling down, clasping the feet, etc., are actions witnessed every day. I have had this done to me often before I could prevent it. So, also, the

[1] 2 Kings iv. 8–10.   [2] 2 Kings iv. 19.   [3] 2 Kings iv. 26.

officious zeal of the wicked Gehazi, who would thrust the broken-hearted mother away, probably thinking her touch pollution, agrees perfectly with what we know of the man, and of the customs of the East; and so, likewise, are the injunctions to Gehazi, *Gird up thy loins* that you may run; if *thou meet any man, salute him not;* and if any salute thee, answer him not—this is no time for idle compliments. The mother followed with the man of God in company; and when he had brought back her son to life, she *fell at his feet, bowed herself* to the *ground*, took up her son, and went out. Nothing can excel the touching simplicity of this narrative.

How came it to pass that the good Shunamite lost her land by merely going to reside during the famine in the country of the Philistines, as we read in 2 Kings viii. 3?

It is still common for even petty sheikhs to confiscate the property of any person who is exiled for a time, or who moves away temporarily from his district. Especially is this true of widows and orphans, and the Shunamite was now a widow. And small is the chance to such of having their property restored, unless they can secure the mediation of some one more influential than themselves. The conversation between the king and Gehazi about his master is also in perfect keeping with the habits of Eastern princes; and the appearance of the widow and her son so opportunely, would have precisely the same effect now that it had then. Not only the *land*, but all the *fruits of it* would be restored. There is an air of genuine verisimilitude in such simple narratives which it is quite impossible for persons not intimately familiar with Oriental manners to appreciate, but which stamps the incidents with undoubted certainty. The thing happened just as recorded. It is too natural to be an invention or fabrication.

Elisha seems to have had no settled place of abode. We read of him in Carmel, in Sulam, in Jezreel, in Gilgal, on the banks of the Jordan, in Dotham, in Samaria, and even in Damascus.

Among his many miracles, I have long wanted to inquire what sort of wild gourd it was that poisoned the "pottage."[1] Is there any thing satisfactory known about it?

COLOCYNTH.

Not much more than the prophet's son that gathered them knew. The Septuagint does not *translate* but gives the Hebrew word, showing that those learned men did not know *what* it was; and if they could not determine the question it is not likely that we can at this day. My Latin Bible calls it wild colocynth. I am not aware that there is any *tame* colocynth. The English renders it by the vague word *gourd*. I can not believe it was colocynth, because this is so well known, so bitter, and so poisonous, that the most ignorant peasants never dream of eating it. He must have been a very stupid son of a prophet, indeed, to have filled his lap with them. Various other herbs have been selected by "critics," as the Cucumus prophetarum, a small prickly gourd, very rarely met with. The Hebrew root seems to point to some herb that bursts or splits open, and I have

[1] 2 Kings iv. 38-41.

thought that it might be the Elaterium, which is found all over the country, looks like a young squash, and is extremely poisonous. When green it might be mistaken for an edible "gourd" or cucumber, but when ripe it can not be "gathered" at all, for it bursts on the slightest pressure, with great violence, scattering the seeds in all directions. But all these are mere conjectures, and we had better turn our thoughts to these sorry representatives of Jezreel, to which our climb up this steep and rocky hill has brought us.

There is certainly nothing royal about it now except its position. That, however, is very fine. East of it rises the high mountain called Jebel Jalûd, and also Jebel Nûris, from a village of that name. Below it the valley of Jezreel sweeps round southward to the Jordan. On the north, Jebel ed Dûhy (Little Hermon) swells up like another Tabor, and to the west and south is the magnificent Esdraelon, surrounded by the mountains of Galilee, the "excellency of Carmel," and the fat hills of Samaria. There is little to claim attention in the village itself. A few stones, built here and there in the rude huts, seem to claim the honors of antiquity; and these large sarcophagi are certainly relics of old Jezreel. The city could never have been large or splendid. The greater part was probably mere mud hovels, and yet there must have been some well-built palaces when Ahab resided here with his bold, but wicked queen. This apology for a castle may now stand upon the spot of that watch-tower from which the rebel Jehu was first seen driving furiously up the valley of Jezreel.[1] The south part of the plain at Beisan is marshy, and farther this way the great fountain of Jalûd, with its spongy banks, renders the same side impassable. This fountain flows out from the base of the mountain below Nûris, and is immediately collected into a large pool by a dam of very ancient work, and from it the water is carried to a succession of mills stretching down the plain to the east. To avoid these mill-ponds, the road must have then passed along the valley, as it now does, not far from Kûmia. Jehu and his party could therefore be seen

[1] 2 Kings ix. 17.

JERUEL.

for at least six miles, and there was time enough to dispatch messenger after messenger to meet him. He, of course, came past Beisan. Ramoth Gilead was south-east of it, on the other side of Jordan, and he was commander of the garrison there when proclaimed king by his fellow-officers. Immediately he sets out in hot haste to slay Joram, and seize the government. The whole history of this revolution shows Jehu to have been a man of vehement energy and desperate daring. When he met his victim, he drew a bow with his *full strength* and smote Joram between his arms, and the arrow went out at his heart.[1] Nor did he hesitate a moment to kill Ahaziah the king of Jùdah also. Then, entering the city, he ordered the eunuchs to tumble the infamous Jezebel out of the window of her palace; so they threw her down, and her blood was sprinkled on the wall and *on the horses*, and *he trode her under foot*.[2]

After this terrible day's work, Jehu went in to eat and drink; and, remembering Jezebel, he said, Go, see now this cursed woman, and bury her, for she is a king's daughter.[3] But they found no more of her than the skull, and the feet, and the palms of the hands. The word of the Lord by his servant Elijah was fulfilled, In the portion of Jezreel shall dogs eat the flesh of Jezebel.[4] .

The field of Naboth which Ahab coveted was doubtless near the great fountain of Jalûd, at the bottom of the valley east of the city. Water was necessary for a garden of *herbs*, and there is no other perennial fountain in this neighborhood. Joram, Ahab's son, went out against Jehu, who was coming up the valley of Jezreel, and they must have met somewhere near the fountain; and Jehu, having killed Joram, ordered his body to be cast into the portion of the field of Naboth, the Jezreelite; for, said he, the Lord laid this burden upon him, Surely I have seen yesterday the blood of Naboth and of his sons, saith the Lord.[5]

The entire narrative in 2 Kings ix. is full of most emphatic lessons of instruction and warning to tyrants. The

[1] 2 Kings ix. 24.   [2] 2 Kings ix. 33.   [3] 2 Kings ix. 34.
[4] 2 Kings ix. 36.   [5] 2 Kings ix. 26.

blood of Naboth was trebly avenged; first upon Ahab himself, then upon his son Joram, and finally on the wicked Jezebel who had instigated the murder.

It must have been a strange state of things when dogs were so abundant and unscrupulous as to devour a human carcass in the streets of this city during the short time that elapsed before search was made for Jezebel's body; but the canine race always bear some resemblance in disposition to the character of the times and of their keepers. We may readily believe, therefore, that those under the palace of Jezebel were sufficiently savage. They may have been *taught to devour* the wretched victims of her cruelty, in which case the retribution would be remarkably appropriate and striking. What is meant by "making her eyes with paint," as the Hebrew has it?

Simply that which has been and is still the favorite mode of beautifying the face among the ladies of this country. They "paint" or blacken the eyelids and brows with *köhl*, and prolong the application in a decreasing pencil, so as to lengthen and reduce the eye in appearance to what is called *almond shape*. The practice is extremely ancient, for such painted eyes are found in the oldest Egyptian tombs. It imparts a peculiar brilliancy to the eye, and a languishing, amorous cast to the whole countenance. Brides are thus painted, and many heighten the effect by application to the cheeks of colored cosmetics. The powder from which *köhl* is made is collected from burning almond shells, or frankincense, and is intensely black. Antimony, and various ores of lead, are also employed. The powder is kept in phials or pots, which are often disposed in a handsomely-worked cover or case; and it is applied to the eye by a small probe of wood, ivory, or silver, which is called *meel*, while the whole apparatus is named *mŭkhŭly*.

This neighborhood is celebrated for its wheat, and a peculiar kind is called Nûrsy, from this village of that name on the mountain. The *grain* is long and slender, while that of the Hauran is short and *plump*. The latter bears the highest price in market. The name Jezreel—*God will sow*—seems to have reference to the adaptation of this place for growing grain.

Hosea[1] intimates that the final overthrow of Israel should be in this valley of Jezreel, where it is farther said that God would punish the house of Jehu for the blood there shed by him. Treason and murder must be remembered and avenged, even though vengeance slumbers through many generations. What is the explanation of that singular passage in Hosea ii. 21–23: It shall come to pass in that day I will hear, saith the Lord. I will hear the heavens, and they shall hear the earth, and the earth shall hear the corn, and the wine, and the oil, *and they shall hear Jezreel*.

You may read thus: the Lord will hear the heavens calling for the vapor and the cloud. These clouds shall hear the parched earth calling for rain. The earth, in turn, shall hear the languishing corn, and wine, and oil, and grant the nourishment required. Jezreel, also, the valley of vengeance and destruction, shall in that happy time be heard calling for the peaceful products of husbandry. Jezreel—God himself will sow her with the seed of peace and righteousness. The Orientals are delighted with this sort of hazy, indistinct figure. There is evidently a play upon the name Jezreel, and an unexpressed blending of the bloody tragedies enacted in this valley with promises of better things in reserve for the true people of Israel. The passage begins with another most obscure, but pregnant figure: I will give her—Israel—the *valley of Achor for a door of hope*. That valley runs up from Gilgal toward Bethel. There Achan was stoned to death, and by that act the anger of the Lord was turned away from Israel, and the door of entrance to the

[1] Hos. i. 4, 5.

promised inheritance thrown open. Achor means *trouble*, affliction, from whence comes our word ache, perhaps. Thus the valley of affliction was the door through which Israel at first entered the land of Canaan. And thus again the Lord, by his prophet, promised to lead Israel to peace and rest through the valley of trouble. The very indistinctness makes this mode of speaking the more suggestive. The *valley of Achor—a door of hope*. Not a bad motto for those who through much tribulation must enter the promised land —the Canaan of eternal peace and rest. But it is time to pass away from Jezreel, with all its lessons of wisdom. There is nothing of interest in the plain itself from this to Jenîn. That village to which we are coming, called Jelâmy, is prettily situated, but nearly ruined; and Em Gabeleh (or Mukeibileh), southwest of it, is quite deserted. The one on the left among the hills is Arrâmy, celebrated for its wheat and tobacco. Between it and Jenîn the plain runs far up into the eastern hills, and at the head of it is Beit Kod. The mountain of Gilboa is that just in front of us to the southeast—that is, the name Jelbûn is now specifically attached only to this part, but in ancient times, I think, the whole rocky region between Jelbûn and the valley of Jezreel was so called. Saul and Jonathan were probably slain somewhere farther north, possibly on the lofty promontory of El Mazar. There may even be an allusion to this very conspicuous place in the opening stanza of David's lament. "The beauty of Israel is slain *upon thy high places*." And this very name Mazar (a sacred tomb to which pilgrimages are made) may have been given to it because the daughters of Israel went thither to weep over Saul, who clothed them in scarlet, and put an ornament of gold upon their apparel.[1]

This dry channel proves that a large stream flows from Beit Kod and the mountains above it during the winter rains. The soil appears to be eminently fertile, and how beautifully the orchards of Jenîn stretch this way down the plain! but I can not yet see the town itself.

It is hid away in a ravine, and farther concealed by the

[1] 2 Samuel i. 24.

JEDDA.

gardens and orchards. Both they and the town owe their flourishing character to the fountain which bursts out in the centre of the valley; and this, again, received its Hebrew name (En Gannim)—*Fountain of Gardens*—from the flourishing orchards which anciently, as well as now, distinguished the place. This is the most distant permanent source of the Kishon, but during summer and autumn the water is all exhausted by irrigation, and none of it reaches beyond the margin of these green fields.

Is Jenîn mentioned in the Bible?

It is, as I already remarked, the *En Gannim* which was given to Issachar.[1] *Gannim* is near enough to Jenîn, and the *En* is for the fountain. As the place grew in importance the prefix of *Ain* was dropped, and it became simply *Gannim*. Josephus calls it Ginnea, and the Arabs Jenîn. It is now the chief town between Nazareth and Nablûs, contains about two thousand inhabitants—nearly all Moslems; has a governor, secretaries, and a custom-house posse. It deals largely in all the products of the country, and with the Bedawîn on the east of Jordan; but the people are fanatical, rude, and rebellious. They are almost always fighting among themselves, or with their neighbors. There are three leading families who keep up perpetual strife and bloodshed throughout all this region—the 'Abd el Hâdy, and Beit Tokân of Nablûs and 'Arrâby, and the Beit Jerrar of this place. They are now actually fighting with each other between this and Nablûs, and the travelers whom we met this morning assert positively that we shall not be able to pass through the country in that direction. We shall know more about this to-morrow.

[1] Joshua xix. 21.

XXXI. JENIN TO SINDIANY.

April 1st.

What does all this uproar mean? We have had a most unquiet night.

I have been out to ascertain the cause, and it seems that the various parties that passed through in the evening with such barbarous uproar were Bedawîn from the ghor, and from Jebel 'Ajlûn, east of the Jordan. They have been brought over by the *Beits* Jerrar and Tokân to aid them against 'Abd el Hâdy; and there has been a skirmish during the night, near Jeb'a, with the partisans of the latter from 'Arrâby. The people of Jenîn, who are of the Jerrar party, say that 'Abd el Hâdy was beaten; but the bloody work is still going on, and the smaller villages are being deserted. If you look out along the paths down the mountains, you will see women and children hastening hither with their miscellaneous furniture on donkeys, mules, and camels. This place is safe only because 'Akil Aga, who refuses to join in this war, lies encamped out on Esdraelon, and our guard is one of his relatives. I once before had to pass this plain when the Arabs were up in arms, when my own horse was seized by a robber; and I shall long remember the cool way in which my guard (also a cousin of the aga) told that party of marauders that if they touched any thing or person under *his* protection *there would be no more khûbs (bread) for them on this side the Jordan.* The same assurance will protect us to-day, but we shall have to make a long detour to get round the places where the people are actually fighting. They are divided among themselves. For example, one half of Seely—that village on the edge of the plain—is for 'Abd el Hâdy, and the other is for Beit Jerrar; and you can see the flash of their guns at this moment, as they fire at each other from their houses.

The women about us are terribly enraged against 'Abd el Hâdy. Some of his party not long ago attacked the villages in the district of Er Rohah, killed some of the people, burned their houses, and drove off their cattle and flocks.

But what most excites their wrath is that these wretches maltreated, and even killed women and children. This is an enormity which they loudly declare has never been known among them before, and, so far as my knowledge extends, they are correct. During the civil wars that desolated Lebanon in 1841 and in 1845, the women were not molested even in battle. I have repeatedly seen them on both sides running with water to their friends who were hard pressed with thirst, and I never knew any of them to be injured or insulted. The same deference to the women has always been shown in this region until the present outbreak, and hence the extreme exasperation of the different parties. If any of 'Abd el Hâdy's men fall into their hands, these women have vowed to roast them alive! This universal exasperation renders it more than ordinarily dangerous to travel through this district, and our wisest policy is to get beyond the range of their bloody quarrel as soon as possible. Hassein is hurrying the muleteers, and now summons us to mount and be off.

He is leading us directly back over our route of yesterday. Would it not be much nearer and more interesting to pass down the southern side of the plain, past Taannach and Megiddo?

Certainly it would; but the people are fighting with one another all along that line, and it would not be safe. We shall have a good view of these places and of many others by the longer route, and there are no antiquities at any of them to exaggerate our regret. Seely, where they are shooting each other, is surrounded by splendid groves of the "peaceful olive;" but neither the whispers of the groves, nor the innocent cultivation of the soil, nor the kindly offices of the shepherd can subdue the innate ferocity of these barbarians. Alas! that such a country should be wasted by wild Arabs, and consumed by the fires of domestic war. But thus it has been for ages, and I fear it will continue thus for ages to come. In fact, this plain has always been a great battle-field. The Canaanites and Philistines, Jews and Egyptians, Chaldeans and Persians, Greeks and Romans, Moslems and Christians, of almost every age and nation, have encamped around Megiddo, because of its commanding position, its abundant supply of water, and its rich pastures. There Ahaziah, who fled from Jehû, died of his wounds; and there, also, the good king Josiah was defeated and slain by Pharaoh Necho. Under the name of Legio it is mentioned very often by the classic historians and geographers, and its modern name Lejjûn is merely the Arabic form of the same word. Of the many villages on the neighboring mountains of old Samaria, the only ones of much importance are Kefr Kûd, the Capercotia of the Greeks; 'Arrâby, the original seat of the 'Abd el Hâdy family; and Em el Fahm, on this side of it. 'Arrâby is a large place, and capable of sending out a *thousand guns*, as they say in this country, and *there* is the centre of the present war.

I greatly regret that we have not been able to pass through these hills to Samaria and Nablûs.

We may yet visit those places from Jerusalem, if this feud quiets down as rapidly as they generally do. In the mean while I will give you an account of them as we ride over this uninhabited plain. I have traveled the route from Jenîn to Samaria many times, but it is almost always disturbed by just such quarrels as the present. On leaving Jenîn, the road follows the Wady Bel'amy for the first half hour, passing on the right an ancient ruin of the same name. This wady is full of fountains in winter, and very muddy, but hot as a furnace in summer. Rising out of this, over a long hill, you come down again to a considerable town called Kŭbatîeh. The hills about this place are covered with groves of flourishing olive-trees, and the net-work of vales and plains west of it is extremely pretty and fertile. In one of them is the site of Dothan, called now Tell Dothaim. This *tell* was once inhabited, and at its base is a fountain where the brethren of Joseph may have watered their flocks. The neighborhood affords the very best pasturage, and this was the reason, no doubt, why they came to it from Nablûs.[1] I am not aware that there still exist old

[1] Gen. xxxvii. 14–17.

cisterns about Dothaim, but there are very few ancient sites where they are not found; and, I presume, a careful search would reveal the very pit (*Beer*) into which Joseph was cast. It is in pleasing agreement with the narrative in Genesis to find that the great highway from Gilead to Egypt still passes near this place. The caravans come up the ghor Beisan, pass by Zer'in and Lejjûn, enter the hill country of Samaria by the wady of Dothaim, and thence go on to Ramleh, Gaza, and Egypt. The large caravansary north of Beisan, called Khan el Ahmar, marks one important station on this route. It was along this road that those "Ishmaelites came from Gilead with their camels bearing spices, and balm, and myrrh, going to carry them down to Egypt," to whom the poor lad Joseph was sold by his cruel and envious brethren. It is worthy of remark that these modern Ishmaelites would not now hesitate to make just such a purchase, and actually do in certain parts of the country; and it is also interesting to find *balm* connected with Gilead at that early day. Jeremiah, long after, exclaims, Is there no balm in Gilead? is there no physician there?[1]

What was this balm?

Not known with any certainty. Josephus frequently mentions it, and says that the tree which bore it grew about Jericho, and there only. In this he must have been mistaken, or the balm, or balsam he speaks of, was of a different kind from that mentioned in the Bible; for that was gathered at Engedi, in Gilead, and at other places. Josephus also says that the Queen of Sheba first brought the balsam-bearing tree into the country as a present to Solomon, which must also be a mistake of our historian, if he means that the balm-tree was unknown in Palestine until her visit. However, it is probable that the balm he describes as so *very scarce* and *precious*, was a different kind from that which the Midianites were taking to Egypt. I was shown, in the jungle about the fountain of Elisha, near Jericho, a rough thorn bush, like a *crab* or *haw* tree, which the monks said yielded balm, and I actually purchased some at the time, but with-

[1] Jer. viii. 22.

out supposing it to be the Biblical article. The Hebrew word has been translated very variously. According to the Septuagint, it may mean any kind of *resinous gum;* the Latin has opobalsamum; the Arabic has *snubar* (pine), meaning apparently the pine-nuts, still an important article of traffic. Some suppose it was the gum or juice of the *turpentine*-tree, which still abounds in Gilead, and the resinous distillation from it is much celebrated by the Arabs for its healing virtues. Josephus says that this balm of Jericho was "an ointment, of all the most precious, which, upon any incision made in the wood with a sharp stone, distills out thence like a juice." I suppose that the balm which Jacob sent to Joseph,[1] and that which Jeremiah refers to for its medicinal qualities,[2] was the same as that which our trading Ishmaelites were transporting to Egypt, and that it was some resinous extract from the forest-trees of Gilead.

Elisha was residing in this Dothan on that memorable occasion when the king of Syria sent horses, and chariots, and a great host to take him; and when the servant of the man of God was risen early and gone forth, behold, a host encompassed the city, and he cried out, Alas! my master, how shall we do?[3] The position appeared desperate. The tell was completely surrounded by the army, and escape seemed impossible; but the mountains above were full of chariots of fire round about Elisha. Well might he say to the terrified servant, "Fear not: they that be with us are more than they that be with them." And so it in reality is with the servants of God at all times; and they alone of all men have no reason to fear. However many or threatening their enemies, they that are with and for them are more numerous and more powerful. This narrative seems to draw aside for a moment the veil which conceals the spirit world, and affords us a hasty glimpse of those ministers of flaming fire which are sent forth to minister for them who shall be heirs of salvation.[4] At the prayer of Elisha the Syrian host were smitten with blindness, and then guided by the prophet himself into the midst of Samaria. I have traveled

[1] Gen. xliii. 11. [2] Jer. viii. 22. [3] 2 Kings vi. 13-23. [4] Heb. i. 14.

SAMARIA.

along the path which this blinded army must have followed for several hours, and such a march has no parallel in history. Indeed, this entire transaction is replete with instruction to all—of rebuke to proud enemies of God, and of delightful encouragement to those who put their trust in Him.

But we must not enter Samaria with this Syrian army, but go back and travel the road more leisurely. From Kŭbatîyeh we ascend a very rocky hill, and then pass down through a low plain to Sanûr, which is two hours from Jenîn. In winter this plain is a lake many miles in circumference, but it dries up, and is sown with corn and vegetables in summer. The village of Sanûr is within a castle, on an isolated hill, at the southwest corner of this plain; and it is, and long has been, occupied by a rude, fanatical population, ever ready to insult travelers, and to stir up rebellion against the government. Jeba is another large village, about an hour farther on, strongly located on the brow of the mountain; and there the road to Samaria parts from that to Nablûs, inclining to the right along the base of the hill of Jeba. The whole route is beautifully and endlessly diversified with hill, and dale, and fertile plain, even now well cultivated, and thickly settled. The villages stand out on every conspicuous position, and by the side of every gushing fountain. At the end of five hours from Jenîn you are at the base of the "hill of Samaria."

The site of this celebrated capital is delightful, by universal consent. It is a very large, isolated hill, rising, by successive terraces, at least *six hundred* feet above the valleys which surround it. In shape it is oval, and the smaller and lower end unites it to the neighboring mountain on the east. There is no fountain on the hill, and during a siege the inhabitants must have depended entirely upon cisterns. Water, however, is abundant in the neighborhood. There is a good spring a short distance below to the southeast, and a brook from the mountains in the same direction, large enough to drive a mill; and in winter a fine millstream also flows past the north side of the hill. All these unite at the bottom of the plain northwest of the city, and, as I am told, form part of the river which, at the sea south of Cæsarea, is called Abu Zabûra.

The view from the topmost terrace of Samaria over the rich plains and hills around it, and far away to the blue Mediterranean, is truly magnificent. The remains of the ancient city consist mainly of colonnades, which certainly date back to the time of the Herods, and perhaps many of the columns are much older. There is a group of sixteen standing in a recess low down on the northeast side of the hill, and a similar group of sixteen on the top, though these last are larger; and there are many lying prostrate. The grand colonnade, however, runs along the south side of the hill, down a broad terrace, which descends rapidly toward the present village. The number of columns, whole or broken, along this line is nearly *one hundred*, and many others lie scattered about on lower terraces. They are of various sizes, and quite irregularly arranged, but when perfect it must have been a splendid colonnade. The entire hill is covered with rubbish, indicating the existence and repeated destruction of a large city. The modern village is on the southeastern slope, adjacent to the ruined church of St. John. You have seen so many views of what these ruins are *not*, that I despair of giving an accurate idea of what they *are*. The church, however, is an interesting specimen of mediæval architecture, which all look at with respect, and many with deep emotion. This is natural, though the tradition that associates the martyrdom of the Baptist with this spot is sufficiently doubtful, yet it augments the reverence with which one explores the vaults of this fine old ruin.

Nearly every thing that is known about ancient Samaria is derived from the Bible and Josephus. This latter historian mentions it very often, and from him we learn that it derived its present name, Sebastia (or Sebustia, as the Arabs call it), from Herod, and in honor of Augustus. Herod rebuilt it after some one of its many overthrows, and most of the columns now visible are supposed to be remains of his edifices; but, as it was celebrated a thousand years before his time, and was for centuries the capital of a kingdom, I think it not unlikely that he built with the ruins of castles and temples much older than himself. It is remarkable that this place took its original name, Samaria, from the man who owned the hill, and not from Omri, the king who built the city.[1] It continued to be the capital of the "Ten Tribes," until they were carried captive into Assyria; and during the *twenty-five centuries* which have passed since that event its fortunes have been very various; often destroyed and again rebuilt, growing smaller by degrees, though *not beautifully* less, until it finally subsided into the insignificant village which now clings to the name and the site.

Like many other visitors, I have uniformly found the inhabitants of Sebustia rude, insolent, and sometimes even dangerous. They seem never to have had a good character, if we form our opinion from the language of the prophets. Many of the wonderful passages in the lives of Elijah and Elisha are connected with Samaria and her idolatrous and bloody rulers. I imagine that the level space on the topmost terrace of the hill, where are the sixteen large columns, marks the site of the great temple of Baal, which Jehu utterly "broke down," after that treacherous slaughter of Baal's priests and worshipers recorded in the tenth chapter of 2 Kings. It was to Samaria that Naaman, the Damascene leper, came to be healed—a very remarkable narrative, and very suggestive. This terrible disease still cleaves to Damascus, and is now, as it was then, incurable by man. It was this latter fact that alarmed the King of Israel in regard to the motive of Benhadad. See how he seeketh a quarrel against me; am I God, to kill and to make alive, that this man doth send unto me to recover a man of his leprosy![2] exclaimed the perplexed king. One is tempted to inquire why this power of healing the leprosy, which so signally honored the God of Israel in the eyes of all nations, should have been so rarely exercised. There were other lepers at that very time in Samaria under the eye of Elisha, as we learn from the next chapter. Indeed, Christ

[1] 1 Kings xvi. 24.   [2] 2 Kings v. 15.

says there were *many* of them, and of the children of Israel, too, and yet none of them were cleansed except Naaman the Syrian.[1] It is obvious, however, that this reserve in putting forth divine power is in strict accordance with the entire economy of miraculous manifestation. Gehazi, for his cupidity, had this terrible disease laid upon him, with the fearful doom added that it should cleave unto his seed *forever*;[2] and who can tell but that the victims of this horrid plague, now seen about this city and at Nablûs, the present home of all the Samaritans, may be the heirs of this heritage of Gehazi.

The lepers mentioned in chapter vii. seem to have been shut out of Samaria even when it was closely besieged by Benhadad. Is it common now to compel lepers to dwell outside of the city?

Not in all places, but they are every where regarded as unclean, shunned as dangerous, and obliged to live by themselves. Where there are considerable numbers of them, as at Jerusalem, there is a separate quarter to which they are confined, just *at* the gate, though *within* the walls of the city. At Samaria they were outside, and I have seen them thus cast out of the villages where they resided.

What have you to say about that extraordinary article of food called "doves' dung," which was sold at a high price during that terrible siege of Benhadad?

I believe that the Hebrew Chirîyonim, or Khir yonim, was a name for a coarse and cheap sort of food, a kind of bean, as some think, to which this whimsical title was given on account of some fancied resemblance between the two. Nor am I at all surprised at it, for the Arabs give the most quaint, obscure, and ridiculous names to their extraordinary edible mixtures. I would, therefore, not translate at all, but let the passage read thus, A fourth part of a cab of Khir yonim for five pieces of silver; and be content with that, until we know what Khir yonim really is.

From Samaria to Nablûs is two hours' easy riding, first south, over the shoulder of the mountain, and then east-

---

[1] Luke iv. 17.   [2] 2 Kings v. 27.

ENTRANCE TO NABLOUS.

ward, up the lovely vale of Nablûs. Nothing in Palestine surpasses it in fertility and natural beauty, and this is mainly due to the fine mill-stream which flows through it. The whole country is thickly studded with villages, the plains clothed with grass or grain, and the rounded hills with orchards of olive, fig, pomegranate, and other trees. Coming from Samaria, the ascent to the city from the valley is quite steep, and it climbs up the side of Gerizim to a very considerable elevation; indeed, the perpendicular cliffs of the mountains overhang the upper part of the city. Travelers generally seek out the Samaritan quarter, which is near the southwestern corner, and sufficiently elevated to afford a good view of the whole town. Nablûs is a queer old place. The streets are narrow, and vaulted over; and in the winter time it is difficult to pass along many of them on account of brooks which rush over the pavement with deafening roar. In this respect, I know no city with which to compare it except Brusa, and, like that city, it has mulberry, orange, pomegranate, and other trees, mingled in with the houses, whose odoriferous flowers load the air with delicious perfume during the months of April and May. Here the bilbûl delights to sit and sing, and thousands of other birds unite to swell the chorus. The inhabitants maintain that theirs is the most *musical* vale in Palestine, and my experience does not enable me to contradict them.

Imagine that the lofty range of mountains running north and south was cleft open to its base by some tremendous convulsion of nature, at right angles to its own line of extension, and the broad fissure thus made is the vale of Nablûs, as it appears to one coming up the plain of Mukhna from Jerusalem. Mount Ebal is on the north, Gerizim on the south, and the city between. Near the eastern end, the vale is not more than sixty rods wide; and just there, I suppose, the tribes assembled to hear the "blessings and the curses" read by the Levites. We have them in extenso in the 27th and 28th chapters of Deuteronomy; and in Joshua[1] we are informed that it was actually done, and how.

[1] Joshua viii.

Simeon, and Levi, and Judah, and Issachar, and Joseph, and Benjamin, stood on Gerizim; and Reuben, Gad, Asher, Zebulon, Dan, and Naphtali, on Ebal; while all Israel, and their elders, and officers, and their judges, stood on this side of the ark and on that side before the priests which bare the ark of the covenant of the Lord; the whole nation of Israel, with the women and little ones, were there. And Joshua read all the words of the law, the blessings and the cursings; there was not a word of all that Moses commanded which Joshua read not before all the congregation of Israel. This was, beyond question or comparison, the most august assembly the sun has ever shone upon; and I never stand in the narrow plain, with Ebal and Gerizim rising on either hand to the sky, without involuntarily recalling and reproducing the scene. I have shouted to hear the echo, and then fancied how it must have been when the loud-voiced Levites proclaimed from the naked cliffs of Ebal, "Cursed be the man that maketh any graven image, an abomination unto Jehovah." And then the tremendous AMEN! tenfold louder, from the mighty congregation, rising, and swelling, and re-echoing from Ebal to Gerizim, and from Gerizim to Ebal. AMEN! even so let him be accursed. No, there never was an assembly to compare with this.

It was part of the command of the Lord, and of Moses to Joshua, that, having placed the "blessings and the cursings" on Gerizim, and on Ebal, he should write the whole law upon pillars of stone which he should rear up at this place. Do you suppose that the whole five books of Moses were thus engraven upon stone?

I suppose not; perhaps none of it was *engraved* on stone. A careful examination of Deuteronomy xxvii. 4, 8, and Joshua viii. 30–32, will lead to the opinion that the law was *written upon* or *in* the *plaster* with which these pillars were *coated*. This could easily be done, and such writing was common in ancient times. I have seen numerous specimens of it certainly more than *two thousand years old*, and still as distinct as when they were first inscribed on the plaster. There seems to have been an unnecessary amount

THE LAW WRITTEN ON THE STONES AT MOUNT EBAL. 205

of learning bestowed upon this matter, and difficulties imagined where none exist. Michaelis, in his Commentary on the Laws of Moses,[1] enters into a labored examination of the passage. He gives and refutes various explanations, among others, that of Kennicott, who supposes that the letters were cut out in black marble, the letters being raised, and the hollow intervals between them filled with white lime plaster. His own opinion, however, is that Moses commanded Joshua to do as Sostratus, the architect of the Pharos did, who cut his own name on the solid marble, then plastered it over, and grooved the name of the King of Egypt on the cement. Moses, in like manner, ordered the law to be cut in the solid stone, and then to be plastered over with hard cement, so that when this plaster fell off, in after ages, the engraven law would be discovered entire and perfectly legible! Now the main objection to these speculations is that there is not the slightest foundation for them in the text. The direction there is perfectly plain, and needs none of these recondite devices to render it intelligible and reasonable. That the Egyptians were accustomed to engrave on stone in various ways is well known, and Moses must have been familiar with it; but he was also familiar with the mode which he here commands to be followed, and he knew it to be sufficiently durable for all practical purposes. He therefore did not order such a herculean labor as to grave the whole law in marble, but simply to write it *on* or *in* properly prepared cement. In this hot climate, where there is no frost to dissolve the cement, it will continue hard and unbroken for thousands of years, which is certainly long enough. The cement on Solomon's pools remains in admirable preservation, though exposed to all the vicissitudes of the climate, and with no protection. The cement in the tombs about Sidon is still perfect, and the writing on them entire, though acted upon by the moist, damp air always found in caverns, for perhaps two thousand years. What Joshua did, therefore, when he erected these great stones at Mount Ebal, was merely to write *in* the still soft cement with

[1] Michaelis, vol. i. book iii.

a stile, or, more likely, *on* the polished surface, when dry, with red paint, as in ancient tombs. If properly sheltered, and not broken away by violence, they would have remained to this day. But every thing that could be destroyed has been long since, and again and again overthrown, in the countless convulsions of this most rebellious neighborhood; and the hope expressed by Michaelis that these (imaginary) marble slabs, with the law engraven upon them, were still in existence, buried beneath the rubbish of Nablûs, and might one day be discovered, crumbles into dust, along with the plaster upon which the commandments of the Lord were really written. Nor need we mourn over the loss. The printing-press preserves this same law to us far more securely than could any monument, though built of bronze or solid adamant.

If Nablûs occupies the place of Shechem (and I suppose it does), it is one of the oldest cities in the world; nor is there any thing improbable in this, for its natural advantages, great beauty, and abundant supply of water mark out the site for a city. This latter fact, however, seems to prove that Shechem was not the Sychar mentioned in the 4th chapter of John. It is incredible that the "woman of Samaria" would have gone two miles away from these delicious fountains to draw water out of an immensely deep well. If we admit the identity of the present well of Jacob with that mentioned by John, there can be but little doubt that Sychar was a small Samaritan town not far from that spot; and there is a village north of it now called Aschâr. This is so like John's Sychar that I feel inclined to adopt it. Of course, the "woman of Samaria" belonged to the country or people of Samaria, not to the city of that name, which is some eight miles to the northwest of it.

I see no good reason to question the identity of this well with that of the patriarch; nor do I intend to disturb the bones of Joseph, concerning which he expressed so much solicitude when about to die in Egypt.[1] The Moslems point out his tomb at the base of Ebal in this vicinity; and this

[1] Gen. l. 25.

JACOB'S WELL.

agrees well enough with Joshua xxiv. 32, where it is said that "the bones of Joseph which the children of Israel brought up out of Egypt, buried they in Shechem, in a parcel of ground which Jacob bought of the sons of Hamor." Of course, this " parcel of ground" must have been adjacent to the well; and tradition has located the sepulchre near enough to meet all the requirements of the history. Let his bones, therefore, rest in peace.

There is, after all, a mystery about this well which is not easily cleared up. Although we know that the patriarchs were given to well-digging, yet it is strange that Jacob should be at the expense of such a work when there is a fine fountain a little west of it, and the whole vale of Nablûs abounds in them beyond almost any other part of Palestine. The well, however, is a very *positive fact*, and it must have been dug by somebody, notwithstanding this abundance of fountains, and why not by Jacob? He was as likely to need it as any one, and as competent to execute the work. As to the reason for it, we may suppose that the fountains within the valley of Shechem were so appropriated as not to be available for Jacob's large family and larger flocks. Even now the inhabitants would not allow the flocks and herds of such an opulent tent-dwelling tribe to frequent their pretty vale; and, as there are no fountains in that part of the eastern plain, and the streams from those within the valley run *westward*, Jacob probably found it necessary to dig this deep well for his own use. It is now deserted, and the surrounding terrace of rude masonry broken down, so that there is nothing distinctive or striking about it.

The ancient city of Shechem, I suppose, stood where Nablûs does now, and it is easy to comprehend how Jotham could stand above it, and deliver his cutting allegory in the hearing of the people, and then "run away" before they could take him.[1] Several lofty precipices of Gerizim literally overhang the city, any one of which would answer his purpose. Nor would it be difficult to be heard, as every body knows who has listened to the *public crier* of villages

[1] Judges ix. 7–21.

on Lebanon. In the stillness of evening, after the people have returned home from their distant fields, he ascends the mountain side above the place, or to the roof of some prominent house, and there "lifts up his voice and cries," as Jotham did; and he gives forth his proclamation with such distinctness that all can hear and understand it. Indeed, the people in these mountainous countries are able, from long practice, so to pitch their voices as to be heard distinctly at distances almost incredible. They talk with persons across enormous wadies, and give the most minute directions, which are perfectly understood; and in doing this they seem to speak very little louder than their usual tone of conversation. Jotham, therefore, might easily be heard by the greater part of the inhabitants of Shechem. The costume of his allegory is simple and natural, and the allusions are to the very trees which most abound at Nablûs, the olive, the fig, the vine, and the bramble.

The Samaritans (and their patrons) claim for the site of their temple above Nablûs two very important Biblical events: that *here*, and not at Jerusalem, Melchizedek met Abraham; and that *on Gerizim*, and *not Moriah*, the patriarch offered his son Isaac; and if I understand Mr. Stanley aright, he concurs in the justness of these pretensions.

He does, and even devotes a long note of several pages to substantiate the claims; but this is not the most successful effort of that pleasant traveler and very clever writer. Mr. Stanley is a gentleman who yields cheerfully to the paramount authority of the Bible on all points where its indications are clear and decisive, and it seems to me that the positive assertion that Melchizedek was king of *Salem*, makes it certain that Abraham did not meet him in *Gerizim*. *Shechem* was never called Salem, nor was there ever any place on Gerizim that bore this name. There was a Shalîm east of it, toward Jordan, and Jerome, after Theodotus, *supposed* that Melchizedek reigned there, but even this does not favor the cause of the Samaritans. The philological argument drawn from *Ar*-Gerizim has no appreciable weight in the case; and as to the probable route which Abraham would follow in returning from Dan to Hebron, I must dissent entirely from the opinion of Mr. Stanley. Abraham would naturally return on the *western* side of the lakes Huleh and Tiberias. I have been round the eastern side of both, and affirm that he could not have selected that road, encumbered as he was with a large company of rescued prisoners and their baggage, nor could he have followed the valley of the Jordan. No one who has ever traversed that impracticable *ghor* will believe that this great company took that path; and, after wandering over these regions in all directions, I am quite sure that the way by which Abraham led back the people of Sodom was along the ordinary road from Galilee to Jerusalem. This, it is true, would bring him near Nablûs, and if there was the remotest evidence that Melchizedek reigned there, the meeting might have taken place on Gerizim, as the Samaritans affirm; but there is *no* such evidence, and this route would bring Abraham to Jerusalem, where the King of Sodom would most naturally meet him. Mr. Stanley supposes that the King of Sodom went round the *eastern* shore of the Dead Sea; but that is quite impracticable, unless one makes a long detour through the interior. On the whole, I have not a doubt but that Abraham met Melchizedek at Jerusalem, and having restored the goods and the captives to the King of Sodom, he returned by way of Bethlehem to his home on the plain of Mamre. I can not avoid the impression that the author of the "Hebrews" believed that *the* Salem of which the "priest of the most high God" was king was Jeru-*salem*, and in the 76th Psalm the Holy City is expressly called *Salem*. Add to this, that Josephus positively asserts that Jerusalem was founded by Melchizedek, and we have a chain of evidence which can not be broken by the weight of a hundred Samaritan traditions, detailed with so much confidence by "our friend Jacob Shelaby" of Nablûs, sheikh of all the holy Samaritans, etc., etc.

I can not comprehend the motive for this partiality on behalf of Gerizim, nor by what authority Mr. Stanley asserts that the original sanctuary of the most high God was on that mountain, and not at Jerusalem. This is contrary to all the Biblical indications, so far as I can understand them. Salvation was of the *Jews*, not of the Samaritans; the spiritual worship of the Father was in Jerusalem, not in Gerizim; and from the days of Sanballat, and before, so far as we know, devout worshipers of Jehovah regarded the temple on Gerizim with abhorrence. Now, if this had been the original shrine, why was not this most important fact urged by Sanballat and Co. in their angry disputes with Nehemiah and Zerubbabel? and if Melchizedek reigned in Shechem, and Abraham offered up Isaac on Gerizim, why do we hear nothing of these things to strengthen their cause?

In regard to the question about the true site of that most wonderful act of Abraham, I believe it was on Mount Moriah, where the altar of burnt sacrifice was erected by Solomon, and near the spot where the greater sacrifice of an infinitely greater Son was finally offered, and it would take a vast amount of contrary evidence to force me to abandon this idea. Mr. Stanley's geographical argument is more than feeble. It is almost absurd to maintain that Abraham could come on his loaded ass from Beersheba to Nablûs in the time specified. On the third day he arrived early enough to leave the servants "afar off," and walk with Isaac bearing the sacrificial wood to the mountain which God had shown him—there build the altar, arrange the wood, bind his son, and stretch forth his hand to slay him; and there was time, too, to take and offer up the ram in Isaac's place. That all this could have been done *at Nablûs* on *the third day* of their journey is incredible. It has always appeared to me, since I first traveled over the country myself, that even Jerusalem was too far off from Beersheba for the tenor of the narrative, but Nablûs is two days' ride farther north! Nor will the suggestion of Mr. Stanley that Abraham came up through Philistia and then turned eastward into the mountain bear examination. The supposition is entirely gratuitous, and at variance with all the lines of patriarchal travel through the country, nor does it render the achievement of the journey in three days any more feasible. If

SAMARITAN TEMPLE ON GERIZIM.   213

Mr. Stanley had traveled over those interminable plains of Philistia and Sharon as I have, he would not select this route for Abraham on his sad errand. Let us rejoice in being permitted to rest with entire confidence in the correctness of our received tradition, that the priest of the most high God reigned in Jerusalem, and that Abraham made that typical sacrifice of his son on Moriah and not on Gerizim.

In regard to the famous temple of the Samaritans on Mount Gerizim, little need be said in addition to the information addressed to the eye by the plan of the *existing foun-*

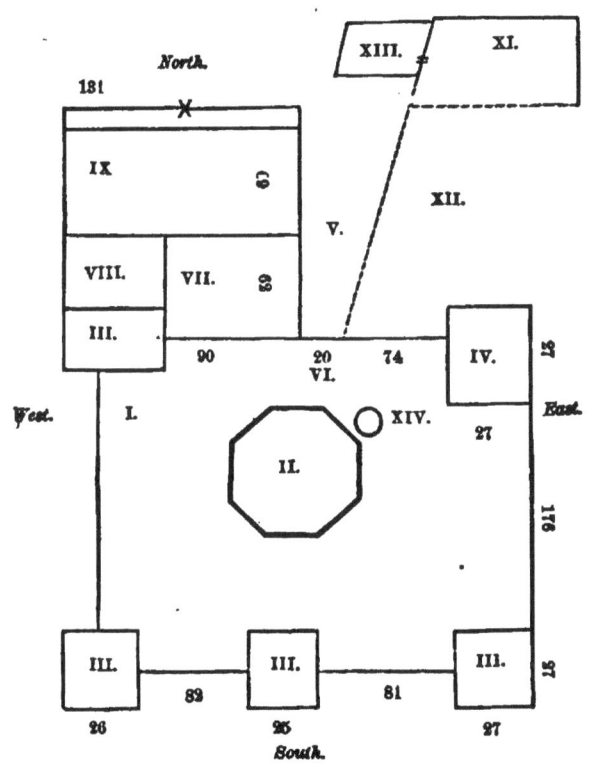

FOUNDATIONS OF SAMARITAN TEMPLE ON GERIZIM.

dations. The main edifice (I.) was nearly a square, being two hundred and forty-one feet from east to west, and two hundred and fifty-five from north to south. In the centre of the court was an octagon (II.), and near it a small but beautifully-rounded tank or cistern (XIV.). On the corners were square rooms (III.), and the one on the northeast (IV.) is covered with a white dome, and is used as an oratory. (V.) is a passage up from a lower platform on the northeast. (VI.) entrance to the grand court. (VII.) an open terrace, a few feet lower than the main court. (VIII.) used apparently as a cemetery. (IX.) a room about eighteen feet lower than No. (VII). (X.) portico or passage to the room (IX.). (XI.) shapeless ruins. (XII.) now unoccupied, perhaps originally a yard or outer court. (XIII.) a room in ruins, object of it doubtful.

The walls are about six feet thick, and from seven to fifteen feet high. There are no ornamental carvings on any of the stones, but they are well cut and *beveled* after the Jewish or Phœnician manner. On the north there is a lower terrace of the mountain, covered with ruins, as of a village, and west of the main edifice is a smooth plat, now used by the Samaritans for their tents, when they go there to celebrate their feasts. For vastness and variety the prospect from this temple is not surpassed by any in Palestine, unless it be the view from Tabor, and many visitors think this from Gerizim the most interesting.

It was doubtless to this mountain, with its ruined temple, that our Saviour pointed when he enunciated that cardinal truth in religion, Woman believe me, the hour cometh when ye shall neither in *this mountain* nor yet at Jerusalem worship the Father. . God is a spirit, and they that worship him must worship him in spirit and in truth.[1] Josephus tells us that this temple was destroyed about a hundred and twenty-nine years before the birth of Christ; but the site of it has been the place where the Samaritans have continued to "worship the Father" from that day to this, *not* in spirit nor in truth, it is to be feared, but in form and fanaticism, according to the traditions of their elders.

There are not now two hundred Samaritans, all told, in the world. They themselves mention one hundred and fifty

[1] John iv. 21, 24.

as the correct census. They are a strange people, clinging to their law, and to the sepulchres of their fathers, with invincible tenacity. Their chief priest will show you, with any amount of sham reverence, their ancient copy of the Pentateuch; but though, like all other travelers, I have given my *būksheesh* for the privilege of turning over its time-stained pages, I have no faith in their legends in regard to it, estimate its real value at a very low figure, and leave to others the minute description of this curious relic of antiquity.

But it is time we should return from our long digression, and give some attention to this great plain through which we are led by our indefatigable guide and protector. The central parts of Esdraelon seem to be entirely destitute of water, and this is the reason, I suppose, why it was never thickly inhabited.

That may have been one reason; another is that it is hot in summer, and unhealthy. As to water, I believe that it could be obtained in any quantity by digging, as in all other great plains of this country. But it is by no means certain that the central parts were always sparsely inhabited. There are traces of many mud villages in it, and some of these have names, and a traditional history among the Arabs. There is a Lûd far down to the left, which was probably settled by a colony from the Lûd which is near Jaffa; and perhaps Jaffa, or Japhia, yonder on the hill-side below Nazareth, and Beit Lahm, in the woods farther west, were also colonized from the celebrated cities of the same name in the south of Palestine.

Esdraelon is far from being a *dead* level, the western half having a decided dip toward the sea, while its different parts roll up in long swells like gigantic waves, terminating in Jebel ed Dûhy in the centre, and the rocky ridges of Zer'in, and Em Gabileh toward the south. I have seen nothing to compare it with except some of our rolling prairies in the West, and these lack Tabor, and Little Hermon, and Gilboa, and Carmel, and a hundred other natural beauties and historic memories with which this is every where surrounded and glorified.

The French engineer who proposed to dig a ship canal from the Bay of Acre, fill up the ghor, and thus open a channel to the Gulf of Akabah, must have been profoundly ignorant of the topography with which he was dealing. The "cutting" for this canal along the bed of the Kishon would gradually deepen, until, at the water-shed of the valley of Jezreel, it would be several hundred feet. This gigantic difficulty overcome, the sea must rush in with volume sufficient to fill up the ghor from near Jisr Benat Yacobe to the Gulf of Akabah, burying Tiberias six hundred feet deep, and all below it deeper still, until, over the Dead Sea, it would be more than thirteen hundred feet, and even then there would be required enormous excavation at the south end before the connection with the gulf could be effected! We may safely conclude that if there is no other way to unite the Red Sea and the Mediterranean than this, the thing will never be done, and Tiberias, Gennesaret, and the splendid valley of the Jordan are safe from this desolating inundation.

What is the name of this ruined castle which we are approaching?

Fûleh, and west of it is 'Afûleh, both now deserted, though both were inhabited twenty-five years ago when I first passed this way. Fûleh was occupied by the French in the time of Bonaparte, and about it were fought many skirmishes with the Turks and Arabs. Many years ago, I spent a night at Sejera, in the oak woods north of Tabor, and found several old men there who remembered the battle of Kleber, and the wild rout of the Turks at the close of it, when Bonaparte, with a troop of horse, came galloping up from Acre to the scene of action. These people of Sejera spoke in the most exaggerated terms of the desperate daring of these French cavaliers, a party of whom was stationed at their village. This castle of Fûleh was circular, with a high wall and a deep ditch. There was no water inside, but directly below it small fountains *ooze* out of the ground in sufficient quantity for the demands of the garrison, which could not have been large. The Bedawîn now resort to them with their flocks and camels, and it was to secure this privilege that they sacked and destroyed the castle; and by the same process the whole of Esdraelon will soon be abandoned to them. Their system of desolation is worked out after this fashion. They pitch their tents in the vicinity of a village, and in such numbers as to bid defiance to the inhabitants. Of course, their camels and flocks roam over the unfenced plain, and devour a large part of the grain while growing; and when it is ripe, they either steal it, or compel the farmers to *present* them a heavy percentage as the price of their *protection*. From the village itself chickens, eggs, sheep, cows, and even horses disappear, and can never be recovered. Many of the inhabitants soon move off to escape from these annoyances, and the village being thereby weakened, the Arabs provoke a quarrel; some one is wounded or killed, and then the place is sacked and burned. The end aimed at is now reached, and the land belongs henceforth to the lawless Ishmaelite. In ten years more there will not be an inhabited village in Esdraelon, unless this wretched work is checked; and even now it is unsafe to traverse this noble plain in any direction, and every body goes armed, and prepared to repel force by force.

But a small portion of the plain is under cultivation, and there are scarcely any traces of antiquity upon it.

That is true, particularly in the centre and western part of it, and there never were any very substantial buildings in those farming villages, I suppose. The houses appear to have been made of unburnt brick, and, of course, it is useless to look for them in our day. From the nature of the country and its relative position it was always subject to invasion, as the great highway for armies, the battle-field of contending nations. The plain, therefore, was mainly cultivated by those who resided in towns upon its border, and there you will find ruins, as at Ksalis, Debûrieh, Nain, Endor, Beisan, Sulam, Zer'in, Jenîn, Lejjun, Tell Caimon, and many other sites. At this place directly ahead of us, now called El Mezrah, there are many sarcophagi of a most antique fashion, yet there is no other trace of an extinct city near it; and the soil among the sarcophagi is plowed and sowed like the rest of the plain. There are also other sites where nothing but the tombs of those who lived there remain to tell the story of their inhabitants.

Our guide, I see, is turning to the south, and intends to take us through Wady Kŭsab, midway between Tell el Mutsellîm and Tell Caimon; and now, before we enter this wady and bid adieu to Esdraelon, let us take a survey of the lower end of it. It has become perfectly level, and I can tell you from experience that in wet seasons it is extremely muddy; and then the Kishon causes great tribulation to the muleteers. Rarely, indeed, do they get over it without some of their animals sticking fast in its oozy bottom. You observe that the hills of Samaria bend round to the base of Carmel, while those of Galilee do the same on the opposite side, leaving a vale between them for the Kishon only a few rods wide. The great tell, which, from our position, seems to close up the entrance entirely, is called Kŭssîs (mound of the priest), a name probably commemorative of the slaughter of Baal's priests near its base. The hills of Galilee are clothed, down to the bank of the river, with a forest of oak, terebinth, mock-orange, and other trees and bushes. Hour after hour you wander delighted through these lovely woods, over hills and through wadies quite up to the Buttauf; and the same kind of grove reappears on the south of Carmel, and still forms the "ingens sylva" of the Roman geographers.

If you look down the Kishon, you can see a huge *double tell* at the farther end of the narrow vale. It is now called Harothîeh, and marks the site, I doubt not, of the old Harosheth of the Gentiles. The present village of that name is in a recess of the hills, a short distance to the east of the tell. On that bold promontory of Carmel directly facing us is the *Mŭkhrakah*, where the great sacrifice was offered by Elijah. The shapeless ruins of El Mansûra are on a lower terrace to the southeast of it, and similar ruins are below on the north side of the mountain. The great Wady Milhh passes southward round the end of Carmel, and through it, I believe, ran the ancient Roman road to Tantûra and Cæsarea. The large *tell* on this side of it is Caimôn, often mentioned by ancient geographers and itineraries. This lower end of Esdraelon is not more than six miles wide, and most of it is too flat and wet for cultivation; but the Arabs delight in it, particularly in winter, and it is even now dotted over with their black tabernacles. Overgrown as it is with tall thistles and long grass, it is the favorite haunt of the gazelle; and there goes a family of them, bounding gayly toward Sheikh Bureîkh on the western margin of the plain. The solemn stork, too, frequents the more marshy parts of it, and adds much to the interest of this rather monotonous scene.

Around this northwestern side of Esdraelon are clustered a number of interesting sites which we may notice in passing. That large *tell* with a village upon it is Jibbata; and directly north of it, half an hour, is Semmûnia, on an immense *tell*, partly hid in a recess of the mountain. In the plain between the two Josephus fought one of his battles with the Romans. Semmûnia is entirely deserted, but there is an excellent fountain of water at the southwest base of the tell; and the traveler along that road in summer will be thankful to know where he can slake his thirst and fill his "bottle." Two miles west of Semmûnia is Jeîda, on an old site full of rock tombs and surrounded with oak glades and rich vales of the most exquisite loveliness. West of this are Kŭskŭs and Tell'aum; and in the woods north of it are Zebda, Beît Lahm, and Em el 'Amed, all ancient, and some of them historical. Beautiful as paradise, yet that whole region is deserted; as in the days of Shamgar, the son of Anath, in the days of Jael, the inhabitants of the villages cease, the highways are unoccupied, and the travelers walk through by-ways;[1] and so we are doing at this moment, and for the same reason. The present state of the country is no novelty.

We are now passing through the scene of Barak's great battle with Sisera; and this same neighborhood witnessed

[1] Judges v. 6, 7.

another contest more remarkable and vastly more important and impressive than the overthrow of that oppressor of Israel. It occurred during the reign of that wicked king Ahab, and his more wicked queen Jezebel; and the scene shifts from Esdraelon to Carmel, and from mountain to plain, in rapid succession. Elijah, the Tishbite, is the principal actor. Jezebel had successfully employed the power and patronage of the government to corrupt the faith of Israel, and the whole kingdom was overrun with the priests of Baal, that abomination of the Zidonians, while his idolatrous temples reared their insulting heads in every part of the land. To effect this apostasy, Jezebel had waged a bloody persecution against the prophets of the Lord. The Tishbite thus states the case, in reply to the question, What doest thou here, Elijah? I have been very jealous for the Lord God of hosts, said he, because the children of Israel have forsaken thy covenant, thrown down thine altars, and slain thy prophets with the sword, and I, even I only am left, and they seek my life to take it away.[1]

To arrest this ruinous revolt, the Lord interposed by a series of awful judgments and stupendous miracles. At the prayer of the prophet he shut up the heavens for three years and six months, so that there was neither rain nor dew during all these years.[2] Near the close of this dreadful drought the king said to Obadiah, the governor of his house, Go into the land, unto all fountains of water, and unto all brooks; peradventure we may find grass to save the horses and mules alive, that we lose not all the beasts. So Ahab went one way by himself, and Obadiah went another way by himself.[3] The latter went westward from Jezreel to the marshy grounds near Carmel, at the bottom of Esdraelon, and there Elijah met him, and said, Go tell thy lord, Behold, Elijah is here.[4] The good man was terrified at the thought of carrying such a message to the enraged king. As the Lord thy God liveth, said he, there is no nation or kingdom whither my lord hath not sent to seek thee.[5] Elijah replied, As the

---

[1] 1 Kings xix. 10.   [2] 1 Kings xvii. 1.   [3] 1 Kings xviii. 5, 6.
[4] 1 Kings xviii. 8.   [5] 1 Kings xviii. 10.

Lord of hosts liveth, before whom I stand, I will surely show myself unto him to-day. Ahab seems to have been near at hand, for he quickly obeyed the summons; and when he saw Elijah he exclaimed, in anger, Art thou he that troubleth Israel?[1] I have not troubled Israel, was the reply of the Tishbite, but *thou* and thy father's house, in that ye have forsaken the commandments of the Lord, and thou hast followed Baalim. Now, therefore, send and gather me all Israel unto Mount Carmel, and the prophets of the groves, four hundred, which eat at Jezebel's table.[2] The wicked but weak-minded king sank before the daring servant of God, his more wicked and resolute wife not being by his side. He hastily gathered the people to a remarkable and well-known spot on the eastern end of Carmel, where sacrifice had been offered to Jehovah in ancient times. But never before was there such a meeting as this, never such a momentous question to be discussed, such a mighty controversy to be settled. Elijah came unto all the people and said, If the Lord be God follow him, but if Baal then follow him.[3] But the people, conscience-smitten, yet afraid of the king, answered him not a word. Then the prophet, to compel a choice, proposed the test of sacrifice, and the God that answered by fire let him be God. The irresolute multitude ventured to approve; the king could not resist; the priests dared not refuse. Quickly the victims are upon the altars, and the priests call upon the name of Baal from morning until noon, saying, O Baal, hear us! But there was no voice, nor any that answered. Then Elijah mocked them, "Cry aloud, for he is a god; either he is talking, or he is pursuing, or he is on a journey, or, *peradventure, he sleepeth and must be awaked.* The poor priests, goaded to madness by this scorching irony, leaped in frantic despair upon the altar, crying aloud, O Baal, hear us! and they cut themselves with knives and lancets after their manner, till the blood gushed out upon them. But in vain. There was neither voice, nor any to answer, nor that regarded. Thus they continued until the time of the evening sacrifice. Then

[1] 1 Kings xviii. 15–17.   [2] 1 Kings xviii. 19.   [3] 1 Kings xviii. 21.

Elijah repaired the *altar of Jehovah, which was broken down*, placing twelve stones, according to the number of the tribes of the sons of Jacob. A trench was dug round it, the wood arranged, the sacrifice upon it, and all was ready for the great decision; but, to make the trial doubly convincing, barrel after barrel of water was poured on until it ran round about the altar and filled the trench. Then comes the solemn invocation, Lord God of Abraham, Isaac, and of Israel, let it be known this day that thou art God in Israel, and that I thy servant have *done all these things at thy word*. Then the fire of the Lord fell and consumed the burnt sacrifice, and the wood, and the stones, and the dust, and licked up the water that was in the trench. The whole multitude fell on their faces, crying out, Jehovah he is the God! Jehovah he is the God! And Elijah said to the people, Take the prophets of Baal; let not one of them escape. They did so, and brought them down to the brook Kishon, and slew them there, near the base of that high Tell Kussis which you see in the mouth of the valley. Then Elijah said to Ahab, Get thee up, eat and drink, for there is a sound of abundance of rain. Elijah himself returned to the top of Carmel, cast himself upon the ground, put his face between his knees, and prayed—prayed earnestly for the rain; but it came not until his servant had gone up to the top and looked out on the Mediterranean seven times. Then the little cloud, as large as a man's hand, was seen to rise out of the sea, and Elijah sent word to the king, Prepare thy chariot, and get thee down, that the rain stop thee not. In the mean while the heaven was black with clouds and wind, and there was a great rain. Thus the long drouth of three years and a half was brought to a close; but the work of the prophet on this most eventful day was not yet ended. Ahab rode and went home to Jezreel; and the hand of the Lord was on Elijah; and he girded up his loins and ran before Ahab to the entrance of Jezreel. This is the last, most strange, and most unexpected act of this great drama; and perhaps there is no one day's work in the whole history of man more wonderful than this.

Have you any confidence in the tradition which fixes the site of these scenes at the place called El Mŭkhrakah, near the ruined village of El Mansûrah?

I have, and for many reasons. From the very nature of the case, it is nearly incredible that such a site should have been lost or forgotten. The narrative itself locates the scene on Carmel, and, by necessary implication, on the southeastern end of it, looking off toward Jezreel. Within these narrow limits there is not much room for uncertainty or mistake. Again, it is clear from the 30th[1] verse that the place was sacred to the worship of Jehovah before the days of Elijah. There had been an altar there, which some one, most likely Jezebel, had caused to be thrown down; and, after these stupendous miracles, it is not to be believed that the scene of them would be forgotten. They took place before all the people, and not in some far-off desert, difficult of access and rarely visited, but in the most conspicuous portion of a densely-inhabited country, and one which has never ceased to be inhabited from that day to this. Accordingly, I believe it can be proved that the tradition of this site has never died out of the country. I have little doubt that this was the spot of the oracle on Carmel mentioned by Tacitus in his history of Vespasian, p. 410. His description is very remarkable: "Between Syria and Judæa stands a mountain known by the name of Mount Carmel, on the top of which *a god* is worshiped under no other title than that of the place, and, according to the *ancient* usage, *without a temple* or *even a statue.* An altar is erected in the *open air*, and there adoration is made to the presiding deity. On *this spot* Vespasian offered a sacrifice," etc., etc. Let us carefully consider this bit of history.

1. As to the precise place. The historian tells us that after their sacrifice Vespasian went to Cæsarea. Now I have already given my reasons for believing that the great Roman road down the coast from the north passes round the southeastern end of Carmel. This conclusion I had reached long before I thought of its bearing on the point before us.

[1] 1 Kings xviii. 30.

But, whether it did or not, the road from the interior did certainly follow this route to Cæsarea, and Vespasian marched along it. *This would bring him directly beneath this Mŭkhrakah.*

2. The place is simply designated as "*the spot.*" There was no temple, no image, only an altar in the open air, and this was according to the *ancient custom* of the place. All this is precisely what we should expect at the seat of Elijah's wonderful miracle, and in striking agreement with what we now actually find there. There is no temple, and no evidence that there ever was one. There is only a "spot" on a natural platform of naked rock, surrounded by a low wall, which, from appearance, may have been there in the days of Elijah, or even before. Within this uncovered inclosure is the *sacred spot*, without a mark, without a title, as Tacitus has it.

3. It is mentioned by pilgrims in subsequent ages, briefly according to their custom, yet in such a way as to leave no doubt that the site was still kept in remembrance. One of the "*stations*" of ancient pilgrimage derived its name from it.

4. It is still well known and reverenced by all the inhabitants of this neighborhood, Jews, Christians, Moslems, Druses, and Bedawîn, and *as the site of these miracles of Elijah.* My guide to it, a Druse, approached it with great reverence, and even awe; and this present veneration of all sects tallies admirably with the history of Tacitus. It was then in the hands of heathen priests or of corrupt Samaritans, but was so celebrated that pilgrims and worshipers of all nations resorted to it. This is natural, and in -agreement with even the present customs of this country. Very many shrines of the Moslems, and other races, owe all their sanctity to events recorded only in Biblical history. In this particular case it is highly probable that those mingled people who were transported hither from Assyria, "who feared the Lord and served Baal," would immediately appropriate to the uses of their superstitions this most celebrated "spot." Their descendants may have held possession of it when Ves-

pasian passed this way, and the fame of its oracle induced even him, the master of the Roman world, to consult it.

5. The name Mŭkhrakah, signifying the place that was *burned*, or the place of *burning*, is so far confirmatory of the tradition. Such native and significant names do not fasten upon any spot without an adequate reason, and there is, in almost every case, some foundation in truth for them. In this instance it is the very name we should expect, and is applied to the spot most likely of all to be the true one.

6. Lastly, there is no other place with opposing claims. It has no rival. This is remarkable in a country where there are so many conflicting traditions in regard to almost every celebrated site. But not only is there nothing to contradict its claims or disturb its title, but the closest scrutiny into the history, even to the most minute incidents and implications, will corroborate and confirm them. Why, therefore, should there be a doubt about the matter? I confess, with hearty good-will, that I am troubled with none.

Mr. Van de Velde, who visited this place in company with Dr. Kalley, was the first in our day, so far as I know, who has published a description of the Mŭkhrakah, and his account is sufficiently accurate. I can not agree with him, however, that the water poured upon the sacrifice was procured from the fountain he mentions. That fountain was nearly dry when I saw it, nor do I think it could hold out through the dry season, even of one ordinary summer. How, then, could it last through three years and a half of total absence of rain? Nor are there any marks of antiquity about it. The water was obtained, as I suppose, from those permanent sources of the Kishon, at the base of Carmel, which I have before mentioned. It is even doubtful whether any of these, except the great one of Saadîeh, could stand such a protracted drouth, and the distance even to that is not so great as to create any difficulty. Perhaps there might have been water in the marshes about Tell Thora, east of Tell Kŭssîs. The path from the place of sacrifice brought me to the Kishon at this great tell, and, from the nature of the mountain, the priests must have been brought down the same track. They were, therefore, in all probability, actually put to death near it, and, naturally enough, the act would fasten its name to the tell as the most conspicuous permanent object in the neighborhood. If Elijah returned to the place of sacrifice after the slaughter of the priests, his servant would have to go but a short distance to obtain an extensive view of the sea, both toward Cæsarea, and also over the plain of Acre to the northwest. I suppose that both Elijah and Ahab did return to the Mŭkhrakah: Ahab to partake of the feast prepared and spread somewhere near at hand, which always formed part of these sacrifices, and Elijah to pray for rain. This is implied by the words of the prophet to the king, Get *thee up*, eat and drink; and again, Get *thee down*, that the rain stop thee not.

The best way to reach the Mŭkhrakah is to go from Haifa, along the base of Carmel, past Tell Harothîeh, to Tell Kŭssîs, and then ascend the mountain by some ruins on a bold swell of Carmel, which my guide said bore the name also of El Mansurah, the same as on the southeastern end of the mountain. But without a guide it is next to impossible to find the spot, so dense is the jungle of thorn-bushes on that part of Carmel. I once undertook to reach it from the southwest, got lost, and finally had to procure a guide from Idjzîm, and then scramble across frightful gorges and up steep precipices, to the no small danger and fatigue of both horse and rider.

How large a portion of these wonderful actions are we to suppose took place on the day of the sacrifice?

The whole of them after the people assembled to the return of the king to Jezreel.

This reminds me of the feat performed by the prophet at the winding up of this wonderful drama. The hand of the Lord was upon Elijah, and he girded up his loins, and ran before Ahab to the entrance of Jezreel. This has always appeared to me most extraordinary conduct for a man of his age, character, and office.

And yet, when rightly understood, it was beautiful, and full of important instruction. Elijah, as God's minister, had overwhelmed the king with shame and confusion in the presence of his subjects. The natural tendency of this would be to lower him in their eyes, and lessen their respect for his authority. It was not the intention, however, to weaken the government nor to encourage rebellion. The prophet was therefore divinely directed to give a testimony of respect and honor to the king as public and striking as from necessity had been the opposition and rebuke to his idolatry. The mode of doing honor to Ahab by running before his chariot was in accordance with the customs of the East, even to this day. I was reminded of this incident more than twenty years ago at Jaffa, when Mohammed Aly came to that city with a large army to quell the rebellion of Palestine. The camp was on the sand-hills south of the city, while Mohammed Aly stopped inside the walls. The officers were constantly going and coming, preceded by runners, who always kept just ahead of the horses, no matter how furiously they were ridden; and, in order to run with the greater ease, they not only "girded their loins" very tightly, but also tucked up their loose garments under the girdle, lest they should be incommoded by them. Thus, no doubt, did Elijah. The distance from the base of Carmel across the plain to Jezreel is not less than twelve miles, and the race was probably accomplished in two hours, in the face of a tremendous storm of rain and wind. It was necessary that the "hand of the Lord should be upon" the prophet, or he would not have been able to achieve it.

It is easy to fancy the place of meeting between Elijah and the angry king of Israel. The prophet was returning from Sarepta along the common highway which led up this wady of Kishon to Megiddo, and had reached that immediate neighborhood where the permanent fountains of the river begin. There he found Obadiah, with part of the "beasts" seeking grass to keep them alive. It is evident that Ahab himself was not far off. Probably he had gone out on that marshy part of the plain, near Tell Thora, hoping also to meet with grass. The only other part of this region where grass could be sought at the end of such a drouth would be down the Wady Jezreel, east of the city, around the great fountain now called 'Ain Jalûd. But the narrative does not countenance the idea that Ahab was at such a distance from Carmel. The place of meeting was therefore at the southeast end of this mountain, not far from Tell Kŭssîs.

Are we to suppose that the *drouth* extended over all this country?

I think not. Probably only over the kingdom of Israel, on whose account it was sent. It, however, involved the plain of Sarepta, but that lies within the proper territorial limits of Israel. In order to understand how it was possible to keep any part of this kingdom from being absolutely depopulated, we may remember that, although all the crops fail even when there is a drouth of only a few months in spring, and that in a single dry summer all the ordinary fountains cease, yet there are others, such as 'Ain Jalûd, in the valley of Jezreel, and some of the sources of the Kishon at the base of Carmel, which have never been known to dry up entirely. Moreover, there is no reason to suppose that the drouth extended to Hermon and Lebanon, and hence the great fountains of the Jordan would keep the lakes and the river full and strong, and water could be brought from these sources of supply on camels and mules, and by other means of transportation. It is certain, too, that a portion of the people would remove to the vicinity of these supplies, and to more distant neighborhoods. As to provisions, the Mediterranean was on their western border, and corn from Egypt could be brought in any quantity, as is still done in seasons of scarcity. By these and other means a remnant would be preserved; but we are not to lessen the calamity too much in our account of these resources. The wandering of the king in search of grass; his angry salutation to the prophet; the dying destitution of the widow at Sarepta, all show the fearful extent and severity of the famine. And now we are about to leave this interesting region for one almost a desert.

It may be desert, but it is very green and inviting; and what a beautiful brook comes babbling down the wady!

If it derived its name, *Kŭsab*, from the abundance of *cane* on its banks, they seem all to have disappeared; but here are splendid oleanders in their place, and I see that the guide has halted for our noonday rest and lunch under a pyramid of these flowery bushes. We shall not be detained long, I dare say, in this solitary place. Hasseîn is evidently uneasy, and looks suspiciously at those horsemen coming down the wady. They are acquaintances, however, I perceive; and, while they discuss Arab politics, we will discuss bread and cheese, chicken and ham.

As I expected. These men advise us to be moving, and to keep close together until we reach the next village, after which there is no danger; and so we are off. It is well we improved the time, or we might have had a long ride on an empty stomach.

These hills are entirely naked, and mostly barren, or, rather, uncultivated, for I see nothing to prevent their being planted with orchards and vineyards.

Nothing but insecurity, and the ferocity of the people in this region. As we advance, you perceive that the wady splits into many branches. We take this one on the west, and our track opens on to beautiful views of Carmel in the north. That village about three miles to the west of us is called Um Ezzêinat, and the one south of it Rehanîeh. The name of the district is Belad er Rohah, and it includes all the southeastern border of Carmel down to Cæsarea. As we are taking leave of Carmel, let us while away the time spent in climbing these tedious hills with a few facts and remarks in regard to that celebrated mountain. It is steep and lofty only at the northwest corner, and on that face which overlooks the plains of Acre and Esdraelon. The ascent is comparatively easy from the sea, and it sinks down gradually to the south into the wooded hills of Samaria and the rich plain of Cæsarea. There are, however, deep ravines, in some of which I became entangled on my way from Tantura to the Mŭkhrakah, and had no small trouble to extricate myself from their perplexing sinuosities and abrupt precipices. There is no special "excellency" in Carmel at present, whatever may be said of Sharon.[1] Its name, *Kerm el*, signifies vineyard of God; and we read that Uzziah, who loved husbandry, had vine-dressers in Carmel.[2] These vineyards have all disappeared, and, in fact, so have the *forests*, which were celebrated in ancient song. It is a glorious mountain, however—one to swear by, according to Jeremiah: As I live, saith the King, whose name is the Lord of hosts, surely as Tabor is among the mountains, and *as Carmel by the sea*, so shall he come.[3] Amos lets us know that in his day the top of it was a famous place to hide in, nor has it changed its character in this respect: Though they dig into hell, thence shall my hand take them; though they climb up to heaven, thence will I bring them down; and though they hide themselves in the top of Carmel, I will search and take them out thence.[4] My experience would not have prompted me to place the "top of Carmel" third in such a series of hiding-places, but yet I can fully appreciate the comparison. Ascending it from the south, we followed a wild gorge, through which my guide thought we could get up, and therefore led us on into the most frightful chasms, overhung by trees, bushes, and dark creepers, until it became absolutely impracticable, and we were obliged to find our way back again. And even after we reached the summit, it was so rough, and broken, and the thorn-bushes so thick-set and sharp, that our clothes were torn, and our hands and faces severely lacerated; nor could I see my guide ten steps ahead of me. It was a noble pasture-field, however, and, in reference to this characteristic, Micah utters this sweet prayer: Feed thy people with thy rod, the flock of thy heritage, which dwell solitarily in the wood in the midst of Carmel.[5] From these and other hints we may believe that Carmel was not very thickly inhabited. There are now some ten or eleven small villages on and around it, occupied by Moslems and Druses; and, besides these, I have the names of eight ruins, none of which, however, are large or historical. Carmel was a habitation

---

[1] Isaiah xxxv. 2.   [2] 2 Chron. xxvi. 10.   [3] Jer. xlvi. 18.
[4] Amos ix. 2, 3.   [5] Micah vii. 14.

TOP OF CARMEL—DECEITFUL BROOKS.

of shepherds,[1] and it is implied that its pastures were not liable to wither. This may in part be occasioned by the heavy dews which its great elevation, so near the sea, causes to distill nightly upon its thirsty head. I found it quite green and flowery in midsummer. Our road now begins to descend toward the southwest, and the village to which we are coming is called Dalia er Rohah, to distinguish it from another of the same name on the top of Carmel, settled by Druses from Lebanon.

This is a singular brook which we are following down the wady. Back yonder I thought of watering my horse, but, supposing the stream would become larger, I omitted it, and here it has vanished altogether, like one of Job's[2] deceitful friends—I mean brooks.

The phenomena of streams in this country aptly illustrate the character of his false friends. In winter, when there is no need of them, they are full, and strong, and loud in their bustling professions and promises; but in the heat of summer, when they are wanted, they disappoint your hope. You think your fields will be irrigated, and yourself and your flocks refreshed by them, when lo! they deal deceitfully and pass away. Nearly all the streams of this country, "what time they wax warm," thus vanish, go to nothing, and perish. Such were Job's friends. There is another illustration equally pertinent. You meet a clear, sparkling brook, and, so long as you follow it among the cool mountains, it holds cheerful converse with you by its merry gambols over the rocks; but, as soon as you reach the plain, "where it is hot," it begins to dwindle, grow sad and discouraged, and finally fails altogether. Those which suggested the comparison of Job probably flowed down from the high lands of Gilead and Bashan, and came to nothing in the neighboring desert; for it is added that the "troops of Teman looked, the companies of Sheba waited for them, and were confounded because they had hoped." It was in those high mountains only that Job would become familiar with the winter phenomena, where the streams are "black-

[1] Amos i. 2.   [2] Job vi. 15–19.

ish by reason of the ice;" for not only are Lebanon and Hermon covered with snow in winter, and the brooks there frozen, but the same is true also of the higher parts of the Hauran, and of the mountains to the south of it, where Job is supposed to have resided. We shall follow this Wady Dalia, called also Shukkah, for an hour at least, and, owing to some peculiarity in the strata, the water repeatedly sinks away and then reappears lower down. The pastures on either side are extremely rich, and, when I passed along it in February, it was all glowing and blushing with an infinite number and variety of flowers, sending up incense to the skies, and offering their honeyed cups to millions of bees. I saw here a flower altogether new to me; the stem resembles a strong rank pea, but the flowers hang in pendent clusters like hops. The upper part is a light bronze color dashed with purple, the rest pure white. I could get no name for it. We now leave this Wady Dalia, and take over the hill southward for half an hour to Sŭbbarîn, near the head of another valley, which bears the name of Sindiany, from a village of that name farther down toward Cæsarea. Perhaps both wady and village are so called from the *oak* woods with which the whole country is clothed. I shall not soon forget the ride on that lonely evening of February when I first passed this way. The setting sun glowed and trembled among the tree-tops, and, streaming down aslope, filled the valley with transparent gold and living emerald full up to the brim and running over. It seemed like fairyland, and I no longer questioned the unequaled charms of Cæsarea and her surroundings. From our present position we can gaze through this glorious vista of oak glades, and along many a solemn aisle, leading every way far into the deep forests. I was taken by surprise, having anticipated nothing but a barren desert, where I met with rural beauty unsurpassed by any thing in this country. The scene now is changed; the fields are white for the harvest, the flowers have faded and fallen, and the grass is sear and dead, but the same round hills are here, and the grand old oaks, with their robes of fadeless green. It never can be less than lovely while they remain. But our guide beckons us onward, and with reason, for there is yet another hour to Sindiany, and this neighborhood has a villainous reputation.

> "Every prospect pleases,
> And only man is vile."

However, my experience enables me to trust the people of Sindiany, and there is a charming camp-ground just north of the village. Take notice of this fountain of Sŭbbarîn. We shall meet it to-morrow where one would least expect it.

XXXII. SINDIANY—CÆSAREA.

April 2d.

I have had a delightful ramble this morning in these grand old forests, and now understand perfectly how Absalom could be caught by the thick branches of an oak. The strong arms of these trees spread out so near the ground that one can not walk erect beneath them; and on a frightened mule, such a head of hair as that vain but wicked son "polled every year" would certainly become inextricably entangled.

No doubt; and it is interesting to know that the region where that battle was fought is still covered with such forests—that "wood of Ephraim," with thick oaks and tangled bushes, and thorny creepers growing over ragged rocks, and ruinous precipices down which the rebel army plunged in wild dismay, horses and men crushing each other to death in remediless ruin. Thus 20,000 men perished in that fatal wood, which devoured more people that day than the sword devoured.[1]

The great heap of stones over the pit into which Absalom was thrown was not raised in honor of the king's son, but in detestation of the traitor's enormous crime; and you will find miniature heaps of the same kind and significance all over the country. It is a widespread custom for each one as he passes the spot where any notorious murderer has been buried, to cast a stone upon it. I have often seen this done, and, yielding to the popular indignation, have thrown my stone with the rest. I am reminded of all this by the conduct of my guide, who has actually dismounted to *spit* upon this heap, and add his pebble to the growing pile. He says the wretch who lies buried there was a notorious robber who infested this road, and committed many cruel murders, and he is using the incident to enforce his admonitions upon us to keep together in this part of our ride, which we will of course conform to as long as it suits our purpose.

Yesterday I thought your description of this valley ex-

[1] 2 Sam. xviii. 7, 8.

travagant, but withdraw the criticism this morning. When the early light began to reveal the character of the scene around me, the country from north to south was buried under a dense, low-lying fog, which left the many-shaped hill-tops peering above it like green islets in the bosom of a placid lake. I was breathless with surprise and admiration. When the sun arose, this gray silvery sea, as if startled by some invisible spirit, became agitated in an extraordinary manner, and vast pyramids of shining vapor burst up from beneath, swelling higher and higher among the oaks, until it escaped through their thick boughs, and vanished away in the clear vault of heaven. All this commotion and gorgeous display I found was owing to a brisk breeze which came up the valley from the sea of Cæsarea. Acting from below, and itself turned about by every bend and swell of the hills, it swayed and twisted the yielding waves of vapor according to its own eccentric will.

There was something of the kind in February last, and it is indeed singularly beautiful. Such fogs, however, are quite common on the great plains along the coast, as we shall see in the land of the Philistines. But let us follow our company down the valley, for we have a busy day, with just enough of danger to make it exciting. That village on our left is called Khŭbbaizy, the Arabic name for the *malva*, the Hebrew nearly for the *rose*, and both malvas and wild roses adorn this sweet vale. Many other hamlets repose in the bosom of these glorious woods, but we can not load our memories with their obscure and ignoble names. Did you observe that the dew rolled off our tent this morning like rain? And now the early sunbeams "sow the earth with pearls and diamonds," as Milton's muse describes these pendent drops that glitter and sparkle from every leaf in the forest and blade in the field.

If I remember correctly, this place on our right bears the ominous name of 'Ain Maiety (Dead Fountain), and the tell east of it is *sit Leîla*, a name more frequently heard in Arab song than any other. We now turn westward toward Cæsarea, leaving the main road, which keeps on southward through the plain of Sharon to Lẏdd and Ramleh. The whole of this region is as fertile as beautiful, but most of it is uncultivated, and all infested with robbers. When at Sindiany last year, I wanted to send my baggage directly across to Tantûra, while I came round this way to Cæsarea, and I had to hire a guard sufficiently large not merely to protect my muleteers in going, but also the men themselves in returning. The people could not then venture from village to village but in companies and well armed. It is not so bad now, and we shall send our tents on to the mills of Zerka, three miles north of Cæsarea, where alone we can pass the night in safety. Left to ourselves for the day, with our faithful guard to watch for us, we will ramble about *ad libitum* among these remains of antiquity.

That large building some two miles to the northwest of us is the kŭsr we heard so much about from our friends at Sindiany, and to reach it we must pick our way through these bushes and tall reeds, over a country not a little infested with bottomless mud. Ignorant of these treacherous bogs, on my first visit I struck directly across the plain for the kŭsr, and was soon floundering in unsubstantial mire up to the belly of my horse, and was glad to get safely out again on the same side by which I entered. Here we are at one of these brooks, sluggish and black as ink, but the bottom is not very *distant*, and we can easily pass over.

Where does this stream come from? There was no water in the wady down which we have traveled this morning.

It is the joint contribution of many springs which rise out of this spongy plain in all directions, and we shall soon see more of them. Between this and the kŭsr are immense fountains, now called Miamās, the water of which was collected in a large pool, and then carried by an aqueduct to Cæsarea. These works are of course broken, and we must pass round them on the north in order to find a practicable path to the kŭsr.

There seem to have been many substantial buildings hereabout; and, indeed, we are floundering over the grass-covered ruins of a considerable city. The kŭsr itself must have been an immense affair, and in a style of architecture quite peculiar.

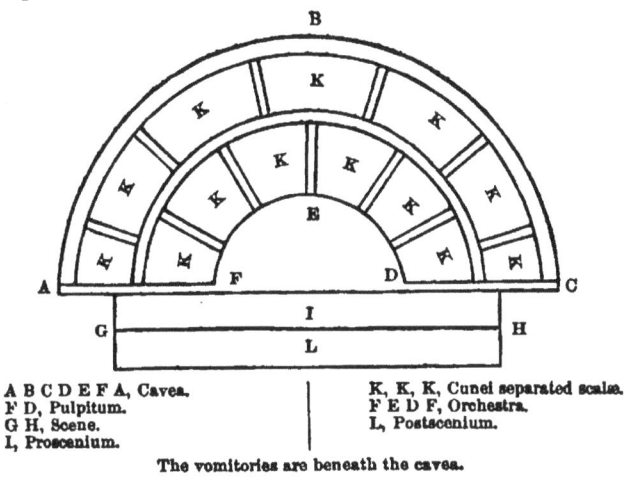

A B C D E F A, Cavea.
F D, Pulpitum.
G H, Scene.
I, Proscenium.

K, K, K, Cunei separated scalæ.
F E D F, Orchestra.
L, Postscenium.

The vomitories are beneath the cavea.

PLAN OF THEATRE.

It was doubtless one of Cæsarea's theatres, and the plan of a *Roman* theatre, which I brought along for the purpose, will enable you to comprehend at once the details of the edifice. It is semicircular, and the *chord* is a hundred and sixty-six feet. The seats are all gone, and the *cavea* much changed, but the vomitories and vaults beneath are in good preservation, and are now used for stables and granaries by the peasants. This tower on the southeastern corner, and these huts inside, are comparatively modern, and were erected probably when the building was turned into a Moslem castle. The prospect over the wooded hills of Samaria and the far-spreading plain of Sharon is very beautiful, and hither flocked the laughter-loving Greeks of Cæsarea to enjoy the excitement of theatric games and the pleasures of the open country at the same time. The topography of the place is decidedly interesting. Directly north of the kŭsr terminate the last spurs of Carmel in a bold promontory called Khŭshm en Nazûr. South of it is the great marsh Ez Zoar, fading out into the sandy downs and brushy slopes of the upper Sharon. The ruined villages of Em el 'Alŭk and Muallŭkah (both names suggestive of "the horse-leech," which greatly abounds in this marsh of Zoar) appear on the northern ridge; and Bureikîeh, three miles distant in the same direction, is inhabited by the peasants who cultivate the land around these fountains of Miamās. The fountain near Subbarîn, which I pointed out to you yesterday, was in former times led down by Bureikîeh to the kŭsr, where it was associated with the stream from Miamās, and the two united were carried along the perpendicular base of Mount Khŭshm, across the swamp of Zoar, to the shore, and thence southward to the city. This was a remarkable work, and most of it is still quite perfect. Our road is now upon, or, rather, *within* this aqueduct until we get over the various brooks which, passing beneath it, are lost in the general marsh.

This is, indeed, a narrow and somewhat *nervous* pathway, especially as one sees on either side of him bogs of bottomless mud.

There is some danger, no doubt, but with nerves sufficiently steady we might follow on the top of this *double* aqueduct quite to the western side of the marsh; for, if I remember aright, there is not a broken arch in the entire line. I, however, have no fancy for such *high* ways, and the ground south of it is here sufficiently solid to justify the attempt to reach the sandy plain beyond. Safely through! Look back now at the long file of arches on columns which span the entire width of the Zoar. But the difficulties of our position are not yet ended. Here is a very suspicious-looking stream *soaking* its way through tall reeds and flags, and beyond it is a second and a third, all pouring their blackish water into the marsh. The largest of these brooks, called Shukeiŭk and Shŭkkauk, is said to rise in Wady Sŭfsâfy about two hours to the southeast. All these streams run northward into the swamp, and not to the sea, in consequence of that low rocky ridge which extends parallel to the coast and about half a mile from it. This formation is the same fossiliferous *sandy* limestone as that out of which nearly all the cities on the sea-board are built, and it has been hewn and cut up by quarriers in the most extraordinary manner; indeed, the cuttings and quarrying are more extensive than those of any other city on this coast. I once spent several hours searching among them for inscriptions, but found none; and the only important discovery was that such enormous quarryings were never made by the short-lived city of Cæsarea, and that this was merely the Roman name for a more ancient city. I had read this before, but I was convinced that the original name could not have been *Strato's Tower*, for that was Latin, and these quarries were opened long before they ever appeared in Syria. This primitive city, I suppose, was the frontier town in this direction of the Phœnicians, and I leave to the lovers of antiquarian research the discovery of its name and history.

And there lie the ruins of all your three cities together, directly in front of us. What could have induced Herod to select this place for a harbor, as it is an open coast without projecting headland or protection of any kind?

The rich country back of it to Samaria and Nablûs probably furnishes the explanation. It is also in the centre of a long *reach* of coast entirely destitute of harbors, and this offers another reason; and, moreover, it is not quite true that there is no natural protection to serve as the basis for an artificial harbor. Several ledges of rock run out into the sea from the shore, and the king took advantage of two, between which the water was deepest, and there constructed great moles, *inclosing a space larger than the Piræus:* Josephus says so, not I. It never could have been sufficiently long to protect a single first-class Boston clipper.

Cæsarea has always been invested with a peculiar interest to my mind, not so much for its own eventful history, nor because it was the capital of Palestine, but chiefly on account of its honorable and most important connection with the Apostolic Church. It was here that the good Cornelius fasted, prayed, and gave alms, which came up before God as a memorial, until an angel of the Lord appeared, and directed him to send unto Joppa for Simon, whose surname is Peter. There another vision revealed to that apostle the great fact that God is no respecter of persons, but that in every nation he that feareth him and worketh righteousness is accepted of him;[1] and thereby prepared this bearer of the "keys of the kingdom of heaven" to unlock the door to the Gentile world. Here the "apostle of the circumcision" first learned that he must not call *any man* common or unclean;[2] *here* the Holy Ghost was first granted to the heathen; and *here* took place the first Gentile baptism. Certainly we Gentiles have abundant reason to cherish the memory of Cæsarea. Paul, the apostle of the Gentiles, and greatest of foreign missionaries, often visited it, and was here held prisoner for two whole years. Standing in chains where some of these ruins now lie, he made his noble speeches before Felix, and Festus and Drusilla, Agrippa and Berenice, characters somewhat famous, and most of them not a little infamous in their day. Eusebius, the historian, was born and lived in Cæsarea, and here Origen studied and wrote commentaries. But we need not prolong the list of her honors. They do but exaggerate her present utter desolation.

These ruins remain precisely as they were twenty-five years ago, upon my first visit. The area inclosed by the wall extends along the shore about the fourth of a mile, and is some forty rods wide from east to west. The wall was built of small but well-cut stone, was strengthened by sixteen square towers, and protected by a broad ditch; but still it could not have been a place of much strength, nor is it celebrated for any great military events. We are not to suppose that its vast population, stated as high as 200,000, was confined within these narrow limits. On the contrary, there are abundant traces of suburbs scattered all over the plain, and the inclosed area was little more than the acropolis of the city. The harbor was at the southwest corner of this citadel, and we can trace its whole extent by the existing remains. Look at them, and then turn to Josephus,[3] and see if you can discover any resemblance. Beyond all doubt, much of that description is magniloquent Josephian hyperbole. Who can read of the *mole*, two hundred feet broad, built of stones more than fifty feet long, eighteen

[1] Acts x. 34, 35.   [2] Acts x. 28.   [3] Ant. xv. 9, 6.

wide, and nine deep, without a smile? Why, the whole harbor inclosed by it is not much broader. But it is use-

MOLE OF THE HARBOR OF CÆSAREA.

less to criticise this extraordinary piece of exaggeration; I can not refrain, however, from remarking that the historian must have forgotten that there is no appreciable *tide* at the head of the Mediterranean when he says "the sea itself, upon the flux of the tide from without, came into the city and washed it all clean!" There is enough here, however, besides the name, to convince us that the historian is actually speaking of this place, though the exaggeration is so egregious that one seems to be walking in his sleep. It was doubtless this southwestern mole which Herod named

Procymatia—wave-breaker. Exactly where the tower of Drusus stood I am at a loss to decide.

In one respect, these remains of the first century of our era are extremely interesting and important. They present the best criterion by which to judge *architecturally* of other ruins, and show conclusively that many of them are far more ancient. A moment's examination will also prove that Herod built with materials furnished to his hands by ruins of a city older, and, I believe, much more magnificent than his own. This immense number of granite columns built into his moles speaks of an antecedent and wealthy metropolis, with splendid temples, which had been overthrown long before Herod began his work. Nor do I believe that Strato's Tower (as the place was then called, and which he changed to Cæsarea) was the original name. That is of foreign derivation, given by the Romans, while these columns and other relics speak of Greek or Phœnician times and architects. Josephus says that Herod built a temple on this southern mole, and a splendid theatre near the harbor, and without the city, on the south side, an amphitheatre capable of holding a vast multitude of people. All have disappeared. These tall buttresses, which make the most show of any part of the present ruins, evidently belonged to a Christian church, possibly of Crusader times. Cæsarea has the misfortune to be inseparably associated with the incipient causes and first outbreaks of that dreadful war in which Jerusalem, the Temple, and the Jewish nation were destroyed. Herod, by erecting heathen temples and theatres, and placing idol statues in the city, greatly displeased the Jews, and the disputes between them and their idolatrous fellow-citizens finally became so bitter and exasperated that they rushed blindly into open revolt. One of the first acts of the bloody tragedy was the massacre of 20,000 Jews in this city by the Greeks. The whole Jewish nation then flew to arms, and ceased to fight only when they ceased to be a people.

How comes it that Cæsarea has for many ages been utterly deserted? It is the only considerable city on the coast that has been thus absolutely forsaken.

Several things have conspired to work out this result. The mole being overthrown, the harbor became utterly unsafe. Not a single ship could ride securely in it. This destroyed her commerce. The aqueducts broken, there was no longer an adequate supply of water; and this gone, the surrounding country relapsed into its natural state of a barren desert, and the sand, constantly accumulating from the sea, buried up every green thing. Thus solitary in itself, it early became infested with robbers, so that no one could live here in safety, and thus it continues to this hour; nor is there much reason to hope that it will again become an important city, for it has not a single natural advantage.

But it is time to seek our tent at Towahîn ez Zerka, an hour to the northeast of us. Let us follow the line of these lofty canals—two in one—by which we shall obtain a better idea of the ancient suburbs, and likewise observe the great size of the aqueducts, which were carried along parallel to the shore for about two miles. They served as a defense against the sands of the sea, and the whole space on the east of them seems to have been occupied with buildings. We can see into the covered canals in many places; and the stories of the natives, that a man could pass inside of them on horseback from the city to the mills of Zerka, do not seem to be incredible fables. They are in such preservation that it would not cost a large sum to clear them of the sand, and again bring the water to the harbor. It is not true, however, as some travelers assert, that ships frequently put in here to obtain water from these aqueducts, for they have been broken for many centuries. Boats often call in summer to load with stones from the ruins, and much of the recent building in Jaffa and Acre is constructed out of them. I once spent a day here while my boat was thus being freighted for Jaffa, and this is the only *trade* carried on with this ancient capital of Palestine. Shepherds, who water their flocks from the well near the southern gate, visit it by day, and robbers, by night, lie in wait to plunder any unprotected traveler who may chance to pass, which, however, is of rare occurrence. Comparatively few now follow this desolate coast, and none venture alone, if they can in any way avoid it.

Here are the mills, and, by the advice of the miller I dare say, our tent is pitched in a very good position for defense. There is no disguising the fact that we must pass the night surrounded by robbers, and for once it will be necessary to keep a strict guard. We have time enough before sunset to examine this extraordinary locality. It appears that the River Zerka, whose various branches we crossed in the morning, had here broken through the low rocky ridge which runs parallel to the shore, and in some remote age this opening was shut up by this powerful wall, thus raising the water twenty-five feet high. This wall is two hundred and thirty paces long, and twenty feet thick, and the road still passes along its top—the grandest mill-dam I have ever seen. The water falls directly from the top on the wheels below. There are some eight or ten mills now in motion, and many are in ruins, and at least twenty might be ranged side by side below the wall. It is this dam that causes the marsh of Zoar, the whole of which would be effectually drained by simply breaking it down, and many thousand acres of the richest land would thus be regained to cultivation.

This Zerka is undoubtedly the Crocodile River of the ancients, and you will be surprised to hear that there are now living crocodiles in the marsh at our side; but such is the fact. These millers say they have seen them often, and the government agent, a respectable Christian, assures me that they recently killed one eighteen spans long, and as thick as his body. I suspect that, long ages ago, some Egyptians, accustomed to worship this ugly creature, settled here, and brought their gods with them. Once here, they would not easily be exterminated, for no better place could be desired by them than this vast jungle and impracticable swamp. I was delighted, on my first visit many years since, to find these creatures still on hand to confirm the assertions of Greek and Roman geographers. The historians of the Crusades speak of this marsh, which they call a lake, and also say that there were crocodiles in it in their day. If the locality would admit, I should identify this Zerka with the Shihor Libnath of Joshua xix. 26, for Shihor is one of the names of the Nile—the very home of the crocodile; but the river in question was given to Asher, and is probably the Naaman (the Belus of ancient geographers), and the marshes at its source are as suitable for this ugly beast as these of Zoar.

CROCODILE.

By taking the interior route on the east and south of Carmel, we have missed a long stretch of the coast. Is there any thing of interest on the shore from Haifa to Cæsarea?

The best answer is to pass it in review; and it is about as profitable, and far more pleasant, to traverse this nine hours in imagination than to ride them on horseback. By way of introduction, listen to some remarks on the general character of the Syrian sea-board. From Carmel and northward there are numerous headlands, with bays on the north of them more or less deep, by which the line of the coast falls back to the east, as it were, by successive steps. Carmel itself, with the Bay of Acre, is not only the first, but one of the most striking. North of Acre is the Ladder of Tyre, which consists of three such capes: el Musheîrifeh, en Nakûrah, and el Baiyod. Between Tyre and Sidon is the low headland of Sarafend, and from Sidon to Beirût are three rocky *Nakûrahs*, with the retreating coves of Rumeîleh, Neby Yûnas, and Damûr. Then comes the projecting cape Ras Beirût, with its Bay of St. George falling back to the deeper cove of Jûn. The next salient point is the Theoprosopon of the ancients, north of Bŭtrŭn, beyond which, by successive steps, at Cape Enfeh and the *mina* of Tripoli, the coast enters far eastward into the plain of Akkar. With lesser indentations at Ruad and Balinas, we come to the long low promontory of Ladakîyeh. Finally, stretching across the open sea at the so-called Bay of Antioch, we pass Ras el Khanzîr, and enter the Bay of Scandaroon. Such is the configuration of the northern half of this coast; but from Carmel southward it runs in a direct line a little west of south, in long unvaried *reaches*, far as the eye can see, and farther too, past Athleet, past Tantûra, Cæsarea, Jaffa, Askelon, Gaza, and quite on round to Egypt.

After this rapid survey we will begin again at the point of Carmel. It is three hours thence to Athleet, with no important villages or ruins intervening. Athleet, however, presents the greatest historic and architectural puzzle found at the head of this sea. I can not identify it with any ancient site whatever. Neither the Bible, nor Josephus, nor any profane historian or geographer mentions it, nor does its name appear in any of the old Itineraries; and yet the remains of antiquity at it are more numerous, more striking, and in better preservation than at any other city of Phœnicia. The exterior wall, built of great stones, and protected by a ditch cut through the solid rock where necessary, inclosed a large quadrangular space reaching quite across the headland on which the city stood. Most of *this* wall has been carried away to build those of Acre during the long centuries of the past. The Acropolis was the extremity of the cape, cut off from the outer city by a wall prodigiously strong, whose heavy stones are beveled after the purest Phœnician style. Large sections of it remain entire, and just as they were first put up. There is no *patch-work*, no broken columns or other fragments, as in the oldest Greek and Roman structures in Syria. It is pure unmixed Phœnician. Just within this wall stands a portion of a gigantic building, whose character it is difficult to comprehend. It was erected on *vaults* of very great strength, and the fragment of the east wall towers up at least *eighty* feet high. There it stands in its loneliness, unbroken by a hundred earthquakes, the first object that strikes the eye of the traveler either up or down the coast. Near the top on the interior, so high that it strains the neck to look at them, are the flying buttresses (finished off below with the heads of men and beasts) from which sprung the arches of the *great dome*. It must have been superb—sublime. Now who erected this magnificent temple, and when? The only history we have of Athleet begins with the Crusaders, who call it Castellum Perigrinorum (Pilgrims' Castle), because they used to land there when Acre was in the hands of the Saracens. But they built none of these edifices. There are also other remarkable indications of extreme antiquity about Athleet. This low rocky ridge on which we are encamped, and which occasions this marsh of Zoar, begins a little to the north of Athleet, and in front of the city it rises to a considerable elevation, and is there cut up in a singular manner by old quarries. Directly east of the city a broad road was hewn through the ridge, which is still the common highway for the surrounding country, and well-worn tracks of chariot-wheels are still to be seen along this remarkable passage. Mr. Van de Velde supposes that these were for *rail-road* cars, and makes some farther *guesses* on the subject, which must have required a good deal of nerve to pen and publish.

Now the question returns, What is Athleet, either by this or any other name? I have no answer. The Hebrew writers may have had no occasion to mention it, because that part of the coast was not in their possession. The Roman and Greek writers and travelers generally passed round on the east of Cæsarea, as I believe, and did not visit it. Strabo says, "After Acre is the tower of Strato, having a station for ships. Between them is Mount Carmel, and *names* of cities, but nothing besides: the city of Sycamenon, Bucolon, and the City of Crocodiles." The ruins of this last town are here at the mouth of this River Zerka. This silence of Strabo with regard to both Athleet and Dor favors the idea that the Roman road passed on the east of Carmel. Sycamenon is probably Caimon. The Bible repeatedly mentions Tantûra and her towns by the name of Dor; and Athleet may have been one of her "towns," though it was immensely superior to Dor. But enough about Athleet, except that her people are great villains, and so are those of Et Tirêh, at the foot of Carmel, northeast of it. En Haud, on the brow of the mountain, may possibly mark the site of En Haddah, given to Issachar. It is nearly three hours from Athleet to Tantûra, and the two villages, Kefr Lam and Sarafend, both apparently ancient, are between them. Farther inland are Yebla and 'Ain Gazzal. The name Yebla resembles Ibleam, which was assigned to Manasseh, though belonging to the lot of Issachar.

Tantûra merits very little attention. It is a sad and sickly hamlet of wretched huts, on a naked sea-beach, with a marshy flat between it and the base of the eastern hills. The sheikh's *palace* and the public *menzûl* for travelers are the only respectable houses. Dor never could have been a large city, for there are no remains. The artificial tell, with a fragment of the *kŭsr* standing like a column upon it, was probably the most ancient site. In front of the present village are five small islets, by the aid of which an artificial harbor could easily be constructed, the entrance to which would be by the inlet at the foot of the kŭsr; and should "Dor and her towns" ever rise again into wealth and importance, such a harbor will assuredly be made.

Twenty minutes south of Tantûra, a considerable stream, called Mufjûr, enters the sea. It descends from Belad er Roha, and is probably the same as Wady Dalia. The beach is thickly strewn with pretty shells, and the sand is solid enough to make the ride along the rippling surf delightful. It is two hours to the mouth of the River Zerka, where are the remains of the old City of Crocodiles; and thus we have reached our camp-ground, and the hour when wearied travelers seek repose.

XXXIII. CÆSAREA TO JAFFA.

April 3d.

The hurry and bustle of our early start have crowded out our usual morning worship. Let us therefore turn aside, and take a lesson from the works and ways of nature, while the gray dawn grows into the full broad day. This is the season, and this the hour when poets love to sing,

> "Sweet is the breath of morn, her rising sweet,
> With charm of earliest birds."

The lark is already on high, saluting the first ray that gilds the dappled east with his cheerful matin. All nature hears the call, shakes off dull sleep, and hastens to join the general welcome to the coming king of day; and yonder he comes, over the head of Carmel, rejoicing as a strong man to run a race. See! even the vegetable kingdom shares the universal joy. Notice these flowers all around us, how they turn smiling to his ardent gaze, *bend forward* in seeming reverence, *throw open their pretty cups*, and cast abroad *their sweetest perfume.* This silent adoration of ten thousand thousand flowers is most beautiful and impressive, and nowhere else beheld in higher perfection than among the lilies and roses of this sacred plain of Sharon.

Now this "powerful king of day" is but the faint shadow of his Maker—the Sun of Righteousness; and when He rises with healing under his wings,[1] may we be ever ready to meet him with analogous welcome and superior joy. Let us even now listen to the many voices around us calling to prayer. Oh come, let us worship and bow down; let us kneel before the Lord our Maker; for he is our God, and we are the people of his pasture, and the sheep of his hand.[2]

We have done well to commence our ride with the dawn, for it is the longest, and will be the most fatiguing which we have yet accomplished. He who goes not to bed will be early up, says an Oriental proverb, and so it has been with me. I can never sleep in such a place as this, and therefore merely wrapped my cloak about me, and sat down

---

[1] Mal. iv. 2. [2] Ps. xcv. 6, 7.

patiently to watch our boastful guard, for I never yet found them faithful through a whole night. Talking, smoking, and joking, they managed to stave off sleep until one o'clock, and then all except Hammûd gave up the effort. He held on for nearly another hour, humming to himself more and more drowsily, till finally his head subsided on his chest, and his song into a gurgling snore. Poor fellow! let him sleep and dream of home.

Lifting his gun quietly from his knee, I walked out on this ancient causeway, and set myself to count the stars, and listen to the sounds that startle the dull ear of night. I deemed myself familiar with every noise and note that mark the transit of these leaden hours: the surf's low murmur dying out on the shore—the sobbing of the winds among the trees and rocks—the monotonous response of the night-hawk to his mate—the muffled flutter of the circling bat—the howl of the wolf—the jackal's wail—the bark of the fox—and the ban-dog's cross bay from the distant fold. To these and such as these I have listened with the listening stars a thousand times, and again last night. But there was something additional to render my solitary watch upon this old dam strange, and doubtful, and expectant. Above the clattering of mill-stones and the rush of water-wheels there came, every now and then, a loud splash and hollow roar never heard by me before. Did they come from the slimy crocodiles which crawl through this hideous swamp in search of prey? The idea made me nervous. Ere long, however, my musings wandered off to more interesting themes. I recalled the day and night I spent among Cæsarea's broken walls and prostrate columns more than twenty years ago. Fresh from scenes of war, and earthquake, and sickness, and death in Jerusalem, I then felt a mysterious sympathy with these sad and forsaken ruins. Cæsarea is, in some respects, the most interesting site on the earth to the missionary. Here the Holy Ghost was first poured out upon Gentiles as upon the Jews, and thus the middle wall of partition broken down. From this spot the glad tidings set forth to run among the nations north, and south, and east, and west—west, far west—and, after eighteen centuries, from that New World, westward, far beyond the dream of prophet or apostle, returns the herald of that Gospel to mingle his tears with the dust and ashes of this cradle of the Gentile Church.

How wonderful the ways of God! In this place the greatest missionary that ever lived was shut up in prison two whole years, and at a most critical time in the history of the Church, when his presence and preaching seemed indispensable. One can not help feeling that Paul made a mistake when he came here from Acre en route to Jerusalem. He should have listened to Philip's four prophetic daughters, and to Agabus, who took Paul's girdle, and bound his own hands and feet, and said, Thus saith the Holy Ghost, so shall the Jews at Jerusalem bind the man that owneth this girdle.[1] But the lion-hearted apostle could not be persuaded. "What mean ye," saith he, "to weep and to break my heart? for I am ready not only to be bound, but to *die* at Jerusalem for the name of the Lord Jesus." And speedily and right nobly did he redeem his pledge.

Having escaped terrific mobs and horrible conspiracies at Jerusalem, he was brought back to this place in chains, and here held prisoner by Felix, that corrupt and tyrannical governor. How often he must have dragged his chain to the top of the castle during those two long years, and gazed on the green hills of Palestine, and out upon the blue sea over which he had sailed many times on messages of mercy to heathen nations along its distant shores. One longs to know something of the musings and occupations of that wonderful man during the tedium of those many months. But inspiration is silent, and even tradition fails us. The supposition that he superintended the writing of Luke's Gospel is a mere guess, with no historic basis.

Here we are again within Cæsarea's prostrate walls. Doubtless some of these mounds of rubbish mark the exact site of Paul's prison, and from this sandy margin of the harbor he stepped on board that ship of Adramyttium in which

[1] Acts xxi. 8–11.

he sailed for Italy to prosecute his appeal before Cæsar.[1] Repeatedly have I passed over these same seas, and followed the apostle step by step in that tedious and unfortunate voyage. They evidently had a pleasant run to Sidon, where they touched the next day, and Paul was allowed to go on shore and refresh himself among his friends. The wind must have then hauled round to the west, for the ship could not pursue the direct course to Italy south of Cyprus, but ran north between the island and the Syrian coast, and then west over the sea of Silicia and Pamphylia; working westward in the teeth of the wind, it was a tedious and dangerous passage. But we may not follow that celebrated voyage any farther at present, nor longer linger here at Cæsarea; so take your last look at these remains of the city, and harbor, and sandy suburbs, and let us hasten after our luggage, now far ahead of us.

In passing through from Cæsarea to Jaffa, we do but follow the example of ancient geographers and Itineraries. They stretch their lines from the one to the other as though there was nothing worth attention in the twelve intervening hours. Nor were they much mistaken, for there is, perhaps, no ride of so many miles in any other part of Palestine more solitary and barren of historic interest. Strabo says, "After Strato's Tower there is a great wood, and then Joppa." The Roman road was evidently carried east of these sandy downs which lie along the shore, both to avoid them, and also to find suitable places to throw their bridges over the rivers which enter the sea. Following that route, we should first pass through a dreary wood of dwarfish pines and entangled bushes, and then down the long plain of Sharon direct to Lydd, the Diospolis of the ancients. But, as this would be much longer, we shall keep to the coast, although the sand is deep and heavy.

Before taking leave of this interesting site, let us examine these traces of a city on the south of it, whose remains appear to be much older than those of Cæsarea. Those inlets along the rocky shore, I suppose, were the harbor of that

[1] Acts xxvii. 2.

ANCIENT HARBOR OF CÆSAREA.

primitive city which was called Strato's Tower before and at the time of Herod, but this could scarcely have been its original name. It was somewhere in this vicinity, south of the city and near the sea, that Herod built his great amphitheatre, and these half-buried foundations may have belonged to that vast edifice.

We have now taken leave of Phœnicia and entered the territory of the Philistines. These people came from Egypt, and we shall see, as we go south, that even the present inhabitants approach more and more closely to the Egyptian type in physiognomy, in costume, language, manners, and customs. Dr. Kitto has a long and labored article to prove that they were the "Shepherd Kings" expelled from Egypt. Others more competent must decide whether or not he makes good his hypothesis, but the mere supposition adds fresh interest to this people and to the country which they occupied.

What are these high *tells* ahead of us, overhanging the sea?

They are one hour from Cæsarea, and are called Abu Zabûr. The encroachment of the sea has worn them half away, but on the top of this first one are some half dozen very large columns of bluish marble, which must have formed part of a temple, or possibly of a mausoleum. The spot is still used as a burying-ground by some of the Arab tribes in this region. It commands a noble view of the sea westward, and of Strabo's "ingens sylva" in the interior. This wilderness is covered by shifting sand, which has overflowed the country, and whose presence is easily explained. The rock of the shore is a loose friable sandstone, constantly washed to pieces by the waves, and driven inward by the west winds. This holds good along the entire coast wherever loose sand encumbers the plain, but here it is unusually abundant and troublesome; and we shall have high hills of it on our left, and this soft beach to wade through for two full hours yet, therefore let us put on the garments of patience, and plod steadily onward.

There is always something to amuse and instruct in this

country. Look at those clouds, which hang like a heavy pall of sackcloth over the sea along the western horizon. From them, on such windy days as these, are formed *water-spouts*, and I have already noticed several incipient "spouts"

WATER-SPOUT.

lengthening downward from their lower edge. These remarkable phenomena occur most frequently in spring, but I have also seen them in autumn. They are not accompanied with much rain, and between the dark stratum above and the sea, the sky is clear and bright. Here and there fragments of black vapor, shaped like long funnels, are drawn down from the clouds toward the sea, and are seen to be in violent agitation, whirling round on themselves as they are driven along by the wind. Directly beneath them the surface of the sea is also in commotion by a whirlwind, which travels onward in concert with the spout above. I have often seen the two actually unite in mid air and rush toward the mountains, writhing, and twisting, and bending like a huge serpent with its head in the clouds and its tail on the deep.

They make a loud noise, of course, and appear very frightful. Deep calleth unto deep at the noise of thy water-spouts; all thy waves and thy billows are gone over me, saith David, when his soul was cast down within him.[1] But, though formidable in appearance, they do very little injury. I have never heard of more than one instance in which they proved destructive even to boats, though the sailors are extremely afraid of them. As soon as they approach the shore they dissolve and disappear.

That kind of water-spout which bursts on the mountains, generally in the dry months of summer, does immense mischief. In a few minutes the wadies along its track are swollen into furious rivers, which sweep away grain, olives, raisins, and every other produce of the farmer. I have frequently known them to carry off and drown flocks of sheep and goats, and even cows, horses, and their owners also.

This is one of those days when the sea is just sufficiently disturbed to set the flying-fish in motion, and I have already seen several flocks of them frightened out of their proper element to try their glossy wings in the air. They are generally supposed to do this to escape some ravenous fish that is pursuing them; but there are no voracious dolphins in this sea, and they often start up in shoals before Arab boats. Their flight is always short, spasmodic, and painful; and when their *web-wings* become dry, they instantly collapse, and the poor little aeronaut drops into the water like a stone. I have had them repeatedly fall into my boat when attempting to sail over it.

[1] Ps. xlii. 7.

FLYING-FISH.

How melancholy is this utter desolation! Not a house, not a trace of inhabitants, not even shepherds, seen every where else, appear to relieve the dull monotony. I wonder if it was thus when Peter came along from Joppa to Cæsarea?

The coast itself was doubtless what it is now, but the road could not have been so utterly deserted. Cæsarea was then a great capital and a grand commercial emporium, and this now solitary track was crowded with multitudes hastening to the grand centre of business, pleasure, and ambition.

Did Paul travel this route to and from Jerusalem?

I suppose not. As I said before, the Roman road, even to Joppa, took inland from Cæsarea, and no doubt it united with the great highway which came down by Sindiany, and continued along the plain southward to Lydd, Ramleh, Eleutheropolis, and onward into the desert toward the Red Sea at Akabah. A few miles farther down, a branch took off to the southeast through the mountains to Jerusalem, and we know that Paul was brought down that way by the Roman soldiers, and this was the direct route which he always pursued unless turned aside by some special call. Antipatris lies between Cæsarea and Lydd, and its site, restored to its original name, Kefr Saba, is now well known.

Here we come to what is called Minet Zabûr, or Harbor of Zabûra, and around this small inlet was once a village of some size, as is indicated from the quantity of broken pottery scattered over the surface. This is an infallible sign of an ancient site. If there ever were any but mud hovels here, however, every stone has been carried away, or has dissolved to sand and dust. The River Abû Zabûra enters the sea a short distance ahead of us, but, as this has been a remarkably dry season, we can doubtless cross on the beach, though, when I passed this way in 1833, I had to make a long detour into the interior over these sand-hills, and finally got across with great difficulty. It is celebrated for quicksands and bottomless mud, and it was partly to avoid such impracticable rivers that the Romans carried their highways down the interior, for it was their system never to make a road where they could not construct bridges. I have an idea that this Abû Zabûra is the River Kânâh, which formed the southwestern border between Ephraim and Manasseh. The country on the north of it belonged to Manasseh, that on the south to Ephraim.[1] Dr. Robinson, however, thinks he has identified this river with a wady now called Kanah, west of Nablûs, which, he says, "turns southwest, joins the Aujeh, and so enters the sea near Jaffa." But I can scarcely believe that the lot of Manasseh reached so far south. The text in Joshua intimates that the border followed the River Kanah to the sea, which it may have done if this Abû Zabûra is it, but not if the River Kanah became swallowed up in the 'Aujeh. The doctor may possibly have been misled in regard to the final direction of his wady Kanah, for nothing is more eccentric than the course of the streams after they enter these plains. Kitto makes the river of Arsûf, which enters the sea between Em Khâlid and El Haram, to be the Kanah of the Bible, and this is certainly far more probable than that the Aujeh is, but even this seems to carry the border of Manasseh too far south.

[1] Josh. xvii. 9.

We must allow our horses to drink at the ford, for it is a long stretch to the next brook. Here is a shepherd with some cattle to relieve this utter solitude. Hammûd exclaimed, when he saw this wild Arab shepherd, *El hamdulillah shûfna ensân*—Thank God! we have seen a man. He may be thankful also that the Bedawy is *one* and that we are many, for every denizen of these wild downs is a robber by profession.

These cliffs, below which we have been trailing our slow and weary march since crossing the Zabûra, are very singular geological specimens—absolutely perpendicular—composed of very thin strata, piled up like *dog-eared paste-board* in a book-bindery; not horizontal, but crumpled, twisted, and *bulging* out in all possible angles and shapes.

Yes, and the same extraordinary formation continues almost to Jaffa. This long line of cliffs is called Durb el Kheît—*road of a chord*—probably because they stretch in a straight line for so many miles. But our horses are becoming quite exhausted with this deep sand; let us therefore take out into the country, and pass over these sand-hills to a village called Em Khâlid, forty-five minutes to the southeast of us. There has been a fight there this week between the villagers and the Arabs, as I was told at the mills last night; but we are a strong party, and they will not venture to molest us. There we shall find water, take our lunch, and refresh our weary horses.

What sort of birds are these which make such a noise among the trees and bushes?

They are field-sparrows, and this is the largest congregation of them I have ever seen. The trees and even the shrubs are stuffed full of their nests; and these hawks, which are soaring about seeking whom they may devour, cause all this alarm and hubbub among the sparrows. You remember we saw something like this on the Hûleh, only the birds are ten times more numerous here; in fact, they seem to be without number. They live upon the wild oats which cover these sand-hills as if they had been sown by man. Now we have gained the summit, see what a splendid prospect opens upon the eye. The great plain of Sharon stretches southward quite beyond the range of vision, while the mountains of Manasseh and Ephraim, crowded with villages, picturesquely perched upon their many-shaped declivities, bound the horizon in that direction. Below us, to the southeast, is Em Khâlid, and most welcome to man and beast, for we have been riding five hours, and at a rapid pace.

Twenty-three years ago I arrived at this village from Tantûra, and slept under this identical old sycamore, which the west wind has forced to spread its branches down the hill to the east. How little of the romance of that first journey through Palestine can I now get up, with all the appliances and luxuries of modern travel! Without tent, canteen, or even cook, sleeping under trees, hedges, or rocks, as it happened, I passed from Beirût to the Dead Sea, and back through the interior by Nablûs, Nazareth, and Tiberias. But there was more romance than common sense in the matter, and before that first summer was over I lay on my bed for many weeks, consumed by that low, nervous, Dead Sea fever, which has proved fatal to so many Syrian travelers.

This Em Khâlid is famous for watermelons beyond almost any village in Palestine, and vast quantities are taken by boat to Beirût, and other towns along the coast.

Are these melons the *abattachim* of Egypt, the remembrance of which augmented the murmurs of the Israelites in the wilderness?[1]

In all probability the same. The Arabic name *bŭtteekh* is only a variation of the Hebrew, and nothing could be more regretted in the burning desert than these delicious melons, whose exuberant juice is so refreshing to the thirsty pilgrim. It is among the most extraordinary eccentricities of the vegetable kingdom that these melons, so large and so full of water, should flourish best on such soil as this around Em Khâlid. Into this dry sand the vine thrusts its short root, and that in the hottest season of the year. Yet a thou-

[1] Numb. xi. 5.

sand boat-loads of this most juicy melon are gathered from these sand-heaps for market every summer. The leaves themselves must have the power of absorbing moisture from the heavy dews of the night. The villagers are telling our people that, for fear of the Arabs, they have not dared to plant their more distant fields this spring, and therefore there will be few of their melons in the city markets, which bit of information has stirred the wrath of the muleteers, and they are pouring maledictions upon them—upon their heads, their eyes, their beards, and every thing else pertaining to them. And really one feels a sort of sympathy with these imprecations. I am conscious of a degree of dislike toward these Bedawîn robbers more intense than I allow toward any other of God's creatures, nor have I any patience with them; but let us leave them before I am startled out of all due decorum. Our lunch over, we must ride steadily and fast, for it is yet more than six hours to Jaffa.

Look well before your horse's head, or you may fall into some of these open-mouthed cisterns. The whole face of the hill is pierced with them.

I see; but what are they for? Not to hold water certainly, for there is no way in which they could be filled.

They are wells or cisterns for grain. In them the farmers store their crops of all kinds after the grain is threshed and winnowed. These cisterns are cool, perfectly dry, and tight. The top is hermetically sealed with plaster, and covered with a deep bed of earth, and thus they keep out rats, mice, and even ants, the latter by no means a contemptible enemy.

By the way, I read lately, in a work of some pretension, that ants do not carry away wheat or barley. This was by way of comment on the word of the wise man, that the "ant gathereth her food in the harvest."[1] What have you to say of the criticism?

That it is nonsense. Tell it to these farmers, and they will laugh in your face. Ants not pilfer from the floor and the granary! They are the greatest robbers in the land.

[1] Prov. vi. 8.

Leave a bushel of wheat in the vicinity of one of their subterranean cities, and in a surprisingly short time the whole commonwealth will be summoned to plunder. A broad black column stretches from the wheat to their hole, and you are startled by the result. As if by magic, every grain seems to be accommodated with legs, and walks off in a hurry along the moving column. The farmers remorselessly set fire to every ant city they find in the neighborhood of their threshing-floors.

Are these Eastern granaries mentioned or alluded to in the Bible?

The custom is doubtless an ancient one, and it extended from this country through the Carthaginians of North Africa into Spain. They seem to be alluded to by those ten men who said to Ishmael, Slay us not, for we have treasures in the field, of wheat, and of barley, and of oil, and of honey,[1] and thus they saved their lives from that treacherous Ishmaelite. These cisterns not only preserve the grain and other stores deposited in them from insects and mice, but they are admirably adapted to conceal them from robbers. These ten men had doubtless thus hid their treasures to avoid being plundered in that time of utter lawlessness; and in a similar time I found people storing away grain in cisterns far out in the open country between Aleppo and Hamath, and they told me it was to hide it from the government tax-gatherers. It is quite dangerous to come upon a deserted site full of these open cisterns and wells, especially at night, as I have often found. Frequently they are entirely concealed by the grass, and the path leads right among them. They must always be dug in dry places; generally, as here, on the side of a sloping hill. They would not answer in a wet country, but in these dry climates stores have been found quite fresh and sound many years after they were thus buried. The farmers also resort to various expedients to keep the grain from injury. One of the most common is to mingle quicksilver with oil, or with the white of an egg, and rub it in well with the wheat. This will pre-

[1] Jer. xli. 8.

serve it free from insects of all kinds. Joseph in Egypt must have understood how to preserve grain, at least for seven years; and I suppose that in ancient times, when cities and fortresses *were liable to very long sieges*, it was of the utmost importance to know the best methods of preserving their stores. Askelon is said to have been besieged *twenty-eight years*, and of course the people must have had immense provisions laid up and well preserved. That this was common is implied in the parable of the rich fool, who built greater store-houses and laid up provisions for *many years*.[1] If there had been no such store-houses in the land, and the custom of laying up grain for many years was unknown, the terms of the parable would have lacked verisimilitude, a defect in construction which attaches to none of our Lord's sayings.

Are we to suppose that these vast downs have really been formed by sand blown in from the sea-shore? All the way from Cæsarea we have had them, and here they are three miles broad and several hundred feet high.

Yes; and they continue, with only partial interruptions, far down the coast beyond Gaza toward Egypt. But, extensive as they are, they are all the work of the winds and waves, acting in the same manner through countless ages. The gradual encroachment of the sea is slowly wearing away this underlying rock, as we have seen in the strange cliffs along the shore, and the new-made sand is being driven farther and farther inland. If this process goes on long enough, the entire plain will be buried under this slow-creeping desolation. There are many parts of the coast where this has actually been accomplished, and the sea now lashes the perpendicular cliffs of the mountains, and along this valley of Sharon are places where the sandy deluge has reached nearly to the foot of the hills, leaving only a narrow strip of fertile soil between them. These shifting banks greatly perplex the brooks which cross the plain. They are not sufficiently powerful to keep their channels open during summer, and hence they are often dammed up at the mouth,

[1] Luke xii. 18, 19.

and form large marshes along the very margin of the sand. We shall encounter one of these a short distance ahead of us. Strong permanent streams like the 'Aujeh maintain their right of passage at all times, and have done so in all ages. The 'Aujeh, in fact, effects an entire break in this line of sand-hills, but, south of Joppa, the weaker and less permanent brooks are constantly shut up during summer, and when swollen by winter rains, flood the country, until they can force open a channel to the sea.

The plain here has evidently been buried deep under this sand long ages ago, precisely as at Beirût, and here are the

STONE PINE.

usual pine forests growing upon it. These are the finest specimens we have seen in Palestine, though every sandy ridge of Lebanon and Hermon is clothed with them, and often of a much larger growth. They are not seen on the *mountains* of Palestine, because that peculiar sandy formation is not found there. This tree the Arabs call *snubar*, and in my opinion it is the Hebrew *berosh*, concerning which there is so much confusion in the various translations of the Bible. In the English it is generally rendered *fir*, but many modern critics think that it should be *cypress*. I, however, suppose that *berosh* is the generic name for the pine, of which there are several varieties on Lebanon. Cypress is rarely found there, but pine every where, and it is *the* tree used for beams and rafters. *Ers* is the distinctive name for the cedar, *berosh* for the pine.

This tree bears a very large and compact cone, from which is obtained the *nut* of the market. This cone, when ripe, is gathered by the owners of the forests, and when thoroughly dried on the roof, or thrown for a few minutes into the fire, it separates into many compartments, from each of which drops a smooth white nut, in shape like the *seed* of the *date*. The *shell* is very hard, and within it is the fruit, which is much used in making pillau and other preparations of rice, and also in various kinds of sweetmeats. In the Arabic Bible, the *myrrh*, which the Ishmaelites who bought Joseph were carrying into Egypt, is called *snubar;* and if this is in truth the *berosh* of the Bible, scarcely any other tree is more frequently mentioned, and this would be in exact correspondence with its actual value.

CONE OF THE PINE.

The variety of pine which we saw on the north of Em Khâlid, and in which the field-sparrows have made their

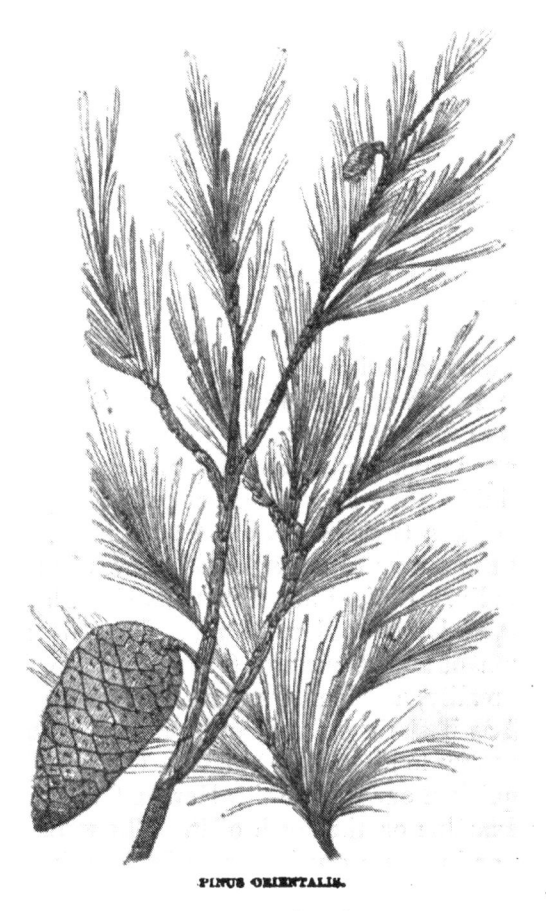

PINUS ORIENTALIS.

nests, is found all over Lebanon, but it never grows tall, and is but little used in building or in the arts; and the same is true of all other kinds in this country, except the stone pine of this grove.

There is your sand-perplexed brook, with its accompanying marsh, I suppose?

Yes; it is called Nahr Falej—the Palsy River. On the shore near its mouth is Arsûf, and from it the river takes that name on many maps. Arsûf is generally supposed to mark the site of the ancient Apollonia. You observe that the banks of the Falej are shaded with a dense jungle of those mop-headed canes called *babeer*, which cover the great marshes of the Hûleh. By keeping up the bank for some distance we shall find an easy ford near some old mills, where the river breaks through a ledge of rocks and enters this verdant vale. It has taken an hour and a half from Em Khâlid, and another hour and a half will bring us to El Haram, on a bold cliff overhanging the sea.

Do you know, I was very suspicious of those Arab horsemen who joined us out of the jungle upon our left. But you seemed to enjoy their society amazingly.

They had no intention of molesting us. The main speaker was the sheikh of a tribe whose tents are concealed by the bushes to the southeast of us. He was very anxious to hear the news from the Crimea, and, to judge from his talk, you would think him a most zealous partisan of the Sultan and the Ingleese (English); but he soon turned from war to discuss the merits of the splendid mare upon which he sat so proudly. He had heard that the English were buying horses, and was anxious to sell. He only asked the modest sum of 18,000 piastres (720 dollars) for his mare. She is, in reality, a splendid creature, and walks over this sandy soil as if she were built on springs; nevertheless, I should be sorry to give 18,000 piastres for her.

Let us quicken our pace to this Haram, for there is something to examine on the north of it. The walls of an ancient city, or immense quadrangular fort, can be traced all round; and on the northwest corner was a citadel overhanging the sea, and cut off from the rest by a deep ditch. It must have been a very strong place. There are also other traces of antiquity in various directions.

What an extensive view this elevation commands! The precipice breaks sheer down to the sea, while to the east the country declines gently over many a mile of this sandy desert. Isaiah says that Sharon shall be a wilderness,[1] and

---
[1] Isaiah xxxiii. 9.

the prediction has become a sad and impressive reality. And so these flocks of the Arabs fulfill that other prophecy, Sharon shall be a fold of flocks.[1] Why is Sharon always joined with Carmel?

Because, as we remarked when turning round the extreme end of it to Cæsarea, the broad vale which stretches southward to this distance and a great deal farther does actually commence at the base of that mountain. This long plain seems always to have been celebrated for its flocks and herds. David appointed one of his great officers—Shitrai, the Sharonite[2]—over the herds that fed in Sharon.

By the way, we have skirted this plain for so many miles without meeting any of those roses about which Solomon sings so sweetly.[3]

There are wild roses enough in some parts, with their ever-accompanying thorny thickets; and, if the Hebrew word khŭbbaizly may be interpreted by the Arabic khŭbbaizy (malva), I have seen thousands of Solomon's roses on Sharon; and, before you explode in a passion at the thought of degrading the poetic *rose* into *marsh-mallows*, let me tell you that certain kinds of mallows grow into a stout bush, and bear thousands of beautiful flowers. However, I will not contend for the identity of *khŭbbaizly* and *khŭbbaizy*, for that would exclude our favorite rose from the Bible altogether, a calamity which the critics seem determined to bring about at any rate, for some of them maintain that the khŭbbaizly is the *narcissus*, others that it is the *asphodel*, and some translators call it *lily*.

But come, bid adieu to El Haram, and, for the present, to Sharon also, and slide down this steep declivity to the shore, along which our track lies all the way to Jaffa, a distance of three hours. You may go to sleep for the first two, for there is nothing to attract attention except the infinite quantity of shells, of which there are banks many miles long and several feet thick. A whole fleet might be loaded with them.

And now we shall have to wait at this 'Aujeh, and take

[1] Isaiah lxv. 10.   [2] 1 Chron. xxvii. 29.   [3] Song ii. 1.

off the loads from our mules, for I see, by that horseman who is fording it, that the water will come up to the sides of the mules, and wet our clothes and books. I never before attempted to cross at this place; but the people of El Haram said that, owing to the scarcity of rain, it could easily be done; and so it can, by all except the loaded animals. However, we shall quickly pass the things over on the shoulders of the men, and then another hour will bring us safely to the *biarah* of our worthy and hospitable friend Mr. Murad.

Jaffa appears well, bathed in the soft light of sunset. We see almost every house, for they are built on the steep northern declivity of the cape, and the roof of the range below is on a level with the street of those above. The city therefore shows to best advantage from the sea as one comes from the north. The cape itself is merely a sand conglomerate, like the cliffs of Durb el Kheît; it is, in fact, the continuation of that ridge, broken up for a short distance by the joint influence of the 'Aujeh and the sea.

JAFFA FROM THE NORTH.

XXXIV. JAFFA.

April 10th.

Jaffa is one of the oldest cities in the world. It was given to Dan in the distribution of the land by Joshua, and it has been known to history ever since. It owes its existence to the low ledge of rocks which extends into the sea from the extremity of the little cape on which the city stands, and forms a small harbor. Insignificant as it is, and insecure, yet there being no other on all this coast, it was sufficient to cause a city to spring up around it even in the earliest times, and to sustain its life through numberless changes of dynasties, races, and religions, down to the present hour. It was, in fact, the only harbor of any notoriety possessed by the Jews throughout the greater part of their national existence. To it the timber for both the temples of Jerusalem was brought from Lebanon, and no doubt a lucrative trade in cedar and pine was always carried on through it with the nations who had possession of the forests of Lebanon. Through it also nearly all the foreign commerce of the Jews was conducted until the artificial port of Cæsarea was built by Herod. Hither Jonah came to find a ship in which to flee from the presence of the Lord, and from it he sailed for Tarshish.

By-the-by, do you think there is any foundation for the idea of Reland and others, that the story about Andromeda and Perseus originated from some confused account of Jonah and the whale which had reached the Greeks through sailors of Tarshish?

Possibly; and it is certainly curious that Pliny, after alluding to the story of Andromeda, says that M. Scaurus, among other wonderful relics, showed the bones of a wild beast brought, during his ædileship, to Rome from Joppa, a walled town of Judæa. The length was forty feet, the elevation of the ribs greater than the height of an Indian elephant, and the thickness of the skin was a foot and a half! This may well have been *a* whale, if not the identical one in whose belly Jonah passed three days. The fact, also, that in the mythical fable of Perseus and Andromeda the name Iapolis frequently occurs as that of a city connected with the same, strongly favors the original identity of the stories. But we leave all such questions to the learned. Joppa has a history not made up of fables, but alas! for the most part, written in blood. Scarcely any other town has been so often overthrown, sacked, pillaged, burned, and rebuilt. It would be tedious to enter into minute detail of these disasters, and they may be gathered from the Bible—the books of the Maccabees, Josephus, the Greek and Roman historians, Eusebius, Jerome, and others of the fathers, and from the chronicles of the Crusades in the Gesta Dei per Francos. In our day it has acquired an unhappy notoriety in connection with Bonaparte, the plague, and the poisoning of sick soldiers. I myself was held prisoner in it for forty days in 1834, while it was besieged by the mountaineers in revolt against Ibrahim Pasha. Mr. Arutîn Murad, our consul at the time, told me that the present city was then not a hundred years old. In consequence of the pirates which infested this coast during the early life of his father, Jaffa was entirely deserted, and the inhabitants retired to Ramleh and Lydd. He himself remembered when there was only a single guard-house, occupied by a few soldiers, who gave notice to the merchants in Ramleh when a ship arrived. With this agrees the account of the desolation of Tyre at the same period and from the same cause. Such facts lay open the wretched state of the country during those times of utter anarchy. When Bonaparte came along, however, Jaffa had again risen to some importance, and it has been growing ever since. Twenty-five years ago the inhabitants of city and gardens were about 6000; now there must be 15,000 at least, and commerce has increased at even a greater ratio. Several sources of prosperity account for the existence and rapid increase of Jaffa. It is the natural landing-place of pilgrims to Jerusalem, both Christians and Jews, and they have created a considerable trade. The Holy City itself has also been constantly rising in importance during the present generation. Then there are extensive soap factories, not only here, but in Ramleh, Lydd, Nablûs, and Jerusalem, much of which is exported from this port to all the cities along the coast, to Egypt, and even to Asia Minor through Tarsus. The fruit trade from Jaffa is likewise quite considerable, and lately there have been large shipments of corn to Europe. Add to this that silk is now being cultivated extensively along the River 'Aujeh, and in the gardens about the city, and the present prosperity of Jaffa is fully explained. And unless European enterprise shall hereafter construct a rail-road which will carry off those sources of wealth to some more secure harbor, Jaffa must continue to rise in importance for ages to come. The harbor, however, is very inconvenient and insecure. Vessels of any considerable burden must lie out in the open roadstead, a very uneasy berth at all times; and even a moderate wind will oblige them to slip cable and run out to sea, or seek anchorage at Haifa, sixty miles distant. The landing also is most inconvenient, and often extremely dangerous. More boats upset, and more lives are lost in the breakers at the north end of the ledge of rocks that defend the inner harbor, than any where else on this coast. I have been in imminent danger myself, with all my family in the boat, and never look without a shudder at this treacherous port, with its noisy surf tumbling over the rocks, as if on purpose to swallow up unfortunate boats. This is the *true monster* which has devoured many an Andromeda, for whose deliverance no gallant Perseus was at hand.

Jaffa is celebrated in modern times for her gardens and orchards of delicious fruit more than for any thing else. They are very extensive, flourishing, and profitable, but their very existence depends upon the fact that water to any amount can be procured in every garden, and at a moderate depth. The entire plain seems to cover a river of vast breadth, percolating through the sand en route to the sea. A thousand Persian wheels working night and day produce no sensible diminution, and this inexhaustible source of wealth underlies the whole territory of the Philistines down to Gaza at least, and probably much farther south.

276   THE LAND AND THE BOOK.

Have we any reason to believe that these Persian wheels were here in ancient days of Jewish history? I have been greatly interested in them, and they seem admirably adapted for the purpose intended—simple in construction, cheap, quickly made, soon repaired, easily worked, and they raise an immense quantity of water.

NA'URA—PERSIAN WATER-WHEEL.

Many efforts have been made to introduce pumps, but they always fail and get out of repair; and as there is no one able to mend them, they are thrown aside, and the gardener returns to his *na'ura*. The whole of this machinery is quickly enumerated and described. A wide cog-wheel is carried round horizontally by a mule with a *sweep*. This turns a larger one perpendicularly, which is directly above the mouth of the well. Over this revolve two rough hawsers, or thick ropes, made of twigs and branches twisted together, and upon them are fastened small jars or wooden buckets. One side descends while the other rises, carrying the small buckets with them; those descending empty, those ascending full, and as they pass over the top they discharge into a trough which conveys the water to the cistern. The length of these hawsers and the number of the buckets depend, of course, upon the depth of the well, for the buckets are fastened on the hawser about two feet apart. The depth of wells in Jaffa varies from ten to forty feet. If the mule turns the wheel rapidly, which he rarely does, a bucket with about two gallons of water will be carried over the top of it, and be discharged into the trough every second; and it must be a good pump that will steadily do as much. The hawser is made of twigs, generally of myrtle branches, not merely because it is cheap and easily plaited by the gardener himself, but because its extreme roughness prevents it from *slipping* on the wheel, as an ordinary rope would do, and thus fail to carry up the loaded buckets.

There are other kinds of water-wheels in this country. The shadûf, so conspicuous on the Nile, is nowhere to be seen in Palestine, but the well-sweep and bucket are used in many places; and I once saw an Egyptian working an

SHADÛF.

apparatus much like the shadûf on the shore of the lake a little north of the city of Tiberias.

Another apparatus is common in this land of Philistia, which I have also seen on the plains of Central Syria. A large buffalo skin is so attached to cords that, when let down into the well, it opens and is instantly filled, and, being drawn up, it closes so as to retain the water. The rope by which it is hoisted to the top works over a wheel, and is drawn by oxen, mules, or camels, that walk directly from the well to the length of the rope, and then return, only to repeat the operation until a sufficient quantity of water is raised. This also is a very successful mode of drawing water.

The wheel and bucket (of different sorts and sizes) is an apparatus much used where the water is near the surface, and also along rapid rivers. For shallow wells it is merely a wheel, whose diameter equals the desired elevation of the water. The *rim* of this wheel is large, hollow, and divided into compartments answering the place of *buckets*. A hole near the top of each *bucket* allows it to fill, as that part of the rim, in revolving, dips under the water. This, of course, will be discharged when the *bucket* begins to descend, and thus a constant succession of streams falls into the cistern. The wheel itself is turned by oxen or mules.

This system of wheels is seen on a grand scale at Hums Hamath, and all along the Orontes. The wheels there are of enormous size. The diameter of some of those at Hamath is eighty or ninety feet. The great advantage of this apparatus is that it is driven by the river itself. Small *paddles* are attached to the rim, and the stream is turned upon them by a low dam with sufficient force to carry the huge wheel around with all its load of ascending buckets. There is, perhaps, no hydraulic machinery in the world by which so much water is raised to so great an elevation at so small an expense. Certainly I have seen none half so picturesque or so musical. These wheels, with their enormous loads, slowly revolve on their groaning axles, and all day and all night each one sings a different tune, with every imaginable variation of tone—sobs, sighs, shrieks, and groans—loud, louder, loudest, down to the bottom of the gamut—a concert wholly unique and half infernal in the night, which, heard once, will never be forgotten.

THE NA'URA, OR WATER-WHEEL, AT HAMATH.

To what does Moses refer in Deuteronomy xi. 10? For the land whither thou goest in to possess it is not as the land of Egypt from whence ye came out, where thou sowedst thy seed, and wateredst it with thy foot as a garden of herbs.

The reference, perhaps, is to the manner of conducting the water about from plant to plant, and from furrow to furrow, in irrigating a garden of herbs. I have often watched the gardener at this fatiguing and unhealthy work. When one place is sufficiently saturated, he pushes aside the sandy soil between it and the next furrow with his foot, and thus continues to do until all are watered. He is thus knee-deep in mud, and many are the diseases generated by this slavish work.

Or the reference may be to certain kinds of hydraulic machines which were turned by the feet. I have seen small water-wheels, on the plain of Acre and elsewhere, which were thus worked, and it appeared to me to be very tedious and toilsome, and, if the whole country had to be irrigated by such a process, it would require a nation of slaves like the Hebrews, and taskmasters like the Egyptians to make it succeed. Whatever may have been the meaning of Moses, the Hebrews, no doubt, had learned by bitter experience what it was to *water with the foot*, and this would add great force to the allusion, and render doubly precious the goodly land which drank of the rain of heaven, and required no such drudgery to make it fruitful.

The fruits of Jaffa are the same as those of Sidon, but with certain variations in their character. Sidon has the best bananas, Jaffa furnishes the best pomegranates. The oranges of Sidon are more juicy and of a richer flavor than those of Jaffa; but the latter hang on the trees much later, and will bear to be shipped to distant regions. They are therefore more valuable to the producer. It is here only that you see in perfection fragrant blossoms encircling golden fruit. In March and April these Jaffa gardens are indeed enchanting. The air is overloaded with the mingled spicery of orange, lemon, apple, apricot, quince, plum, and china trees in blossom. The people then frequent the groves, sit on mats beneath their grateful shade, sip coffee, smoke the argela, sing, converse, or sleep, as best suits their individual idiosyncrasies, till evening, when they slowly return to their homes in the city. To us of the restless West, this way of making *kaif* soon wearies by its slumberous monotony, but it is elysium to the Arabs.

Are these orchards remunerative in a pecuniary point of view?

I am informed that they yield ten per cent. on the capital invested, clear of all expense. Our friend Murad tells me that a *biarah* (the technical name of a watered garden) which costs 100,000 piastres will produce annually 15,000; but 5000 of this must be expended in irrigation, plowing, planting, and manuring. This allows the proprietor 10,000 piastres, which is a very fair percentage on capital invested in agricultural pursuits.

I have been strolling along the streets, or rather *street* of Jaffa, for there seems to be but one, and a more crowded thoroughfare I never saw. I had to force my way through the motley crowd of busy citizens, wild Arabs, foreign pilgrims, camels, mules, horses, and donkeys. Then what a strange rabble outside the gate, noisy, quarrelsome, ragged, and filthy! Many are blind, or at least have some painful defect about their eyes, and some are leprous. The peasants hereabout must be very poor, to judge by their rags and squalid appearance. I was reminded of Dorcas and the widows around Peter exhibiting the *coats* and garments which that benevolent lady had made, and I devoutly hoped she might be raised again, at least in spirit, for there is need of a dozen Dorcas societies in Jaffa at the present time.

Did you find her house? No! Well, our consul discovered *her grave* in one of his gardens, and gave it to the Armenian convent of Jerusalem. I examined the sarcophagus in its original bed, and there was this *negative* evidence in favor of Tabitha that there was no counter claim whatever. If not Tabitha's, whose tomb was it, pray?

Though not so fortunate as you, I was taken to the house where *Simon the tanner* resided. It is certainly by the seaside, and that is something, but then so is all Jaffa. A stout earthquake might shake half of it into the sea.

If Simon lived near his business, his house was probably on the shore *south of the city*, where the *tanneries* now are located, and most likely were in Peter's day. These manufacturing establishments are generally removed to a distance beyond the walls, and with good reason, for they are extremely offensive, as well as prejudicial to health. But there is no reason to suppose that Simon's *dwelling-house* was near his tannery, and it *may* have occupied the identical site now assigned to it.

I have been out on the shore again, examining a native manufactory of pottery, and was delighted to find the whole

282 THE LAND AND THE BOOK.

Biblical apparatus complete, and in full operation. There was the potter sitting at his "frame," and turning the

THE POTTER AND WHEEL.

"wheel" with his foot. He had a heap of the prepared clay near him, and a pan of water by his side. Taking a lump in his hand, he placed it on the top of the wheel (which revolves horizontally), and smoothed it into a low cone, like the upper end of a sugar-loaf; then thrusting his thumb into the top of it, he opened a hole down through the centre, and this he constantly widened by pressing the edges of the revolving cone between his hands. As it enlarged and became thinner, he gave it whatever shape he pleased with the utmost ease and expedition. This, I suppose, is the exact point of those Biblical comparisons between the human and the Divine Potter: O house of Israel, can not I do with you as this potter? saith the Lord. Behold, as the clay is in the potter's hand, so are ye in my hand, saith the Lord.[1] And the same idea is found in many other passages. When Jeremiah was watching the potter, the vessel was marred in his hand, and so he made it again another vessel as seemed good to the potter to make it.[2] I had to wait a long time for that, but it happened at last. From some defect in the clay, or because he had taken too little, the potter suddenly changed his mind, crushed his growing jar instantly into a shapeless mass of mud, and beginning anew, fashioned it into a totally different vessel. This idea Paul has expounded, and employed in the ninth chapter of the Romans, to soften some of those things which Peter says are hard to be understood: Shall the thing formed say to him that formed it, Why hast thou made me thus? Has not the potter power over the same lump to make one vessel to honor and another to dishonor?[3] Certainly he has, and I saw him do it, but I did not see thereby much farther into the great mystery which the apostle was illustrating. That, I fear, will ever remain among the "hard things" which the unlearned and unstable will wrest unto their own destruction.[4]

It is evident, from numerous expressions in the Bible, that the potter's vessel was the synonym of utter fragility; and to say that the wicked should be broken to pieces as a potter's vessel was to threaten the most ruinous destruction. In this day of glass and other fragile fabrics, and of strong stone pottery, we should hardly have adopted this language.

Perhaps not; but for this country it is still as appropriate and forcible as ever. Arab jars are so thin and frail that they are literally "dashed to shivers" by the slightest

[1] Jer. xviii. 6.
[2] Jer. xviii. 4.
[3] Rom. ix. 20, 21.
[4] 2 Pet. iii. 16.

stroke. Water-jars are often broken by merely putting them down upon the floor, and nothing is more common than for the servant to return from the fountain empty-handed, having had all his jars smashed to atoms by some irregular behavior of his donkey.

To what does Isaiah refer in the 14th verse of the 30th chapter, where he says, He shall break it as the breaking of the potter's vessel that is broken in pieces. He shall not spare; so that there shall not be found in the bursting of it a sherd to take fire from the hearth, or to take water withal out of the pit?

Your inquiry refers, I suppose, to the *sherd to take fire from the hearth*, or to *take water out of the pit*. This last you must have seen many times during our rambles. It is very common to find at the spring or the "pit" pieces of broken jars, to be used as ladles, either to drink from or to fill with; and bits of fractured jars are preserved for this purpose. But the destruction mentioned by Isaiah was to be so complete that there would not be a piece left large enough for that. The other allusion in this passage you may not have noticed, but I have a hundred times and more. Take your stand near any of the public ovens in Sidon (or here in Jaffa, I presume) in the evening, and you will see the children of the poor coming with "sherds" of pottery in their hands, into which the baker pours a small quantity of hot embers and a few coals with which to warm up their evening meal. Isaiah's vessels, however, were to be broken into such small bits that there would not be a sherd of sufficient size to carry away a few embers from the hearth. These comparisons are exceedingly expressive where the actions referred to are of constant occurrence, as they are in all our cities to this present day.

The only building about Jaffa that has the slightest claims to even Saracenic beauty is the fountain near the gate. This is really striking; and its surrounding courts furnish admirable specimens of Arab countenances and costumes for the pencil of the artist and the study of the phrenologist. I rarely pass out of the city without turning aside there to

FOUNTAIN IN JAFFA.

taste its cool water, and amuse myself with the ever-shifting scene.

Did you not also notice the "void space" about Jaffa's only gate, and the crowds of people that always gather there in the afternoon? I have seen both the governor and the kady, with their suites, sitting there, decreeing and executing judgment precisely as such things are spoken of in the Bible. As the city is surrounded by a wall and ditch, and has but this one gate, all must go in and out through it, and hence the great crowd that chokes up the passage, and hence, too, it happens that there is scarcely an allusion in the Bible to matters transacted "in the gate" but what you may see enacted every day about this one of Jaffa.

April 13*th*. I am quite satisfied with Jaffa, and it is a relief to get beyond this sea of green trees into open plain. How many hours' ride have we before us to-day?

That depends upon the rate of travel. It is about three hours to the main source of the 'Aujeh at Er Ras, nearly the same distance back to Lydd, and three quarters of an hour farther to Ramleh, where we are to find our tent.

This is truly a magnificent plain, much larger than those of Tyre, Acre, or even Esdraelon.

In its whole extent it certainly is the largest on the west side of the Jordan, for it includes the entire territory of the Philistines. Far from being a flat, dead level, it is, like Esdraelon, agreeably varied by long swells, growing into sandy ridges, and even rocky tells and hills, which afford sightly positions for villages. Of these there are more than in other plains, more populous also, and surrounded often by olive and fruit orchards, which impart an air of cheerfulness not seen elsewhere in Palestine. Yonder, on the plain to the southeast of us, is a beautiful mirage. This optical illusion is often so perfect that even the experienced traveler finds it difficult to believe that he is not approaching an actual lake of transparent water. Dr. Wilson tells us that the name for mirage in Sanscrit means "the thirst of the antelope," and nothing could be more poetical. I once gave chase to a flock of gazelles on the plain of Tireh, southeast of Aleppo. The day was intensely hot, and the antelopes made direct toward a vast mirage, which covered the whole eastern horizon. To me they seemed to be literally leaping through the water, and I could see their figures *below* the surface, and *reversed*, with the utmost distinctness. No wonder *they* were deceived, for even their pursuers were utterly confounded. But the pursuit of a mirage is like chasing the rainbow, which retreats as you advance, and can never be overtaken. The Arab name is *serab*, and it is doubtless to this deceitful phenomenon that Isaiah refers,[1] where the promise is that this *serab* shall become a real lake. Our translators have missed the exact meaning of this most emphatic figure. *Serab* is not "parched ground," but a simmering, tantalizing phantom of a lake. Sale, in his Koran, chapter xxiv., translates serab by *vapor:* "The works of unbelievers are like the *vapor serab* in a plain which the thirsty thinketh to be water, until, when he cometh thereto, he findeth it nothing." Mohammed meant the mirage, and gave the proper name for it.

The peasants of Sharon differ strikingly from those in the north. All these around us appear to me to be of Egyptian origin. Do you suppose that there is sufficient of the old Philistine blood in their veins to account for their peculiar physiognomy?

There is enough of the Egypto-African about them to explain all peculiarities of color, contour, and character. I hold that the Philistines came from the neighboring coast of Africa, perhaps from Lower Egypt, though Josephus seems to place Caphtor, their ancient home, higher up the valley of the Nile. There is much plausibility in the theory which identifies the shepherd kings who conquered Lower Egypt about the time of Abraham with the Philistines. They may have been a great roving race of Bedawîn until the time of that conquest. By remaining masters of that highly enlightened people for so many generations, they acquired much of their civilization; and when finally expelled, they came north into Palestine, drove the original in-

[1] Isaiah xxxv. 7.

habitants from the coast and the great plain of Sharon, and there built their cities, carried on agriculture and commerce, and became a powerful confederacy, quite able to protect themselves from their neighbors. This seems to me best to agree with the various notices of them found in the Bible, in the fragments of Manetho, the history of Josephus, and with all other hints which can be gathered up from ancient authors, the traditions of nations, and the architectural indications derived from the monuments which still exist. I can not think that the Philistines emigrated originally from Crete, or from Cappadocia, nor even from Cyprus. Such theories show the skill and learning of their inventors more than they illustrate the true origin of nations. Who can believe that these islands were so overstocked with inhabitants at that *very early* age after the Deluge as to require, or even to admit such an emigration? And if they had been forcibly expelled from either of those countries, would there not have been some tradition of such a great fact in their national history?

To which of the tribes did this part of the plain belong?

The border over against Jaffa was assigned to Dan, and Ephraim was north of it. The 'Aujeh *may* have been the boundary betwixt them. The Jews do not seem to have obtained possession of this neighborhood, at least not until the time of David. There, to the south of us, on the road from Jaffa to Lydd, is Beit Dujan, the house of Dagon, which was probably held by the Philistines, and named from their famous god.

Within the last fifteen years certain persons from Beirût planted along this fertile valley of the 'Aujeh large mulberry orchards, which are succeeding well, and the cultivation of silk is extending rapidly to many other parts of this plain. The attempt was made to introduce this valuable crop many years ago, but for some reason or other failed. The fountains here at the *Ras* rise low in the earth, and the engineers of Ibrahim Pasha decided that the water could not be carried to Jaffa at a sufficient elevation to irrigate the gardens, and the project was therefore abandoned. If it could be achieved, such a canal would relieve the farmers from a very large part of the expense of cultivating their orchards, and would irrigate them much more thoroughly. I think it by no means fully ascertained that the water could not be elevated at this great source, as it is at Ras el 'Ain, near Tyre, and at other places, by building strong cisterns. They would, of course, be very large and expensive; but then the supply of water, greater than even that near Tyre, would be invaluable, and convert the whole of Sharon into a paradise. Let us ride up to that mosque, and take a bird's-eye view of the country. About an hour to the north is Jiljulieh, probably the site of that Gilgal whose king is called king of the nations in Joshua (xii. 23). If this is the Gilgal of the Onomasticon, there seems to be a mistake of *south* for *north* in that invaluable work, because Gilgal is placed six Roman miles north of Antipatris, whereas it is that much south of it. The latter place, now called Kefr Saba, is seen beyond it on the edge of the plain.

It is useless to endeavor to remember these non-historic names which our guide is rattling off at such a rate, so we will turn our horses southward, and pursue the regular old Roman road toward Lydd. It was along this route, doubtless, that Paul was brought by the soldiers who guarded him to Cæsarea. Here we have the village Renthieh before us, and, as Dr. Robinson remarks, it is sufficiently like Arimathea to be assumed as the site of that place; and from what Jerome says, it seems to me quite probable that this was realy the city of that honorable counselor "which also waited for the kingdom of God, who went in boldly unto Pilate and craved the body of Jesus."[1]

The map of Dr. Robinson has some mistakes in this region which deserve to be corrected. The situation of Lydd is correctly laid down with respect to Jaffa and Ramleh, but Kubab is where Beit Dujan should be, and Safuriyeh is too near Lydd. Kubab is between Ramleh and Latron; Amwas (Emmaus, Nicopolis) is half an hour *north*, not south of Latron. On the north of Beit Dujan is a village called Yafa,

[1] Mark xv. 43.

and south of Safuriyeh, a little off the road to Ramleh, is Sarafend, the third of the name between this and Sidon. We are now approaching the orchards of Lydd, that village where Peter was when summoned to Jaffa on account of the death of Dorcas. Its greatest celebrity, however, is derived from St. George, who is said to have been both born and buried there. Dr. Robinson has given an excellent description of the church as its ruins now are, and a rapid sketch of the long and somewhat eventful history of the city. No

CHURCH OF ST. GEORGE.

one will examine the remains of the church without being impressed with a certain air of grandeur which it wears. The arch of the south aisle is particularly fine and striking. The edifice is at the southwest corner of the village, and it seems always to have been outside the ancient city or on its wall. It was a little more than seventy feet wide, and one hundred long, though it is impossible to get the exact length on account of a mosque which is built on the corner of it. The material is a pale yellow rock, cut from quarries on the road to Jerusalem. It takes a good polish, and is very hard and durable.

Lydd is a flourishing village of some two thousand inhabitants, imbosomed in noble orchards of olive, fig, pomegranate, mulberry, sycamore, and other trees, and surrounded every way by a very fertile neighborhood. The inhabitants are evidently industrious and thriving, and the whole country between this and Ramleh is fast being filled up with their flourishing orchards. Rarely have I beheld a rural scene more delightful than this presented in early harvest, when I rode from Ramleh hither through the fields on the east of the common path. A thousand reapers, gleaners, and carriers were abroad and busy when the morning sun shot his first rays down through the olive-trees upon the animated groups. The wheat and barley grow among the olive-trees, which half hid, half revealed the merry harvesters—men, women, and children—the first reaping, the second gleaning and guiding the loaded camels, and the children at play, or watching the flocks and herds, which were allowed to follow the *gleaners.*, But no description can reproduce such a tableau. It must be seen, heard, and enjoyed to be appreciated.

Lydd, like most other towns in this country, has seen better days, and that, too, in times not very remote., There are remains of large and well-constructed buildings mingled in with the modern huts, and several extensive soap factories are now also deserted and falling to decay. These times of recent prosperity were probably when Jaffa was abandoned on account of the pirates, for in those days the trade of Syria and Palestine was carried on over land. Large caravans came from Aleppo through the Bŭk'âh, and down Wady et Teim to Khan Minieh; from Bagdad and Damascus across the Jaulan, by Jisr Benat Yacobe, to the same place; and from the Hauran by Beisan and Zer'in. All these lines, meeting near Lejjun, passed down by Antipatris to this place, and thence, by Ramleh and Gaza, to Egypt. That was the time when the long lines of khans, *caravanserais*, and castles were needed and maintained. But no sooner did the sea, freed from pirates, offer a cheaper conveyance, than this entire system was abandoned. Commerce sought the nearest ports along the coast, and was thence shipped to its destination. Hence all these khans have gone to ruin, and those great highways are deserted. Many other towns besides Lydd and Ramleh have lost by this change of route, and the cities on the coast have gained in equal if not greater proportion.

Let us ride through the village to get a better idea of a place which has figured so largely in Jewish, Macedonian, Roman, Saracenic, Frank, Arab, and Turkish dynasties. From the earliest ages of the Church to the present hour it has been frequented by pilgrims, and during the Crusades it was specially honored on account of St. George.

This little circuit has afforded me a beautiful illustration of Scripture. Two women are sitting before the door of their house, upon a large piece of sackcloth, grinding on a

WOMEN GRINDING AT A MILL.

hand-mill. I heard the ring of this apparatus some time before I saw it, and I now understand what is meant by the preacher when he says, The sound of the grinding is low, because the grinders are few.[1] Jeremiah also saddens his picture of Israel's desolation by Nebuchadnezzar by adding that the sound of the mill-stones should cease.[2] And upon Babylon, whose king thus stilled the voice of the grinding in Jerusalem, John, with apocalyptic thunders, denounces the like desolation, The sound of a mill-stone shall be heard no more in thee.[3]

From this on southward through Philistia there are no mill-streams, and we shall not cease to hear the hum of the hand-mill at every village and Arab camp morning and evening, and often deep into the night. I like it, and go to sleep on it as a child to its mother's lullaby. It is suggestive of hot bread and a warm welcome when hungry and weary. When at work with it *two women* sit at the mill facing each other; both have hold of the handle by which the upper is turned round on the "nether" mill-stone. The one whose right hand is disengaged throws in the grain as occasion requires through the hole in the upper stone, which is called the rekkab (rider) in Arabic, as it was long ago in Hebrew. It is not correct to say that one pushes it half round, and then the other seizes the handle. This would be slow work, and would give a spasmodic motion to the stone. Both retain their hold, and pull *to*, or push *from*, as men do with the whip or cross-cut saw. The proverb of our Saviour[4] is true to life, for *women* only grind. I can not recall an instance in which men were at the mill. It is tedious, fatiguing work, and slaves, or lowest servants, are set at it.[5] From the king to the maid-servant behind the mill, therefore, embraced all, from the very highest to the very lowest inhabitants of Egypt.[6] This grinding at the mill was often imposed upon captives taken in war. Thus Samson was abused by the Philistines,[7] and, with Milton for his poet, bitterly laments his cruel lot:

"To grind in brazen fetters under task,
 Eyeless, in Gaza, at the mill with slaves."

What is the foundation for the comparison, Hard as the *nether* mill-stone?[8] Is the lower harder than the upper?

[1] Eccl. xii. 4. [2] Jer. xxv. 10. [3] Rev. xviii. 22. [4] Matt. xxiv. 41.
[5] Ex. xi. 5. [6] Is. xlvii. 2. [7] Judg. xvi. 21. [8] Job xli. 24.

Not always. They are often both of the same porous lava, brought from the Hauran; but I have seen the *nether* made of a compact sandstone, and quite thick, while the upper was of this lava, probably because, from its lightness, it is the more easily driven round with the hand.

What tree is this mingled with the olive and the almond, and loaded with a pale green berry?

That is the *tût shamy*—the Damascus mulberry. It is grown for its fruit, not for the silk-worm. Pass this way in the middle of May, and you will find these trees bending under a load of berries so exactly resembling our largest blackberries in America that you can not distinguish them from each other. There are more of these Damascus mulberry-trees here than all I have seen elsewhere in my life, and they yield their glossy black fruit more abundantly than in other places. It has a sharper acid than that of the ripe blackberry, and when eaten in large quantities is unhealthy. It is one of those fruits now found all over Palestine which is not mentioned in the Bible; and the same remark applies to the prickly-pear, which flourishes in such impenetrable thickets around these villages.

Let us incline a little to the right, pass round to the west of Ramleh, and examine that tower which overlooks the whole country. Here we cross the road from Jaffa, and you observe this large open cistern in ruins to the south of it. There are many vaulted cisterns between this and the tower, and other indications that this vicinity was once either the seat of Ramleh itself, or of some more ancient town. These cisterns may be almost of any age, and a city at this place would have them, of course. In Mohammedan times we can find an adequate cause for them in the fact that there were here large *khans* for the accommodation of the trading caravans which passed this way into Egypt.

This noble tower is generally believed to be a minaret, but the style of architecture differs from that of any minaret known to have been erected by the Moslems, at least so far as I have seen. There are a few minarets in some of the cities of Syria which resemble this, but they are in every

VIEW OF RAMLEH.

case attached to mosques which were originally Christian churches. In my opinion this tower is one of them, and was the campanile of a magnificent church. Of its age I know nothing. That there is an Arabic inscription over the entrance to the interior stairway, bearing date A.H. 710, A.D. 1310, establishes only the fact that this record was placed there at that date, for Mohammedan rulers often insert slabs with pompous inscriptions over entrances to buildings which they did not erect. There are scores of such vaunting records on castles, temples, and churches which are much older than the era of Mohammed. The nature of those ancient buildings renders this matter quite easy, and the architects of this country are so skilled in these insertions that the forgery can not readily be detected. I am inclined, therefore, to ascribe an early date to the cisterns found all through the olive orchards hereabout, and the same to the tower itself. That the Moslems did destroy Christian churches at Ramleh is certain, and in doing this it would be quite natural to leave the tower standing, to serve as a minaret to mosques, which, after their usual custom, they erected at or near the same site. These mosques, being less substantial, subsequently fell into decay, or were thrown down by earthquakes or by the Crusaders. The confused tradition of such events, mingled up with fables of various ages, have therefore, as I suppose, a foundation in fact. Dr. Robinson has a long and learned epitome of these historical and traditionary notices, and, though we may not always fully sympathize with him in his depreciation of ecclesiastical tradition, nor feel anxious to strip all these cherished sites of their sacred associations, yet we can never fail to be instructed by his learned researches.

These vaults beneath the area inclosed by the ancient buildings are in themselves, and apart from all historical questions, very remarkable. The one under the south side is about one hundred and fifty feet long, forty wide, and twenty-five deep. The roof is sustained in the centre by a row of nine square columns. The cistern on the west end is nearly seventy-five feet *square* and twenty deep, and the roof is supported by a *double row* of columns. The *third* is parallel to the *first*, which it also resembles in its details. Besides these, there are smaller vaults and cisterns, so perfect, even yet, as to hold water. The great vaults, well plastered with hard stucco, are dry, lighted from above, and may have been used as store-houses for the caravans; but if so, the case is unique, for there is no other example of the kind in Syria, and no reason can be assigned why resort should have been had to such expensive subterraneous magazines in Ramleh alone. In all other khans the magazines were built round the hollow square inclosed by the exterior walls, nor can I believe that the Moslems constructed these vast vaults for that purpose. Probably they were connected with the more ancient cathedral or convent, or both united, of which they and the tower are the only remaining monuments. But enough of this antiquarian discussion. Here lies a heavy marble slab, or, rather, square column, written over from end to end with an Arabic inscription which refers to the erection of mosques on this spot subsequent to the times of the Crusades.

Let us now enter and ascend this *campanile* by its winding stairs of one hundred and twenty-six steps. The entire height can not be much less than one hundred feet. Twenty-three years ago, after this tower had been rudely shaken by an earthquake, which cracked nearly all the houses in Ramleh, and threw down many, I ascended to see if it had been injured; but it stood precisely as before, not a rent or crack from bottom to top, and thus it has stood a hundred earthquakes uninjured. It is twenty-five feet square at the base, and diminishes by graceful offsets, dividing it into different stories, with various-shaped windows and architectural embellishments. The summit has been accommodated with a round tower and balcony, to fit it for the muezzin of the mosque, but this is obviously an anomalous addition to the original structure, and most of it has been shaken down by those earthquakes which have had no effect on the body of the tower.

At the time I speak of the whole of this country was in revolt against Ibrahim Pasha and Mohammed Aly of Egypt. I was shut up in Ramleh for many anxious days, and often came to this lofty look-out to watch the movements of the opposing forces with a heavy heart, for my family was in Jerusalem—the only Franks there, with one exception—and the city was in the hands of the rebels. After returning from one of these sad and solitary watchings, I wrote in my journal as follows: "The view from the top of the tower is inexpressibly grand. The whole plain of Sharon, from the mountains of Judæa and Samaria to the sea, and from the foot of Carmel to the sandy deserts of Philistia, lies spread out like an illuminated map. Beautiful as vast, and diversified as beautiful, the eye is fascinated, the imagination enchanted, especially when the last rays of the setting sun light up the white villages which sit or hang upon the many-shaped declivities of the mountains. Then the lengthening shadows retreat over the plain and ascend the hill-sides, while all below fades out of view under the misty and mellow haze of summer's twilight. The weary reapers return from their toil, the flocks come frisking to their folds, and the solemn hush of nature shutting up her manifold works and retiring to rest, all conspire to soothe the troubled heart into sympathetic repose. At such an hour I saw it once and again, and often lingered until the stars looked out from the deep sky, and the breezes of evening shed soft dews on the feverish land. What a paradise was here when Solomon reigned in Jerusalem, and sang of the 'roses of Sharon!' Better still will it be when He that is greater than Solomon shall sit on the throne of David his father, for in his days shall the righteous flourish and abundance of peace so long as the morn endureth. The mountains shall bring peace to the people, and the little hills by righteousness.[1]

> 'Fly swifter round, ye wheels of time,
> And bring the promised day.'"

Lovely Sharon, good-night! our tent awaits us at the Birkeh on the eastern side of the village.

Is there reason to believe that Ramleh is the Arimathea of Joseph?

Some understand Jerome to mean this place when he speaks of Arimathea as being near to Diospolis—that is, Lydd; but he may have had in mind Renthieh, on the north of Lydd. The tradition which connects Joseph with this place, however, is quite ancient, confused, and doubtful, though it may be. Dr. Robinson discusses the question with his usual learning, and with his usual distrust of tradition he settles it against Ramleh. There is too little resemblance between the names of Ramleh—*sand*—and Arimathea, derived from a root which means *high*, and is applied to towns on elevated sites, to build any thing upon the mere name; but those who have faith in ecclesiastical tradition will scarcely give up Ramleh on this account. The assertion of Abu el Fida that *Ramleh* as it now is was

[1] Ps. lxxii. 3, 7.

built after Mohammed, scarcely touches the question, for the Mohammedans rarely built entirely *de novo*, and I am quite sure they did not here. The old city *might* have been called Ramathaim; and the form of the word, not being according to Arab taste and idiom, was changed to Ramleh for their new town. I am unable to decide the question, because I can not be certain that both Eusebius and Jerome do not speak of this as the Arimathea of Joseph. They must have had better opportunities for correct information than we can procure, and if they locate it here I shall not dispute their decision.

Ramleh is a larger town than Lydd, and has now about three thousand five hundred inhabitants, a greater proportion of whom are Christians than in any other place on this plain. There are many good houses, several churches and convents for pilgrims, and some large well-built soap factories. An immense old church, once dedicated to St. John, is now the chief mosque of the place. It always fills me with indignation to see these ancient edifices thus perverted, and I believe it would be an act of real justice if the Christian nations would compel the restitution of this, and all others like it, to the native Christians. Most of the European nations have consular agents here, and there is more wealth and a greater approximation to the style and manners of a city than in other towns of the same size in Palestine. This is doubtless owing to constant intercourse with pilgrims and European travelers.

XXXV. RAMLEH TO ASHDOD.

April 14th.

A ramble through the streets this morning has not increased my respect for Ramleh. I got bewildered among narrow crooked lanes which lead nowhere in particular; and with dogs, hairless and scabby, had a regular battle, until a one-eyed man kindly drove them away, and guided me out of the perplexing labyrinth. Are these large mounds of gray rubbish the ashes of soap factories?

They are, and they speak of an extensive business continued through many centuries. You will see similar heaps at Gaza, Jerusalem, and many other places, but by far the largest are at Edlip; and there, too, are the most extensive olive orchards in the country. I can not account for these immense hills of ashes, except on the supposition that the *kŭly* (alkali) used in the manufacture of soap has been very impure, leaving a large residuum to be cast out upon these heaps.

From whence is this *kŭly*, and by what process is it manufactured?

In Syria it is obtained mostly from the Arabs of the frontier deserts, where it is made by burning the *glasswort* and other saliferous plants that grow on those arid plains. The *kŭly* resembles in appearance cakes of coarse salt, and it is generally adulterated with sand, earth, and ashes, which makes the residuum very large, and from it these vast *tells* of rubbish gradually accumulate around the places where soap is manufactured. The growth of these mounds, however, is so slow that it must have taken hundreds, if not thousands of years for those at Edlip to reach their present enormous size. The mineral alkali, called *natron*, found in Egypt, and employed from remotest antiquity for various purposes besides making soap, as we learn from Herodotus and other old authors, is not used in this country.

Both kinds of alkali are mentioned, I suppose, in the Bible. Jeremiah says of the degenerate Jews of his day, Though thou wash thee with *nitre*, and take thee much soap, yet thine iniquity is marked before me, saith the Lord God.[1] This *borith*, here translated soap, was doubtless some cleansing preparation of vegetable alkali, and the *nitre* was the mineral *natron* of Egypt. Malachi also speaks of "fullers' soap,"[2] where the same word *borith* is used. Solomon was acquainted with the natron of Egypt, and also with the fact that it effervesced violently when brought into contact with vinegar; and he says that this is like singing songs to a heavy heart[3]—that is, it throws the heavy heart into a sour, angry fermentation, as when *natron* is cast into a pot of vinegar. The wise king's own heart seems to have been in such an effervescing state when he indited his "Ecclesiastecal" complaints and confessions.

In one respect, at least, these ashes are very mischievous. They not only add to the heat of summer, which renders Ramleh almost uninhabitable, but on the occurrence of the slightest wind the air is filled with a fine pungent dust which is very injurious to the eyes. I once walked the streets counting all that were either blind or had defective eyes, and it amounted to about one half of the *male* population. The women I could not count, for they are more rigidly veiled in Ramleh than in any other town in the country. I never saw the faces of those in whose house I resided for a month. Whenever I had occasion to go out or come in, a servant, or one of the sons, always preceded me, calling out, *Et tarîûk, et tarîûk—the way! the way!* when the women fled and concealed themselves in their own apartments. But we must leave Ramleh, and I fear we shall encounter a sirocco to-day, for there are premonitory puffs of hot air which rarely deceive.

The muleteers will go directly to Ashdod, while we make a detour, to gain a better knowledge of the plain, and also to visit Jamnia, which lies to the west of the regular road from Ramleh. We will ride through these olive orchards to an elevated point in the ridge, which commands a prospect of great rural beauty and rich historic interest. On the east you can trace the road from Lydd to Jerusalem, far up

[1] Jer. ii. 22. [2] Mal. iii. 2. [3] Prov. xxv. 20.

the mountain toward Bethhoron; and to the southeast the path that goes by Emmaus quite to Latron, at the entrance into Wady 'Aly. As we do not take either of these roads to the Holy City, this is the spot from which to point out to you what there is to be seen along them. I have been over them so often that every salient rock and stunted bush is perfectly familiar to me. From Lydd the path leads down into a wady, which it partly follows for three miles, to a place called Jimzû, no doubt the Gimzo reconquered by the Philistines, with other cities in the low country, in the days of Ahaz.[1] Neby Danyāl—Prophet Daniel—is some two miles in this direction, and on the north of Jimzû is a large tell covered with rubbish, and now named Daheriyeh or Duheîry. The road keeps up a valley north of Jimzû, which I heard called Wady Zicherîyeh—Zechariah—and in it are some remarkable caverns and old foundations, marking an ancient site, which also bears the name of this prophet. The extensive quarries along this wady were probably made by the builders of Lydd and Ramleh. Bufilîya lies over the ridge to the south, in a wady called Suleiman, along which there is a road leading to Jîb. Above Zicherîyeh is Shilta, a ruin on the left, and east of it another called Kŭrakûr. Half an hour farther is an extensive site called Keferrût, possibly the Chephirah of the Gibeonites who deceived Joshua.[2] There is a willy there called Khŭrîyeh. Sŭffah is a village one mile southeast of Keferrût, and in about an hour more Beit Ur et Tahta, a site manifestly ancient, and admitted on all hands to be the lower Bethhoron, so often mentioned in the Bible. I have always found the Moslems there particularly austere and uncivil. It is just an hour from this to the upper Beit Ur—heavy climbing over extremely rough road. This place we shall visit from Jerusalem, and may now return by a track leading southwest into a broad wady called Merj Ibn Omeir, on the south side of which is situated Yalo, the modern representative of that Ajalon over which Joshua commanded the moon to stand still on that memorable day when his victorious army

---

[1] 2 Chron. xxviii. 18.   [2] Josh. ix. 17.

WELL NEAR ENNADA.

VALLEY OF AJALON—EMMAUS. 307

pursued the routed host of the five kings. They evidently fled from Gibeon down by the upper Bethhoron to the lower, and then southward into this Merj Ibn Omeir. All these places are still found, and in exact agreement with the account of that great victory recorded in the tenth chapter of Joshua. The water from this Merj, *when it flows at all*, runs down a narrow channel, passes off to the *north*west along Wady Atallah, east of Lydd, and thence across the great plain to the 'Aujeh. Wady 'Aly bends round Latron, and then *northward* below Kebab to the same valley east of Lydd, and not *southwest* toward Ekron, as in most maps of this region, in which, also, Amwas is placed *south* of Latron, whereas its true position is north.

What a nest of Biblical sites are in view! but that which interests me most is Amwas. Do you suppose it is the site of the Emmaus toward which the two disciples were pursuing their sad walk when the risen Saviour joined them, and in which he was made known to them by the breaking of bread?

So thought Eusebius and Jerome, but there are almost insurmountable objections against it. Luke says it was *threescore* furlongs from Jerusalem,[1] and this site is twice that distance as the crow flies. Besides, if we were at liberty to correct the text, as has been suggested, and make it read one hundred and sixty furlongs instead of sixty, that might bring you to Amwas, but how were the disciples to get back to Jerusalem that same night, before the people had retired to sleep, as we are told expressly that they did?[2] "The day was far spent" when the three reached Emmaus. They had their meal to get ready, and it was certainly evening when they sat down to meat. They could not, therefore, have started back before dark, and it is six hours hard walking over rough mountains from this Emmaus to Jerusalem. If this had been the place, they could not have reached home until after midnight. This is certainly possible, but not probable, and therefore I can not believe that we have before us the scene of that interesting conversation and miracle re-

[1] Luke xxiv. 13.   [2] Luke xxiv. 33.

corded in the 24th chapter of Luke. This is yet to be found somewhere much nearer the Holy City, and Josephus states[1] that Cæsar, after the destruction of Jerusalem, gave Emmaus, a village *sixty* furlongs from the city, to eight hundred of his soldiers, whom he had dismissed from his army. This I believe to be identical with the Emmaus of Luke.

I regard with respect the tradition that the Emmaus of Luke is Kuryet el 'Ainub, which Dr. Robinson identifies with Kirjath Jearim. It is the right distance from Jerusalem, and it would be a very appropriate situation to plant a colony of disbanded troops, for they would command the road from the sea-board to Jerusalem. The two things do not clash, for Kuryet el 'Ainub *may* be both Kirjath Jearim and Emmaus, and it renders the place more interesting to find it not only the resting-place of the *ark*, but, long after, of *Him* who was infinitely greater than the ark.

But, though this is not the Emmaus of Luke, it early became celebrated, and there are still the remains of a church there, and other indications of antiquity. It was called Nicopolis by Julius Africanus, who caused it to be rebuilt early in the third century, and under this name it is often mentioned by Eusebius, Jerome, and other early writers. It also figures largely in the Crusades, as does also Beit Nuba, that village a short distance north of it, which marks the end of Richard the Lion-hearted's wild career in this country. He loitered weeks there, and then returned crestfallen to Ramlch. There are fine fountains below Emmaus, which Pliny mentions;[2] and good water in this neighborhood is most acceptable even in spring, as the pilgrims have abundant reason to remember, for the road is lined with boys and girls with jars of it, which they sell at exorbitant prices.

Where is Modin, so celebrated in the Maccabees and in Josephus?

The site has not yet been discovered, but I suspect that it is identical with Latron, seated about two miles south of Amwas, upon a high hill directly in front of the entrance

[1] Wars, vii. 6, 6.   [2] Book vi. 14.

into Wady 'Aly. This site seems best to agree with all the notices of Modin which we have; and the *pyramids*, built there by the Maccabean family, could well be seen from the sea, as they are said to have been; and the large ruins now covering the hill at Latron require something of the kind to account for them. It was a strong castle, and an important station during the Crusades, for which its position is admirably adapted, for it completely commands the entrance into Wady 'Aly, up which is the ordinary road to Jerusalem. The monks say that this Latron was the city of the penitent thief, whom they call Disma, and who, according to their legends, used to rob pilgrims and travelers in Wady 'Aly. Hence the name of the place, Latron or Ladrone—robber.

Wady 'Aly is the easiest route to Jerusalem, but there is neither water nor any monument of antiquity in it except the tomb of the Imam 'Aly, below Saris, from which the valley takes its name. After gaining the top of the mountain—three good hours from Latron—you descend to Kuryet el 'Ainub, which, for the last half century, has had a bad notoriety as the seat of the mountain robber Abu Gush. We shall visit that neighborhood from the Holy City, and now let us turn westward to Yebna. This little village to the south, with its pretty gardens, is 'Akir, no doubt the modern heir of the celebrated Ekron. Josephus says the god of Ekron was a fly, and I certainly found plenty of them there when I visited it two years ago. From this place the ark of God was sent back, and the unbroken and unguided kine took the direct road across the plain to Bethshemesh, which city was near the mouth of Wady Sûrar, behind that long rocky spur which puts down from the mountains south of Latron.[1] There is *'Ain* es Shems at the present day, and somewhere near it was the city to which came the cart with its mysterious burden. We can now easily understand how the lords of the Philistines could follow until they saw it taken possession of by the Bethshemites, and then return the same day to Ekron. It might

[1] 1 Sam. vi. 10-12.

be said by those ignorant of the country that, the whole distance being a level plain, there was no great miracle needed to secure the safe transmission of the ark over this comparatively short distance; but let them make a similar experiment, and stake their skepticism upon its success, if they have the courage to do so, or let them even try to reach 'Ain es Shems themselves without a guide, and see how they will succeed.

My thoughts have often followed Philip and the eunuch in their ride across this plain; and I have wished to know what sort of country they passed through?

If the eunuch came down Wady 'Aly from Jerusalem, he would follow nearly the same track from Latron that I once took, and this is now regarded as the easiest and safest route. If he came by Wady Sûrar, entering the plain near Bethshemesh, he would cross it farther south; and if he descended by Eluetheropolis, his route would be still nearer the southern desert. Then another question is whether Philip set out from Samaria or from Jerusalem; most probably from Samaria, as I think, for he appears to have been in that city when he received the command to go.[1] He would then have met the chariot somewhere southwest of Latron. There is a fine stream of water, called Murŭbbah, deep enough even in June to satisfy the utmost wishes of our Baptist friends. This Murŭbbah is merely a local name for the great Wady Sûrar, given to it on account of copious fountains which supply it with water during summer. Above them the wady was entirely dry in the month of April, at which time the transaction took place, I suppose. I know of no brook on the route from Bethshemesh to Gaza, but there may be one. Dr. Robinson found water in the wady below Tell el Hâsy, which is midway between Beit Jibrîn and Gaza, and on the direct line between them. This route would lead them near, if not quite into the desert. The same, however, might have been true of either of the routes, out in the centre of the plain, as it is at this day. Some, perhaps most people, suppose

[1] Acts viii. 5, and 25-27.

that it was Gaza which was desert, and not the country through which the road passed; and the Greek is as indefinite as the English; but Philip did not go to the city, neither was it desert or deserted at the time when the angel commanded him to take this excursion; nor do I believe it has ever been an *eremos*—desert—since the earliest days of history. It has often been sacked, plundered, and sometimes burned, and it suffered one of these reverses about thirty years after the journey of Philip; but these Oriental cities spring up from their ashes, like the phœnix, with wonderful rapidity; and I can not suppose that Gaza itself could, with any propriety, be called desert either then or at any other time from that day to this.

That Philip was found at Azotus, which is Ashdod, after the baptism of the eunuch, seems to imply that it took place not far from that city, which is rather against the idea that they followed the road from Beit Jibrîn to Gaza, since that would carry them many miles south of Ashdod.

These filmy apologies for clouds which lounge about the sky seem to act rather as condensers to concentrate the heat than as a cooling shadow. There is something extremely oppressive in this air.

We have two kinds of sirocco, one accompanied with vehement wind, which fills the air with dust and fine sand. I have often seen the whole heavens veiled in gloom with this sort of sand-cloud, through which the sun, shorn of his beams, looked like a globe of dull smouldering fire. It may have been this phenomenon which suggested that strong prophetic figure of Joel, quoted by Peter on the day of Pentecost.[1] Wonders in the heaven and in the earth; blood, and fire, and pillars of smoke; the sun shall be turned into darkness, and the moon into blood.[2] The pillars of smoke are probably those columns of sand and dust raised high in the air by local whirlwinds, which often accompany the sirocco. On the great desert of the Hauran I have seen a score of them marching with great rapidity over the plain, and they closely resemble "pillars of smoke."

[1] Joel ii. 30, 31.   [2] Acts ii. 19, 20.

The sirocco to-day is of the quiet kind, and they are often more overpowering than the others. I encountered one a year ago on my way from Lydd to Jerusalem. Just such clouds covered the sky, collecting, as these are doing, into darker groups about the tops of the mountains, and a stranger to the country would have expected rain. Pale lightnings played through the air like forked tongues of burnished steel, but there was no thunder and no wind. The heat, however, became intolerable, and I escaped from the burning highway into a dark vaulted room at the lower Bethhoron. I then fully understood what Isaiah meant when he said, Thou shalt bring down the noise of the strangers as the heat in a dry place, as the heat with the shadow of a cloud[1]—that is, as such heat brings down the noise and makes the earth quiet—a figure used by Job when he says, Thy garments are warm when he quieteth the earth by the south wind.[2] We can testify that the garments are not only warm, but *hot*. This sensation of dry hot clothes is only experienced during the siroccos, and on such a day, too, one understands the other effects mentioned by the prophet, bringing down the noise and *quieting* the earth. There is no living thing abroad to make a noise. The birds hide in thickest shades, the fowls pant under the walls with open mouth and drooping wings, the flocks and herds take shelter in caves and under great rocks, the laborers retire from the fields, and close the windows and doors of their houses, and travelers hasten, as I did, to take shelter in the first cool place they can find. No one has energy enough to make a noise, and the very air is too weak and languid to stir the pendent leaves even of the tall poplars. Such a south wind with the heat of a cloud does indeed bring down the noise and quiet the earth.

Here we are at Yebna, as the Jamnia of the classic geographers is now pronounced. Yebna, however, was the ancient Hebrew name, as appears from 2 Chron. xxvi. 6, and the Arabs have restored it to its proper place. It has always been a flourishing town, and is so still. There are

[1] Isa. xxv. 5.   [2] Job xxxvii. 17.

traces of old buildings about it, but no remains of any remarkable edifice, yet the ancient inhabitants must have had temples and idols in abundance, for when Judas Maccabeus had overthrown Gorgious here at Jamnia, he found under the coats of every one that was slain things consecrated to the idols of the Jamnites. Then every man saw that this was the cause for which they were slain.[1] Strabo says that Jamnia and its vicinity were so densely inhabited that it sent forth forty thousand armed men. Pliny mentions two Jamnias—this before us, and another on the sea-board. This last is mentioned in 2 Macc. xii. 9; and there Judas is said to have set fire to the haven and the navy, so that the light of the fire was seen at Jerusalem! The sea is behind these sandy downs about three miles distant, but the harbor has entirely disappeared.

From Yebna to Jaffa is three hours and a half. Coming this way, the road leads through gardens for more than half an hour, and then keeps along the border of these downs of white sand for nearly two hours to Wady Haneîn, in which are traces of ancient buildings at different places. The remains of old Sarafend are up this wady to the northeast, and the wady runs down to the sea on the north side of a remarkable tell called Rubîn, where is also a willy of the same name. A considerable ridge extends back eastward, and spreads out in different directions, on the southern slope of which is Kebab, and El Mughar twenty minutes east of it. Between these and Yebna is a deep valley, through the centre of which descends the brook of Wady Surar, which turns round to the northwest, and then unites with Wady Haneîn near the tell Rubîn. The ancient harbor of Yebna was at the mouth of this wady.

Yebna is pleasantly situated on this hill, which declines westward toward the sea; and there may be three thousand inhabitants, all Moslems, and all given to agriculture. Their territory is large and of surpassing fertility. Our steam plows would work wonders in the plain of Philistia, and the time must come when they, or something better, will

[1] 2 Macc. xii. 40.

314 THE LAND AND THE BOOK.

take the place of these ridiculous Arab machines; and yet, with even this imperfect mode of cultivation, the harvests of Yebna are very abundant. When I passed this way two years ago there were hundreds of men, women, and children reaping, gleaning, and carrying away the grain to their great threshing-floors. Long lines of camels, bearing on their backs burdens many times larger than themselves, were slowly converging to a point here at Yebna from every part of the plain, and the grain lay in heaps almost mountain-high.

The threshing-floors were arranged all round the town,

SUMMER THRESHING-FLOOR.

MOWREJ.

MODES OF THRESHING, SYRIAN AND EGYPTIAN. 315

and the scene was picturesque and novel even to me. The most common mode of threshing is with the ordinary slab, called *mowrej*, which is drawn over the floor by a horse or yoke of oxen, until not only the grain is shelled out, but the straw itself is ground up into chaff. To facilitate this operation, bits of rough lava are fastened into the bottom of the *mowrej*, and the driver sits or stands upon it. It is rare sport for the children to sit on these slabs, and even our own delight to get out to the *baidar*, as the floor is called, and ride round on the mowrej.

The Egyptian mowrej is a little different from this, having rollers which revolve on the grain, and the driver has a seat upon it, which is certainly more comfortable. In the

plains of Hamath I saw this machine improved by having *circular saws* attached to these rollers. It is to this instrument, I suppose, that Isaiah refers in the 41st chapter of his prophecies: Behold, I will make thee a new sharp threshing instrument *having teeth*. Thou shalt thresh the mountains, and beat them small, and shalt make the hills as chaff. Thou shalt fan them, and the winds shall carry them away, and the whirlwind shall scatter them.[1] This passage has

[1] Is. xli. 15, 16.

several allusions which we can readily understand and explain in this country. The intention of the farmer is to beat and grind down his hills of grain to chaff, and much of it is reduced to fine dust, which the wind carries away. Very little use is now made of the *fan*, but I have seen it employed to *purge the floor* of the refuse dust, which the owner throws away as useless. The references to the wind which drives off the chaff are numerous in the Bible and very forcible. The grain, as it is threshed, is heaped up in the centre of the "floor," until it frequently becomes a little mound much higher than the workmen. This is particularly the case when there is no wind for several days, for the only way adopted to separate the chaff from the wheat is to toss it up into the air, when the grain falls in one place and the chaff is carried on to another. Isaiah here speaks of the whirlwinds, and it is a curious fact that whirling currents are extremely common on the plains. They start up as if by magic or spirit influence, and rush furiously onward, swooping dust and chaff up to the clouds in their wild career.

The sacred writers speak of *treading out* the corn. Is this mode still practiced by these farmers of Philistia?

On some floors here at Yebna there was no machine of any kind, and boys rode and drove horses round on the grain, somewhat as we did in our barns when I was a boy. It was this, in part, which made the scene so peculiar. Some ran round from left to right, and others the reverse, and no one continued long in the same direction, but changed every few minutes, to keep the animals from getting dizzy.

The command of Moses not to muzzle the ox that treadeth out the corn is literally obeyed to this day by most farmers, and you often see the oxen that draw the mowrej eating from the floor as they revolve. There are niggardly peasants, however, who *do muzzle* the ox, enough to show the need of the command, and Paul intimates that there were just such in the Church in his day: Doth God take care for oxen, or saith he it altogether for our sakes? For

вадаи.

our sakes no doubt this is written, that he that ploweth should plow in hope, and he that thresheth in hope should be partaker of his hope.[1]

The Peutingerian Tables make the distance between Yebna and Ashdod to be ten miles, and we shall find it two hours and a half fair riding over the level plain. The only village that divides with Yebna the produce of this region is El Hamamy, just visible to the east of us. Here is a deep channel coming down toward the sea, with a bridge over it, for which I have no name but that of Usdûd. In the plain above it has various branches, one of which passes down by a ruin called Mukhazin, and another comes from Mesmia, two hours east of Usdûd. I hope our tent will be under the shady trees near the large ruined khan of Usdûd, on the west of the village, for there alone we shall find refuge from this persecuting wind.

There seem to be extensive orchards and large groves of sycamore about it, but the sand from the shore comes quite up to the town.

Yes; and at no distant day it will entirely overwhelm it, and Ashdod will then be nothing but a heap of barren moving sand. The site, however, is protected by these groves, which break the course of the wind, and is farther sheltered by this artificial tell, on the eastern side of which most of the houses are built. The tell was most likely the acropolis of the old city.

Hot as it is, I must take a stroll round this ancient capital of the Philistines.

As you like; but I have seen enough of it on former occasions to dispense with a farther survey in such air as this.

Well, you are soon satisfied. Did you find the marble columns of the temple of Dagon, or the grassy hill of Volney?

You may as well stop. I saw nothing ancient, and think there is nothing to be seen except a few old stone buildings stowed away among the wretched mud hovels, so as not to be easily examined. The people, too, are so rude, that I was glad to escape from their impertinent curiosity. The

[1] 1 Cor. ix. 9, 10.

village is buried beneath forests of cactus, and overshadowed by sycamores, which impart a singular aspect to the place. I saw camels drawing up water from deep wells with the Persian water-wheel. The plain eastward seems boundless, very fertile, and well cultivated. This is the extent of my discoveries; and there is more evidence of antiquity at this old khan and *mazar* than any where else about Ashdod.

You have enumerated nearly every thing that is to be seen, and we can not do better just now than discuss our dinner, which has been waiting this last half hour. And yet I would not imply that Ashdod, even in ruins, is destitute of interest. This high and ample mound, I suspect, constituted that impregnable acropolis which it took Psammetichus of Egypt *twenty-nine years* to subdue. Herodotus says this was the longest siege that any city ever sustained. Ashdod, like Jamnia, had a port, which, like that, also, has entirely disappeared. The sea is some two miles distant, and the intervening space is a desert of moving sand, which has reached the outskirts of the town. If you are anxious to see what vicissitudes this city of Dagon has passed through, and on what occasions it has played a part in the great drama of history, you can consult Joshua, and 1st Samuel, and 2d Chronicles, and Nehemiah, and the Maccabees, and Josephus, and Luke, who calls it Azotus in the eighth chapter of Acts.[1] The Greek and Roman historians and geographers often speak of it, as also Eusebius, Jerome, and other Christian fathers, under the same name. It figures likewise largely in the Crusades, and, indeed, in nearly all other wars that have ever desolated the country of the Philistines. This long and eventful story proclaims its inherent importance and the tenacity of its life; but it has finally fallen under the heavy "burden" of prophecy, and sunk to the miserable village from which you have just escaped.

You are quite correct about the eastern plain, for it is exceedingly fertile, and crowded with flourishing villages, more so than any part of Philistia. I once came from Latron

---

[1] Josh. xv. 46, 47; 1 Sam. v. vi.; 2 Chron. xxvi. 6; Acts viii. 40; Neh. xiii. 23, 24.

diagonally across the country to this place in a little more than six hours. The whole distance must be about twenty-five miles, for I rode fast. For the first hour and a half the country was diversified by alternate fat valleys and low rocky spurs from the mountains west of 'Ain es Shems. Leaving Khŭlda on a high hill a little to the right, I crossed the brook Murŭbbah—a name for this part of Wady Sûrar—and, after following down its reedy bank for a mile, I left it where it inclines to the northwest, and, riding nearly two hours farther, through an ocean of ripe wheat, came to Mesmia just as the sun set. There I pitched for the night. It is a large agricultural village, mud hovels packed together like stacks in a barn-yard, and nearly concealed by vast mounds of manure on all sides of it. During the night a dense fog settled down flat upon the face of the plain, through which you could not see ten steps, and the scene in the morning was extraordinary and highly exciting. Before it was light the village was all *a buz* like a bee-hive. Forth issued party after party, driving camels, horses, mules, donkeys, cows, sheep, goats, and even poultry before them. To every body and thing there was a separate call, and the roar and uproar were prodigious. The parties separated in all directions out into the plain, shouting for the same reason that steamers whistle, blow horns, and ring bells in foggy weather. Ere long all were lost in the dense mist, and by degrees the thousand-tongued hubbub died away in the distance. Taking a guide from Mesmia, we also set out for this Usdûd, directing our course a little north of west. It was a strange ride, for, during the gray and foggy dawn, we saw camels in the air, and "men as trees walking," and often heard all sorts of noises about us without seeing any thing. At length, a sea-breeze coming to the assistance of the sun, the fog began to rise and wheel about, now hither, now thither, in fantastic evolutions, until, at the end of an hour, we came out into the clear light of day near Yazûr. This village is seated at the south end of a high ridge, is better built, and has more trees about it than Mesmia, but is not so populous. Turning somewhat to the south of west, we came in half an hour to Bûtany es Sharkîyeh, and thence to Bûtany el Gharbîyeh, and from this last to Usdûd—two hours and a half in all from Mesmia, through as fertile a country as the sun ever shone upon.

Isaiah makes the Lord say, I will take my rest, I will consider in my dwelling like a clear heat upon herbs, and like a cloud of dew in the heat of harvest.[1] This latter comparison I have no doubt was suggested by some such cloud as this which I have described. In the morning it absolutely *reposed* upon the vast harvest-field of Philistia, lying on the corn serene and quiet as infancy asleep. I have never seen such a cloud in this country except "in the heat of harvest." To exactly what natural phenomenon the poetic prophet refers in the preceding clause is doubtful; "like a clear heat upon herbs" is scarcely intelligible in this connection. I at least have noticed nothing of this kind which could suggest the thought of repose and meditation. Nor does it improve the matter to read, "like a clear heat *after rain*," as it is in the margin. The Hebrew itself is obscure, but in the Arabic it is "like the shining light of *noonday*." This is very suggestive of retirement to some cool, quiet place of rest, and there are many references to it in other passages of the Bible. I have often been struck with the quietude of sultry noon. Neither man, nor beast, nor bird is astir. The flocks gather under shady trees, or behind walls and great rocks, and drowsily ruminate, the feeble breeze slumbers among the tree-tops, and the very shadows appear stationary and dreamy. If the allusion is to these phenomena, it is very expressive indeed.

It is during such rides that one sees life as it is in Philistia. When the fog dispersed the whole plain appeared to be dotted over with harvesting-parties, men reaping, women and children gleaning and gathering the grain into bundles, or taking care of the flocks which followed closely upon the footsteps of the gleaners. All seemed to be in good-humor, enjoying the cool air of the morning. There

[1] Isaiah xviii. 4.

was singing alone and in chorus, incessant talking, home-made jokes, and laughing long and loud.

The grain is not bound in sheaves as in America, but gathered into large bundles. Two of these, secured in a large net-work of rope, are placed a few feet apart. The camel is made to kneel down between them, the large bundles are fastened to his pack-saddle, and at a signal from the driver up rises the peaceful beast and marches off toward the threshing-floor near the village. Arrived there, the patient beast kneels down again, and is relieved of his awkward load only to repeat the same operation all day long, and for many weeks together, for the Syrian harvest extends through several months. On the plain of Philistia it commences in April and ends in June, and this not only gives ample time, but it has this great advantage, that the villagers from the mountains can assist the farmers on the plain, since their own crops are not yet ripe. I was struck with this fact when at Mesmia. Several Christians from Bethlehem, who had thus come to reap, spent the evening at my tent, and one of them explained to me the advantages derived from thus laboring on the plain. He not only received wages for his own and his wife's labor, but his children were permitted to follow after them and glean on their own account, as Boaz allowed Ruth to do in their native village.

In that ride through Philistia I saw many villages built entirely of unburned brick, made by tramping up the soil into thick mud mixed with *tibn* from the threshing-floor. It was this kind of brick which the Israelites were required to make in Egypt, and the manufacture of them is certainly the most dirty and slavish work in which the peasant engages.

It would be easy to dig through houses built of these soft bricks, as did Ezekiel when enacting the signs of captivity before the people.[1]

Or as robbers and other bad men, bent on evil errands, did in Job's day.[2] The fact is that these mud houses and

[1] Ezek. xii. 5. [2] Job xxiv. 16.

mud villages are ephemeral, insecure, and every way uncomfortable; low, filthy, and earthy, without light or ventilation, all packed together; no privacy of any kind possible; no relief from incessant noise from man, and beast, and creeping things; no shelter from a burning sun; no escape from clouds of dust; in a word, they are dens of wretchedness and endless discomfort. . The natives, however, seem insensible to these annoyances, and are measurably happy. They have also some wise and good *institutions* among them. One is the public wells, where the water is raised by *wheel and bucket-work*, called sâkîeh, at the common cost and for common use. The one near my tent at Mesmia had four stout mules allotted to it, and was kept in motion night and day. The well was one hundred and twenty feet deep, and the water was cool, sweet, and inexhaustible.

RUINS OF ASKELON.

XXXVI. ASHDOD TO GAZA.

April 15th.

Fortunately our sirocco has subsided into a soft southwest wind, and without rain, giving us a bright morning and the prospect of an agreeable day. This plain over which we have ridden from Usdûd is constantly being encroached upon by this desolating sand, along the border of which the path has led, rising occasionally over the advanced swells of the coming flood. The first village on our left was Beit Daras, the next farther out is Jûlis, eastward of which a little more than an hour is Gustiny, all of them rich agricultural towns, which sit very prettily on the rolling plain. We shall now turn off from the regular road to Gaza, which keeps more inland, and make for Askelon, by that village called Hamamy. It is about six miles from Usdûd, and, like it, seems just about to be overwhelmed by the sand. It is a thriving village, however, and has traces of a more prosperous antiquity. By the direct line over the sand-hills it is three miles to Askelon, but much farther by the regular road from Hamamy. We shall take the former, not because it is the nearest, but because there is something sadly appropriate in this approach to Philistia's capital over such swells and ridges of barren sand. The modern village is a little north of the old site, and the houses which are not made of sun-dried bricks are built out of the fragments of old Askelon. It will take us two hours to run even hastily over the ruins, and the baggage had better pass on to some sycamore-trees near a large Moslem willy on the southeast side of the city. There we will lunch and rest, for I give you warning that the ramble will be very fatiguing. We will pass down here on the north side to the shore, and there hand our horses to these boys to be taken to our lunching-ground, for it is impossible to explore the interior on horseback.

Askelon differs from the other celebrated cities of the Philistines, being seated on the sea, while Ekron, Gath, Jamnia, Ashdod, and Gaza are in the interior. It never could have had a harbor of any considerable size, however, and what once existed appears to have been filled up by Sultan Bibars of Egypt, that great scourge of mankind, and destroyer of cities in this country. The topography of this place is very peculiar. A lofty and abrupt ridge begins near the shore, runs up eastward, bends round to the south, then to the west, and finally northwest to the sea again, forming an irregular amphitheatre. On the top of this ridge ran the wall, which was defended at its salient angles by strong towers. The specimens which still exist along the southeast and west sides show that it was very high and thick, built, however, of small stones, and bound together by broken columns of granite and marble. This clearly proves that it is patchwork, and not Askelon's original rampart. These extraordinary fragments, tilted up in strange confusion along the sandy ridge, are what generally appear in the pictures of Askelon, and impart such an air of desolation to the view. The position, however, is one of the fairest along this part of the Mediterranean coast; and when the interior of this amphitheatre was crowded with splendid temples and palaces, ascending, rank above rank, from northwest to southeast, the appearance from the sea must have been very imposing. Now the whole area is planted over with orchards of the various kinds of fruit which flourish on this coast. It is especially celebrated for its apples, which are the largest and best I have ever seen in this country. When I was here in June quite a caravan started for Jerusalem loaded with them, and they would not have disgraced even an American orchard. Dr. Kitto has labored in several of his works to prove that the Hebrew word taffûah, translated apples, means citron, but I think this is one of his least happy criticisms. The Arabic word for apple is almost the same as the Hebrew, and it is as perfectly definite, to say the least, as our English word, as much as the word for grape, and just as well understood; and so is that for citron; but this is a comparatively rare fruit. Citrons are also very large, weighing several pounds each, and are so hard and indigestible that they can not be used except when made into preserves. The tree is small, slender, and must be propped up, or the fruit will bend it down to the ground. Nobody ever thinks of sitting under its shadow, for it is too small and straggling to make a shade. I can not believe, therefore, that it is spoken of in the Canticles. It can scarcely be called a *tree* at all, much less would it be singled out as among the choice trees of the wood. As to the smell and color, all the demands of the Biblical allusions are fully met by these apples of Askelon, and no doubt, in ancient times and in royal gardens, their cultivation was far superior to what it is now, and the fruit larger and more fragrant. Let taffûah, therefore, stand for apple, as our noble translation has it.

The sycamore fig grows larger here, and of a darker blue color than in any other place I have visited. They are gathered, and carried in baskets to Gaza. None of these fruits are ripe yet, but the orchards promise a generous crop. There are no buildings of the ancient city now standing, but broken columns are mixed up with the soil, and the number of old wells and cisterns still kept in repair enables the peasants to water their orchards and gardens abundantly, without which all would quickly perish.

Let us climb to the top of these tall fragments at the southeast angle of the wall, and we shall have the whole scene of desolation before us, stretching, terrace after terrace, quite down to the sea on the northwest. The walls must have been blown to pieces by powder, for not even earthquakes could toss these gigantic masses of masonry into such extraordinary attitudes. No site in this country has so deeply impressed my mind with sadness. O man, savage, ferocious, brutal, what desolations thou hast wrought in the earth! They have stretched out upon Askelon the line of confusion and the stones of emptiness. Thorns have come up in her palaces, and *brambles in the fortresses thereof*, and it is a habitation of dragons and a court for owls.[1]

This is the impression "before dinner." Let us descend to our cheerful lunch, spread on the clean sand under those

[1] Isaiah xxxiv. 11, 13.

giant sycamores, and the view after dinner will be much less gloomy. Askelon will surely be rebuilt at some future day of prosperity for this unhappy land. The position is altogether too advantageous to allow it to sink into total neglect. The inhabitants call the place El Jore, but they are also acquainted with the name Askelon, and in some degree with her ancient story, which closely resembles that of her neighbors, Ashdod and Gaza, and is to be found in the same books, sacred and profane. In the Crusades it played a more illustrious part than either of them, but we shall not enter into details, which may be found in the same authors referred to for the history of Usdûd. If this place were ever celebrated for aromatic plants, as Strabo, Pliny, and Dioscorides assert, they probably grew on these sand-hills north and south of the city.

Askelon was famous for the worship of Venus under the name of Derceto, as Herodotus informs us; but if there ever was a deep lake near it, abounding in fish, into which she, ashamed of some of her misdeeds, plunged, and was transformed into a fish, it has totally disappeared. It is a curious fact, however, that there are still sacred fish kept in consecrated fountains in several parts of this country. Is this a remnant of the old fish-worship of Syria, springing originally from, or connected with these fables about Venus? I think so; for it is difficult to account for these sacred fish on any other supposition. I have visited several of these fountains, but the largest and most remarkable is situated a short distance north of Tripoli.

We must now pursue our journey, and for the first half hour over this naked ridge to N'alia, a village nearly surrounded by sand-hills. Mejdel, buried up in a forest of tall olive-trees, lies nearly due east of Askelon, but it has exchanged places with Hamamy on modern maps. Mejdel is a large town, with mosque and minaret, and some good houses. It has also a governor and Kady, and is regarded as a sort of capital for the region about Askelon. The direct road from Usdûd to Gaza keeps farther inland, having Beit Timah, El Jfyeh, and Beit Jirjia on the east of it, in the order named. Beit Timah is a considerable distance out on the plain; the others are near the road; and all of them are surrounded by large olive-groves. The next village southward is Deir Senad, and near it is a bridge, broad and substantial, over a deep channel, always dry when I have been here, but which has a vast volume of water during the winter rains. It is called Senad from this village, but higher up it takes the name of Wady Simsim. This river does not run northwest, as put down on maps, but breaks through the sand ridge to the sea, west of Deir Senad. Here is Beit Hanûn on our left, and between us and the sea is Beit Lahia, and farther on is Jebala. These villages are famous for their fruit and vegetables, with which the markets of Gaza are supplied. Jebala is a sort of suburb to Gaza, and at it a great part of the oil gathered from these immense groves is made into soap. And now the tall palm-trees and taller minarets of this last city of Palestine toward Egypt come into view. We shall seek quarters in a khan, in order to escape annoyance from this rude population. They bear a bad character, and have lately shown symptoms of Moslem fanaticism and insubordination, which render it safest and wisest to avoid all occasion of trouble.

In wandering over the ruins of this curious city I came upon an immense serpent, which had just caught one of these pretty crown-larks. The screams and fluttering of the poor captive drew me to the spot, and I succeeded in killing the snake, but the bird was dead. This adventure reminded me of an inquiry I have often wished to make in regard to the curse pronounced upon the serpent in Eden: Dust shalt thou eat, etc., etc.[1] Are there any snakes in the East that eat dust or earth? In our country they are carnivorous or insectivorous—gather their food from the grass, the rocks, the trees, the water—insects, worms, frogs, birds, and mice, while the larger devour squirrels and hares. We know that in Africa and the East the gigantic anaconda and boa crush to death and swallow whole gazelles and other animals, but I never heard or read of any that eat dust.

[1] Gen. iii. 14.

SERPENT AT GAZA.

Perhaps the phrase "eat dust" has a metaphorical meaning, equivalent to "bite the dust," which from time immemorial has been the favorite boast of the Eastern warrior over his enemy. To make him eat dust, or, as the Persians have it, *dirt*, is the most insulting threat that can be uttered. In pronouncing sentence upon the serpent, we need not suppose that God used the identical *Hebrew* words which Moses wrote some thousands of years afterward, but the Jewish lawgiver was guided to a proverb which fully expressed the purport of that divine commination. We may paraphrase it after this fashion: Boast not of thy triumph over a feeble woman, proud, deceitful spirit; you shall be overthrown, and reduced to the most abject degradation. The seed of this feeble victim of thy treachery shall yet plant his heel upon thy accursed head, and make thee bite the dust. This explanation agrees well with the manner in which Isaiah uses the proverb. Speaking of the triumph of the Redeemer's kingdom, he adds, And dust shall be the serpent's meat, what time the wolf and the lamb shall feed together, and the lion shall eat straw like the bullock. Then shall this most ancient and most glorious prophecy and promise receive its full accomplishment, and the old serpent, with all his evil brood, be made to bite the dust. May we not find here an allusion to the manner in which the serpent has always been killed—by crushing his head into the earth?

Moses speaks repeatedly of fiery serpents,[1] and Isaiah mentions fiery flying serpents:[2] are there any kind of snakes which can properly be said to fly?

In all these cases the Hebrew word is suraph, and Arab scholars identify it with a kind of serpent that *darts* with prodigious velocity upon its victims, and, when enraged, against its enemies. A thousand incredible stories are related in reference to it. I have been assured by those who professed to speak from personal knowledge, that it will spring, leap, or, as they call it, *fly* to an immense distance, and with such force as literally to penetrate and pass quite through any soft substance with which it comes in contact. The children of Israel encountered these flying serpents in the *wilderness;* and, in strict agreement with this, the scene of all these marvelous stories is laid in the great deserts. Though I by no means credit all these anecdotes, at least in their exaggerations, yet they are too numerous and consistent to be mere fictions. Niebuhr, and many other respectable travelers into Arabia and Chaldea, also speak of them, not as fables, but as well-known realities. The name, *flying serpents*, does not necessarily imply that they had wings, as Orientals familiarly apply this to multitudes of things to which such appendages do not, and are never supposed to belong. The epithet *fiery* would be given to them either from their fiery temper, color, and motions when enraged, or from the burning pain of their bite. They are regarded as very dangerous, and even mysteriously dreadful.

16*th*. We have had a pleasant excursion through the different parts of this celebrated city. How many inhabitants is it supposed to contain?

There are one hundred and fifty taxable Greeks, which

[1] Numbers xxi. 6. [2] Isaiah xxx. 6.

may give seven hundred for the entire Christian population. The kady told me last night that there were *fourteen thousand males* among the Moslems. This, if applied to the *whole province*, may be correct; if restricted to the *city*, it is simply absurd, as it would give a population of about fifty thousand Mohammedans. Both Christians and Moslems maintain that Gaza is larger than Jerusalem, and the entire population may be sixteen or eighteen thousand. The city is built partly on an oblong hill, partly in the valleys south and north of it. There are now neither walls nor forts, but the places of certain gates belonging to ancient walls are pointed out. The only one that interests me is that which bears the name of Samson, from the tradition that it was from that place he carried off the gate, bars and all. It is on the east side of the hill-part of the city, looking toward Hebron, and near it is a mazar, or willy, to his honor. Gaza is municipally divided into five *haras*, or *wards*. Two are in the broad vale on the southeast, and both called *Sejariyeh—woody*. They are the *new* town, and indicate growth and advancement. The other three are *et Tuffah*—the *apples*; *Daraj—steps*; and *Zeitûn—olive*.

The original city stood on the hill where the palace, mosques, khans, and nearly all the stone houses now are. This was its position when Alexander besieged and took it, according to Arrian; and many granite and marble columns, and heavy old stones, mingled with more recent work, on this hill, go to confirm the fact. This, too, is the tradition of the place; and the people know of no other site for ancient Gaza. I suppose, therefore, that Dr. Keith is mistaken in his theory on that subject. There is, however, an old tradition, given by Reland, that the original city was deserted, and a new Gaza erected on another spot. Jerome also seems to intimate something of this kind; but perhaps nothing more is meant than some new suburb around the old site on the main hill, just as the two *haras* or wards, called *Sejariyeh*, have arisen in the vale to the southeast of the present town. An air of decay hangs over Gaza, partly because many buildings are really falling to ruins, and part-

GAZA.

ly because the stone out of which it is built is old and saturated with saltpetre, which effloresces, and disintegrates with great rapidity. A house soon comes to look old that is built of these rotten ruins. On the southwest of the city are the quarantine buildings, erected by the present government out of this same description of stone, and they already show signs of decay. The mosque, most conspicuous for its massive minaret, is believed to have been a Christian church, and is still known by the name of Dier Hannah. Dr. Robinson gives a particular description of this church, and thinks it may possibly date back as far as the *beginning* of the fifth century. Bonaparte is said to have destroyed this castle east of our *khan*, and, at any rate, its overthrow is comparatively recent. Those travelers are mistaken who say that the sea is not visible from Gaza. We have seen it from various points, over and beyond the great olive-groves; but, of course, it can not be seen from lower parts of the city. The harbor is a little north of west, near two willys, now called 'Adjlûn and Sheikh Hasan. The ancient name seems to have been Majumas. It is a mere open roadstead, and there is no village, nor even a magazine on the shore.

The wells at Gaza are very deep, some of them one hundred and fifty feet, but the natives greatly praise the quality of the water. I found the air cool in June, and all agree that the city is healthy. The houses are full of sparrows, and the gardens alive with doves and other birds, which keep up a constant *roar* of music, aided by rooks in abundance from the tops of the feathery palm. The commerce of Gaza with the Arabs is considerable, but the great trade of the city is in soap, which is carried over the desert to Cairo. They send none by ship, as the sea air damages the soap. A *cantar*—about five hundred and fifty pounds—is transferred on camels to Cairo for four dollars and a half, though the journey takes fifteen days. Latterly a large trade in wheat, barley, and sesamum has sprung up with Europe, shipped mostly from Jaffa. With a harbor at hand and a government to protect from the Bedawîn, Gaza would rapidly rise in importance. It is admirably situated for trade with all the eastern tribes of Arabs, and with Egypt. At no very distant day a railroad will pass down from the plains of Northern Syria, and the valleys of the Euphrates and Tigris, to Egypt, and then again Gaza, as the frontier city, will become populous and flourishing.

Gaza is among the very oldest cities in the world. The name occurs in the tenth chapter of Genesis,[1] and in Joshua[2] it is mentioned as one of the three cities in which alone Anakims still existed. In the distribution of the land it was assigned to Judah, and after the death of Joshua it was actually conquered by that tribe, but they did not long keep possession of it, for when it again appears in sacred history it is as a city of the Philistines, in connection with the romantic adventures and exploits of Samson.

That reminds me that he was here imprisoned and made to grind at the mill. I saw this operation going on in several places during our ramble about the city, and we heard its ringing "sound" until a late hour last night. To what an abject condition that renowned champion of Israel was reduced,

> "To grind in brazen fetters under task,
> Eyeless, in Gaza, at the mill with slaves!
> Oh, change beyond report, thought, or belief!
> See how he lies at random, carelessly diffused!
>   Can this be he
> Who tore the lion as the lion tears the kid;
> Ran on embattled armies clad in iron,
> In scorn of their proud arms and warlike tools;
> Spurned them to death by troops? The bold Ascalonite
> Fled from his lion ramp; old warriors turned
> Their plated backs under his heel,
> Or, groveling, soiled their crested helmets in the dust.
> Then, with what trivial weapon come to hand,
> The jaw of a dead ass his sword of bone,
> A thousand foreskins fell, the flower of Palestine,
> In Ramath-lechi, famous to this day.
> Then by main force pulled up and on his shoulders bore
> The gates of Gaza, post, and massy bar,
> Up to the hill of Hebron, seat of giants old."

[1] Gen. x. 19.   [2] Josh. xi. 22.

SAMSON IN GAZA—OVERTHROW OF DAGON'S TEMPLE. 339

Thus Milton sings his glorious deeds.

Yes, and with what shame, remorse, and horror he is made to bewail his unequaled folly in having divulged the secret gift of God

> "To a deceitful woman. . . . Delilah,
> That specious monster, my accomplished snare,
>   who shore me,
> Like a tame wether, of my precious fleece,
> Then turned me out ridiculous, despoiled,
> Shaven, and disarmed among mine enemies.
>   Tell me, friends,
> Am I not sung and proverbed for a fool
> In every street?"

By far the most wonderful exhibitions of his giant strength he ever made was in this city, not only in walking off with the gates to the top of yonder hill toward Hebron, though any one who knows what the doors of a city gate are will not think this a small achievement, but chiefly in pulling down the vast temple of Dagon, by which he himself perished, with three thousand of his enemies. I looked at some of the old columns near the brow of Castle Hill with great interest, and I fancied that they once formed part of Dagon's Temple. I suppose that the three thousand were partly on the flat roof and partly below, and all were crushed together in an unparalleled calamity. Have you never felt it difficult to believe that such strength could reside in or be put forth by any combination of human bone and sinews?

It was divine power acting through these limbs of Samson. This renders it easy and simple. Samson himself, according to Milton, was rather disposed to understate the gift.

> "What is strength without a double share
> Of wisdom? Vast, unwieldy, burdensome.
> God, when he gave me strength, to show withal
> How slight the gift was, *hung it in my hair.*"

It is one of those pleasant coincidences that here at Gaza, where we read so incidentally of the "grinding at the mill" in that ancient story, we still have the same operation ringing in our ears. The reason is that this city has no mill-stream near it; there are no wind nor steam mills, and hence the primitive apparatus is found in every house, and heard in every street. Nor can it be mere fancy that these modern Philistines bear a close resemblance to their proud, vindictive, and licentious ancestors.

How do you understand the matter about the three hundred foxes? I have often heard it quoted as proof of the incredibility of some of the Bible narratives by skeptics, who deny the possibility of one man's catching so many foxes.

It is probable that by foxes jackals are intended, and these are even now extremely numerous. I have had more than one race after them, and over the very theatre of Samson's exploit. When encamped out in the plain, with a part of Ibrahim Pasha's army, in 1834, we were serenaded all night long by troops of these hideous howlers. But if we must limit Samson to the ordinary meaning of fox, even these are to be found here. I started up and chased one when I passed over that part of the plain where Timnah is believed to have been situated. It must be admitted, however, that the number seems not only large in view of the difficulty of capturing them, but also far too great for the purpose intended. The object was to set fire to the dry corn which covered the plains of the Philistines. Now a spark would seem sufficient to accomplish this. During the summer months the whole country is one sea of dead-ripe grain, dry as tinder. There is neither break, nor hedge, nor fence, nor any cause of interruption. Once in a blaze, it would create a wind for itself, even if it were calm to begin with; and it would seem that a less number could have answered all the purposes of Samson; but to this it is obvious to remark that he meditated no limited revenge. He therefore planned to set the fields of a great many towns and villages on fire at the same moment, so that the people would be confounded and bewildered by beholding the conflagration on all sides of them, and, each being intent on saving his own crop, no one could help his neighbor. Besides, the text implies that certain parts were already reaped, and this would produce interruptions in the continuity of the fields; and, also, we know not the modes of cultivation at that early period. Part of the land may have been permitted to lie fallow, or might have been planted with "summer fruits," which, being green, would stop the conflagration, and render necessary a greater number of fire-brands. As to the difficulty of capturing so many foxes, we must remember that Samson was judge or governor of Israel at that time. He no more caught these creatures himself than Solomon built the Temple with his own hands; and if we take two or three other facts into account, it will not appear incredible that the governor of a nation could gather such a number of foxes when he had occasion for them. The first is, that in those days this country was infested with all sorts of wild animals to an extent which seems to us almost incredible. This is evident from almost numberless incidental allusions in the Bible; but the use of fire-arms for so many centuries has either totally exterminated whole classes, or obliged them to retire into the remote and unfrequented deserts. No doubt, therefore, foxes and jackals were far more numerous in the days of Samson than at present. The second fact is, that, not having fire-arms, the ancients were much more skillful than the moderns in the use of snares, nets, and pits for capturing wild animals. A large class of Biblical figures and allusions necessarily presuppose this state of things. Job, and David, and all the poets and prophets continually refer in their complaints to snares, nets, pits, etc. We are justified, therefore, in believing that, at the time in question, the commander of Israel could, with no great difficulty, collect even three hundred foxes. He was not limited to a day or a week; and though it may be true that in the whole country there are not now so many killed in an entire year, yet this does not prove that this number could not have been then gathered by Samson from the territories of Judah, Dan, and Simeon, over which his authority more particularly extended. We therefore want no correction of the text to render the whole account credible, nor need we call in the aid of miracles. It was merely a cunning device of Israel's champion to inflict a terrible chastisement upon his enemies.

That it was felt to be a most serious calamity is shown by

the cruel punishment inflicted upon the indirect cause of it. Not being able to reach Samson, they wreaked their vengeance upon his wife and all her house, and they destroyed them with the same element which had consumed their harvest. And when we remember that so great is the dread of fire in harvest-time that the Arabs punish with death any one who sets fire to a wheat-field, even though done by accident, we will not greatly wonder that the Philistines should have thus dealt with the family whose injurious conduct had excited their dreaded enemy to this ruinous exploit.

Have you been able to discover any remnants of that famous temple which Samson overthrew with such terrible slaughter of the laughter-loving Philistines?

I have never seen them except in pictures, with the mighty man "bowing himself with all his might" between two of the toppling columns.

The edifice must have been of enormous size, for there were *upon the roof* about three thousand men and women that beheld while Samson made sport.[1] It is not easy for me to understand how the tearing of a column or two from so vast a temple could have brought the whole to the ground.

The roofs in Gaza were then flat as they are now, and it does not require a *very* large space for three thousand people, who stand as close as they can be packed. So much for the size of the building. A farther explanation may be found in the peculiar topography of Gaza. Most of it is built on hills, which, though comparatively low, have declivities exceedingly steep. The temple was erected over one of these, beyond a doubt, for such was and is the custom in the East; and in such a position, if the central columns were taken out, the whole edifice would be precipitated down the hill in ruinous confusion. There is such a steep declivity on the northeast corner of the present city, near the old dilapidated castle and palace, and the houses in that vicinity have fragments of columns wrought into the walls and laid down as *sills* for their gates. Somewhere in that neighborhood, I suppose, the temple stood, and it coincides with this

[1] Judg. xvi. 27.

conjecture that the *willy* of Samson is in a garden a little east of it.

Is it not a fair deduction from the story of the overthrow of this temple that *columns* large enough to sustain immense roofs were common at that very early day? And may not those which are found in many of the ruined cities of Palestine date back to the same age? Such has long been my opinion, and I am farther inclined to believe that the immense roof which rested upon these columns was sustained by *arches*. If this were so, and the centre columns stood on the brow of the declivity, near the old castle, the whole edifice would be precipitated down the hill merely by tearing away those centre supports.

There seems to be an unusual amount of noise and confusion in the street. To what is this owing?

Salim says it is a procession in honor of the marriage of the governor's oldest son. Let us take our stand on the roof of the *khan*, from which we can have a full view of this Oriental cavalcade. Playing the jereed is the most animating spectacle of the whole, but this, I perceive, has already taken place out on the plain, for their panting steeds are still covered with froth and foam. There are a thousand pictures of this sport, but none that does justice to it, and, indeed, it must be seen to be understood and appreciated. The sheikhs and emeers of Lebanon and Hermon are the best jereed-players. Gayly dressed, and superbly mounted, they take their stations at opposite ends of the hippodrome. At length one plunges his sharp *shovel* stirrups into the quivering side of his horse, and away he bounds like a thunderbolt until within a short distance of his opponent, when he wheels sharp round as if on a pivot, flings his "reed" with all his might, and then darts back again, hotly pursued by his antagonist. Others now join in, until the whole hippodrome resounds with the general melee. Many are the accidents which occur in this rough play, and what begins in sport often ends in downright earnest; but, notwithstanding this, the young emeers are extravagantly fond of it, for nowhere else can they exhibit either their horses or

344   THE LAND AND THE BOOK.

themselves to so great advantage; and from every latticed window that looks out upon the hippodrome they well know they are keenly watched by the invisible houris of their midnight dreams. Some of the players perform almost incredible feats of daring and agility. Not only will they catch the "reed" of their antagonist in their hand while on the run, but I have seen them hang to the saddle by the upper part of the leg, throw themselves down so low as to catch up from the ground their own reed, and regain their seat again, and all this while their horse was at the top of his speed. There is always more or less of this jereed-playing at the weddings of the great, and upon all important state occasions.

SHIELD AND SPEAR.

Here comes a new farce: musicians in harlequin attire, with fox-tails dangling from conical caps, blowing, beating, and braying any amount of discordant music. Following them is a company of dancers at sword-play. They are fierce-looking fellows, and their crooked Damascus blades flash around their heads in most perilous vehemence and vicinity. This, I suppose, is the first time you have seen a real shield, or heard its ring beneath the thick-falling blows of the sword. The next in this procession are genuine Bedawîn Arabs, with their tremendous spears. This is because Gaza is on the borders of the desert, and the governor finds it to his interest to court the sheikhs of these powerful robbers. And now comes the governor and suite, with the bridegroom and his friends—a gay cavalcade, in long silk robes; some of them are olive-green, and heavily loaded with silver and gold lace. Such is high life in Gaza.

The whole night will be spent in feasting, singing, dancing, and rude buffoonery, in the open court by the men, and in the *harem*, in equally boisterous games and dances, by the

DANCING-GIRLS.

women. These are great occasions for the dancing-girls; and many, not of the "profession," take part in the sport. We see little to admire in their performances. They move forward, and backward, and sidewise, now slowly, then rapidly, throwing their arms and heads about at random, and rolling the eye, and *wriggling* the body into various preposterous attitudes, languishing, lascivious, and sometimes indecent; and this is repeated over and over, singly, or in pairs or groups. One thing is to be said in their favor: the different sexes do not intermingle in those indecorous sports; and I hope you will not be greatly scandalized if I venture the opinion that the dances spoken of in ancient Biblical times were in most points just such as we have been describing.

XXXVII. GAZA TO BEIT JIBRIN.

April 17th.

I am now more than ready to leave this rude and fanatical city. What sort of country have we before us to-day?

Beautiful in itself, but monotonous—wheat, wheat, a very ocean of wheat. Our road to Beit Jibrîn leads diagonally across the whole territory of Philistia, and offers an opportunity to become familiar with its physical features and its present productions, but there is not a single site of much importance along the entire distance.

This I shall not regret, for I am almost disgusted with ruins, and fatigued by the effort to trace out the history of extinct races and magnificent cities among mud hovels and semi-savage Arabs. Give me for one day the open country, and soil unpolluted by these vulgar people, and unencumbered with shapeless heaps of unmeaning rubbish.

I can not promise freedom from Arabs, not even from Bedawîn robbers, for we ride along the very borders of their desert homes, and they frequently make inroads quite beyond our track. Neither is the country any thing like what we mean by virgin soil in America. It has been plowed for thousands of years, and probably very much as it is at present; but in one very remarkable respect it is not what it once was. There was doubtless a time, long, long ago, when it was covered with dense primeval forests, and there have been ages of prosperity and peace since then, when it was crowded with towns and villages, inclosed in and surrounded by beautiful gardens and orchards. But, ever since Moslem rule began, the land has become the property, not of the cultivator, but of the government, and while this ruinous régime lasts, this splendid country will remain as it is. No man will plant orchards and make improvements on land not his own; but give him a secure title, and under the crude husbandry of even these ignorant peasants, Philistia will quickly be studded with villages, and beautified with vineyards, olive-yards, and orange-groves. This, however, will never be realized until a strong government subdue or drive back the Bedawîn to their deep deserts. Neither vineyards, nor fig orchards, nor vegetable gardens can exist while these wretches are allowed to roam at will with their all-devouring herds and droves of camels.

The first time I came into this region I was agreeably surprised to find it not a flat, barren country, approaching to a sandy desert; but one must go much farther south to encounter any thing resembling that. From the distant mountains it indeed has the appearance of a level plain, but the view is so vast that even very considerable hills are lost to the eye. In reality, Philistia closely resembles some of the most beautiful regions of our own glorious West. True, it lacks our fine forests, and one misses our charming country-houses, with their orchards, but that is owing to the inhabitants. The country is equally lovely and no less fertile than the very best of the Mississippi Valley. Nay, owing to something in the nature of the soil, or of the climate, or both, the sources of its fertility are even more inexhaustible than in any part of our own land. Without manure, and with a style of plowing and general culture which would secure nothing but failure in America, this vast plain continues to produce splendid crops every year, and this, too, be it remembered, after forty centuries of such tillage.

In what part of this plain was Gerar, where Isaac resided so many years? It seems to have been extremely fertile, for he reaped a hundred-fold in that valley: And the man waxed great, and went forward, and grew until he became very great,[1] as any other farmer would who reaped such harvests.

The site has not yet been discovered, but I doubt not it can and will be, just so soon as it is safe to travel in that region. It must be somewhere to the southeast of us, and not above fifteen miles distant. According to the Onomasticon, it was twenty miles to the south of Eleutheropolis. Beginning, therefore, at Beit Jibrîn, and going southward about seven hours, the traveler encounters the great Wady Sheriah, called by some Wady Gaza, and in it, or in one of its

[1] Gen. xxvi. 12, 13.

fertile branches, there is little doubt but that the lost site will be found. Arabs who frequent Gaza from that neighborhood speak of a ruined city somewhere there, which careful examination may yet decide to be the ancient Gerar. Isaac went there from Beersheba, the site of which is now known to be a few hours to the east of this region. There was a Wady Gerar in ancient times, which no doubt took its name from the city, and, with such data to guide the future explorer, the place will surely be found.

It is perhaps scarcely proper to speak of this site as even now absolutely unknown. The Rev. J. Rowlands believes that he not only found Gerar, but also the lost Kadesh Barnea. He thus writes to his friend Mr. Williams: "From Gaza our course was to Khalasa. On our way we discovered ancient Gerar. We had heard of it at Gaza under the name of Joorf el Gerar—the Rush or Rapid of Gerar, which we found to lie three hours south-southeast of Gaza. Within Wady Gaza, a deep and broad channel coming down from the southeast, and running a little higher up than this spot, is Wady es Sheriah, from the east-northeast. Near Joorf el Gerar are the traces of an ancient city, called Khirbet el Gerar—the Ruins of Gerar. Our road beyond Khalasa lay along a plain slightly undulating. This plain must be the land of Gerar. Here we sojourned for two days (one of which was Sunday) with Abraham in Gerar." This is rather a meagre account of such a celebrated and unknown region and city, but it is the best we have at present. Mr. Rowlands then went southward to Suez, passing by Khalasa, or Khulasah as Dr. Robinson spells it, and identifies it with the Greek Elusa; but Mr. Rowlands thinks it marks the site of the Chesil of Joshua xv. 30, one of the cities in the south of Judah. Both may be correct. Mr. Rowlands does not seem to have been aware that Dr. Robinson not only visited the place, but gave an extensive description and history of it. Our fortunate traveler, passing in a direct line across the desert from Khalasa to Suez, came, in two hours and a half, to an old site called Sebâta, which he identifies with Zephath, called Hormah—"destruction"—in Numbers

xxi. 3, where the Israelites vowed a vow to utterly destroy the place, on account of the attack of King Arad; and subsequently, in Judges i. 17, after Judah and Simeon had utterly overthrown it, this name "destruction" was attached to it a second time. Near this place is also a well, called Bir Rohebeh, and the ruins of a city with the same name, which he has no doubt was the Rehoboth of Genesis xxvi. 22. The ruins are extensive, and in remarkably good preservation. Ten camel-hours (25 miles) farther toward Suez, Mr. Rowlands found Moilâhi, which he believes, for half a dozen reasons, to be Beer-Lahai-roi, where Hagar found water, and called it after the name of the Lord that spake unto her, Lahai-roi—Thou God seest me.[1] Our traveler is now in the vast wilderness, plain, or desert of Paran, called also wilderness of Kadesh, so famous in early Bible story, and he discovers more than one interesting locality. We shall only refer to Kadesh Barnea. He finds it twelve miles east-southeast of Moilâhi; and as he stood at the base of the rock that was smitten by Moses, and gazed upon the beautiful brook of delicious water still gushing forth from it and leaping down into the desert over many a lovely cascade, he was quite wild with enthusiastic excitement, and well he might be, with his firm faith in the identification.

The history of Isaac's sojourn in Gerar is very curious and instructive. Combining both pastoral and agricultural industry, it is not strange that he grew very great. The vast grazing plains around and south of his position enabled him to multiply his flocks indefinitely, while the "hundred-fold" harvests furnished bread for his numerous servants; and, in addition to these advantages, the blessing of the Lord was on the labor of his hands in a manner altogether extraordinary. These things made the Philistines envy and fear him; and therefore Abimelech, king of Gerar, demanded and obtained a covenant of peace with him. Just so at this day the towns, and even cities, such as Hamath and Hums in the north, and Gaza and Hebron in this region, cultivate with great care friendly relations with the sheikhs of pros-

[1] Gen. xvi. 13, 14.

DIGGING OF WELLS—VALUE OF THEM. 351

perous tribes on their borders. It appears that the country was deficient in water, and that wells, dug at great expense, were regarded as very valuable possessions. Isaac was a great well-digger, prompted thereto by the necessities of his vast flocks; and in those days this was an operation of such expense and difficulty as to be mentioned among the acts which rendered illustrious even kings.[1] The strife for possession of them was a fruitful source of annoyance to the peaceful patriarch, as it had been the cause of separation between Abraham and Lot before him; and such contests are now very common all over the country, but more especially in these southern deserts. It was the custom in former times to erect towers or castles to command and secure the possession of valuable watering-places. Thus Uzziah built towers in connection with "his many wells;"[2] and to stop up wells was the most pernicious and destructive species of vengeance, the surest way to convert a flourishing country into a frightful wilderness. Israel was commanded thus to destroy the land of the Moabites by stopping all the wells of water.[3] It would be a curious inquiry for the explorer to seek out these wells; nor would it be surprising if they should be found still bearing the significant names which Isaac gave them. All travelers agree that water is so scarce and valuable in that region that the places where it is to be found are as well known by the Arabs as are the most flourishing towns in other parts of the country. Isaac's place of residence was the well Lahai-roi, as we read in Genesis xxv. 11, and xxiv. 62, the same that was so named by Hagar.[4] It may have been first discovered by her, or miraculously produced by "the God that saw her" for the salvation of the maternal ancestor of the Arab race and her unborn son, as the fountain of Kadesh afterward was for all Israel,[5] and perhaps that of Lehi for Samson.[6] It seems to have been the usual mode to designate the dwelling-place in patriarchal times, and indeed long after, by some circumstance or fact which made it memorable. Abraham dwelt under *the* oak

[1] 2 Chron. xxvi. 10. [2] 2 Chron. xxvi. 9. [3] 2 Kings iii. 19, 25.
[4] Gen. xvi. 14. [5] Numb. xx. 11. [6] Judg. xv. 19.

at Mamre, Isaac at this well, Jacob hid the idols of his family under *the* oak at Shechem,[1] and, long after, Joshua took a great stone and set it up under the same oak, as I suppose.[2] Thus, also, Deborah dwelt under *the palm*-tree of Deborah.[3] The angel of the Lord that was sent to Gideon came down and sat under an oak which was in Ophrah.[4] King Saul is said to have tarried under a pomegranate-tree[5] in Migron, and it is yet quite common to find a village better known by some remarkable tree or fountain near it than by its proper name. The knowledge of these places and things is perpetuated from generation to generation, and I doubt not many of these wells in the south could be discovered, if one had time and liberty to explore.

There are some curious coincidences in the patriarchal connections with Gerar. Both Abraham and Isaac came from Beersheba to that city; both adopted the same prevarication in regard to their wives, for the same reason, and with the same result. It would appear that these ladies must have been beautiful in comparison with the darker daughters of Philistia, and this even when they were far advanced in life. Both were taken into the *harem* of the king, and both rescued by similar divine interpositions. The king, in either case, was called Abimelech, and each had a chief commander called Phicol. Both Abraham and Isaac made covenants with these Abimelechs; the place of meeting in both cases was a well; and from the seven ewe lambs the well was called Beersheba—the well of seven, or well of the oath.

How do you account for these strange coincidences?

It is fair to conclude that Abimelech was the royal title, just as Pharaoh was in Egypt, and Cæsar in Rome. *Phicol* may also have been a name of office, as mudîr or mushîr now is in this country. If one of these officers is spoken of, his *name* is rarely mentioned. I, indeed, never know any but the official title of these Turkish officers. I suppose it was the custom of these Abimelechs to augment their state

---
[1] Gen. xxxv. 4.   [2] Josh. xxiv. 25–27.   [3] Judg. iv. 5.
[4] Judg. vi. 11.   [5] 1 Sam. xiv. 2.

and glory by introducing into their *harems* illustrious ladies, and that often without respect to their age. To enable them to do this they sometimes killed their husbands, and such things are not unknown even in our day. I could point to more than one such transaction among the emeers and sheikhs of this country. This was the temptation which led both Abraham and Isaac to that culpable deception which is recorded of them. As to the other repetitions of similar acts, there is no difficulty in understanding them. After the lapse of many years, it would be quite in accordance with Oriental usages for the successors of the first Abimelech to renew the covenant of peace with Isaac, who had grown so great as to be both envied and feared. The *mode* of contracting alliance was the same, because in both cases an established custom was followed; and that the well should have been twice named Beersheba from this double transaction made at it is not surprising. It may have been intended also by that divine providence which guided all such proceedings of the patriarchs, to settle, by these remarkable acts, a well-known point to determine in future ages the extreme southern border of the promised land.

The character of Isaac is very marked and peculiar. He never traveled far from this spot during his long life of one hundred and eighty years—probably never removed from Wady Gerar and its neighboring city. There are but few acts of his life on record, and several of these are not much to his credit. He seems to have been an industrious, quiet man, disposed to wander alone and meditate, at least when he had such an interesting theme to think about as the coming of the camels with his expected bride. He preferred peace to strife, even when the right was on his side, and he was "much mightier" than those who annoyed and injured him. This silent submission to injury was objected to by Abimelech in the question of the wells, and with much apparent justice. The king, when reproved about those which his servants had violently taken away, replied, in substance, Why did you lay up this grudge in your heart all this while? You should have had more confidence in my justice, and, instead of tacitly implying that I was a party to this violence, you ought to have reported the case to me. I do not feel flattered by this concealment, nor very well pleased that it should be cast in my teeth on this particular occasion. The same injurious suspicion is more prominent in Isaac's conversation about his wife. He there distinctly states his apprehension that Abimelech was a lawless tyrant, who would not stick at murder in order to get Rebekah into his harem. Neither Isaac nor Rebekah appear to advantage in this discussion with Abimelech. I say *appear*, because it is by no means certain that the king was not capable of doing just what Isaac feared; while Isaac would sooner have lost his right hand, or even his life, than be guilty of such enormous wickedness. And it is often the case that a very bad man may be able to set his conduct in such a light as to seem more honorable and generous than those much better than himself. This should be remembered when we study the exhibitions of character made by Jacob and Esau at their meeting in Gilead. Esau carries off the whole credit of the interview, and his brother seems cold, suspicious, cunning, unbrotherly. And while I do not pretend to admire certain traits in Jacob's character, yet he was far more upright and religious than Esau. Jacob knew him and his four hundred men too well to venture into his society and power. Hence all the shuffling and backing out, and even deception, which he gave in return for his injured brother's forgiveness, warm-hearted welcome, and generous offers of assistance. Jacob *dared* not accept them, and yet to reject them under such circumstances could not but place him in great embarrassment.

How could Isaac have been so grossly deceived by Jacob and his mother?

He was not only blind, but old, so that he could not distinguish with accuracy, either by the touch of his shriveled hand or by the ear, now dull of hearing. It must be farther remembered that Esau was, from his birth, a hairy person. He was now a man, full grown, and no doubt as rough and shaggy as any he-goat. Jacob was of the same age, and his whole history shows that he was eminently shrewd and cunning. He got that from his mother, who on this occasion plied all her arts to make the deception perfect. She fitted out Jacob with Esau's well-known clothes, strongly scented with such odors as he was accustomed to use. The ladies and dandies in ancient times delighted to make their "raiment smell like the smell of a field which the Lord had blessed;" and at this day they scent their gala garments with such rich and powerful spicery that the very street along which they walk is perfumed. It is highly probable that Jacob, a plain man, given to cattle and husbandry, utterly eschewed these odoriferous vanities, and this would greatly aid in the deception. Poor old Isaac felt the garments, and smelled the still more distinguishing perfumes of Esau, and, though the voice was Jacob's, yet he could not doubt that the person before him was—what he solemnly protested that he was—his first-born. The extreme improbability of deception would make him less suspicious, and, so far as the hair and the perfume are concerned, I have seen many Arabs who might now play such a game with entire success.

All this is easy and plain in comparison with the great fact that this treachery and perjury, under most aggravating accompaniments, should be in a sense ratified and prospered by the all-seeing God of justice. It is well to remember, however, that, though the blessing, once solemnly bestowed, according to established custom in such cases, could not be recalled, yet, in the overruling providence of God, the guilty parties were made to eat the bitter fruit of their sin during their whole lives. In this matter they sowed to the wind and reaped the whirlwind.

We set out on this line of remark by saying that in several of the known incidents of Isaac's history, few though they be, he does not appear to advantage. Even in this transaction, where he, now old, blind, and helpless, was so cruelly betrayed by his wife and deceived by his son, he is unfortunately at fault in the main question. He was wrong and Rebekah was right on the real point of issue; and, what is more, Isaac's judgment in regard to the person most proper to be invested with the great office of transmitting the true faith and the true line of descent for the promised Messiah was determined by a pitiful relish and longing for "savory meat." Alas for poor human nature! There is none of it without dross; and mountains of mud must be washed to get one diamond as large as a pea.

We have taken no note of time during this long digression, nor have I even noticed the face of the country.

Not much lost thereby, for our track has been the ordinary road to Beit Jibrîn. After emerging from the great olive-grove north of Gaza, we had Beit Hanûn on our left; then Demreh, on the same side, upon the bank of Wady Simsim, and Nejid on the south of our path. The village we have just passed is Simsim, and this one to which we are coming is Burier. Time from Gaza three hours; direction northeast; country a rich, rolling, agricultural plain. Our next village is Um Lakis, which, I have little doubt, *derives its name* from the Lakish so celebrated in Bible story and prophecy. The city itself seems to have been more to the south, and nearer Beit Jibrîn, according to the Onomasticon and other notices. Even that is not certain, however, and the great similarity of name, for a site so close to the locality of the ancient city, is not to be forgotten. My company at Mesmia gave me names of villages, ruins, old sites, tells, and wells sufficient to fill two pages. None in this direction, however, seemed to be of any historic interest except 'Aglan and this Lakis. We shall come to 'Aglan in half an hour. There are no ruins at either of these places to remind one of ancient glory, but the same remark applies to all the sites on this plain, and that for two reasons: the cities were built chiefly of unburned brick; and such parts as were of stone were either taken from that soft arenaceous formation which is found all along the coast, or from that cretaceous rock which is so characteristic of all these southern hills of Judæa, and which is often nothing more than indurated marl. We are not, therefore, to expect ruins; and the name, with a tell of greater or less height, composed of such debris, pottery scattered over the neighborhood, and a well or two, with a sarcophagus or a stone trough—these are the things by which we identify old sites in Philistia.

The plain from this to Beit Jibrîn is destitute of villages and barren of historic interest; and, after taking our lunch at this 'Aglan, we must quicken our pace, or we shall be out on this desert later than is exactly safe. The whole distance, at our rate of riding, is nine hours, and this may be taken as the utmost breadth of the proper territory of the Philistines. The great Wady Simsim branches out to the northeast and south, but it is everywhere destitute of water except in winter. The largest of these branches, called Wady el Hasy, wanders about in a general direction toward the southeast, and drains the western slopes of the mountains of Hebron.

What sort of vegetable is this whose stems our muleteers are cutting up and chewing with so much relish?

It is the wild artichoke. We can amuse ourselves with it and its behavior for a while, and may possibly extract something more valuable than the insipid juice of which our men are so fond. You observe that in growing it throws out numerous branches of equal size and length in all directions, forming a sort of sphere or globe a foot or more in diameter. When ripe and dry in autumn, these branches become rigid and light as a feather, the parent stem breaks off at the ground, and the wind carries these vegetable globes whithersoever it pleaseth. At the proper season thousands of them come scudding over the plain, rolling, leaping, bounding with vast racket, to the dismay both of the horse and his rider. Once, on the plain north of Hamath, my horse became quite unmanageable among them. They charged down upon us on the wings of the wind, which broke them from their moorings, and sent them careering over the desert in countless numbers. Our excellent native itinerant, A—— F——, had a similar encounter with them on the eastern desert, beyond the Hauran, and his horse was so terrified that he was obliged to alight and lead him. I have long suspected that this wild artichoke is the *gulgal*, which, in Psalms lxxxiii. 13, is rendered *wheel*, and in Isaiah xvii. 13, a *rolling* thing. Evidently our translators knew not what to call it. The first passage reads thus: "O my God, make them like a wheel—*gulgal*—as the stubble before the wind;" and the second, "Rebuke them, and they shall flee far off, and shall be chased as the chaff of the mountains before the wind, and like a rolling thing—*gulgal*—before the whirlwind." Now, from the nature of the parallelism, the *gulgal* can not be a "wheel," but something corresponding to chaff. It must also be something that does not fly like the chaff, but, in a striking manner, *rolls* before the wind. The signification of *gulgal* in Hebrew, and its equivalent in other Shemitic dialects, requires this, and this rolling artichoke meets the case most emphatically, and especially when it rolls before the whirlwind. In the encounter referred to north of Hamath, my eyes were half blinded with the stubble and chaff which filled the air; but it was the extraordinary behavior of this "rolling thing" that riveted my attention. Hundreds of these globes, all bounding like gazelles in one direction over the desert, would suddenly wheel short round at the bidding of a counter-blast, and dash away with equal speed on their new course. An Arab proverb addresses this "rolling thing" thus: "Ho! 'akkûb, where do you put up to-night?" to which it answers as it flies, "Where the wind puts up." They also derive one of their many forms of cursing from this plant: "May you be whirled, like the 'akkûb, before the wind, until you are caught in the thorns, or plunged into the sea." If this is not the "wheel" of David and the "rolling thing" of Isaiah, from which they also borrowed their imprecations upon the wicked, I have seen nothing in the country to suggest the comparison.

April 18*th.* How is it ascertained that this Beit Jibrîn is the site of the ancient Eleutheropolis?

The identification is due to the skill of Robinson and Smith, and the process of discovery and verification is detailed with great care in their "Researches." Owing to the fact that Eusebius and Jerome take this as the central station from which to mark the direction and distance of many

BEIT JIBRIN.

other places, there are few geographical points in the country of greater value, and Dr. Robinson very justly magnifies its importance. Having myself derived the highest gratification in following out his results in my own excursions in this region, I gladly embrace every opportunity to express my obligations. There is a whole nest of sacred sites scattered around this important centre. On the east we have Beit Nusib—Nezib—and farther over the hills to the northeast Jeb'a—the Gibeah of Judah—and north, a little east, we find Shochoh in Shuwiekeh, and beyond it Jarmuth in Yarmuk. 'Ain Shemsh is Bethshemesh, and northwest of this, Tibneh is the Timnath of Samson's wife. Northeast of this is Zorah, the city of his father, and southeast of that is Zanuah. The wady in which Zorah lies is called Wady es Sumpt, and this is probably the battle-field of David and

Goliath of Gath. Dr. Robinson thinks that Gath may have been at or near Deir Dubban, where are very remarkable excavations and other indications of an ancient city. It appears to me that Bethogabra—Eleutheropolis—Beit Jibrîn, and *Gath* are all one and the same city. Khurbet Get—ruins of Gath—is the name now applied to one of the heaps of rubbish a short distance westward from the castle of Beit Jibrîn. The Hebrew word Bethogabra and the Arabic Beit Jibrîn may be rendered *house of giants*, which reminds us of Goliath of Gath and his family. And farther, I think that the Moreshah of Joshua xv. 44, which was rebuilt by Rehoboam, and is repeatedly mentioned in connection with Gath,[1] was a suburb of this great capital of the Philistines. Benjamin of Tudela makes Moreshah and Beit Jibrîn identical, and Jerome places them so near each other that they may be regarded as one and the same place. Micah probably wrote Moreshah-gath in order to fix the location of the suburb by the name of the main city.[2] All these identifications lend additional interest to this vicinity. Not only did Goliath and his family of giants reside here, but in this beautiful valley King Asa achieved that grand victory over Zera the Ethiopian, with his host of a thousand thousand, and three hundred chariots; for the battle was at Moreshah, in the valley of Zephatha. These facts and suggestions will be sure to quicken your zeal for this day's explorations, notwithstanding your growing disgust with old ruins. There are, in fact, many things about Beit Jibrîn which merit a careful examination. The most striking is this immense quadrangular inclosure which marks out the boundaries of an old castle. It is about six hundred feet square, and was built of large heavy stone. Then, too, the castle within this inclosure has points of interest. Some parts of it appear very ancient, while this confused mass of arches, vaults, and broken walls speaks of Saracenic and crusading times. Besides this building there are immense artificial caverns hewn out of these cretaceous hills, and some of them carefully ornamented. They are found chiefly in the wady which runs

[1] 2 Chron. xi. 8.   [2] Micah i. 14.

up south by east, and in which is situated the ruined church called Mar Hannah. Dr. Robinson has given a detailed account of these remarkable excavations, the object of which he is at a loss to comprehend. Some of them were undoubtedly cisterns, and it is not impossible that all were originally such, but subsequently some of them may have been enlarged into temples and underground chapels, and others made into granaries.

In traveling through this sacred territory, few things please me more than to light upon those circumstances which prove the accuracy of ancient Bible narratives even in the most incidental remarks and the minutest allusions. We are now not far from Zorah, the birth-place of Samson,[1] and it is pleasant to find his home still in existence, in that secluded mountain village above 'Ain Shemsh. On one of the hard rocks of that village Manoah placed his sacrifice, and the angel of the Lord did wondrously while Manoah and his wife looked on; for it came to pass, when the flame went up toward heaven from off the altar, that the angel of the Lord ascended in the flame.[2]

Josephus has a curious addition to the Bible narrative of these transactions, in which, after extolling the beauty of Manoah's wife, he says that her husband was exceedingly jealous; and when he heard her expatiate upon the beauty of the man who had appeared to her and announced the birth of a son, he was so consumed with this terrible passion that he besought God to send the messenger again, that he might see him—and much more to the same purport. But to return to the history. It is said that Samson went *down* to Timnah, and there saw the woman whom he desired to marry. Now Timnah still exists on the plain, and to reach it from Zorah you must *descend* through wild rocky gorges, just where one would expect to find a lion in those days, when wild beasts were far more common than at present. Nor is it more remarkable that lions should be met with in such places than that fierce leopards should now maintain their position in the thickly-settled parts of Lebanon, and

[1] Judg. xiii. 2.   [2] Judg. xiii. 20.

even in these very mountains, within a few hundred rods of large villages. Yet such I know is the fact.

There were then vineyards belonging to Timnah, as there now are in all these hamlets along the base of the hills and upon the mountain sides. These vineyards are very often far out from the villages, climbing up rough wadies and wild cliffs, in one of which Samson encountered the young lion. He threw the dead body aside, and the next time he went down to Timnah he found a swarm of bees in the carcass. This, it must be confessed, is an extraordinary occurrence. The word for bees is the *Arabic* for *hornets*, and these, we know, are very fond of flesh, and devour it with the greatest avidity. I have myself seen a swarm of hornets build their comb in the skull of a dead camel, and this would incline me to believe that it was really our *debabir—hornets*—that had settled in the carcass of Samson's lion, if it were known that they manufactured honey enough to meet the demands of the story. However, we find that not long after this, bees were so abundant in a wood at no great distance from this spot that the honey dropped down from the trees on the ground; and I have explored densely-wooded gorges in Hermon and in southern Lebanon where wild bees are still found, both in trees and in the clefts of the rocks. It keeps up the verisimilitude of the narrative that these are just the places where wild beasts still abound, and though *bees* ordinarily avoid dead carcasses, it is possible that they on this occasion selected that of the lion for their hive.

The circumstances of the wedding-feast in Timnah are also in keeping with such occasions at the present day. Even the weddings of ordinary people are celebrated with great rejoicings, which are kept up several days. Samson, however, was not an ordinary peasant, but the son of an emeer or nobleman, and the marriages of such are attended with quite as much display as that of Samson. The games and sports, also, by which the companions of the bridegroom pass away the time, are not unlike those mentioned in the 14th chapter of Judges, and such occasions frequently end in quarrels, and even bloodshed. I have known many fatal feuds grow out of the sports of these boisterous festivals.

And yet one thing more: Samson's wife was a weak and wicked woman, who had no real love for her husband, and this is certainly common enough at the present day. Wives are procured now as then by the intervention of parents, and without any of that personal attachment between the parties which we deem essential. They are also very often ready to enter into any treacherous conspiracy against their husbands by which they can gain some desired advantage either for themselves or their friends. Indeed, there are very many husbands in this country who neither will nor dare trust their wives. On the contrary, they watch them with the utmost distrust, and keep every thing locked up for fear of their treachery. And yet these distrusted but cunning wives have wonderful power over their husbands. Though uneducated in all that is good, they are perfect masters of craft and deceit. By their arts and their *importunity* they carry their point often to the utter and obvious ruin of their husbands, and this, too, when there is really no love between them. It is not at all contrary to present experience, therefore, that Samson's wife should conspire against him in the matter of the riddle, nor that she should succeed in teasing him out of the secret.

We are now in the neighborhood where David began his illustrious career by slaying Goliath of Gath. The Philistines went up against Judah and pitched near Shochoh, which site is ascertained to be at Shuwiekeh, about six miles to the northeast of us. Beit Netif is on a hill some three miles nearly north of it, and between them is the deep Wady es Sumpt, which passes down the plain, by Timnath, to the great Wady Surar. Dr. Robinson identifies this Wady Sumpt with the Elah of 1 Samuel xvii. 2, by which Saul encamped, probably on the north side, opposite the Philistines; and it was into this wady that the champion of the "uncircumcised" descended every day to defy the armies of the living God: his height nearly ten feet, his proportions enormous, his visage terrible; covered with a shining coat of mail weighing five thousand shekels, a helmet of brass on his head, a target of brass between his shoulders, and greaves of brass on his legs, he appeared like a brazen statue of colossal size, holding a spear whose staff was like a weaver's beam. No wonder the stoutest heart quailed, and all the men of Israel, when they saw the man, fled from him and were sore afraid. Forty days did this terrible giant come into the valley, morning and evening, to defy the hosts of Israel, exclaiming, with impious insolence, "Give me a man, that we may fight together." Thus he stood and cried in the morning when the youthful David drew nigh with parched corn, and the ten loaves which his father had sent to his elder brothers. He hears the tumult, and the defiance, and his heroic soul takes fire. Eagerly he inquires into the case, and, undeterred by the rebukes of his envious brothers, he offers to meet the dreadful champion. He is brought before Saul, who said unto him, Thou art not able to go against this Philistine to fight with him; thou art but a youth. David modestly replies that, though young, he had already performed, by God's aid, deeds as daring and desperate as this could be. He had killed both a lion and a bear with his empty hands: And the Lord that delivered me out of the paw of the lion and out of the paw of the bear, will deliver me out of the hand of this Philistine.[1] Declining armor and helmet, coat of mail and sword, he took merely his shepherd's staff, and the sling with which he had often practiced while tending his father's sheep on the mountains. He came down into the wady, put five smooth stones into his scrip, and went on boldly to meet the giant. One of these, hurled with his whole force and with unerring aim, sank deep into the giant's insolent forehead. He staggers convulsively, and with a mighty clang falls prostrate upon his face. David is upon him in a moment, and with his own great sword strikes off his head, which he bears back to Saul in triumph. Thus were verified David's confidence and piety. He fought "that all the earth might know that there is a God in Israel."

[1] 1 Sam. xvii. 37.

How do you account for the fact that neither Saul nor Abner, either before or after the battle, recognized David? In the verses immediately preceding the account of Goliath we are informed that David had been summoned from Bethlehem to play on his harp before Saul, when the evil spirit from the Lord came upon him, and Jesse had sent him upon an ass, laden with bread, and a bottle of wine, and a kid. It is added that Saul loved David greatly, and he became his armor-bearer. He also requested his father to leave David with him, for he had found favor in his sight; but the very next notice is that David is quietly tending sheep at Bethlehem, and his three oldest brothers are with the army. David reappears before the king, and is not recognized either by him or by his servants. To me this has always appeared very strange.

It is, indeed, so strange as to suggest the query whether the incidents in this part of David's life are arranged in the exact order of time in which they occurred. The account in the 17th chapter has throughout the air of first acquaintance. Abner said, in reply to the inquiry of the king, As thy soul liveth, O king, I can not tell who he is. David himself gives not the slightest hint, either before or after the fight, that he had ever seen the king before. This is a reserve—a stretch of modesty utterly unparalleled, upon the supposition that he had not only been with him before, but had been greatly beloved by him, and selected to be his armor-bearer—implying the closest intimacy and largest confidence. It is no part of Oriental character to refrain, through modesty, from claiming previous acquaintanceship with superiors, and the present instance is so far beyond the bounds of probability that I hesitate to believe it while there is any other possible explanation. How could the king, and Abner, and all the other attendants of the royal household, have so utterly forgotten the wonderful harper, who had charmed away the evil spirit, and had been so beloved? It seems to me much more probable that this incident of playing on the harp before the king belongs to some period subsequent to the battle with Goliath. This is rendered more credible from the fact that there are some circumstances introduced into the account of that day's adventures which could not have taken place until long after; as, for example, in the 54th verse, where it is said that David took the head of the Philistine and brought it to Jerusalem, but he put his armor in his tent. Now David *had no tent at the time*, and did not *go to Jerusalem* until after the lapse of many eventful years.

If, however, we were shut up to the necessity of accepting the narrative as to time just in the order in which it is recorded, I have only to remark that we do not know how long a period intervened between the return of David to his father's house and his appearance before the king on the morning of the *duel* with Goliath. If it were two or three years, it is possible that David had, in the mean while, suddenly shot up from boyhood to youth, tall and robust, and his personal appearance might have so changed as to bear little resemblance to the ruddy lad who played skillfully on the harp. It is a fact that lads of this country, particularly of the higher classes, are often very fair, full-faced, and handsome until about fourteen years of age, but during the next two or three years a surprising change takes place. They not only spring into full-grown manhood as if by magic, but all their former beauty disappears; their complexion becomes dark, their features harsh and angular, and the whole expression of countenance stern and even disagreeable. I have often been accosted by such persons, formerly intimate acquaintances, but who had suddenly grown entirely out of my knowledge, nor could I, without difficulty, recognize them. David had become a shepherd after leaving the king's palace, an occupation which of all others would most rapidly change his fair complexion into a dirty bronze. He appeared before Saul in his shepherd's attire, not in the gay dress of a courtier in the king's palace, and he *may*, therefore, not have been recognized. But, as before remarked, if this were so, it is not only remarkable in itself, but it follows that David was at an early age possessed of a wisdom, modesty, and self-control without a parallel in the history of mankind.

In after life David had much to do with this part of the country. Twice he fled to Gath for fear of Saul. Is it not strange that he should select the city of Goliath for his asylum?

He was hard pressed, and had only a choice of dangers. Gath was near his native mountains, and probably had more friendly relations with the Israelites than the more distant cities of the Philistines. King Achish, also, appears to have been an open-hearted, unsuspecting, and generous character, probably of that chivalrous temperament which led him to admire such a hero as David. At any rate, he treated him very kindly, and presented him with Ziklag, a village which seems to have been long retained and highly prized by the royal family.

How do you dispose of the deception practiced by David toward his protector in the matter of the excursions against the Amalekites and others down south of us?

That David acted under the pressure of very powerful motives, and was by them urged aside from the plain, open path of rectitude. We are under no obligation to justify all his conduct. It is but common justice, however, to give him the benefit of all palliating circumstances, and when these are duly weighed we shall not find occasion to pass a severe judgment upon him. He was an exile, hunted out of his home like a partridge on the mountains, and obliged to reside among enemies—was surrounded on all sides by difficulties and dangers, and with a large troop of friends and followers, for whom he must find the means of support—he had also been set apart by God himself to be the deliverer of his people from these very Amalekites, who had been condemned to total destruction for their enormous wickedness by the Sovereign Ruler of all nations. David therefore felt that he had a divine warrant for attacking and exterminating them, and they were actually within the borders of his own tribe of Judah as settled by Joshua. The wrong, therefore, if wrong there were, was in the deception practiced upon Achish, and not in the invading and destroying of the Amalekites. This God had sternly enjoined upon the Israelites to do. Let it be remembered, however, that Achish had no real right to know where David went, nor was David under any obligation to tell him the whole truth. What he did say was true in the letter of it, for David did really make an inroad into those places which he mentioned, though not against the Jews.

Ziklag, you suppose, was somewhere in this neighborhood?

We infer this from the notices of it in the Bible, but the site has been long lost. Connected with it is one of the most remarkable incidents in the life of David. While he was with Achish, and the Philistine army in the plain of Esdraelon, these bordering Amalekites invaded the south, and Ziklag, which they burned with fire, and carried all the inhabitants away captive. This terrible calamity threw David and his whole company into the most violent transports of grief. They lifted up their voices and wept until they had no more power to weep, and the people, in their madness and despair, even talked of stoning David.[1] He, however, succeeded in inspiring them with courage to pursue their enemies. They overtook them in the night some distance south of the brook Besor, and falling suddenly upon them while they were eating, and drinking, and dancing because of the great spoil they had taken, the victory was complete, and all that had been taken from Ziklag were recovered, together with a vast amount of booty, which these Amalekites had gathered up from the land of the Philistines. There is a remarkable resemblance between this victory of David and that of Abraham over the kings who had carried Lot away captive.

I was reminded of the poor Egyptian whom David found half dead and brought to life again by giving him "a piece of a cake of figs and two clusters of raisins to eat," and water to drink, by an incident which occurred to me when crossing the plain to Askelon. Far from any village, a sick Egyptian was lying by the road side in the burning sun, and apparently almost dead with a terrible fever. He wanted

[1] 1 Sam. xxx. 3–6.

nothing but "*water! water!*" which we were fortunately able to give him from our traveling-bottle; but we were obliged to pass on and leave him to his fate, whatever that might be.

This victory over the Amalekites was probably achieved on the very day that Saul was defeated and slain on Gilboa; and David, when he had heard of that event—by which the way to the throne of Israel was open to himself—took of the spoils, and sent presents to all the towns and villages where he used formerly to resort. He acted in this matter upon a principle which his wise son has expressed after this fashion: A man's gift maketh room for him, and bringeth him before great men.[1] His gifts speedily made room for him in Hebron, and prepared the hearts of all Judah to welcome him as their king.

It seems to have tasked all David's firmness and tact in government to control his heterogeneous troop of followers.

There were certainly some churlish sons of Belial among them, but this was not their general character. The servants of Nabal, in Carmel, gave a very different testimony concerning them: The men were very good unto us, and we were not hurt, neither missed we any thing as long as we were conversant with them when we were in the fields.[2] They were, therefore, in no sense a lawless set of robbers. Nabal's taunt to the messengers, Who is David, and who is the son of Jesse? there be many servants nowadays that break away every man from his master,[3] was as unjust as it was insolent; but he was, in fact, such a son of Belial that a man could not speak to him; or, as his not very polite wife has it, As his name is, so is he. Nabal is his name, and folly is with him.[4] It does not follow that because every one that was in distress, and every one that was in debt, and every one that was discontented, or, rather, *bitter of soul*, gathered themselves unto David,[5] that therefore they were the refuse and offscouring of the land, like a troop of irregular Turkish cavalry, or the followers of an outlawed Druse

[1] Prov. xviii. 16. [2] 1 Sam. xxv. 15. [3] 1 Sam. xxv. 10.
[4] 1 Sam. xxv. 25. [5] 1 Sam. xxii. 2.

sheikh. The government of Saul had degenerated into a cruel despotism. David himself, and all his relations, had been obliged to flee from his outrageous and murderous jealousy, and there is abundant evidence that they were honorable and respectable people. Nor is it any wonder that many were in distress, and bitter of soul, under a king who could employ a savage Edomite to kill the whole family of the chief priest of the nation, merely because David had been innocently entertained for a night by them. The madness and ferocity of such a king would compel the noblest spirits in the land to flee unto David, and a large proportion of his retinue was actually composed of such men.

Even the debtors, in such a time of misrule, were, in most cases, better men than their creditors. Nearly every body is in debt in these Oriental countries, and, owing to the tenure of land, the modes of raising taxes, and the claims of feudal chiefs, it is impossible for the villagers to keep free from it, either personally, or as part of a community loaded with heavy liabilities, and, even in the cities, the number who are more or less involved is far greater than those who stand square with the world. I hardly ever knew an estate in this country which was not found thus encumbered when the death of the owner brought out the truth, and very generally those who are the creditors are cold, cunning usurers, hated and hateful. The fact, therefore, that a man is in debt is no reflection on his character; and in times of misrule and apprehension like that of Saul, the best families are suddenly reduced by extortion to utter poverty. To raise the enormous sums demanded of the head of the house, and enforced by the bastinado, the wife and children sell and pledge every thing they possess to these lenders, and raise money at ruinous rates of interest. The tyrant, also, from motives easily understood, enforces the collection of such debts with a rigor that knows neither delay nor mercy. That some of David's company fled from just such extortion is highly probable, and they may have been the most estimable people of the land. It is pleasant to believe that the noble and generous David was surrounded by a fair pro-

BEIT JIBRIN—CHARACTER OF INHABITANTS.

portion of kindred spirits, and that in the midst of his sore trials and perplexities his heart was sustained and comforted by the reflection that he was able to furnish an asylum to many innocent victims of regal oppression. This is distinctly stated in the case of Abiathar, who escaped from the slaughter of the priests at Nob, and must have been equally so in regard to his own father and all his family.

These modern dwellers about old Gath appear to be actually taller and more warlike than the average inhabitants of this region.

The sheikh and his family might well be descendants of the ancient giants, for they are rough, fierce-looking fellows, and, indeed, the whole population now make a very savage display of guns, pistols, crooked swords, double-edged *khanjars*, long knives, and whatever else can aid them to cut,

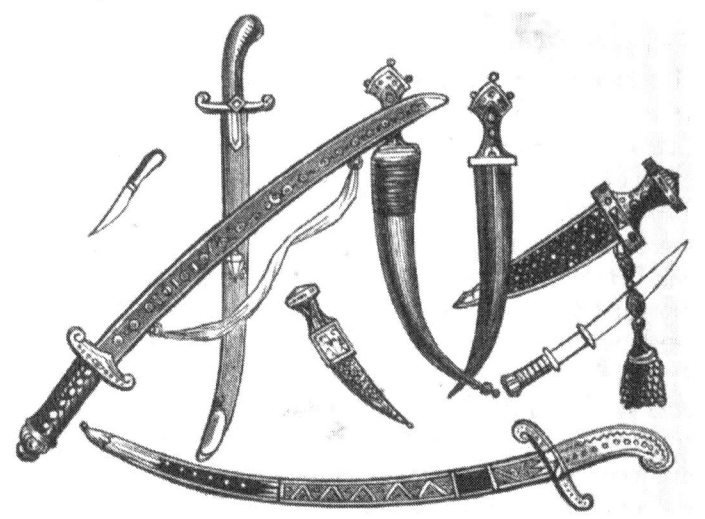

SWORDS, KHANJARS, AND DAGGERS.

stab, and hack the human body to pieces. The sheikh says that they are thus armed in order to keep at a distance the Bedawîn Arabs, who would otherwise eat up their ripening harvests. This may be so, though I have never seen them without arms, and those who can get nothing better carry tremendous clubs, like the weaver's beam of the giant, and in handling them they are as expert as any Irishman with his shillalah, and far more dangerous.

Do these people now make any use of the sling, which, in the hand of David, was so fatal to their famous townsman?

The only place where I have seen the sling used is at Hasbeîya, on Mount Hermon, and there merely in mimic warfare, waged by the boys of the town. The deep gorge of the Busîs divides Hasbeîya into two parts, and when the war-spirit is up in the community, the lads collect on opposite sides of this gorge, and fight desperate battles with their slings. They chase one another from cliff to cliff, as in real warfare, until one of the parties gives way, and retreats up the mountain. I have seen the air almost darkened by their ringing, whizzing pebbles, and so many serious accidents occur that the "authorities" have often interfered to abolish the rude sport; but, whenever there occurs a fresh feud, or a revolt against the government among the old folks, the young ones return again to the fight with slings across the Busîs.

It must have required careful drilling and long practice before the seven hundred left-handed Benjamites could sling stones at a hair-breadth and not miss;[1] but this is a region where such a mode of warfare would be cultivated in ancient times, and be very effective. The stones for the sling are every where at hand, and the country is cut up by deep gorges, with impracticable banks; and, before the invention of guns, there was no other weapon that could carry across these profound depths and reach the ranks of the enemy. David, while following his flocks over these rough mountains, practiced other arts besides that of playing on the shepherd's pipe, for he became as expert in the use of the sling as any of the chosen men of Benjamin. He was manifestly one of nature's noblemen, born to excel in every thing he undertook. Not only was he the most skillful musician, but the greatest poet; not only the most daring shepherd, but the bravest soldier and the most successful general. It is nowhere stated in so many words that he possessed great

[1] Judg. xx. 16.

DAVID'S CONTEST WITH WILD BEASTS. 373

physical strength, but this is implied in several anecdotes of his life. Without this he could not have wielded the sword of Goliath, and yet he chose that of all others for himself; and again, none but the very strongest could kill a lion and a bear in fair fight. What the lion is we all know, or at least imagine, and yet David says I caught him by his beard, and smote him, and slew him.[1] The Syrian bear—still found

SYRIAN BEAR.

on the higher mountains of this country—is perhaps equally to be dreaded in a close personal encounter. The inhabitants of Hermon say that when he is chased up the mountain he will cast back large stones upon his pursuers with terrible force and unerring aim. The stoutest hunter will not venture to attack him alone, nor without being thor-

[1] 1 Sam. xvii. 35.

oughly armed for the deadly strife. David, however, caught him as he was running away with a kid from his flock, and slew him; and this when he was yet but a youth, ruddy, and of a fair countenance, so that Goliath disdained him as an antagonist. It is interesting to remember that these personal adventures of David, both with giants and with wild beasts, took place in these mountains immediately above us.

XXXVIII. HEBRON.

April 19th.

Owing to the wretched headache which tormented me all day, our ride from Beit Jibrîn to this city has left no distinct trace on my memory, except that of a very fatiguing ascent from Idna toward Taffuah.

I can readily refresh your memory this morning by passing in review yesterday's journey, which was one of great interest to me. While the muleteers were packing up and loading, I rode out and again examined the excavations on the southeast of Beit Jibrîn. My guide led me on horseback through a long succession of caverns, all dug out of the white cretaceous rock of the hill above the city. They closely resemble ancient cisterns, having a hole at the top as if to draw water from; but their number and vast size fill the mind with astonishment, and suggest doubts with regard to the original purpose for which they were made. They, however, were hewn out of the rock precisely as cisterns were, and the mark of the pickaxe is distinctly seen on the sides of those that are tolerably perfect. Multitudes of them, however, have fallen in from above, and the partition-walls of others have dissolved by time, thus throwing many into one. Indeed, they appear to have been originally connected by doors and galleries cut through the rock. But it would require a separate memoir adequately to describe these remarkable caverns, and this I certainly have no disposition to write, nor would you have patience to hear. They are all circular, and I measured one which was sixty-five feet in diameter, and ninety-one to the top of the dome from the rubbish which covered the floor ten feet deep at least. The entire height of this cistern must therefore have been more than a hundred feet. On the north side, and about midway to the top, are several figures of idols cut in the rock—rude images of Dagon himself perhaps. In several of the caverns farther south are inscriptions very high up, in a large and mixed Cufic and Phœnician character. I have copies of them, and also of the images, kept rather as curiosities than for any light which they shed upon the mysteries of their location. The only theory I can entertain in regard to these gigantic excavations is that they were cisterns of old Gath, made thus numerous, and on such an immense scale, to secure a supply of water against all emergencies of drouth or of war; and this idea is corroborated by the existence, at the present day, of similar cisterns in more than one of the neighboring villages. At Zikrîn, some six miles northwest of Beit Jibrîn, are vast excavations beneath a broad platform of hard rock which covers several acres, and it is pierced by forty openings or doors—*babs* in Arabic—through which water is drawn up by the villagers. The excavations underneath this flooring closely resemble these of Beit Jibrîn both in shape and size, and the separate cisterns are so connected by galleries and doors that the water passes from one to the other, and stands in all at the same elevation. The overlying rock at Zikrîn is so hard that the roof has nowhere caved in, and the cisterns are therefore in good preservation, and afford an inexhaustible supply of water. This is all I have to suggest on the subject, and now for the ride to Hebron.

I overtook you at Deir en Nukhaz, slowly sauntering up the pretty valley of Senaber, which village we reached in an hour from our camp-ground. The valley, you remember, was broad and fertile, and the ascent for the first three hours very gradual. As we advanced, side valleys came in from the right and left, opening long vistas into the bosom of the surrounding country. In the mouth of the wady which descends from the vicinity of Turkumieh (Tricomia) we saw a large and picturesque encampment of Arabs, with whose goats, and dogs, and naked children we were highly entertained.

Escaping from the half-begging, half-plundering importunity of these Ishmaelites, we rode another hour, and stopped to lunch at 'Ain el Kuf, which is the only fountain in this entire valley. Here we saw many people coming and going with pitchers and jars, and not a few with large "bottles" of skin, an unmistakable evidence that good water is

ARAB CAMP.

very scarce in that region; and, had we not filled our own "bottles," we should have suffered no slight inconvenience in the long ascent, for we found no water from that on to this vale of Hebron.

WATER-JARS AND "BOTTLES."

I remember that ascent with sufficient distinctness, and also that we stopped to rest about half way up Wady 'Ain el Kuf, at a sheepfold under the southern cliff of the ravine, and there, for the first time, I saw the mandrake, with its broad leaves and green "apples," and my curiosity was excited by the discussion which followed about the singular contract between Rachel and Leah for Reuben's mandrakes.[1]

Into that we shall not now enter, nor will we pry with curious eye into the motives which urged Rachel to make

[1] Gen. xxx. 14–16.

the purchase. I, for one, don't know. As to the mandrakes themselves something may be said. Reuben gathered them

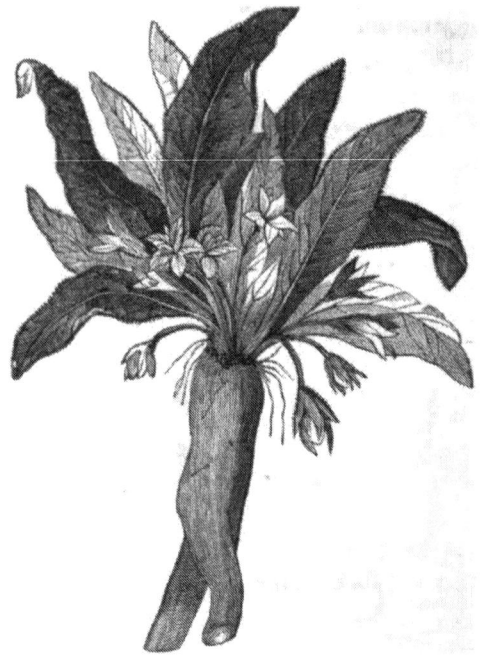

MANDRAKE—LEAF, FLOWER, AND ROOT.

in wheat-harvest, and it is then that they are still found ripe and eatable on the lower ranges of Lebanon and Hermon, where I have most frequently seen them. The apple becomes of a very pale yellow color, partially soft, and of an insipid, *sickish* taste. They are said to produce dizziness; but I have seen people eat them without experiencing any such effect. The Arabs, however, believe them to be exhilarating and stimulating even to insanity, and hence the name *tuffah el jan*—apples of the jan; but we may safely leave the disputed questions concerning mandrakes to those who have time and inclination for such inquiries, and hasten on to our camp-ground in the pretty valley of Mamre, here on the hill-side, near the quarantine of Hebron.

Whatever may be true in regard to the road hither, the

appearance of Hebron itself, lying in deep repose along the vale of Mamre, was quite beautiful. The time of our visit is doubtless most favorable, for nature upon these mountains is now in her holiday dress; and when we began to descend toward the city, the lengthening shadows of the western hills had just dropped their sober curtains over the scene, softening its somewhat rugged features, thereby greatly enhancing its charms. Seen under circumstances not so favorable, the impression might be much less agreeable; but, apart from natural scenery, no intelligent traveler can approach Hebron with indifference. No city in Palestine so carries one back to earliest patriarchal times. Manners and customs, and modes of action, and even idioms of speech, have changed but little since the Bible was written, or from what they were when Abraham dwelt here among "the sons of Heth." Take the account of the death and burial of Sarah, as it is found in the 23d chapter of Genesis, as an example. Sarah died in Kirjath Arba—the same is Hebron—and Abraham came to mourn for Sarah and to weep for her. There is something formal in this remark, but it is in perfect accordance with present customs. Should such a person die here to-morrow, there would be a solemn public mourning and weeping, not as indicating the grief of the family so much as in honor of the dead. The customs of the people demand that there should be loud, boisterous, uncontrollable weeping, mourning, beating of the breast, and every other external manifestation of great sorrow. Such was this funeral mourning of the great emeer Abraham; but, besides this public tribute to the memory of Sarah, he, no doubt, sincerely lamented her death in the privacy of his own tent.

Abraham's negotiation for a sepulchre is also very Oriental and striking. Such a purchase was quite necessary. There has always been in this country the utmost exclusiveness in regard to tombs; and although these polite Hittites said, "Hear us, my lord, thou art a mighty prince among us; in the choice of our sepulchres bury thy dead; none of us shall withhold from thee his sepulchre, but that thou mayest bury thy dead," Abraham was too experienced an Oriental not to know that this was merely compliment. The thing was quite out of the question; nor would Abraham himself have consented thus to mingle his dead with the dust and bones of strangers, even if they had been willing. He knew well how to understand the offer, and therefore pressed his request to be allowed to purchase. Nor is such a negotiation easily arranged. If you or I had occasion to make a similar contract to-day from these modern Hittites, we should find it even more delicate and tedious than did Abraham. I do not believe we could succeed, even with the aid of all the mediators we could employ. In concluding the purchase with Ephron, we see the process of a modern bargain admirably carried out. The polite son of Zohar says, Nay, my lord, hear me; the field *give* I thee, and the cave that is therein, I *give* it thee. In the presence of the sons of my people give I it thee; bury thy dead." Of course! And just so I have had a hundred houses, and fields, and horses given to me, and the by-standers called upon to witness the deed, and a score of protestations and oaths taken to seal the truth of the donation; all which, of course, meant nothing whatever, just as Abraham understood the true intent and value of Ephron's *buksheesh*. He therefore urged forward the purchase, and finally brought the owner to state definitely his price, which he did at four hundred shekels of silver. Now, without knowing the relation between silver and a bit of barren rock at that time and in this place, my experience of such transactions leads me to suppose that this price was treble the actual value of the field. "But," says the courteous Hittite, "four hundred shekels! what is *that* betwixt me and thee!" Oh, how often you hear those identical words on similar occasions, and yet, acting upon their apparent import, you would soon find out what and how much they meant. Abraham knew that too; and as he was then in no humor to chaffer with the owner, whatever might be his price, he proceeded forthwith to *weigh* out the money. Even this is still common; for, although coins have now a definite name, size, and value, yet every merchant arries a small apparatus by which he weighs each coin, to ee that it has not been tampered with by Jewish clippers. In like manner, the *specifications* in the contract are just such as are found in modern deeds. It is not enough that you purchase a well-known lot; the contract must mention every thing that belongs to it, and certify that fountains or wells in it, trees upon it, etc., are sold with the field. If you rent a house, not only the building itself, but every room in it, above and below, down to the kitchen, pantry, stable, and hen-coop, must be specified. Thus Abraham bought this field, *and* the cave that was therein, *and* all the trees that were in the field, *and* that were in all the borders round about, were made sure. I see this negotiation in all its details enacted before me, and hear the identical words that passed between the parties. The venerable patriarch, bowed down with sorrow, rises from beside the couch on which lay the lifeless body of his beloved Sarah. He *stands* before the people—the attitude of respect which etiquette still demands. He addresses them as *beni Heth*—sons of Heth; and in the same words he would address these Arabs about us as *beni Keîs, beni Yemen*, etc., etc., according as each tribe is now designated. Again, Abraham begins his plea with a reference to his condition among them *as a stranger*—the very idiom now in use—I, a stranger, *ana ghurîb;* and this plea appeals strongly to the sympathies of the hearers. It is by such an appeal that the beggar now seeks to enlist your compassion, and succeeds, because all over the East the stranger is greatly to be pitied. He is liable to be plundered and treated as an enemy, and among these denizens of the desert strangers *are* generally enemies, and dealt with as such. The plea, therefore, was natural and effective. Abraham stood and *bowed* himself to the children of Heth; another act of respect in accordance with modern manners, and the next step is equally so. He does not apply directly to the owner of the field, but requests the neighbors to act as mediators on his behalf; and were we anxious to succeed in a similar bargain with these people, we must resort to the same roundabout mode. There is scarcely any thing in the habits of Orientals more annoying to us Occidentals than this universal custom of employing mediators to pass between you and those with whom you wish to do business. Nothing can be done without them. A merchant can not sell a piece of print, nor a farmer a yoke of oxen, nor any one rent a house, buy a horse, *or get a wife,* without a succession of go-betweens. Of course, Abraham knew that this matter of the field could not be brought about without the intervention of the neighbors of Ephron, and therefore he applies to them first. How much manœuvring, taking aside, whispering, nodding of heads, and clasping of hands there was before the real owner was brought within reasonable terms, we are not told, but at length all the preliminary obstacles and conventional impediments are surmounted according to the most approved style of etiquette, and the contract is closed in the *audience of all the people that went in at the gate of the city.* This also is true to life. When any sale is now to be effected in a town or village, the whole population gather about the parties at the usual place of concourse, around or near the gate, where there is one. There all take part, and enter in the pros and cons with as much earnestness as if it were their own individual affair. By these means, the operation, in all its circumstances and details, is known to many witnesses, and the thing is made *sure,* without any written contract. In fact, up to this day, in this very city, a purchase thus witnessed is legal, while the best drawn deeds of a London lawyer, though signed and sealed, would be of no avail without such living witnesses.

Well, Abraham thus obtained the cave of Machpelah for the possession of a burying-place for himself and his descendants, and thus became legal proprietor of a portion of the promised inheritance. There, as Jacob, when dying, said, they buried Abraham and Sarah his wife; there they buried Isaac and Rebekah his wife; and there I buried Leah.[1] And thither, too, his sons carried Jacob out of Egypt when he died, and buried him by the side of his wife.

Dr. Kitto maintains that Joseph carried his father through

[1] Gen. xlix. 31.

the Great Desert, round the south end of the Dead Sea, then through the land of Moab, and, crossing the Jordan near Jericho, there held the great mourning of the Egyptians in the floor of Atad, which he locates between Jericho and the Jordan; and the doctor rather complains that no one has taken the trouble to notice this extraordinary fact. The reason, I suppose, is, that no one believes the story. There is not a particle of evidence for such a wonderful journey in the Bible account of the funeral, nor does Josephus give a hint that he had ever heard of it. Moses, who wrote on the *east* of the Jordan, simply says that the floor at Atad, called Abel Mitzraim, was on the other, or *west* side of it, without stating where. Jerome, indeed, identifies it with Bethagla, and locates that village near Jericho; but this identification has no authority in itself; and, besides, there was another Bethagla in the land of the Philistines, much more likely to be the Abel Mitzraim of Genesis, if the two places had in reality any relation to each other. In a word, nothing less than the positive assertion of the Bible would enable me to believe this theory of Dr. Kitto, for it would be the most extraordinary journey on record.

Do you suppose that this *El Haram* incloses the identical cave, and the graves of the six ancestors of the Hebrew nation?

I have no doubt of it, and therefore I regard it as the most interesting of all spots on the face of the earth. Others might be equally sacred and precious could we be sure of their identity—the manger at Bethlehem, Calvary in Jerusalem, or the last resting-place of Adam or Noah, for example; but doubt and obscurity, absolute and impenetrable, rests on all such sites. Here, however, there is no room for skepticism. We have before us the identical cave in which these patriarchs, with their wives, were reverently gathered "unto their people," one after another, by their children. Such a cave may last as long as the "everlasting hills" of which it is a part; and from that to this day it has so come to pass, in the providence of God, that no nation or people has had possession of Machpelah who would have been disposed to disturb the ashes of the illustrious dead within it.

I have been out examining this venerable edifice as closely as the insolent keepers would allow, and it seems to bear marks of a higher antiquity than any thing I have yet seen in the country.

It is doubtless very ancient—is probably of Jewish workmanship, though I can not think that it dates back to Solomon, or to any time anterior to the captivity. The stones are large, but with a shallow bevel, and the face is worked off smooth, like some parts of the wall about the area of the Temple at Jerusalem. The square pilasters, without capitals or any well-defined cornice, are a feature wholly unique, and marks it off from any other edifice I have examined. There are sixteen of these on each side, and eight on the ends. The height, including the more recent additions of the Saracens, is at least fifty feet, perhaps more. Dr. Robinson gives two hundred feet for the length, one hundred and fifty for the breadth, and sixty for the height, and this is as near the truth as any guess of our own could be. It is located on the declivity of the hill, with the town mostly below in the wady south and west of it. The rock above it is intensely hard, and portions of it are of a pale red color, like that from which books, crosses, and other curiosities are made for the pilgrims. I succeeded, in 1838, in breaking off specimens of it, though not without danger of a mob. The *cave* is beneath this foundation of hard rock. Up to this day we have no good description of the interior of the edifice. I have studied Aly Bey's drawings, and his very unsatisfactory account explanatory of them, but am unable to say whether or not they confirm the following particulars gleaned from other sources. The most interesting items we have are from Benjamin of Tudela, a traveler of the twelfth century, upon whom I have wished on many occasions to be able to rely, and never more than in this instance. He says the real sepulchres are not shown to ordinary visitors, but, if a rich Jew arrives, the keepers open an iron door which has been there *ever since the days of our forefathers*, that is, of the patriarchs themselves! Through this they enter, descend into a first cave, which is empty, traverse a second, which is also empty, and reach a third, which contains six sepulchres—those of Abraham, Isaac, and Jacob, and of Sarah, Rebekah, and Leah, one opposite the other! He says, also, that all these sepulchres have inscriptions, the letters being engraved, that of Abraham thus: "This is the sepulchre of our father Abraham, upon whom be peace;" and so of all the rest. Oh Benjamin! why did you allow yourself to write so carelessly in other instances, where we can follow you, as to shake our faith when we *can not?* Well, the day is not far off when this and every other sacred locality will be thrown open to the inspection of all who wish to know the truth, and until then we must rest contented with what information floats about without any very satisfactory authority. All agree, and my own Moslem servants testify to it, that within this exterior edifice is a large building which may have been an ancient church, but is now used as a mosque. The *cave* is beneath its dome. Monro, the traveler, thus speaks of it, but most certainly from hearsay: "The mosque is a square building, with little external decoration. Behind it is a small cupola, with eight or ten windows, beneath which is the tomb of Esau. Ascending from the street at the corner of the mosque, you pass through an arched way, by a flight of steps, to a wide platform, at the end of which is another short ascent. To the left is the court, out of which, to the left again, you enter the mosque." Not very intelligible; but let that pass. "The dimensions within are about forty paces by twenty-five. Immediately on the right of the door is the tomb of Sarah, and beyond it that of Abraham, having a passage between them into the court. Corresponding to these, on the opposite side of the mosque, are the tombs of Isaac and Rebekah, and behind them is a recess for prayer, and a pulpit. These tombs resemble small huts, with a window on each side, and folding doors in front, the lower parts of which are of wood and the upper of iron, or of bronze plated. Within each of these is an *imitation* of the sarcophagus which lies in the cave below the mosque, and which no one is allowed to enter. Those seen above resemble coffins, with pyramidal tops, and are covered with green silk, lettered with verses from the Koran. The doors of these tombs are left constantly open, but no one enters those of the women—at least men do not. In the mosque is a baldachin, supported by four columns, over an octagonal figure of black and white marble inlaid, around a small hole in the foremost, through which passes a cord from the top of the canopy to a lamp which is kept continually burning in the cave of Machpelah, where the actual sarcophagi rest. At the upper end of the court is the chief place of prayer, and on the opposite of the mosque are two large tombs, where are deposited the two larger sarcophagi of Jacob and Leah."[1] This whole description has the air of something composed from the account of an intelligent Moslem, who had been employed by Mr. Monro to bring back the best account of it he could. If it will not bear a very rigid criticism, it is probably a tolerably close approximation to the reality, and with it we must be content.

Hebron appears to be well built. The houses are generally two stories high, and have flattened domes, such as we saw at Jaffa, Ramleh, Gaza, and other places in the south part of this country.

The same as at Jerusalem, and the reason is that beams are too scarce and dear to admit of flat roofs. I presume it was the same in the days of Solomon, for he had to bring the beams and boards for the Temple from Lebanon, and what is now used in these cities is brought from thence by sea to Jaffa, and afterward carried on camels. Hence the rooms are all vaults, even when there is a second and a third story. The roofs, however, may be made flat by raising the exterior walls and filling in until level with the top of the arch. This is done on the convents and other heavy buildings, by which a fine promenade is secured.

What may be the population of Hebron?

I estimated it at between seven and eight thousand in 1838, and it remains about what it was then. Some think

[1] Summer's Ramble, i. 245.

HEBRON.

this estimate too low, while others speak of only five thousand; but this is certainly below the truth. There are some seven hundred Jews; all the rest are Moslems, and of a most bigoted and insolent character. There are no Christians either in the town or district. Hebron furnishes another refutation of the ancient fable about the cities of refuge, that they were situated in conspicuous positions. Here it lies in this long valley, with no prospect in any direction except toward the southeast, and even that is not very extensive.

If it were of any importance, we might refer to a tradition as old, at least, as Benjamin of Tudela, that the original city did actually occupy the northwestern hill. I do not, however, believe it; there is nothing there to support it; and many things in and about the present town seem to settle its claims to be one of the oldest cities in the world on an immovable basis. These immense *birkehs* or pools are certainly very ancient. The one farthest down the valley is one hundred and thirty-three feet square and about twenty-two feet deep. The upper one is eighty-five by fifty-five, and nineteen feet deep. They are rarely full of water, though I have seen them overflowing in a very rainy season. Stone steps lead down to the water from the corners, and people are constantly descending and ascending with large skin "bottles" on their backs. Indeed, the town seems now to depend entirely upon them, though the water is none of the purest, and there are two or three fountains at no great distance up the valley. It was not always thus, for there are two or three broken aqueducts in the valley to the west and northwest of the city, which must have been in use down to a comparatively recent period.

All the visitors speak of the vineyards of Hebron, and it is a very ancient tradition that the clusters which the spies carried back from Eshcol were from this valley. Certainly in no other part of Palestine are the vineyards so extensive, so well kept, or so productive. They cover the sloping hill-sides for a long distance to the west and northwest of the town. As the Moslems do not make wine, the grapes not disposed of in the market are dried into raisins, or the juice is boiled down into *dibs*, a kind of thick grape molasses, frequently mentioned in the Bible under the kindred name of *debash*, in some places translated honey, and in others manna! Besides grapes, the olive and the fig are the most important fruits of Hebron, but apricots, pomegranates, quinces, apples, pears, and plums also flourish with proper care.

There are some pomegranate bushes in this neighborhood which may even be called trees by way of courtesy, but in reality these large and delicious "apples" grow on a stout thorny bush. There are several kinds of them in this country. In Jebaah, on Lebanon, there is a variety perfectly black on the outside. The general color, however, is a dull green, inclining to yellow, and some even have a blush of red spread over a part of their surface. The outside rind is thin but tough, and the bitter juice of it stains every thing it touches with an undefined but indelible blue. The average size is about that of the orange, but some of those from Jaffa are as large as the egg of an ostrich. Within, the "grains" are arranged in longitudinal compartments as compactly as corn on the cob, and they closely resemble those of pale red corn, except that they are nearly transparent and very beautiful. A dish filled with these "grains" *shelled out* is a very handsome ornament on any table, and the fruit is as sweet to the taste as it is pleasant to the eye. They are ripe about the middle of October, and remain in good condition all winter. Suspended in the pantry, they are kept partially dried through the whole year.

The flower of the pomegranate is bell or tulip shaped, and is of a beautiful orange-red, deepening into crimson on some bushes. There is a kind very large and double, but this bears no fruit, and is cultivated merely for its brilliant blossoms, which are put forth profusely during the whole summer.

This fruit was greatly esteemed in ancient times, and is mentioned by Moses as one of the excellencies of the promised land;[1] and, by divine command, he was to make pomegranates on the hem of the ephod: a golden bell (the blos-

[1] Deut. viii. 8.

POMEGRANATES.

som) and a pomegranate alternately round about the hem of the robe;[1] and they were reproduced in the Temple upon the net-work that covered the chapiters on the top of "Jachin and Boaz"—those noble pillars of brass—two hundred pomegranates, in rows, round about. Solomon, of course, adorns his Song of Songs with allusions to this beautiful and pleasant fruit, and, while admiring it, we may enter more readily into the gorgeous chamber of imagery where that poetic monarch delighted to dwell and to revel.

The only manufacture peculiar to Hebron is that of glass. I was not a little amused, on my first visit, with this business. Having not long before examined the great glass factories at Pittsburg, I entered these with no little curiosity; but what a contrast! In an old rickety room were three or four small furnaces of earth, all in a glow with the melted matter. The men were then making rings for bracelets, or rather armlets, to supply the Jerusalem market. The process was extremely simple: an iron rod was thrust into the melted mass, to the end of which a small portion adhered. This was rapidly twisted and pressed into a circular shape merely by the dexterous use of a long blade like that of a knife. It was a second time thrust into the furnace, and, when sufficiently softened, was stretched to the proper size

[1] Exod. xxviii. 34.

by the aid of another iron rod. This was the entire process. The various colors seen in these rings and seals are mingled into the general mass while in the furnaces, not laid on afterward. Some are nearly black, others quite white, and others variegated with all the intermediate shades. I did not see them make lamps, although they manufacture large quantities for this country and for Egypt.

Hebron, having been built "seven years before Zoan in Egypt," has, of course, a very long history from that day to this; and from the fact that Abraham, Isaac, and Jacob spent much of their lives in and near it, and, with their wives, were buried here, it has always been held in high veneration by their descendants. Not only Jews, but all who claim to be related to them, Arabs and Edomites, and other Oriental tribes, have shared in this veneration; and, since the Gentile world has adopted the religion of Abraham—that father of the faithful—its name and fame have extended to the ends of the earth, and must continue till time shall be no more. When the spies came this way, the giants of the Anakim family resided in it, but they were expelled by Caleb, to whom the place was given by Joshua. After this, we hear but little of Hebron until the time of David, who made it his residence during the seven years in which he reigned over the tribe of Judah. When he became king of all Israel he removed to Jerusalem, made that city the permanent capital of the Jewish commonwealth, and Hebron is rarely mentioned after this in sacred history. Neither the prophets nor the evangelists name it, nor does the Saviour appear to have visited it; yet we know from the Maccabees and Josephus that it continued to be an important city even subsequent to the time of the captivity; and Eusebius, Jerome, and a host of later writers speak of it, generally in connection with the tombs of the patriarchs. The Moslems got possession in the seventh century, and have continued to inhabit it ever since, with short interruptions during the time of the Crusades. Thus its existence and identity have been perpetuated and guaranteed without a break to our day.

Is it not strange that the historians of the Crusades, who must have had free access to the cave of Machpelah, have given us no intelligible description of it?

Not to those who have waded through their confused and rambling annals, where one finds every thing he does not want, and very little of what he does. Every valuable geographical and topographical fact contained in the large folios of the Gesta Dei per Francos might be condensed into a few pages, and yet this collection embodies the most important remaining records of those eventful times. If there had then been a single intelligent student of Biblical geography in the world, we might now have important light from the Middle Ages to guide us in many a doubtful ramble after a lost locality.

The Anakims of ancient Arba seem to have been the proverbial type of those giants so often mentioned in the Bible. We hear of them in Moab under the name of Emims, a people great and many, and tall as the Anakims, which also were accounted giants. The same were found among the Ammonites, and called Zamzummims; and Og, king of Bashan, remained of the giants at the time of Moses. What are we to understand, and how much, from these and other notices of this peculiar race?

Nothing less, certainly, than that there existed men of gigantic stature from the remotest antiquity, even before the Deluge, for these "men of renown" are mentioned in the sixth of Genesis. That there were in times past men of extraordinary size is a tradition wonderfully prevalent to this day all over the East. It not only runs through their legendary lore, but is embodied in numerous monuments of a more substantial character, as the tomb of Noah at Kerak, in the Buk'ah, and that of Seth at Neby Sheet, on the eastern side of the same plain. To what extent such fables corroborate the historic facts of the Bible every one must decide for himself; but the traditions themselves, and these commemorative monuments, are extremely ancient, reaching back to the times of myth and fable. The truth appears to be that there were among the governing races of primitive times certain families of gigantic stature. This peculiarity was carefully perpetuated and increased by such marriage restrictions as tended to that result, and something similar has been found among the inhabitants of the Pacific Islands. For any thing beyond this, tradition, that delights in the marvelous and monstrous, is probably accountable. Every distant object seen through her telescope is distorted and vastly exaggerated.

If we pass from fact to fable, we may pause a moment on the first steps in the scale of exaggeration, and hear the returned spies terrifying their brethren at Kadesh by their false report: All the people that we saw in the land are men of great stature. There we saw the giants, the sons of Anak which came of the giants, and we were in our own sight as grasshoppers, and so we were in their sight.[1] You may now enter any coffee-shop on a mild summer evening, and as twilight shadows settle on the silent auditors, listen to the professional *hakwatieh* amplifying the dimensions of these ancient men of renown, until—the coffee sipped and the argela out—the hearers separate, stroking their beards, and muttering *Ma sha Allah!*—God is great! But the flights of these story-tellers are tame and timid in comparison with the unfettered excursions of rabbinical imagination. Hear what they say about Og, king of Bashan: The soles of his feet were forty miles long, and the waters of the Deluge only reached to his ankles. He, being one of the antediluvian giants, escaped the general destruction, and reappears in subsequent history as Eliezer of Damascus, Abraham's servant. Abraham, who was only of the size of seventy-four ordinary men, could yet scold most terribly. Under his rebuke Og trembled so violently that one of his double teeth dropped out, and this the patriarch made into an ivory bedstead for himself, and ever after slept upon it. When Moses—who was ten ells high—attacked this same Og—by this time King of Bashan—he seized an axe ten ells in length, jumped ten ells high, and then struck with all his might—*where?* why, on *his ankle.* That blow finally killed him; for Rabbi

[1] Num. xiii. 32, 33.

Jochanan says, "I have been a grave-digger, and once, when I was chasing a roe, it fled into a shin-bone. I ran after it, and followed it for three miles, but could neither overtake it, nor see any end to the bone; so I returned, and was told that this was the shin-bone of Og, king of Bashan." But enough of this nonsense. Go to Kanah, and the old Metäwely sheikh there will entertain you till midnight with an account of the process by which Abraham tamed this unruly servant into obedience somewhere in the marshes of the Hûleh, below Tell el Kady. Coming back from such grotesque and monstrous fables, we may be thankful for the sober and credible statements of the Bible, which only require us to believe that there were in primitive times certain persons of very large stature who were called giants.

April 20th. In my rambles about the outskirts of the town last evening, I lit upon a company of Ishmaelites sitting round a large saucepan, regaling themselves with their dinner. As they said "*Tufuddal*" very earnestly, I sat down among them, and, doubling some of their bread spoon-fashion, plunged into the saucepan as they did, and I found their food very savory indeed. The composition was made of that red kind of lentils which we examined in the market, and I can readily believe that to a hungry hunter it must have been very tempting.

It is a singular fact that our Frank children born in this country are extravagantly fond of this same *adis* pottage. Generally, however, it is made out of the brown or bronze-colored, and not of this red kind. I can testify, also, that, when cooking, it diffuses far and wide an odor extremely grateful to a hungry man. It was, therefore, no slight temptation to Esau, returning weary and famished from an unsuccessful hunt in this burning climate. I have known modern hunters so utterly spent as to feel, like him, that they were about to die.

It has always seemed to me an act peculiarly unlovely and unbrotherly in Jacob to seize such an opportunity to cheat Esau out of his birthright.

Doubtless it was so; nor do I suppose that it was the first

time he had overreached his careless brother. This, however, deserved to be recorded, because it was the grand pivot upon which turned all Jacob's life—the antecedent act which led directly on to that odious deception practiced upon poor old blind Isaac, then to Jacob's flight into Mesopotamia, his marriages, etc., etc. It is instructive to notice how one sin prepares the way for and seduces to the commission of greater. This private purchase would do Jacob no good unless the father confirmed the sale. When, therefore, Isaac was about to transmit, by an act of solemn blessing, the birthright, with all its rich covenants and promises, to Esau, Jacob and his mother saw that their whole previous manœuvres to secure these would utterly fail unless they could now succeed in deluding the helpless father also.

It is not difficult to imagine by what process of sophistry Jacob might reconcile his conduct with his conscience. I believe the unsophisticated reason of man always refuses to ratify the rights of mere primogeniture as established by custom or law among many nations. In the case of Jacob and Esau it is also to be remembered that they were twins, born at the same time, and Jacob, no doubt, felt that his brother had really no valid claims of precedence which should entitle him to the inestimable blessings involved, in this instance, in the question of birthright; so also thought his mother; and to that extent I agree with them. Then it is highly probable that Jacob knew that Esau disbelieved, or, at least, despised the religious covenants and promises connected with the line of family descent, and that he was utterly unfit to be trusted with matters of such high import. And in this, also, he judged correctly. And, farther, it is nearly certain that Jacob had largely augmented the common estate, while Esau, by his wild and idle life, had rather squandered than added to it. He therefore felt that he had the best right to it, and so he had. Add to this a spice of chagrin at the obvious partiality of the father for the idle Esau, for no better reason, as appears, than because he ate of his savory venison, and we have materials enough from which Jacob could work out a tissue of specious reasons for self-justification. Success in fraud, as usual, entails a long train of retributive sorrows. Jacob was immediately obliged to fly from his beloved home, and his fond mother, largely implicated in the crime, never again saw her 'darling son. After a long and perilous journey to Mesopotamia, he was subjected to a series of cruel deceptions and frauds practiced upon him by his selfish father-in-law, and, when compelled to flee from this intolerable annoyance, he had to humble himself to the dust and plead for his life before the brother he had so often and so grossly injured; and, long after this, he was again deceived by his own sons in the matter of his lost, beloved son Joseph. Few histories are more instructive than this of Jacob, or better illustrate the, to us, involved and complicated machinery of divine Providence.

There are some curious incidents in this long story which let us into the habits and manners of those primitive times. For example, it appears that Jacob, though the son of a wealthy emeer, was actually cooking his own mess of pottage.

There is nothing in this contrary even to present usage in this country. I have often seen rich and luxurious citizens occupied in the same way, and this is still more common among the Arabs of the desert. So also Esau, one would have thought, might easily have sent some of the numerous servants to hunt for venison on the important occasion of receiving the parental blessing; but this, too, is quite natural in the East. I have had an opportunity to see the great sheikhs of the Anizy, Bini Sukhr, and other tribes of Arabs, and they were in no way distinguished either by dress or manners from their humblest followers. Their garments were even more worn and greasy than those of the servants, and I could not see that they refused to bear their full share of any business that was going on. Indeed, there is a rude etiquette which requires these chiefs to be foremost in all hardships which they and their followers encounter. So, also, the fact that Laban's daughters were keeping the flocks, and Jacob's mother carrying water from the well, and other similar examples, do not contradict the customs of wealthy Eastern shepherds. And who that has traveled much in this country has not often arrived at a well in the heat of the day which was surrounded with numerous flocks of sheep waiting to be watered? I once saw such a scene in the burning plains of northern Syria. Half-naked, fierce-looking men were drawing up water in leather buckets; flock after flock was brought up, watered, and sent away, and, after all the men had ended their work, then several women and girls brought up their flocks and drew water for them. Thus it was with Jethro's daughters when Moses stood up and aided them, and thus, no doubt, it would have been with Rachel, if Jacob had not rolled away the stone and watered her sheep. I have frequently seen wells closed up with large stones, though in this part of the country it is not commonly done, because water is not so scarce and precious. It is otherwise, however, in the dreary deserts.

Cisterns are very generally covered over with a large slab, having a round hole in it large enough to let down the leather bucket or earthen jar. Into this hole a heavy stone is thrust, often such as to require the united strength of two or three shepherds to remove. The same is seen occasionally over *wells* of living water; but, where they are large and the supply abundant, no such precaution is needed. It was either at one of these cisterns, or less abundant and more precious wells, that Jacob met Rachel, and, being a stout man, nearly seventy years of age, he was able to remove the stone and water the flock.

I have repeatedly found wells closed up tight and the mouth plastered over with mortar. Such wells are reserved until times of greatest need, when all other sources of supply have failed. This may illustrate that passage in Zechariah xiii. 1: In that day there shall be a fountain opened to the house of David and to the inhabitants of Jerusalem for sin and for uncleanness. This is, indeed, a beautiful and significant promise, which many actions and customs in this country may shed light upon and render emphatic. Not only are fountains often sealed up until times of utmost need, and then opened for public use, but, when this is not the case, they are commonly far off from the villages, in secluded valleys, and, on account of the difficulty of carrying water to their homes, the women take their soiled clothes, a kettle, and some wood down to them, and there do their washing. Again, the inhabitants of most villages select one or more sheep in autumn, which they feed with the greatest care for their winter's supply of cooking-fat. They not only stuff them with vine and mulberry leaves, as is done in our country with poultry, but every evening they take them to the open fountain, and thoroughly wash them from all defilements. This greatly adds to the richness and sweetness of the mutton. The figure may have been suggested to Zechariah by this custom. Now Christ is not only the Good Shepherd, and his people the sheep of his pasture, but he is also the fountain in which their sins and pollutions are washed away. This fountain, long sealed up, was opened by the nails and the spear on Calvary, and not merely for the house of David and the inhabitants of Jerusalem, but for all whom they represent and include. Millions have been washed in the Gospel fountain, and yet its waters are as abundant and efficacious to cleanse from sin as ever. It is the very heart and core of the glad tidings to all nations that this fountain has indeed been opened, and whosoever will may wash and be clean.

What does this curious and irregular procession signify?

Our friend here says it is a circumcision, and it is generally attended with just such music and buffoonery.

Well, that is interesting, certainly, to find this rite still practiced in the very place where it was first instituted by command of God to Abraham, nearly four thousand years ago. Ishmael, too, the great ancestor of these Arabs, was among the very first to receive the rite.[1]

If you have any curiosity to study this subject in detail, you will find the process, and the accompanying feasts and ceremonies, minutely explained by Lane in his "Modern Egyptians." This before us is evidently a small affair, for the rabble accompanying the victim are rude in the extreme, and poorly clad. The whole thing resembles a drunken

[1] Gen. xvii. 23.

frolic more than a religious ceremony; but, even in the processions of the rich on such occasions, there are commonly two or three buffoons along with the musicians, to make sport by their outlandish costume and ridiculous behavior.

What do you say to the arguments of those who maintain that Abraham was not the first that practiced circumcision—that, in fact, the Father of the Faithful borrowed it from the Egyptians, the Ethiopians, or Colchians?

I have very little interest in such speculations. The Bible is false—let us say so at once—if Abraham did not receive this rite by revelation, and adopt it in obedience to a direct command of God. He received it also as the seal of a most important covenant. I care not whether any body ever used a somewhat similar custom or not before the time of Abraham. It may be so, though there is no satisfactory evidence of the fact. To me it seems far more probable that the rite was communicated to the priests in Egypt through Joseph, who married into their family or tribe, than that the Israelites borrowed it from them. As to the testimony of Herodotus, who came into Egypt *fifteen centuries* after, and, with great learning and research, often writes a good deal of nonsense, I refuse utterly to put it in the same category with that of Moses. The great founder of the Jewish commonwealth—the greatest lawgiver on record—born and bred in Egypt, states the facts in relation to the introduction of circumcision among his people. A mere traveler and historian—a foreigner and a *Greek*—comes along very much later, and makes statements which are partly true, partly erroneous, as Josephus shows in his answer to Apion; and then skeptical authors, more than twenty centuries later than Herodotus, bring up his imperfect statements, and, twisting and expanding them, attempt to prove that Abraham did not receive circumcision from God (as Moses plainly says he did), but from the Egyptians! Not with such weapons can the veracity of Moses be successfully assailed.

It is, however, very remarkable that this singular rite did actually spread into many countries, that it has been retained not only by Jews and Moslems all over the world, but that even some Christian sects have adopted it, as the Copts and Abyssinians. We need not pursue this subject any farther at present, but it is certainly a fine corroboration of the book of Genesis to stand in the plain of Mamre, and witness the ceremonies of that solemn religious rite which Abraham here received as a seal of the righteousness of faith which he had, yet being uncircumcised.[1]

We are reminded by the firing of guns, the beating of the everlasting *tubble*, the singing and clapping of hands, and the general hubbub always attendant upon native weddings, that it was from this place Abraham sent his faithful servant into Mesopotamia to find and to bring a wife for Isaac.

Yes; and the account of this embassy in the 24th chapter of Genesis furnishes many allusions to Oriental customs which modern manners beautifully illustrate. We have already had occasion to notice the great influence and authority which chief servants in the families of emeers and sheikhs still exercise. Such was the confidence and respect accorded to Eliezer, that Abraham at one time seriously contemplated making him his heir, a result not uncommon in these Oriental countries in all ages down to the present time.

Another thing very noticeable, and to which also we have before alluded, is the great solicitude of Abraham to have his son marry *one of his own kindred*. This is in exact correspondence with the customs of the Eastern nobility; nor need we limit the remark to the higher classes. Certain degrees of affinity excepted, a relative always has the preference in matrimonial negotiations. The strict injunction of Abraham, therefore, to bring none but a *relative* from his own family, though enforced by religious considerations, was in no sense a departure from established usages and social laws in regard to marriage.

The mode of swearing fidelity required of Eliezer by placing his hand under the thigh of Abraham seems to have been peculiar to the patriarchs, and *may* have had reference to that promised seed who was to proceed from Abraham's loins, according to the then figurative style of speaking on

[1] Rom. iv. 11.

this subject. In the present case there would be more than ordinary propriety in this significant action, inasmuch as the oath taken had direct and exclusive reference to the preservation of that line of descent through which this promised seed was to come.

The preparation and outfit for this journey agree in all respects with the persons concerned, the nature of the country, and the habits of the people. Eliezer took ten camels loaded with provisions and presents; and such an expedition would not now be undertaken from Hebron with any other animals, nor with a less number. The diligent servant, no doubt, selected the most direct route, which would be through Palestine, along the west side of the Jordan and the lakes, into the Buk'ah, and out through the land of Hamath to the Euphrates, and thence to the city of Nahor in Mesopotamia. Such a journey is both long and dangerous, far beyond what is indicated to a Western reader by the brief statement that Eliezer arose and went into Mesopotamia; but what befell him by the way we know not. The narrative leaps the whole distance, and so must we, with the simple assurance that the Lord God of Israel led him by the right way.

Every phrase of the eleventh verse contains an allusion to matters Oriental. Arrived at the town of Nahor, he made his camels *kneel down without the city by a well of water at the time of evening—the time that women go out to draw water*. He made the camels kneel—a mode of expression taken from actual life. The action is literally *kneeling;* not stooping, sitting, or lying down on the side like a horse, but *kneeling* on his *knees*, and this the camel is taught to do from his youth. The *place* is said to have been by a well of water, and this well was outside the city. In the East, where wells are scarce, and water indispensable, the existence of a well or fountain determines the site of the village. The people build near it, but prefer to have it outside the "city," to avoid the noise, dust, and confusion always occurring at it, and especially if the place is on the public highway. It is around the fountain that the thirsty traveler and the wearied caravan assemble; and if you have become separated from your own company before arriving at a town, you need only inquire for the fountain, and there you will find them. It was perfectly natural, therefore, for Eliezer to *halt at the well.* The *time* was evening; but it is farther stated that it was when the *women* go forth to draw water. True to life again. At that hour the peasant returns home from his labor, and the women are busy preparing the evening meal, which is to be ready at sunset. Cool fresh water is then demanded, and of course there is a great concourse around the well. But why limit it to the *women?* Simply because such is the fact. About great cities men often carry water, both on donkeys and on their own backs, but in the country, among the unsophisticated natives, *women only* go to the well or the fountain; and often, when traveling, have I seen long files of them going and returning with their pitchers, "at the time when women go out to draw water."

Again: the description of Rebekah, the account she gives of herself, and the whole dialogue with Eliezer, agree admirably with Oriental customs. Even the statement as to the manner of carrying her pitcher, or rather jar, is exact—*on her shoulder.* The Egyptian and the negro carry on the head, the Syrian on the shoulder or the hip. She went *down* to the well; and nearly all wells in the East are in wadies, and many of them have steps down to the water—fountains of course have. Eliezer asks water to drink; she hastens and *lets down the pitcher on her hand.* How often have I had this identical act performed for myself, when traveling in this thirsty land. Rebekah's address to the "servant," Drink, my lord—*Ishrub ya seedy*—will be given to you in the exact idiom by the first gentle Rebekah you ask water from. But I have never found any young lady so generous as this fair daughter of Bethuel. She drew for all his camels, and for nothing, while I have often found it difficult to get my horse watered even for money. Rebekah emptied her pitcher into the *trough*—an article always found about wells, and frequently made of stone. The jewels, also, for the *face,* forehead, and arms, are still as popular among the same class of people as they were in the days of Abraham. Not only are the head, neck, and arms adorned with a profusion of gold and silver rings, chains, and other ornaments, but rings are suspended on the face, from the side of the nose, etc., etc.

Laban's address, Come-in, thou blessed of the Lord, is still in good taste. I have often been welcomed in set phrases even more complimentary and sacred. The camels, as appears from the 32d verse, were included in the invitation, and were brought *into the house;* and I have often slept in the *same room* with these peaceful animals, in company with their owner and all his family. *Straw* and provender were given to them; that is, *tibn*, and some kind of pulse or grain. There is no *hay* in the East. Water to wash the feet of the wearied travelers was of course given, and the same kind act will be done to you under similar circumstances. So, also, the mode of negotiating the marriage contract, the presenting of gifts, etc., are all in perfect accordance with modern usages. The parents manage the whole affair, often, however, with the advice of the eldest son and heir, as Laban was in this case. And if the father be dead, the eldest son takes his place, and assumes his authority in the disposal of his sisters. Presents are absolutely essential in betrothals. They are given with much ceremony before witnesses, and the articles presented are described in a written document, so that, if the match be broken off, the bridegroom can obtain them back again, or their value, and something more as a compensation for the injury.

Finally, the behavior of Rebekah, when about to meet Isaac, was such as modern etiquette requires. It is customary for both men and women, when an emeer or great personage is approaching, to alight some time before he comes up with them. Women frequently refuse to ride in the presence of men, and when a company of them are to pass through a town, they often dismount and walk. It was, no doubt, a point of Syrian etiquette for Rebekah to stop, descend from her camel, and cover herself with a veil in the presence of her future husband. In a word, this Biblical narrative is so natural to one familiar with the East, so beautiful also, and life-like, that the entire scene seems to be an affair in which he has himself been but recently an actor.

DESCENT OF JACOB'S SONS TO EGYPT.

XXXIX. HEBRON TO SANTA SABA.
April 21st.

Returning from my ramble down the vale of Hebron this morning, I met a company of men and donkeys going out apparently for grain, and I was struck with the resemblance of the animals themselves to those in pictures now found on the monuments of Egypt. The saddles and sacks of some appeared to be precisely like those used in the days when the sons of Jacob descended along the same valley to get corn from Egypt.

EGYPTIAN DONKEYS.

Doubtless there has been but little change in all these matters from that time to this, and the resemblance is often still more exact from the fact that when the crops of this country fail through drouth or other causes, the people still go down to Egypt to buy corn, as they did in the time of the patriarch. It has also frequently occurred to me, when passing a large company of donkeys on their way to buy food, that we are not to suppose that only the eleven donkeys on which the brethren of Joseph rode composed the whole caravan. One man often leads or drives half a dozen; and, besides, I apprehend that Jacob's sons had many servants along with them. Eleven sacks of grain, such as donkeys would carry, would not sustain a household like his for a week. It is no objection to this supposition that these servants are not mentioned. There was no occasion to allude to them, and such a reference would have disturbed the perfect *unity* and touching simplicity of that most beautiful narrative; and it is in accordance with the general practice of Moses in sketching the lives of the patriarchs, not to confuse the story by introducing non-historic characters. Thus, had it not been for the capture of Lot by Chedorlaomer, we should not have known that Abraham had three hundred and eighteen full-grown men in his household; and so, also, had it not been necessary for Jacob to send company after company to guide his large presents to meet Esau, we might have been left to suppose that he and his sons alone conducted his flocks in his flight from Mesopotamia; but it is certain that he had a large retinue of servants; and so, doubtless, each of his sons had servants, and it is incredible that they should have gone down to Egypt without them; on the contrary, there is every reason to believe that there was a large caravan. The fact, also, that the sons themselves took part in the work, and that each had his sack under him, is in exact correspondence with the customs of tent-dwelling shepherds at this day. The highest sheikhs dress and fare precisely as their followers do, and bear their full share in the operations of the company, whatever they may be.

This leads me to suggest another idea which I have long entertained in regard to the actual number of persons that went down to Egypt with Jacob. It was strictly true that all the souls that *came out of Jacob's loins*, besides his sons' wives, were threescore and six;[1] and these being, so to speak,

[1] Gen. xlvi. 26.

historic characters, are, according to the usual practice, specifically mentioned. But there must have been a very large company belonging to them, of both men-servants, maid-servants, and children; and, beyond a doubt, these remained, were incorporated with, and multiplied as rapidly as their masters. May we not in this fact find an explanation of the vast multitude to which this company had grown in so short a time? I have myself no doubt on the subject. Israel did not sell his home-born servants, but took them into Egypt. There they were absorbed into the Hebrew nation during those generations when all were reduced by their tyrannical masters to one common lot of hard bondage. And thus it came to pass that there were six hundred thousand men that went up harnessed and fit for war. Nor is this custom of absorbing into the different tribes those servants that belonged to them at variance with either ancient or modern practice. That the freedmen were incorporated with and adopted the family name of their masters, is a well-known fact in the history of the great Roman commonwealth.

That company of donkeys you met were doubtless going to the distant fields to bring in to the threshing-floors the *'adis* or lentils from which Esau's pottage was made.— Just below us is a field in which it is not yet ripe, and another yonder, on the southern

LENTILS ('ADIS).

slope of the mountain, where they are gathering it. You notice that it does not grow more than six or eight inches high, and is *pulled* like flax, not cut with the sickle. When green, it resembles an incipient pea-vine, only the leaves are differently arranged, smaller, and more delicate, somewhat like those of the mimosa or sensitive plant.

Our muleteers anticipate a hard day's march to St. Saba, and therefore are more than usually expeditious in starting. Allowing them to pursue the regular road toward the Pools of Solomon, we will pass up to the northwest, and visit the great oak of Abraham.

LOWER POOL OF HEBRON.

Do you suppose that this large pool we are now passing is ancient?

I see no reason to doubt that both this and also the smaller one, higher up the valley, date back to the days of the Jews. Whether either of them is mentioned in 2 Sam. iv. 12, as the place where David hung up the murderers of Ishbosheth, is, of course, doubtful, but both of them may have then been in existence; for works of this kind, and in such localities, last as long as the cities for whose accommodation they were made.

We are now riding through the most extensive and best-kept vineyards that I have seen in this country.

All travelers are struck with them, and no one fails, or can fail, of being reminded by them of that extraordinary cluster of grapes which the spies carried "between two" on a staff; for the valley of Hebron is the place from whence they bore this proof of the fertility of the promised land.[1] I have been here in the season of grapes, and, though they are larger than in most other localities, and the clusters very long, yet I have never seen any so heavy as to require to be borne between two upon a staff.

These houses and rude towers in the vineyards are for the vine-dressers, I suppose?

The houses are for the families of the owners of these vineyards; and should you come this way in September or October, you will find the city deserted, and these gardens crowded with grape-gatherers of every age and sex. The whole population then live abroad, each under his own vine and fig-tree. Most of them sleep beneath these vine-arbors, and the houses are for the safe-keeping of their utensils and their raisins, while they are out gathering grapes. A large part of the crop is eaten or sold at the time; the remainder is dried into raisins, or pressed, and the juice boiled down to a thick molasses, called *dibs;* for the Moslems, as you are aware, make no wine.

These towers stationed around on commanding points are for the *natûrs*, or watchmen, and they are already there, keeping a keen eye upon the entire range of vineyards. One of them is coming toward us from his tower, and his object is to see who we are, and what may be our business out here among the vineyards. We will take him as our guide to the oak; for, although it is in full view, there are innumerable turns yet to be made in our tortuous path before we can reach it. These watchmen are very celebrated characters in the Bible, and figure largely both in prose and poetry. Isaiah has a beautiful reference to them in the 52d chapter of his prophecies: Thy watchmen shall lift up the

[1] Numb. xiii. 23.

voice, with the voice together shall they sing, for they shall see eye to eye when the Lord shall bring again Zion.[1]

Do you believe that the watchmen here mentioned were these *natûrs* over the fields and vineyards? I had supposed that the prophet refers in that passage to the military sentinels in time of danger.

Doubtless the reference is in many places to such sentinels stationed upon lofty mountains or upon the fortifications of the city. Thus, in this 52d chapter, "I have set watchmen upon thy walls, oh Jerusalem, which shall never hold their peace day nor night;" and again, in the 7th verse, "How beautiful upon the mountains are the feet of him that bringeth good tidings, that publishes peace; that bringeth good tidings of good; that saith unto Zion, 'Thy God reigneth.'" If you conceive of Zion as a city defended by walls and towers, and guarded by soldiers, the illustration is natural and striking, particularly in time of war. Then, as I myself have seen at Jerusalem, these watchmen are multiplied, and so stationed that every yard of the wall falls under their surveillance, and thus they literally see eye to eye. They never remit their watchfulness, nor do they keep silence, especially at night. When danger is apprehended they are obliged to call to one another, and to respond every few minutes. The guard on the look-out at the Tower of David, for instance, lifts up his voice in a long call, the one next south of him takes up the note and repeats it, and thus it runs quite round the circuit of the walls. At Sidon the custom-house guards stationed around the city are required to keep one another awake and alert in the same way, particularly when there is danger of smuggling.

There is, however, another set of scenes which seems to me to correspond better to the drapery of the passage from Isaiah. Zion, or the Church of God, is frequently described under the similitude of a garden or vineyard, and such is the case here. Her watchmen are not on walls, but stand upon the mountains, and the costume of the entire

[1] Isaiah lii. 8.

scene is rural, not mural. It breathes of the country, not of the city. To understand and enjoy this noble passage, one needs to go forth to the fields at the time of the vintage. The vineyards are generally planted on the sides of mountains, often climbing, by successive terraces, quite to the summit. As they are far from the village, and without fence or hedge, they must be carefully guarded, and the stoutest and boldest young men are selected for *natûrs*. They take their stations on the highest part of the mountain which they have to watch, and are so arranged that the *eye of one surveys the entire series of vineyards up to the point where the eye of the other reaches.* Thus eye meets eye, and every part is brought under constant surveillance. "They shall lift up the voice," etc. This is very natural and beautiful. When an animal or thief appears, or any other cause of alarm occurs, the watchman who observes it lifts up a long-toned cry at the very top of his voice, and is immediately responded to by his fellows at the other stations; and the attention of all being aroused, it is his duty whose part is threatened with injury to attend to the case at once. Thus it will be with *Zion* in the happy days foreshadowed by this prophecy. The watchmen being sufficient in number, rightly located, all intent upon their work of watching, and ready to afford each other information of danger and assistance in repelling it, then will Zion dwell safely. Wild beasts may threaten to break in and devour, and robbers may prowl about, but the system of defense will be perfect, and the watchmen "scorn surprise."

This explanation coincides best with the 7th verse: "How beautiful on the mountains are the feet of him that bringeth good tidings, that *publishes peace.*" These *natûrs*, standing upon the very pinnacle of the mountain, have a very striking appearance, particularly when seen below, far off, at a great elevation, in picturesque costumes, their outline drawn sharply upon the clear blue sky beyond; they seem in fancy's eye like aerial beings, guardian angels, hovering in mid heaven over their peaceful charge. The *feet* are mentioned, perhaps, because they are seen *standing*, as if alert and prompt to fulfill the duties of their office. They do, in fact, *stand*, *not sit or lounge;* and the same idea is implied in the 5th verse of the 61st chapter of Isaiah: "Strangers shall *stand* and feed your flocks." Good shepherds do not sit down in careless neglect of their charge, and I have often been reminded of this promise to Israel when looking at the shepherd *standing out* in bold relief upon some towering cliff, from which he could see every member of his flock.

It is only on rare occasions that one now finds all the circumstances here alluded to combined in the same scene, and never but in elevated and retired parts of Lebanon, during the months of September and October. When passing through vineyards thus situated and thus guarded on that goodly mountain, I have been suddenly startled by a long, loud note of warning, swelling up the steep cliffs of the mountains, and responded to by others before and behind, "singing together" in concert, and waking the echoes that sleep in the wadies and among the ragged rocks; then one of the watchmen, leaving his lofty station, would descend to meet me with hands laden with the best clusters for my acceptance, and this, too, without money and without price. Courteously accompanying me to the end of the vineyards, he would then dismiss me with a graceful bow, and the prayer of peace on his lips. If, however, one attempts to take without permission, these watchmen are required to resist even unto death, and in the execution of their office they are extremely bold and resolute. I have known many serious and some fatal rencounters of this kind.

Here we are at the famous oak, and a moment's inspection will show to one acquainted with such matters that it can have no connection with Abraham, nor, indeed, with any one else who lived more than a thousand years ago. We have oaks in Lebanon twice the size of this, and every way more striking and majestic. It is a fine old *baluta* (evergreen oak), however, twenty-six feet in girth at the ground, and its thick branches extend over an area ninety-three feet in diameter. Some six feet from the ground the tree *forks* into three great arms, which again divide as they ascend into innumerable limbs. The location is beautiful, near the head of this wady Sebta, and about two miles northwest of the city, and many a pic-nic is achieved by the Jews of Hebron upon the soft sward that is allowed to grow beneath this noble oak of their father Abraham.

We must now pursue our ride to the northeast, and join our company below Beled en Nussarah (town of the Christians), where they are to wait for us. In the valley south of this ruined *Beled* is a fountain of the same name, from which an aqueduct once carried the water to Hebron. Beyond is the *house* of Abraham, which lies some distance to the east of the regular road from Hebron to Bethlehem, on a path that leads to Tekoa, and which we would follow if our men knew the way, as it would take us nearer the cave of Adullam, which we wish to visit. This house of Abraham appears never to have been finished, and at present there remain but two courses of great stones, some of them fifteen feet in length, and more than three thick. The builder, whoever he was, appears to have projected a strong castle or palace, two hundred feet long and a hundred and sixty feet broad; but, like many who begin, he was not able to finish, and has left these courses of hewn stones out on this lone mountain to puzzle the brains of antiquarians and tourists to the end of time.

We now begin to descend northward to Dirweh, where is a fountain of water with large stone troughs, and many old quarries in the neighborhood. The place is doubtless ancient, though its name does not occur in the Bible. Directly east of it, however, is Hŭlhŭl, the ancient Halhûl, which was given to Judah, and which was near Hebron, according to the Onomasticon. From this to the Pools of Solomon one may go to sleep, so far as pretty scenery or interesting historic sites are concerned. We are now coming to a deserted village called Kûfîn, and west of it a short distance is Beit Ummar, while on the east of our path is a considerable ruin called Bazata, or Beth Zeita.

Though our present road is destitute of historic sites, this region of country abounds in them; and if the season was not so far advanced, and the country had been less disturbed, it would have been pleasant to spend a few days in making excursions around Hebron. Scarcely any part of Palestine has preserved so many ancient names as the district of which this city is the centre. On the south are Adoraim, and Anab, and Shochoh, Juttah, Ziph, Eshtemoa, Anim, Maon, and Carmel, from whence David got his wife, after Nabal, "that son of Belial," had died in his drunken debauch, as recorded in the twenty-fifth chapter of 1st Samuel; on the west and north are Beth Tappuah, Ramah, Beth-zur, and Halhûl, and many more, according as we extend the circle. These names, however, are nearly all destitute of Biblical interest, and what there is of ruins about the sites worthy of notice we must commit to the care of tourists and explorers, who make it their business to search out, measure, and describe them. The people of Ziph obtained an odious reputation in the time of David by betraying his hiding-place in the hill of Hachilah to King Saul. One of these rough hills below Ziph must doubtless be the scene of that venturesome visit of David into the camp of his enemy while he and all his troop were asleep.[1] That entire region is now almost deserted except by Bedawîn robbers, who render it at least as dangerous to honest shepherds as it seems to have been before David and his company frequented it. The men of Carmel mention it as something remarkable that they were not *hurt*, neither missed any thing as long as they were conversant with them in the fields. They were a wall unto us night and day all the while we were with them keeping the sheep.[2] It is refreshing to read such a testimony to David's admirable government over the heterogeneous and not very respectable band that followed him; and if there was now such an emeer in that same region, we might have safely extended our rambles down to the Dead Sea, at the famous castle of Masada, and then passed on northward by 'Ain Jidy to Jericho. As it is, we are only able to get some such view of these districts as Moses had from the top of Pisgah. The result of such a

---

[1] 1 Sam. xxvi. 1-12.   [2] 1 Sam. xxv. 15, 16.

survey on my mind, however, has always been far less satisfactory and refreshing than it appears to have been to Moses, for no other part of Palestine is so dreary and uninteresting as this, and it grows more and more so as you approach the Sea of Sodom, until the barren, bronze-colored rocks terminate in the tremendous cliff of Masada. It has never been my privilege to visit that celebrated castle, and the best account I have seen of it is from the pen of Mr. Wolcott, who was also the first in modern times to visit and identify it. The most striking *views* were drawn by his traveling companion, Mr. Tipping, and appear in Mr. Traill's new translation of Josephus. Their visit was made in the winter of 1842, and since then many travelers have been there, including several of the exploring expedition of Captain Lynch. All who visited this terrific crag and strange

ROCK OF MASADA.

castle seem to have been smitten with the spirit of exaggeration, but no one, except perhaps M. de Saulcey, has equaled Josephus. You can read his account in the 8th chapter of the 7th book of his Wars. He thus speaks of the approach to it along the path "called the *serpent*," as resembling that animal in its narrowness and its perpetual windings, for it is broken off at the prominent precipices of the rock, and returns frequently into itself, and, lengthening again by little and little, hath much ado to proceed forward, and he that would walk along it must first go on one leg and then on the other; and there is also nothing but destruction in case your foot slip, for on each side there is a vastly deep chasm and precipice, sufficient to quell the courage of any body by the terror it infuses into the mind, etc., etc.

The historian informs us that Jonathan the high-priest first of all built a fortress on this cliff, and called it Masada; but the great wall around the entire summit, seven furlongs in length, was the work of Herod, who erected a palace there, and spent vast sums in preparing it to be a last retreat for himself in case of need. He, however, died elsewhere, and had no occasion for such a stronghold; but after the destruction of Jerusalem, a band of robbers, whom Josephus calls Siccarii, seized upon it, and dared to set at defiance the conquerors of the world; and upon its hard and blackened summit was enacted the very last scene in the tragedy of Israel's destruction.

The wall built by Silva to hem in the besieged can still be traced quite round the rock, and also the remains of the Roman camp; and when the place was subdued by famine, and the defenses were stormed, the people, unable to escape, and maddened by the speech of Eleazar their chief, "embraced their wives, took their children in their arms, and gave the longest parting kisses," and with bitter tears then plunged their dripping daggers to their hearts, and laid them all dead in one ghastly funeral pile. They then chose ten men by lot to slay all the rest, and every one laid himself down by his wife and children, and, with his arms around their lifeless bodies, offered his neck to the sword of the executioner. This bloody butchery accomplished, one of the ten killed all the rest, and finally himself. Thus perished nine hundred and sixty men, women, and children, the last great sacrifice on the altar of divine retribution, and only two women and five children survived to tell the tale. Such tragedies are far more than mere incidents in man's general history. They are the voice of the Almighty One, setting the seal of truth divine to a thousand admonitions and prophetic warnings scattered every where through his holy Word, and, thus regarded, there is no stronger evidence for the divine origin of the Bible than the seven books of Jewish Wars by Josephus.

There is no other point of much interest along the western shore of the Dead Sea, except 'Ain Jidy—Fountain of the Goat—the En-gedi of the Bible, which was given to Judah, and mentioned by Joshua along with the city of salt.[1] It is in a wild ravine, and the cliffs on either side are full of natural and artificial caves and sepulchres. It was in the strongholds of En-gedi that the persecuted David at one time dwelt, and into one of the caves there Saul went "to cover his feet," when David, who lay hid deep within, arose and cut off the skirt of his robe, and might have slain the wearer also, had he not feared to stretch forth his hand against the Lord's anointed.[2] Owing to copious fountains in this warm ravine, there were, in ancient times, fragrant orchards and spicy gardens at En-gedi, to which Solomon, in his Song of Songs, compares his beloved: My beloved is unto me as a cluster of camphire in the vintage of En-gedi.[3] Just what comphire was can not now be determined, but it must have been very pleasant. In the margin it is translated cypress, something equally unknown to me. Dr. Kitto argues that this *kopher* was the *henneh*, and certainly the long "clusters" of henneh flowers are extremely fragrant. The Orientals, also, are extravagantly fond of their odor, and they have an intimate association with love and marriage, so that Solomon might very appropriately compare his beloved to such

[1] Josh. xv. 62. [2] 1 Sam. xxiii. 29, and xxiv. 1–6. [3] Song i. 14.

a cluster. It is my opinion, however, that *kopher* is merely a poetic name for a very *fragrant species* of grape that flourished most luxuriously in these vineyards of En-gedi. The Arabs of the present day distinguish their choice varieties of grapes by names every way analogous to this.

In the account of Saul's pursuit of David to En-gedi, two circumstances are mentioned which are worthy of a passing remark. The first is, that there were *sheepcotes* there in connection with the cave into which Saul retired. I have seen hundreds of them around the mouth of caverns, and, indeed, there is scarcely a cave in the land, whose location will admit of being thus occupied, but has such a "cote" in front of it, generally made by piling up loose stones into a circular wall, which is covered with thorns as a farther protection against robbers and wild beasts. During cold storms, and in the night, the flocks retreat into the cave, but at other times they remain in this inclosed cote. The cavern may have been full of them when the king entered; nor would his presence have disturbed them—as I have found on many occasions—while their constant tramping about the sleeping Saul would have rendered the approach of David wholly unnoticed. I have had them step over me when resting in such caves, and have seen them actually tramp on their sleeping shepherd without disturbing his slumbers. Moreover, these caverns are as dark as midnight, and the keenest eye can not see five paces *inward;* but one who has been long within, and is looking *outward* toward the entrance, can observe with perfect distinctness all that takes place in that direction. David, therefore, could watch Saul as he came in, and notice the exact place where he "covered his feet," while he could see nothing but impenetrable darkness.

The other fact is, that the cliffs about En-gedi were then called "the rocks of the wild goats," and from them, doubtless, the place received its name, En-gedi ('Ain Jidy)—the Fountain of the Goats. Now it is a remarkable and a pleasing circumstance that these bold and hardy dwellers upon the rocks are still found in the wild ravines about 'Ain

Jidy. I have seen the skin and powerful horns of one that was shot there by an Arab hunter.

WILD GOATS.

But here we are at El Burak, as the Pools of Solomon are now called, and there we will take our noonday lunch, and drink of that "sealed fountain" which furnished the king another pretty figure with which to compare his "beloved;" at least such is monastic identification and exposition of Song iv. 12.

While I arrange for our repast under the wall of this dilapidated old castle, you may satisfy your curiosity by a survey of these great cisterns.—Well, do they equal their name and fame?

They are worthy of Solomon, and that is the highest note I can think of at present.

They are certainly gigantic cisterns, and all the more impressive in this utter solitude, where there are no other structures with which to compare them, or to divide the interest which they inspire. The proportions of the one farthest to the east are truly royal: nearly six hundred feet long, two hundred wide, and fifty deep.— When full, it would float the largest man-of-war that ever plowed the ocean.[1]

The first time I saw these Burak there was very little water in any of them, but I have since been here when the two upper ones were full and overflowing into the third. The stream from the only fountain in this vicinity was then led along an open canal on the north side, directly into the aqueduct east of the pools, and thus carried round the shoulder of the hill, apparently to irrigate gardens in that direction. I examined the underground rooms in the southwest corner of this old castle, where the water first ap-

---

[1] Dr. Robinson, with his usual accuracy, gives the measurement of the three as follows: the 1st is 582 by 207, and 50 feet deep; the 2d is 423 by 250, and 39 deep; the 3d is 380 by 236, and 25 deep. All of them, however, are considerably *narrower* at the upper end, the first being 148, the second 160, and the third 229 feet.

pears, brought there by an artificial channel, many feet below the surface, from the fountain-head, which is some forty rods to the northwest. Tradition makes this "the spring shut up, the fountain sealed," to which the "sister spouse" is compared in Song iv. 12, and if so, the "garden inclosed" was near at hand, perhaps in this little plain which spreads up to the fountain from the pools. If Solomon really constructed these vast reservoirs—and even Dr. Robinson is disposed to admit the fact—it is probable that it was on the neighboring hills, and in the valleys to the northeast of them, that he planted the vineyards, made the gardens and orchards of all kinds of fruits, and made pools of water, to water therewith the wood that bringeth forth trees;[1] by which and other like data he worked out the great problem of human affairs to the final product of "vanity of vanities." Josephus, however, says that these gardens were at Etam, which our friends in Jerusalem have identified with Urtas, its fountains and fine gardens.

Well, at Urtas let it be, or wherever you please: I am tired of doubting every thing. Besides, I think there is good reason to rest in the *general* correctness of this identification; and the thought that the wise king of Israel had often retired to those then well-wooded and well-watered hills and valleys, adds immensely to the charm of this day's most delightful and instructive ramble.

We must now pursue our ride, and the path lies down the valley below Urtas, and we shall follow for some time the line of the canal by which the water was conveyed to Jerusalem. This aqueduct is probably less ancient than the pools; but that is not certain, for I have often noticed that such canals, where the line followed along the surface of the country, was constructed of small stones, laid up in a careless manner, and this, too, where we know that the work dates back at least to the beginning of our era. The ephemeral character of the present aqueduct, therefore, does not *prove* that it is modern. It followed the sinuosities of the hills, passed east, and below Bethlehem and the convent of

[1] Eccl. ii. 4-6.

Elijah, and near Jerusalem was carried along the west side of Gihon to the north end of the lower pool, where it crossed to the east side, and descended around the southern declivity of Zion below Neby Daûd, and finally entered the southwestern corner of the temple area, where the water was employed in the various services of the sanctuary.

I once struck across the wild region east of us to visit Tekoa and the so-called cave of Adullam. Of Tekoa little need be said. The name is applied to a ruined site lying on the northeastern slope of a high ridge, an hour and a half to the southeast of the pools. The whole country is now deserted, except by the Arabs, who pasture their flocks on those barren hills. They are a rude and sinister-looking generation. I hope the herdsmen of Tekoa, with whom Amos says he associated, were better men and more civilized than their present successors. Joab, I am sure, would search Tekoa in vain for a wise woman to fetch about that cunning form of speech by which David was induced to recall Absalom from banishment.[1]

Having passed eastward of Tekoa, we descended a shallow wady for about a mile to some curious old buildings which overhang the tremendous gorge of Wady Urtas, there called Khureitûn, which is also the name of the ruins. Leaving our horses in charge of wild Arabs, and taking one for a guide, we started for the cave, having a fearful gorge below, gigantic cliffs above, and the path winding along a shelf of the rock, narrow enough to make the nervous among us shudder. At length, from a great rock hanging on the edge of this shelf, we sprang by a long leap into a low window which opened into the perpendicular face of the cliff. We were then within the hold of David,[2] and, creeping half doubled through a narrow crevice for a few rods, we stood beneath the dark vault of the first grand chamber of this mysterious and oppressive cavern. Our whole collection of lights did little more than make the damp darkness visible. After groping about as long as we had time to spare, we returned to the light of day, fully convinced that,

[1] 2 Sam. xiv. [2] 1 Sam. xxii. 4, 5.

TEKOA—FUREIDIS.

with David and his lion-hearted followers inside, all the strength of Israel under Saul could not have forced an entrance—would not have even attempted it.

I see no reason to disturb the tradition which makes this the *hold* into which David retired with his father's house and his faithful followers when he fled from Gath. David, as a shepherd leading his flocks over these hills, was doubtless acquainted from his boyhood with all the intricacies of this fearful cavern, just as these Arab shepherds, his successors, now are, and what more natural, therefore, than that he should flee thither in the day of his extremity? It was out in the wild desert, far from the haunts of Saul, and not likely to be visited by him. It was also in the direction of Moab, whither he sent his parents and the women of his train, while he abode still in the hold. Again, we know that many of his subsequent exploits and escapes from Saul were in this region and south of it; and, finally, there is a sort of verbal accuracy in speaking of the topography—David's family are said to have gone *down* to him from Bethlehem. Now this cavern is nearly two hours to the southeast of that village, and the path *descends* rapidly nearly the entire distance. Let us therefore acquiesce in the tradition that this is the Adullam into which David fled from Gath, and in which he first collected and organized his band of trusty followers.

Of course, this is not the *city* Adullam, so often mentioned in the oldest books of the Bible, and which appears to have been in the neighborhood of Gath. But enough about this cave. After escaping from it, we returned up the same shallow wady for a mile or more, and then descended by one of the vilest roads in this world into Wady Urtas, and passed up northward round the western base of Jebel Fureidîs. We had not time to ascend it, but it seemed very high—I should say eight hundred feet from the bottom of the wady—an enormous natural mound, as trimly turned and as steep as a haystack. It is doubtless the Herodium of Josephus, which he somewhat fancifully compares to the breast of a woman. It has every appearance of an extinct crater, and yet I noticed no indication of volcanic agency in that immediate vicinity.

This Fureîdîs was called Frank Mountain by the Crusaders, and must have been a strong fortification during all the ages in which isolated tells afforded the natural platform for castles. There is none of equal height and size in Palestine. Leaving it on the right, we had Bethlehem in full view about three miles westward, and the setting sun threw a mild and subdued light over the plains where the shepherds were keeping watch. Somehow or other we made but slow progress, and night came upon us bewildered in a labyrinth of wadies, while there were yet two long hours to Mar Saba, whither the muleteers had preceded us, and which we had to reach, or otherwise sleep out in the wilderness supperless, and at the mercy of our villainous guides. On we marched, up and down, and down and up, on sharp ridges, in deep wadies, and over slippery rocks, or through stiff mud, but finally, without accident or injury of any kind, we dismounted at the entrance of the convent. I shall never forget that evening ride. Our imaginations had been held wide awake hour after hour by bad roads, doubtful guides, and the dismal notes of owls and jackals. The moon, rising over the brown hills of Moab, flashed and trembled on the Dead Sea, giving just light enough to make the crags appear more stern, and the chasms more horrible. At the convent, two towers, one on either brow of the gorge, loomed up through the misty moonbeams, like grim old giants, to guard the access. We entered through a low iron door, went down, turned round through a second door, then down again by winding stairs, across queer courts, and along dark passages, until we reached at length our rooms, hanging between cliffs that towered to the stars, or seemed to, and yawning gulfs which darkness made bottomless and dreadful. I was struck dumb with astonishment. It was a transition sudden and unexpected, from the wild mountain to the yet wilder, more vague and mysterious scenes of Oriental enchantment. Lights gleamed out fitfully from hanging rocks and doubtful caverns. Winding stairs, with balus-

VALLEY OF NYAM (UNYAMUEZI).

trade and iron rail, ran right up the perpendicular cliffs into rock chambers, where the solitary monk was drowsily muttering his midnight prayers. It was long after that hour before sleep visited my eyes, and then my dreams were of Arabs, and frightful chasms, and enchanted castles.

Daylight next morning stripped off much of the wild and fearful from the midnight view through the pale beams of the waning moon, but even then Mar Saba is the strangest convent that I have ever seen. We, of course, visited the curiosities of the place: St. Saba's sepulchre, beneath an octagon mausoleum; the numerous chapels, covered with pictures and Greek inscriptions; the really splendid church, blazing with silver and gold; the vault, filled with fourteen thousand skulls of martyred monks! and I know not what besides, with which this convent-castle is crowded. No description had in the least prepared me for what I saw, and no pen-picture could do justice to the original. It must be seen, and every visitor will be well rewarded for his three hours' ride. The stupendous cliffs of the Kidron, full of caverns, now the home of bats and owls instead of monks and hermits, are not the least impressive of the many wonders that cluster around this strange retirement of Santa Saba.

Our *present* approach will be by the sober light of day, and must lack every element of romance, so we may as well interest ourselves with this fine valley of Urtas. This is believed to be the Etam of the ancient Hebrew kings, a name which rarely occurs in the Bible, and nowhere in such relation to other places as to indicate this locality, unless it be in 2d Chronicles xi. 6, where it is named along with Bethlehem and Tekoa. The truth is that its celebrity depends upon the fables of the rabbis more than the pages of sober history. The fountain near the village, however, must have always filled the valley below it with orchards and flourishing gardens; and it is not an unreasonable supposition that David, who so intensely longed for even a drink of water from his native Bethlehem, would have shown a similar partiality for this pretty valley below it, where he must have often played while a child. Not unlikely he had purchased it before he died, and when Solomon came into possession, he farther adorned it with his pools and orchards; and in traversing this vale, I always love to reproduce in imagination the gorgeous scene when it was filled with fruits and flowers, and these many-shaped hills on either side, and on all sides, were terraced to their tops, and dotted every where with country villas, amid olive-groves, fig-orchards, and clustering vines. Thus it certainly was through many long ages of peace and prosperity, and it is my belief that thus it will be once more, in that happy day "when the Lord shall bring again Zion."

CONVENT OF SANTA SABA.

XL. 'AIN ES SULTAN—JERICHO.

April 24th.

The tent never was so welcome to me as at the close of this long day's ride. I am glad we have taken it, but shall never wish to repeat it.

The reasons of this unusual weariness are that we have actually been in the saddle more than twelve hours, and then the greater part of the day and of the ride has been in this depressed and hot region of the Dead Sea. The fact is, our visit is nearly a month too late both for pleasure and health. But the fatigue is over, and we may now sit down and review at our leisure this most interesting excursion.

Among the multiplicity of sights and scenes which drew my attention hither and thither in rapid succession, only a few points have impressed their features upon my memory. In the morning, as soon as the gate of the convent was opened, I climbed to the top of the tower on the south of the ravine. From there my eye roamed over a wilderness of rusty brown hills, the most dreary and blasted that I ever beheld. Beyond and below it is the Dead Sea, bordered on the east by the abrupt cliffs of Moab. Turning to what was beneath me, the wonderful chasm of the Kidron struck me with amazement. We have seen nothing so profound or so wild in all our travels.

I am glad you have had an opportunity to spend one night in an Oriental convent, and become acquainted with these remarkable institutions. Santa Saba is among the very best specimens, and, in addition to its distinctive religious character, it seems always to have been a sort of frontier castle in the heart of this stern desert of Judæa. Saint Saba was probably attracted to the spot by those very savage aspects of the scene which strike our minds with such horror—the howling wilderness, the stern desolation, the terrific chasms, the oppressive solitude, the countless caverns, the ever-prevalent dangers from wild beasts and wild robbers, these and such as these were the charms that fascinated his morbid imagination. We would not judge the dead, however, nor ought we to forget the shelter and good dinner which his institution afforded us last night. It is really, in our day, a very respectable hotel, and gentlemen —not ladies—can scarcely do better than to spend one of the two nights there which an excursion from Jerusalem to the Dead Sea and the Jordan necessarily requires. The régime, it is true, partakes of both military sternness and conventual austerity, so far as the fortress itself and the monks within it are concerned; but both are necessary, the one to meet the requirements of the Church, the other to repel the attacks of the Bedawîn, who prowl about at all seasons, watching for an opportunity to force an entrance and to plunder the rich treasures of the establishment.

As to the ride from St. Saba to the Dead Sea, you surely can not have forgotten the path along the perpendicular cliffs of Wady en Nar—*Valley of Fire*—as the wonderful gorge of the Kidron is there called, nor the long descent to and ascent from it, nor the naked hills over which we toiled in the broiling sun for seven hours, frequently losing the path amid tangled ravines and shelving gullies washed out of sand-hills; nor will you cease to remember the delight with which we galloped over the level plain after we had escaped from this perplexing net-work of wadies.

Of all these things I have but a faint recollection, but I remember attempting to shelter my aching head from the burning sun under a stunted juniper-tree.

Yes; and, in your disappointment, said that, if Elijah's juniper afforded no better shade than yours, it was not at all surprising that he requested for himself that he might die.[1] And certainly these straggling bushes cast but a doubtful shade at all times, and lend no effectual protection against such a sun and wind as beat upon us in *our* "wilderness." Still, the prophet slept under one, and the Bedawîn do the same, when wandering in the desert, where they often furnish the only shelter that can be found. Job, as translated, has a curious reference to this tree in the 30th chapter of his remarkable dialogues. He says that those contemptible

[1] 1 Kings xix. 4.

JUNIPER.

children whose *fathers he would have disdained to set with the dogs of his flock*, flee into the wilderness, and for want and famine cut up mallows by the bushes and juniper roots for their meat.[1] These mallows are a coarse kind of *greens*, which the poor boil as a relish for their dry bread. I have often seen the children of the poor cutting them up under the hedges and by the bushes in early spring, so that this rendering seems natural and appropriate to us who reside in the country, and therefore I accept the rendering, without noticing the arguments of learned critics against it. What sort of juniper roots can be used for food is more than I can discover or comprehend. They are excessively bitter, and nothing but the fire will devour them. Burckhardt found the Bedawîn of Sinai burning them into coal, and says that they make the best charcoal, and throw out the most intense heat. The same thing seems to be implied in Psalms cxx. 4, where David threatens the false tongue with sharp ar-

[1] Job xxx. 14.

rows of the mighty—with *coals of juniper*. Perhaps the meaning of Job is, that the poor cut up mallows to *eat*, and juniper roots with which to cook them. This would give a sense in accordance with the known use of these roots, and still preserve the connection with the food of the poor. The Arabic word is *retem*, the same as the Hebrew, and Forskal calls it genista raetam. It is, therefore, a species of broom, and not that kind of juniper which bears the famous berries, and whose oil assists in the composition of certain varnishes. This tree is also found in the country, and, if you had met with it, you would have had less occasion to complain of the want of shade.

Some of these things will certainly be remembered, nor shall I ever forget the unexpected appearance of Mount Hermon towering to the sky far, far up the ghor to the north (which convinced me that Moses also saw it from the mountains of Moab), nor the sombre and shadowy surface and shores of the Dead Sea, nor the indescribable feeling of disappointment at the Jordan. While approaching it over that melancholy desert of soft deep sand, I eagerly watched the line of willow-trees which you said marked out the tortuous line of the river, expecting it to burst on my delighted eyes; but not until we were actually on the very brink did I see water enough to fill a thimble, and when there it was hard to believe that what I saw was the whole Jordan. Finding, however, that it was, I endeavored to reconcile my previous anticipations with the vastly ensmalled reality by noticing the rapidity of the current and the depth of the stream.

This, however, was not your first acquaintance with the river; but I can not smile at your forgetfulness of this fact; for, though I have looked at the Upper Jordan a thousand times, yet down here at Jericho I too am always disappointed. When boys, we used to sing with vast enthusiasm, "On Jordan's *stormy* banks I stand," and supposed that it was big as the Ohio at least, and as stormy as the Northwest Passage; and something like this must have been in the mind of Watts when he applied the word *stormy* to this little river rambling over this low plain where everlasting *summer* abides. It is not an epithet which personal acquaintance would have suggested.

I begin to feel that there is more fancy than fact in the costume and drapery of many of our hymns, but that is allowable perhaps. I found, however, that my traditionary notions in regard to matters of fact were about equally fanciful. What, for example, becomes of one's hereditary ideas of the prodigious fertility of the plain of Jericho? From the river to 'Ain Hajla there was nothing but a most unprofitable extension of simmering sand, bare and barren of every thing except stunted thorn bushes and ugly black lizards.

You must not forget that the day has been excessively hot, you very tired, and, more than all, that the cultivated part of the plain has just been shorn of its luxuriant harvests, and also that the vegetation elsewhere has entirely dried up, except the "summer crops" which are irrigated from 'Ain Hajla, the brook Krith, and this fountain of Elisha. If your temper had not been somewhat like the day, and your anticipations had been moderated by reflection, you would have brought away impressions more just as well as more agreeable.

I see that 'Ain Hajla stands on modern maps for Beth Hoglah.

And correctly, I think; but that the Gilgal, where Joshua made his first encampment within the promised land, and where the ark and tabernacle remained for so many years after the conquest, was immediately above it, as located on some modern maps, remains yet to be proved. Josephus says that Joshua pitched his camp fifty furlongs from the river, and ten from Jericho.[1] Now, *if* he crossed due east of the city, and *if* Josephus is correct in his numbers, then Gilgal must have been very near the present Riha; and this again may have been true, on the supposition that ancient Jericho was in the immediate neighborhood of this 'Ain es Sultan, as I suspect it really was; for Riha is about six

[1] Ant. vi. 4.

miles from the Jordan, and a city below this Fountain of the Sultan would not be much more than ten furlongs from it. All these things are mere suppositions, I admit, and, indeed, there probably never was any permanent *city* called Gilgal in this plain; and if there was it had passed away, and the name and site were lost even before Josephus wrote his history.

I have never seen this plain so entirely deserted as it is at present. Even the few inhabitants of Riha have gone to other parts to labor, since their own harvests are already gathered. On my first visit the whole valley was lively enough, for I was one of several thousand pilgrims drawn hither from all parts of the world to bathe in this holy river.

This is a ceremony which we have missed, somewhat to my regret, as it was one of the scenes I had always associated with my intended visit to the Jordan.

Well, since you can not *see*, the next best thing is to *hear;* and if you will put yourself into the most comfortable position to listen, I will read from notes, taken a quarter of a century ago, the adventures of my first visit to Jericho. Early in the morning of April 16th, 1833, we left the convent of Archangel, and passed down the Via Dolorosa to the palace, where the guard was already in motion, and from thence, with the white flag of the pilgrim in front, and the green of the prophet in the rear, we set forward. It was a merry hour apparently to every body. The whole population of the city, of either sex and of every age, in their best, lined the zigzag path along which the pilgrim host was to pass. With noise and pomp such as Arabs only can affect, we passed out at St. Stephen's gate, wound our way down into the narrow vale of Jehoshaphat, over the south point of Olivet, by the miserable remains of the city of Mary, Martha, and Lazarus, and then prepared ourselves to descend, for you remember that we must go "*down* to Jericho." And, sure enough, *down, down* we did go, over slippery rocks, for more than a mile, when the path became less precipitous. Still, however, the road follows the dry channel of a brook for several miles farther, as if

PLAIN OF JERICHO—NORTH END OF DEAD SEA.

descending into the very bowels of the earth. How admirably calculated for "robbers!"

After leaving the brook, which turns aside too far to the south, we ascended and descended naked hills for several miles, the prospect gradually becoming more and more gloomy. Not a house, nor even a tree, is to be seen; and the only remains are those of a large khan, *said* to have been the inn to which the Good Samaritan brought the wounded Jew. Not far from here, in a narrow defile, an English traveler was attacked, shot, and robbed in 1820. As you approach the plain the mountains wear a more doleful appearance, the ravines become more frightful, and the narrow passages less and less passable. At length the weary pilgrim reaches the plain by a long, steep declivity, and doubtless expects to step immediately into Jericho. But alas! no city appears, and after a full hour's ride he pitches his tent (if he have one) in a dry, sultry plain of sand, sparsely sprinkled over with burnt-up grass. If he have no tent, a shriveled thorn bush is better than nothing; and if he can not get that, let him do as we did—sit down under the burning sun, and bear it as well as he can.

Finding it intolerably hot, we passed through the camp, and went on to the village, about a mile distant, and took shelter under some fig-trees which grew around the sheikh's palace, a square, castle-like house, the only one of any size in the place, and where, tradition says, the little Zaccheus once dwelt. In the immediate vicinity are some forty or fifty of the most forlorn habitations that I have ever seen. And this is Jericho! These houses, or rather huts, are surrounded by a peculiar kind of fortification, made of nubk, a species of bush very abundant in the plain. Its thorns are so sharp and the branches are so platted together that neither horse nor man will attack it.

The Arabs of Jericho and the plain are many shades darker than the same class on the mountains only a few miles distant. This is easily accounted for by the great difference in climate. We shivered in our cloaks upon the hills, and broiled in the shade on the plain.

After looking about the village, and riding a mile or two to the northwest to see the great fountain 'Ain es Sultan, we returned to the camp about sunset for protection. Having sung "The voice of free grace," and "There is a land of pure delight," we wrapped our cloaks about us and prepared to sleep; but the scenes of the day and the circumstances with which we were surrounded were too novel and exciting to allow of sleep. East and west of us, in parallel lines, stretched the mountains of Moab and Palestine, like perpendicular walls reared to heaven by the Creator to guard this favored spot. At our feet flowed the Jordan, the most interesting river on earth; a little to the south slept in mysterious silence the bitter waters of the Dead Sea; while underneath were the mouldering ruins of old Jericho, whose walls fell prostrate at the blast of Israel's priests. What an assemblage of interesting objects! How well calculated to awaken deep and solemn reflection! Here the swellings of the Jordan rolled back, that Israel's chosen race might take possession of the promised land; and thus, "when on Jordan's stormy banks we stand," if the ark of God be there, the angry billows shall flee away at the presence of Him who hath said, When thou passest through the waters, I will be with thee; and through the rivers, they shall not overflow thee.[1] Here, too, the smitten Jordan parted hither and thither when the prophet of the Lord went over to be carried to the skies in a chariot of fire. We drink of the fountain which was sweetened by Elisha's cruse of salt. Here, also, our blessed Saviour was baptized, the heavens were opened, the Spirit descended upon him in the form of a dove, and a voice from the Father said, "This is my beloved Son, in whom I am well pleased." O ye guilty cities of the plain, even here do ye lie sealed up unto the judgment day, suffering the vengeance of eternal fire. Tremble, O my soul, lest thou be overthrown and consumed with that fire which shall never be quenched, and be cast into that other lake of which this is such a solemn type.

[1] Isa. xliii. 2.

About three o'clock in the morning there was a buzz in the camp, which in a short time became like the "noise of many waters," and at four precisely we set forward toward the Jordan, going to the southeast. A large company of guards went before, bearing on long poles flaming torches made of turpentine and old rags, which threw over the plain a brilliant light, revealing double ranks of armed horsemen on either side of the host, careering in genuine Arab style, and plunging with fearless impetuosity through the grass and bushes to drive out any Bedawîn that might be lurking there. The governor, with his body-guard, brought up the rear, and thus we were defended on all sides. Nor was this caution misplaced. One poor fellow from Poland, having fallen behind, was attacked, robbed, and stripped naked.

After a two hours' ride over an uneven plain, we reached the Jordan as the sun rose above the mountains of Moab. Immediately the pilgrims rushed headlong into the stream, men, women, and children, in one undistinguished mass. Many of the men were in a state of shameless nudity, and the females, in changing their scanty dress, were shockingly exposed. The haughty Turk sat upon his beautiful horse, and looked in scorn upon this exposure of the "Christian dogs." The pilgrims, however, were highly delighted with their bath. The men *ducked* the women somewhat as the farmers do their sheep, while the little children were carried and plunged under water, trembling like so many lambs. Some had water poured on their heads in imitation of the baptism of the Saviour, for it is part of the tradition that our blessed Lord was here baptized; and the ruins of an old convent near at hand ascertain the exact locality to the perfect satisfaction of the devout pilgrim. The Latins, however, maintain that the event took place higher up the stream, and hence they bathe there. I hope they have a more convenient place than the Greeks. It could scarcely be more unsuitable. The banks are nearly perpendicular, and very muddy, while the current is astonishingly rapid, and at least ten feet deep. It required the most expert swimmers to cross it, and one less skilled must inevitably be carried away, as we had melancholy proof. Two Christians and a Turk, who ventured too far, were drowned without the possibility of rescue, and the wonder is that many more did not share the same fate where thousands were bathing at once. This sad accident, which would have cast a shade over the whole assembly in America, produced very little sensation among the pilgrims. In fact, this pilgrimaging seems to obliterate every benevolent feeling from the heart. When we left Jerusalem, the guard immediately in front of me, in careering and curvetting with his horse, fired a pistol, and shot a woman dead, and yet I never heard the affair mentioned afterward but with levity. As we came along, if any poor woman fell from her horse, and rolled down among the rocks, it called forth only loud laughter from the passing crowd.

The Jordan would scarcely be dignified with the name of river in America, and its appearance is, in reality, quite insignificant. It is, however, deep, narrow, and very muddy, and hurries away to the sea with great volocity. In approaching the river, you descend several benches or terraces; and, though much swollen with the rains and the melting snows of Lebanon at that time, it was still fifteen or twenty feet below its proper banks. It has also a very winding course, and resembles the streams of the Mississippi Valley, having on one side a perpendicular bluff, and on the opposite a low beach covered with weeds, bushes, and drift, and these alternate constantly. These low flats vary in width. At the bathing-place it was about twenty rods wide, and the whole of it had recently been inundated. These are the banks that were flooded when the Israelites passed over. Nor was the miracle unnecessary. It would be impossible for such a host to cross the Jordan at the same season of the year without either a bridge or a miracle, for boats could do nothing in such a current, and it is too deep to ford. Travelers have differed widely in their description of the Jordan, principally from two causes—visiting it at different *seasons* of the year, and at different

DEAD SEA FROM THE NORTH.

places. When and where I saw it, the width might have been twenty yards, and its depth ten feet.

After the pilgrims had bathed, we left them, and turned down to the south, with three or four English travelers, and a guard from the governor, to visit the Dead Sea, and having ridden across plains of barren sand for an hour and a half, we stood upon the shore of this memorable lake. Without any reference to what others have said, I can testify to the following facts. The water is perfectly clear and transparent. The taste is bitter and salt, far beyond that of the ocean. It acts upon the tongue and mouth like alum, smarts in the eye like camphor, produces a burning, pricking sensation, and it stiffens the hair of the head much like pomatum. The water has a much greater specific gravity than the human body, and hence I did not sink lower than to the arms when standing perpendicularly in it. Although there is evidence in the sand and brushwood thrown upon the beach that in great storms there are waves, still there is some foundation for the reports about its immobility. There was a considerable breeze, yet the water lay perfectly calm and motionless. We saw no fish nor living animals in the water, though birds were flying *over* it unharmed. All of us noticed an unnatural gloom, not upon the sea only, but also over the whole plain below Jericho. This, too, is mentioned by ancient historians. It had the appearance of Indian summer in America, and, like a vast funeral pall let down from heaven, it hung heavily over the lifeless bosom of this mysterious lake. Having gathered some curious pebbles from the shore, and filled our cans with the water, we returned to the camp about noon, highly pleased with our excursion.

In the afternoon we visited again 'Ain es Sultan. This fountain rises at the base of a hill which has the appearance of an Indian mound, though rather too large for a work of art. But there are many similar tells in the plain, and they were probably thrown up for the same purpose as those which are so numerous in America. The water is sufficiently abundant to turn a large mill, is beautifully transparent, sweet, and cool, and swarms with small fish. There seems to be no reason to doubt the tradition that this is the identical fountain whose bitter waters Elisha healed. On the margin of this delightful brook grow great numbers of bushes, bearing a yellow apple about the size, and having very much the appearance, of a small apricot, beautiful to the eye, but nauseous to the taste, and said to be poisonous. I can do as others have done before me—inquire. Is this the apple of Sodom?

Directly west, at the distance of a mile and a half, is the high and precipitous mountain called Quarantania, from a tradition that our Saviour here fasted forty days and nights, and also that this is the "high mountain" from whose top the tempter exhibited "all the kingdoms of this world, and the glory of them." The side facing the plain is as perpendicular, and apparently as high, as the rock of Gibraltar, and upon the very summit are still visible the ruins of an ancient convent. Midway below are caverns hewn in the perpendicular rock, where hermits formerly retired to fast and pray in imitation of the "forty days," and it is said that even at the present time there is to be found an occasional Copt or Abyssinian languishing out his *quarantania* in this doleful place. We found it, however, inhabited only by Bedawîn, several of whom made their appearance, well armed, many hundred feet above us. Leaving the company here, I took southward across the plain, in order to look for the site of ancient Jericho. It appeared to me highly probable that the original city took in the great fountain 'Ain es Sultan, as there was nothing to prevent it, and, if left without the walls, an enemy could compel them to surrender by cutting off their supply of water. Accordingly, the plain to the south and southwest of the fountain is covered in many parts with very ancient remains. There are evidences of walls stretching in different directions, and many indications of decayed buildings. The rocks are black and honeycombed, and the walls can only be traced by continuous elevations of the turf, with an occasional bit of foundation appearing through the grass. Whether these mark the site of old Jericho, of course, can not at present be decided, but they are evidently more ancient than the ruins of Tyre or of Cæsarea, and there are no others visible in this vicinity.

18*th*. Spent the first part of the night in walking about the camp. The scene was very picturesque. Spread abroad over the plain lay men, women, and children, of almost every nation under heaven, of all languages, every variety of costume, and of all colors, from the black of Africa to the white of Poland. All denominations of this sectarian world were there—Mohammedans, Druses, Maronites, Catholics, Greeks, Arminians, Copts, Syrians, Jews, Episcopalians, Lutherans, Presbyterians, Methodists, and infidels, in one vast congregation—faint image of that great congregation when the trumpet shall sound and wake the dead. The camp did not become quiet at all, and about midnight every thing was again set in motion. We hastily mounted our animals to keep from being trampled under foot, and, falling into line with a long train of lights, set forward toward the narrow pass down which we came at first. A similar line of torches, about a mile to the south, marked out the course of another division of the host. The night was exceedingly dark, and, as we approached the defile leading up the mountain, the confusion became horrible. Women screaming in terror when about to be trampled down by a long line of camels coupled together; parents calling for their children, friends hallooing for friends, muleteers beating and cursing their animals to force them up the steep rocks, those above calling to those below, while the guards, stationed upon projecting rocks, kept up a constant discharge of musketry, whose lurid glare and hollow reverberations down the deep ravines startled the "leaden ear" of night, and rendered sublime what would otherwise have been ridiculous. After we were fairly up the mountain we came in view of the southern division, and the prospect was grand beyond description. For miles, the long train of torches rose and sunk in graceful curves, corresponding to the hills and vales over which they marched, while the same discharge of fire-arms continued with even magnified effect.

In about an hour we united our lines and hurried on to the Holy City, which we reached a little after sunrise, shivering with the cold wind of the mountains, but thankful that we had been permitted to perform this interesting tour with so much ease and safety.

Your account of the separation of parents and children in this returning host of pilgrims reminds me of the one single incident in the youthful life of our blessed Lord which is recorded in the New Testament.[1]

It is not, in fact, surprising that, in the midst of such a crowd, Joseph and his mother should suppose that Jesus was in the "company with his kinsfolk and acquaintance," nor is the time that elapsed before they became so alarmed at his absence as to turn back and search for him at all remarkable. I question whether there is ever a pilgrimage made from Jerusalem to the Jordan at this day without the separation of parents and children equally prolonged; and, in the case we are considering, it was the absence of a youth who, his parents well knew, had never done in his whole life one unwise or improper act. They would not, therefore, be easily alarmed on his account.

OVERFLOW OF THE JORDAN.

Among the stupendous miracles that have rendered this neighborhood illustrious, the most wonderful and the most suggestive was the passage of the Hebrew nation through the Jordan to their promised inheritance. The twelve stones that bore witness to the fact have long since disappeared, and even the precise spot where the passage was made is a matter of dispute; and in view of the superstitious abuses to which such sites are perverted, I am quite contented to have them all thus hidden, as was the sepulchre of Moses. We have the hills of Moab on the other side, the river itself that was divided, the sea, into which the water, cut off from above, subsided, and Jericho, over against which the grand miracle was performed, and these are enough for the confirmation of our faith; nor would I walk a mile or turn a

[1] Luke ii. 41–50.

stone to make the identification any closer or more perfect. There is an incidental allusion, however, in the account of the miracle, which infidels have employed to throw discredit on the entire narrative, and even upon the Bible itself, and which it is highly proper that we should explain if we can. It is said in Joshua iii. 15 that Jordan overfloweth all his banks all the time of harvest. This is the statement, and the objections against its accuracy and truthfulness are, that the Jordan is a short and rapid river which soon runs down, and that, therefore, it could not have overflowed all its banks in harvest, for the rains have entirely ceased, and the tributaries of the river have dried up; and this plausible reasoning is strengthened and confirmed by the unqualified assertion that the Jordan does not overflow its banks at all, not even in the rainy season.

To meet and refute these injurious assertions, various suppositions and suggestions have been put forward by the friends of revelation. It has been maintained that the channel of the river has been deepened since the time of Joshua, and this is indeed very probable; and again, that, from various causes, less water now falls upon the country of the Jordan than did anciently, and that the rains cease earlier in the spring; and this may possibly be true, and, if there was any need of such hypothetical assistance to establish the veracity of the sacred historian, we should not hesitate to employ it for what it is worth, but I am persuaded that the matter in question needs no such aid. It is a plain, honest statement of a simple fact, as literally true now as it was when Joshua led the ransomed tribes into Canaan. All we need in order to clear the passage from obscurity or doubt is an adequate acquaintance with the phenomena of the country and the river. Let us subject the passage and the scenery to a careful scrutiny and analysis, and we shall find that here, as in a thousand other places, the Land illustrates and confirms the Book.

The river overflows during harvest; but *where* was the harvest spoken of, and what is the time of it? These inquiries are strictly essential. I visited the scene of this miracle on the 1st of April, and found barley harvest about Jericho already ended. I also found the river full to the brim, and saw evidence in abundance that it had overflowed its banks very recently. Harvest in the vale of the Lower Jordan comes on about the middle of March. This seems early, and it is long before the crops are ready for the sickle on the neighboring mountains, or even around the fountains of the Upper Jordan. But the reason is obvious. The valley at Jericho is thirteen hundred feet below the level of the ocean, is sheltered from cold winds on all sides by mountains of great height, and is open to the warm southern breezes from the deeper basin of the Dead Sea. It has therefore the climate of the tropics, though in the latitude of Jerusalem.

Still, the rains are over, and most of the tributary streams have dwindled down to inconsiderable rills, even at this early season of the year, and how comes it, therefore, that the Jordan alone is full to overflowing? This is easily explained. The Jordan does not depend upon tributaries for its steady supply of water, but is almost wholly formed and fed by certain great fountains, which arise far north, around the base of snowy Hermon. The largest of these is called El Leddan, at Tell el Kady; the next in size is at Banias. These are the two great sources mentioned by Josephus under the names Greater and Lesser Jordan. The one from Tell el Kady is about three times as large as that from Banias, and its course is south, a little west, through the plain of the Hûleh, for about five miles, where it is joined by the Baniasy, and, in less than a mile farther south, by the Hasbâny. The Jordan is thus formed by the union of these three rivers, and, winding southward through extensive marshes, flows into Lake Hûleh—the Merom of Joshua. The Hasbâny is a beautiful river, whose farthest permanent source is near Hasbeîya, some eighteen miles north of Tell el Kady. The torrents from Wady et Teim greatly augment its size in the rainy season, but it depends for its permanent volume of water upon three fountains: the Fuarr, at Hasbeîya, the Sareid, below Kefr Shubah, and the Luisany, at El Ghujar.

To complete the account of the sources of the Jordan, the fountains of Derdara, in Merj Aiyûn, and the Ruahiny, must be mentioned, and also those of Blata and El Mellahah. We need not pause to notice the River Jermuk, nor the fountains which flow directly into the different lakes. Those we have named are sufficient for the purpose of our illustration. The Jordan is thus made up from the joint contributions of great permanent springs, and in this fact we find the explanation of the overflow of the river so late in the season as March. These immense fountains do not feel the effects of the early winter rains at all. It requires the heavy and long-continued storms of mid-winter before they are moved in the least; and it is not until toward the close of winter, when the melting snows of Hermon and Lebanon, with the heavy rains of the season, have penetrated through the mighty masses of these mountains, and filled to overflowing their hidden chambers and vast reservoirs, that the streams gush forth in their full volume. The Hûleh—*marsh* and *lake*—is filled, and then Gennesaret rises, and pours its accumulated waters into the swelling Jordan about the 1st of March. Thus it comes to pass that it does actually "overflow all its banks during all the time of harvest;" nor does it soon subside, as other short rivers do, when the rains cease. These fountains continue to pour forth their contributions for months with undiminished volume, and the river keeps full and strong all through March into April, and the proper banks of the river are still full to overflowing in the time of harvest.

To understand the passage correctly, we must also remember that Jordan has two series of banks, and in some places three, but it is the lower only which are overflowed, either now or at any former period within the history of man, and to these the reference in Joshua is unquestionably made. The low *flat*, or river *bottom*, thus inundated is nowhere wide, and is generally covered with a thick jungle of willow, sycamore, and other trees. It was from these thickets that "the swellings of Jordan," in ancient days, expelled the lion from his lair: a poetic allusion, which bears incidental testimony to the historic statement. At present there are no lions to be roused, but the wild boar, the jackal, and the wolf occupy his place, and, like him, flee before the swellings of this river.

I think it not improbable that the rise and fall of the Jordan are, in reality, *somewhat* earlier now and more rapid than in the days of Joshua. The cutting off of the forests of Lebanon and Hermon may cause the snows to dissolve sooner; and the clearing away much of the marshes at the head of the Hûleh allows the floods a quicker passage, and thus the river *may* be at its height, in ordinary seasons, a few days sooner than was the case three thousand years ago. It is nearly certain, also, that the channel of the Jordan has deepened, and especially near the Dead Sea, so that the *extent* of the overflow may now be less than then, and of shorter duration. But, without referring to these circumstances, the preceding facts and explanations are sufficient to establish the accuracy of the statement in Joshua that the Jordan overflows all his banks all the time of harvest.

It will be easy for us to overtake the company while they are climbing the long ascent out of the valley of the Jordan, and therefore we may linger an hour on this hill to study the features of this melancholy but eminently interesting scene. Jericho was called the city of palm-trees, but the one only palm that a quarter of a century ago stood, like a solitary sentinel, near the old tower is gone, and thus has passed away the last vestige of that great forest which gave name to the city. The forest, however, might be restored, and then the best dates would again come from Jericho. The soil and climate are admirably adapted to this tree, and, indeed, there is nothing required but cultivation and irrigation to make the whole plain of the lower Jordan fruitful as the garden of the Lord. Such it will certainly become at no very distant day. Every acre of it might be watered from the strong brook in Wady Kelt, from this great fountain Es Sultan, from those of Wady Dûk, and from the Jordan itself. This river winds incessantly, falls every where rapidly, and has about thirty distinct cascades.

VALLEY OF THE JORDAN—AGRICULTURAL PRODUCTS. 457

Here is unappropriated water-power to drive any amount of machinery, and elevation sufficient to allow every part of this valley to be irrigated at all times of the year. Thus treated, and subjected to the science and the modern mechanical appliances in agriculture, the valley of the Jordan could sustain half a million of inhabitants. Cotton, rice, sugar-cane, indigo, and nearly every other valuable product for the use of man, would flourish most luxuriantly. There were, in fact, sugar plantations here long before America was discovered, and it is quite possible that this plant was taken from this very spot to Tripoli and thence to Spain by the Crusaders, from whence it was carried to the West Indies. Those edifices to the west of 'Ain es Sultan are the remains of ancient sugar-mills, and are still called Towahîn es Sukkar. They seem to have been driven by a canal brought along the base of Quarantania from Wady Dûk.

Now how desolate and barren! Just around 'Ain es Sultan, and between it and Riha, the plain is covered with a forest of thorn-trees; but look elsewhere, and the eye aches from the glare of naked sand-fields glowing beneath a burning sun.

Many of these thorn bushes through which we have been carefully picking our way are the zŭkŭm. This bush looks like a crab apple-tree, and bears a small nut, from which a kind of liquid balsam is made, and sold by the monks as the balm of Gilead, so famous in ancient times. I purchased a phial of it when on my first visit to the Jordan with the pilgrims, but could not discover that it possessed any particular medicinal virtues. And now we must cross this Wady Kelt, and begin to climb the mountain. In the winter this is a powerful stream, and the remnants of aqueducts in several places show that the inhabitants once knew how to employ its fertilizing powers upon the desert of the Jordan and Dead Sea.

I notice traces of ancient structures on each side of the wady, and some of them were made with small stones, cut and fitted into the wall like tesselated pavement. We have nowhere else seen any such buildings.

Vol. II.—U

It is, in fact, the only specimen of the kind. This must always have been a pass of great importance, and hence these mounds and old castles in front of it. The one nearest the pass is called 'Akabet ed Deir. Turn now and take your last view of the Jordan, as it loses itself in the bitter waters of the Dead Sea. Captain Lynch says that a short distance above the sea it was forty yards wide and twelve feet deep, then fifty yards wide and eleven feet deep, then eighty yards by seven feet, and, finally, one hundred yards and only three feet deep upon the bar. Thus this sweet type of life subsides into the Sea of Death, and is lost forever.

I have still some inquiries to make about the Dead Sea, and we may as well while away this fatiguing climb and this desolate road by discussing them.

Allow me first to call your attention to this gorge of Wady Kelt, on the right of the path. It is grand, wild, and stern, almost beyond a parallel.

Do you suppose that this is the Cherith to which Elijah was sent to be fed by ravens?

The name favors the opinion, but not so the situation. It is far from the prophet's usual abode, and in returning back again to Sarepta he would be obliged to pass through the kingdom of his enemy, which would certainly be a long and critical journey. The brook itself, however, is admirably adapted to the purpose for which Elijah retired to it, and there come sailing down the tremendous gorge a family of ravens to remind us that God can feed his people by means the most unlikely. And now for your inquiries about the Dead Sea.

They refer rather to the south end of it, and concern particularly the location of the cities of the plain which were destroyed. All agree that Sodom and her associated towns were around the south end of this sea, and since the exploration of Lynch and others it has appeared very probable that the shallow part, which is some fifteen miles long, was originally a plain on which the cities stood, and that this plain was submerged at the time they were overthrown.

VIEW AROUND THE NORTH END OF THE DEAD SEA, FROM 'ARARET ED DER.

Admitting this to be true, or at least probable, how are we to understand what is said of the fertility of that region in the time when Lot chose it for his residence? It was well watered every where before the Lord destroyed Sodom and Gomorrah, even as the garden of the Lord, like the land of Egypt as thou comest unto Zoar.[1] Lot resided at the south end of the Dead Sea, and it seems to be implied that the land there belonged to the valley of the Jordan, was watered by that river, and that therefore it was immensely fertile.

And such, I think, was the fact. The River Jordan begins in the valleys of Hermon, and terminates in this sea, and it is my opinion that, until the destruction of Sodom, this was a fresh-water lake, and that its character was changed at that time by the obtrusion from below of rock salt and other volcanic products, which have rendered it so extremely bitter and nauseous. The evidences of such action and obtrusion are to be seen in the ridge of rock salt called Usdum, at the south end of the sea, and in the presence of naphtha and bitumen in its waters. The lake being originally shorter by the length of these plains of Sodom and Gomorrah, would necessarily rise much higher during the rainy season than it does now, and the water being fresh, it would subside by evaporation, and perhaps by irrigation, much more rapidly than at present, though there is a much greater rise and fall in the sea than was formerly supposed. This great southern extension is thirteen feet deep in winter, but late in autumn it is only *three*, and is then forded not only by camels, but even by donkeys. Now for my specific answer to your inquiry. I suppose that this southern plain on which the cities stood was actually flooded by fresh water during the rise of the lake, just as the Nile floods the land of Egypt "as thou comest unto Zoar," and that when the water subsided the whole plain was sown just as Egypt was and is. There are many examples of this operation about smaller lakes and ponds, and places thus overflowed are the most productive in the country. We have only to suppose that the inhabitants knew how to control the rising

---

[1] Gen. xiii. 10.

of the lake by embankments, as the Egyptians did the Nile, and the whole mystery about the fertility of this plain is explained. It seems to me nearly certain that, if this had been then a salt sea, the whole territories of those cities must have been about as blasted and barren as are the desolate shores at present, which would be in flat contradiction to the statement in Genesis. The obtrusion of rock salt at Usdum must, therefore, have been subsequent to, or, rather, it accompanied the catastrophe. I have not examined this matter at the place itself, but I have seen no statement which would render such an obtrusion a geological impossibility, while instances of the submergence of tracts much larger than this plain are well-ascertained historical facts.

Of course, the old and rather taking theory that the Jordan, before the destruction of Sodom, ran through Wady 'Arabah to the Gulf of 'Akabah, must be abandoned. This would demand geological changes, reaching from the Lake of Tiberias to the Red Sea, too stupendous to have occurred within the period of man's residence upon the earth. Still, this grand chasm, valley, or *crevasse*, running, as it does, between the two Lebanons, through the whole length of the Jordan, and along the 'Arabah to the Elanitic Gulf, and even down that gulf itself into the Red Sea, is among the most remarkable phenomena of our globe; and it is not certain to my mind but that there was at one time a water communication throughout this long and unbroken depression.

How do you account for the nauseous and malignant character of the water of the Dead Sea?

This is owing to the extraordinary amount of mineral salts held in solution. The analyses of chemists, however, show very different results. Some give only seventy parts of water to the hundred, while others give eighty, or even more. I account for these differences by supposing that the specimens analyzed are taken at different seasons of the year, and at different distances from the Jordan. Water brought from near the mouth of that river might be comparatively fresh, and that taken in winter from *any part* would be less salt and bitter than what was brought away in autumn.

One analysis shows, chloride of sodium, 8; potassium, 1; calcium, 8. The very last I have seen gives calcium, $2\frac{4}{5}$; chloride of magnesium, $10\frac{1}{2}$; of potassium, $1\frac{1}{8}$; of sodium, $6\frac{1}{4}$. The specific gravity may average about 1200, that of distilled water being 1000. This, however, will vary according to the time and the place from whence the specimens are taken.

XLI. JERUSALEM.

April 26th.

A friend has placed at our disposal a small cottage near the top of Olivet, which commands a charming view of the city in all its extent, and, as we are to remain some time at this true capital of the Christian world, we will accept the kind offer. By this arrangement our time will be as much at command as though we kept to the tent; we shall also escape the annoyance of Jerusalem's inexorable gates, and be able to prolong our walks and rides in the evening at pleasure. To reach the cottage we must take this rather blind path from Bethany over the summit of the mount, and we at once experience the advantage of this arrangement, for it is already too late in the evening to enter the city; nor can we now stop to examine these misshapen ruins that mark the home of that happy family whom Jesus loved. Our cottage, however, will be within a short walk of it, and we shall have opportunities to visit it at our leisure.

27th. From the top of this Mount of Olives, the view eastward and southward, over the regions through which we have wandered for the last few days, is most peculiar and impressive. It is the Creator's own conception realized of desolation absolute—hills behind hills, sinking far down to the Dead Sea, with Edom and Moab beyond. As the rising sun revealed them, I have been watching their worn and haggard features with a strange sort of fascination, for I doubt not it was into this "wilderness" that Jesus was led after his baptism in the Jordan. What particular part of it I care not to know. Enough for me that on these doleful hills the great temptation was borne by the suffering Son of God for forty days and forty nights—that here the Prince of Darkness was baffled at every point, and his accursed dominion overthrown and forever.

Our position on this mount is indeed delightful, and whichever way one turns he sees objects of the highest and most sacred interest. From a dozen points I have been gazing down into the Holy City, and my utmost anticipations

DEAD SEA FROM THE TOP OF OLIVET.

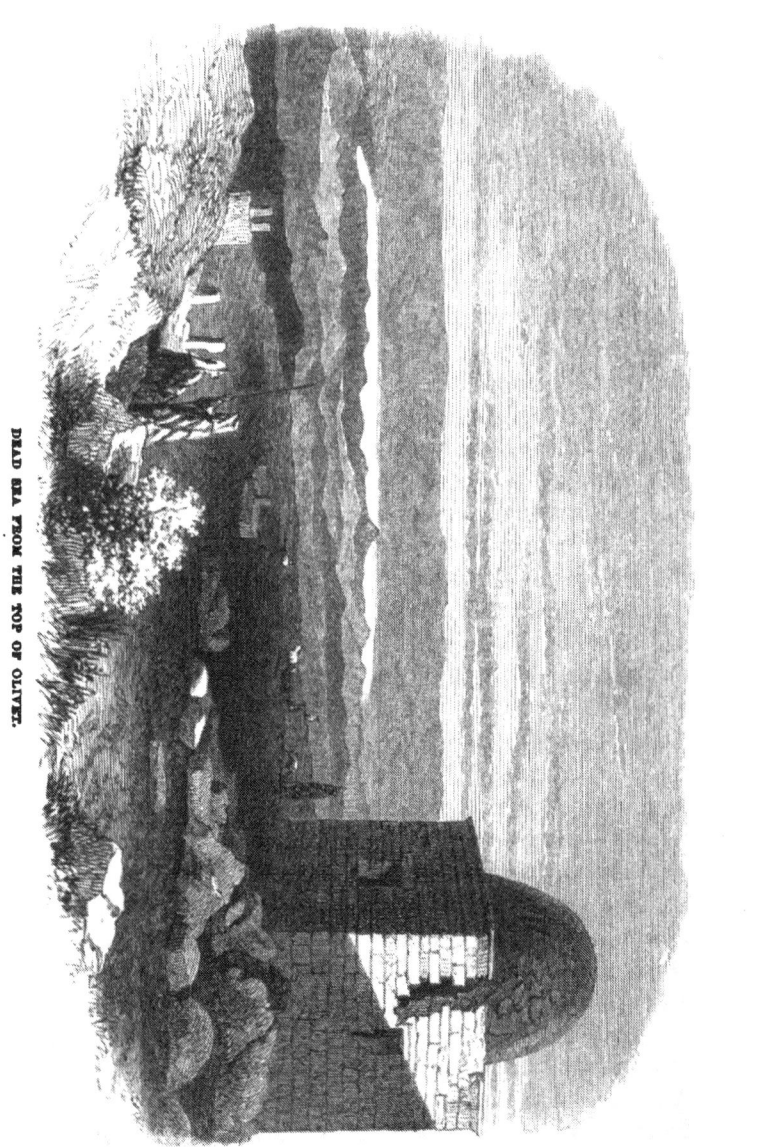

are more than realized. Jerusalem, as I see it this morning, is all I could desire, and, if a nearer acquaintance is going to disappoint and disgust, let me not enter, but depart from this "Mount of Ascension" carrying away the picture already imprinted on my heart.

Such a result is not inevitable, though this your first is by far the best view you will ever have. Your introduction to the Holy City differs widely from mine. Wearied with a long ride from Jaffa, I approached from the west when the shadows of evening were falling heavily over the blank walls and unpicturesque ramparts of Zion. I could see nothing of the city, and entered the gate dissatisfied and sadly disappointed. Subsequently, while residing here, this first impression wore off, and was succeeded by feelings of deep reverence and earnest affection. Be not discouraged, therefore, if you return from the first walk about Zion hungry, weary, half roasted, and with a sensation of disgust tugging desperately at your heart. As you repeat your rambles with less excitement and hurry, and become familiar with the localities and their sacred associations, an intelligent and abiding interest in the very dust and stones of Jerusalem will grow up vigorous and refreshing, you scarcely know how.

At any rate, I am resolved to make myself thoroughly acquainted with the Holy City and its environs, cost what it may.

A very sensible resolution; but I give you fair warning that I am not to be your guide and *cicerone*. It is no child's play, at this season of the year, to walk down and up Mount Olivet, and explore sites and scenes from the bottom of Jehoshaphat to the top of Zion. I have gone the rounds a hundred times, and intend now to rest. Guides in abundance can be procured, and the city is before you. As to "helps and helpers," you are in danger of being bewildered with an *embarras du richesse*. Not to name the Bible and Josephus, here are Eusebius and Jerome, Reland, Maundrell, Chateaubriand, Williams, Wilson, Schultz, Robinson, and any number of minor works. In charts, plans, and views we are equally rich—Catherwood's, Robinson's, Wilson's, Schultz's, Williams's, and many others; and, most satisfactory of all, you have the living original spread out beneath your eye, and ready to be questioned at all hours of day and night. Do not set out, however, like Mr. Solesby, resolved to make *discoveries*. There is not a foot of ground that has not been already scrutinized by a thousand eyes as keen as yours, and the old adage, "If *true* not *new*, if *new* not *true*," may be applied to Jerusalem and her monuments with more propriety than to any other place on earth.

I am in no mood to allow my enthusiasm to be extinguished by such a damper as that. To me every thing is invested with the charm of novelty, and I shall taste all the pleasure of discovery without claiming any of its honors. Jerusalem is the common property of the whole Christian world—belongs neither to Greek nor Latin—is neither papist nor Protestant. *I* claim a share in Zion and Moriah, Olivet and Siloah, Gethsemane and Calvary, and I mean to pursue my studies and researches with as much freedom and zest as though no eye but mine had ever scanned these sacred sites.

So be it; but do not dream of reaching results in all cases clear and satisfactory even to yourself, much less to others.

It would be entertaining at least, if not instructive, to submit the topography of Jerusalem and her environs to a conclave composed of devout padres, learned authors, and intelligent gentlemen from Europe and America now residing in the Holy City. They would scarcely agree on a single point. Poor Josephus would be so tortured, and twisted, and perplexed as not to know what he meant himself; and, by the same process, every text in the Bible that had any bearing upon this topography would be mystified and confounded; and thus, too, would be treated the "fathers," and every pilgrim and visitor who unfortunately published a sentence about Jerusalem. They would be completely bewildered, and then dismissed from the witness-box as incompetent, or otherwise unworthy of credit. Now I would learn from this imaginary congress of conflicting theorizers to walk softly over such doubtful territory, and not to dogmatize where opinions of the learned clash.

It is my own decided impression that no ingenuity can reconstruct this city as our Saviour saw it, or as Josephus describes it. No man on earth *knows* the line of the *eastern* and *southeastern* portions of the *first* wall, nor where the *second* began, nor how it ran after it began, nor where the *third* wall commenced, nor one foot of its circuit afterward; and of necessity, the locations of castles, towers, corners, gates, pools, sepulchres, etc., etc., depending upon *supposed* starting-points and directions, are merely hypothetical. One hypothesis may have more probability than another, but all must share the uncertainty which hangs over the data assumed by the theorizers.

Well, leaving speculations and their results to take care of themselves, may we not find some important points and boundaries about which there can be no reasonable doubts?

Certainly there are such outlines, strongly drawn and ineffaceable, which make it absolutely certain that we have the Holy City, with all its interesting localities, before us. For example, this mount on which our cottage stands is Olivet, without a doubt; the deep valley at its base is the channel of Kidron; that broad ravine that joins it from the west, at the well of Job, is the Valley of Hinnom, which is prolonged northward and then westward under the ordinary name of Gihon. The rocky region lying in between these valleys is the platform of ancient Jerusalem—*the whole of it*. Within these limits there was nothing else, and beyond them the city never extended. Thus I understand the language of Josephus when he is speaking of Jerusalem, *one* and *entire*.

I go a step farther in generalizing, and with considerable confidence. This platform of Jerusalem is divided into two nearly equal parts by a valley which commences to the northwest of the Damascus Gate, shallow and broad at first, but deepening rapidly in its course down along the west side of the Temple area, until it unites with the Kidron at the pool of Siloam. The city, therefore, was built upon two parallel ridges, with a valley between them, and these grand landmarks are perfectly distinct to this day. The eastern ridge is Moriah, on which stood the Temple; the western is Mount Zion, and the valley between them is that of the Cheesemongers. These ridges are parallel to each other, and that of Zion is every where the highest of the two; that is, the part of it without the present south wall towers above Ophel, which is over against it; the Temple area is much lower than that part of Zion which is west of it, and the northwest corner of the city overlooks the whole of the ridge on which the Temple stood. This accords with the express and repeated assertions of Josephus that the hill, which sustained the Upper Market-place, or the Upper City, was much the highest of all. The houses built down the *eastern* slopes of Zion every where face those on the *western* slopes of the opposite ridge, and the corresponding rows of houses meet in this intervening valley just as Josephus represents them to have done in his day. The historian wrote his description with an eye to Titus and the Roman army, and I can not doubt but that, up to our present point of generalization, we have laid down the outlines of Jerusalem *as they saw and conquered it*. If we now proceed from generalities to particulars, we shall encounter obscurity and perplexing difficulties at every turn, and these will thicken around us just in proportion as we descend to details more and more minute. For example, perhaps all *planographists* of the Holy City agree that the lower part of the interior valley is that of the Cheesemongers, but higher up, where, under the name of Tyropean, it must define the supposed position of a certain tower, the course of this valley is very earnestly contested. And thus, too, all agree that the ridge *south* of Jaffa Gate is Zion, but some maintain that it terminates there at the Tower of David, while others believe that Zion continued up northward to the Castle of Goliath, and even beyond it. Some authors assume that the Tyropean commences at the Tower of David, and descends first eastward and then to the southeast, under the Temple area and down to Siloam, and that traces of such a valley can still be seen. Other eyes absolutely fail to discover it, and their owners say that the rain from heaven and the theodolite of the engineer obstinately refuse to acknowledge any such valley. Some place Acra north of Jaffa Gate, and others northeast of the Temple area. But we need not extend the list of conflicting theories any farther, for it includes nearly every rod of the entire city—the line of every wall, the position of every castle, the name of every pool, the place of every gate, the site of every scene, etc., etc. On most of these questions I have my own opinions, but to state and defend them would be a most wearisome business, and as useless as it would be endless; from which *libera nos, Domine.*

It is probable that a considerable part of the present western wall, and possibly some of the northern, occupies nearly the line of the *ancient first wall.* That part east of Damascus Gate may be on the line of the *second wall,* as far as that wall extended in that direction, and from the corner of the Temple area northward it must follow very closely that of the *third wall.* That part which crosses Zion from the lower pool of Gihon to the mosque of El Aksa is modern. These walls, as is well known, were built, or, more correctly, I suspect, largely repaired by Sultan Suleiman in 1542, A.H. 948. They are from ten to fifteen feet thick, and from twenty-five to forty feet high, according to the nature of the ground. They have salient angles and square towers, with battlements and loop-holes. A path, protected by a breastwork, runs all round on the top of these walls, and from many parts of this promenade the tourist obtains his most satisfactory views of the city. The stone employed is evidently the fragments and remains of ancient structures. They vary greatly in size and appearance. Along the eastern line of the Temple area are portions of very ancient walls—huge stones, well cut, and laid down with the utmost regularity, probably the work of Herod. Where the south wall crosses the Tyropean it is built of large irregular blocks, evidently the fragments of the Temple and its substructions. Near the Damascus Gate, also, are some fine specimens of ancient work. The entire length of these walls,

WALL AT SOUTHEAST CORNER OF TEMPLE AREA.

according to Dr. Robinson's measurements, is four thousand three hundred and twenty-six yards—a little less than two miles and a half. This makes nearly twenty of the thirty-three stadii which, Josephus says, was the entire circuit of the exterior walls, and leaves but thirteen stadii for the south end of Zion, the hill Ophel, and the quarter of Bezetha, on the north of the Temple. The ancient third wall, therefore, could not have extended very far to the north of the present city.

Where the gates of ancient Jerusalem were located I do not know, and therefore I will leave it to others to station them according to their different theories. The present city has five gates: that at the Tower of David takes the name of Jaffa or Bethlehem, because from it the roads to those places depart; Damascus Gate on the north, St. Stephen's on the east; Bab el Mugharabeh, leading down to Siloam, and the Gate of Zion. Some of these have other names, but it is not necessary to charge the memory with many titles for the same things. There are also two or three old gates, now walled up, as that of Herod on the northeast, and the Golden Gate, in the east wall of the Temple area. The architecture of all these entrances to the Holy City is Saracenic, except the last, which is ancient, and the interior of it ornamented with rich and elaborate carving in good Grecian style.

GOLDEN GATE—INTERIOR VIEW.

It will facilitate your study of Jerusalem to fix in your memory the names and direction of a few of the leading thoroughfares of the city. The streets are, with rare exceptions, short, narrow, and crooked. A few, however, are sufficiently long and important as thoroughfares to be put down on a chart. I prefer the plan of Mr. Williams, and we will use his division of streets, and, to avoid confusion, his nomenclature also. There are only some half a dozen streets which are much frequented by travelers.

1. The Street of David, entering into Temple Street, which descends from Jaffa Gate, and crosses the Tyropean to the Temple area.

2. The Street of the Patriarch, leading north from David Street to the Church of the Holy Sepulchre.

3. Via Dolorosa, which is a sort of eastern continuation of the Street of the Holy Sepulchre, and leads finally to the Gate of St. Stephen.

4. The Street of St. Stephen, which passes through the markets to the Gate of Damascus. Zion Street is a southern continuation of it.

5. The street leading from the Armenian convent to Zion Gate. There are many more, and a multitude of blind alleys, traversed only by those who are in search of some particular locality. These streets are paved with smooth stone, not a little dangerous to timid riders, especially where the descent is steep.

The only castle of any particular importance is that at the Jaffa Gate, commonly called the Tower of David. The lower part of it is built of huge stones, roughly cut, and with a deep *bevel* round the edges. They are undoubtedly ancient, but the interspersed patch-work proves that they are not in their original positions. I have been within it, and carefully explored all parts of it that are now accessible, but found nothing which could cast any light upon its history. It is believed by many to be the Hippicus of Josephus, and to this idea it owes its chief importance, for the historian makes that the point of departure in laying down the line of the ancient walls of Jerusalem. Volumes have been written in our day for and against the correctness of this identification, and the contest is still undecided; but, interesting

TOWER OF DAVID.

as may be the result, we may safely leave it with those who are now conducting the controversy, and turn to matters more in unison with our particular inquiries. Every thing that can be said about this grand old tower will be found in the voluminous works of Williams, Robinson, Schultz, Wilson, Fergusson, and other able writers on the topography of the Holy City.

After riding through the city, I spent this morning in walking about Mount Zion, particularly that part of it which is without the walls, and have been struck with the wonderful fulfillment of the prophecies of Jeremiah and Micah that Zion should be plowed as a field.[1]

It has so happened that my visits to Jerusalem have been at the season when luxuriant crops of grain were growing

[1] Jer. xxvi. 18; Micah iii. 12.

on all the southeastern face of the mount. The full force of the prophecy is not reached unless we remember what Zion was—the stronghold, by nature and by art almost impregnable. Even the Jebuzites scornfully said to David, Except thou take away the lame and the blind, thou canst not come up hither,[1] so confident were they that it could not be captured. David, having made it the capital of his kingdom, greatly strengthened the fortifications, and other kings, in after ages, added to them, and it was, no doubt, densely-crowded with the best and the strongest edifices in Jerusalem at the time these prophecies were uttered. That such a place should become a common wheat-field, where, generation after generation, the husbandman should quietly gather rich harvests, was, indeed, a most daring prediction, and yet it has long since been most literally fulfilled.

What is there or was there about Zion to justify the high eulogium of David: Beautiful for situation, the joy of the whole earth is Mount Zion, on the sides of the north, the city of the great king?[2]

The situation is indeed eminently adapted to be the platform of a magnificent citadel. Rising high above the deep Valley of Gihon and Hinnom on the west and south, and the scarcely less deep one of the Cheesemongers on the east, it could only be assailed from the northwest; and then " on the sides of the north" it was magnificently beautiful, and fortified by walls, towers, and bulwarks the wonder and terror of the nations: For the kings were assembled; they passed by together. They saw it, and so they marveled; they were troubled, and hasted away. At the thought of it the royal psalmist again bursts forth in triumph: Walk about Zion, and go round about her; tell the towers thereof; mark ye well her bulwarks; consider her palaces, that ye may tell it to the generation following.[3] Alas! her towers have long since fallen to the ground, her bulwarks have been overthrown, her palaces have crumbled to dust, and we who now walk about Zion can tell no other story than this to the generation following.

[1] 2 Sam. v. 6.   [2] Ps. xlviii. 2.   [3] Ps. xlviii. 12, 13.

There is another Zion, however, whose towers are still more glorious, and shall never be overthrown. God is known in her palaces for a refuge.[1] And this God is our God forever and ever. How often is this name synonymous with the Church of the living God, and no other spot but one can divide with it the affection of his people—no other name but one can awaken such joyful hopes in the Christian's heart. This temporal Zion is now in the dust, but the true Zion is rising and shaking herself from it, and putting on her beautiful garments to welcome her King when he comes to reign over the whole earth.

There are very few stations to be visited on Zion. Inside the walls is the Armenian convent, with its fine church and large gardens, and on the outside is the house of Caiaphas, near the gate, an ill-shaped building, in itself meriting no attention, but it is enriched with some choice relics. The Armenians here show the identical stone slab which closed the door of the sepulchre, and the precise spot where the cock stood when he crowed three times before Peter completed his miserable denial of the Lord. You may lay this up along with the olive-tree in which the ram was caught by the horns, and substituted on the altar for Isaac. It is growing near Abraham's chapel, on the north side of Calvary.

The only other building of any note on Zion is the Tomb of David—now a mosque, which has been so often drawn by artists that its appearance is familiar to all. Belonging to it is the Cœnaculum—a large, dreary "upper room" of stone, fifty or sixty feet long, by some thirty in width. An ancient tradition says that our blessed Lord here celebrated his last Passover, and at the close of it instituted the "Supper." Here, too, he gave that most affecting lesson on humility, when he rose from supper, laid aside his garments, girded himself with a napkin, and washed the feet of his disciples.[2] Whether there is any foundation for this, or for the equally old tradition that this was the place where the apostles had assembled on the day of Pentecost, when the

[1] Ps. xlviii. 3. [2] John xiii. 4-17.

miracle of cloven tongues was shown, I care not to inquire. There was an *old* chapel there in the *fourth* century to commemorate these events, and I please myself with the idea that there may be truth in the traditions. What a pity that both it and the reputed tomb of David below should be in the hands of Moslems! No Christian is permitted to enter the latter on any account, and it is guarded with more jealousy than even the Mosque of Omar.

On this south part of Zion are the cemeteries of the different Christian denominations, and, among others, that of our own nation, northwest of the Tomb of David, and that of the English to the southwest, on the very declivity of the mount, above the Valley of Hinnom. The high school of Bishop Gobat is located at the same place, and the whole establishment forms an interesting group in a most remarkable position.

The southeastern face of Zion declines, by many a winding terrace, down to the level of the Kidron at the Pool of Siloam, and the line of the aqueduct from the Pools of Solomon can be traced quite round the shoulder of the mount to the place where it passed under the city wall, some distance east of, and far below Zion Gate.

VALLEY OF JEHOSHAPHAT.

Why the valley of the Kidron has this name, or when it first received it, I believe to be wholly unknown. It commences far round to the northwest, toward the tombs of the Judges, and is there broad and shallow. Passing eastward, it has Scopus and the general platform of the city south of it. Meeting the northeastern corner of Olivet, it turns due south, and pursues this direction to Beer 'Ayub, where it bends again to the southeast. From the Church of the Virgin southward, it becomes a narrow ravine, and sinks down between Olivet and Ophel very rapidly, so that at the Well of Job it is more than five hundred feet below the top of Zion. I had visited this lower part, to the Fountain of the Virgin, previously, and to-day I examined the sepulchral monuments above it. They are in the steep rocky termi-

TOMBS IN THE VALLEY OF JEHOSHAPHAT.

nation of that part of Olivet directly north of Kefr Silwan, and the entire base of the mountain has been cut and hewn into perpendicular faces by Jerusalem's ancient quarriers. In these faces are many sepulchres of the ordinary kind, but the tombs which merit special attention are, first, the monolith of Zechariah. It is a cubical block about twenty feet every way, and surmounted by a flattened pyramid of at least ten feet elevation, so that the entire height is thirty feet. It has no mason-work about it, but is one solid mass hewn out of the mountain, the adjacent rock being cut away, so that it stands entirely detached. Each of the sides has two columns and two demi-columns, and the corners are finished off with square pilasters. The capitals are plain Ionic, and a broad cornice, worked with acanthus leaves, runs round the top below the pyramid. There is no known entrance.

Second, the tomb of St. James, which is near to the north side of this monolith. It shows a fine front to the west, ornamented with four short Doric columns. The entrance is not by these columns, but from a passage cut through the rock, in the northeast corner of the space around the tomb of Zechariah. The *cave* of St. James extends forty or fifty feet back into the mountain.

Some two hundred feet north of this is the tomb of Absalom. The lower part of this monument resembles that of Zechariah. Mr. Willis gives the following description of its architectural composition. The square has a pilaster at each angle, and a quarter column attached to it, and also two half columns between these have Ionic capitals, and sustain an entablature of a singularly mixed character. Its frieze and architrave are Doric, and have triglyphs and guttæ. The metope is occupied by a circular disk or shield, but in lieu of the regular cornice there is one which resembles the Egyptian cornice, consisting of a deep and high corvetto, and a bold torus below it. Above this is a square attic rather more than seven feet in height. Upon this is a circular attic. The whole is finished off with what Dr. Robinson calls a small dome, running up into a low spire, which

ABSALOM'S TOMB (RESTORED).

spreads a little at the top, like an opening flower. The entire height of this very striking "pillar" can not be less than forty feet, but the lower part is not a little encumbered with stones and rubbish. Believing it to be Absalom's tomb, the natives throw stones against and spit at it as they pass by. This tomb has been much broken on the north side, and an opening made into a small sepulchral chamber within the solid part of it.

Close to this monument, on the northeast, is the reputed

tomb of Jehoshaphat, and from it the valley may have taken this name. It has an ornamental portal in the perpendicular face of the rock, but the sepulchre is wholly subterranean, and in no way remarkable. I examined these monuments with special pleasure and interest, not because they really had any connection with the individuals whose names they bear, but because they remain very much as they were at the time of our Saviour. I know not whether there is a single edifice, or part of one, in Jerusalem, upon which his eye of compassion rested, when from this Olivet he beheld the city and wept over it, but these sepulchral monuments appear now just as they did then to Him, and He must have often seen, admired, and spoke of them.

From these tombs I went north to look at the subterranean church and sepulchre of St. Mary. It was closed, and so was the so-called Garden of Gethsemane, a short distance to the southeast of it, and I could only examine the outside wall.

The authenticity of this sacred garden Mr. Williams says he chooses rather to believe than to defend. I do not even choose to believe. When I first came to Jerusalem, and for many years afterward, this plot of ground was open to all, whenever they chose to come and meditate beneath its very old olive-trees. The Latins, however, have, within the last few years, succeeded in gaining sole possession; have built a high wall around it, plastered and whitewashed; and, by planting it with trees, seem disposed to make it like what they suppose it was when our Lord retired thither with his disciples on that mournful night of his "agony." Whatever may be thought of this idea, all travelers regret the exclusiveness which makes access difficult, and renders it impossible for most of them to visit the spot at all. The Greeks have invented another site a little north of it, and, of course, contend that they have the true Gethsemane. My own impression is that both are wrong. The position is too near the city, and so close to what must have always been the great thoroughfare eastward, that our Lord would scarcely have selected it for *retirement* on that dangerous and dismal night. In the broad recess northeast of the Church of Mary there must have been gardens far larger and more secluded, and, as we have before suggested, it is nearly certain that all the gardens around the city were thrown open, during the great feasts, for the accommodation of the pilgrims, so that he could select the one best adapted to the purpose for which he retired from the crowded city. I am inclined, therefore, to place the garden in the secluded vale several hundred yards to the northeast of the present Gethsemane, and hidden, as I hope, forever from the idolatrous intrusion of all sects and denominations. The traditions in favor of the present location, however old, have but little weight, and fail to convince the mind; and there is no reason to think that a single tree, bush, or stone on either of these had any connection with the mysterious agony of the Son of God, when "his sweat was, as it were, great drops of blood falling down to the ground."

As to the church and sepulchre of the Virgin Mary, I have had more than one opportunity to examine it. There is a descent of sixty steps to the church, which, consequently, lies almost entirely under the bed of the Valley of Jehoshaphat. The steps, however, are partly outside and partly within the door which leads down to the body of the church. Seen from above, when this is lighted up, the church presents a most striking appearance. On the right of the descent are shown the chapel and tombs of Joachim and Anna; that of St. Joseph on the left; and toward the east of the church is the supposed tomb of Mary, bearing a general resemblance to the Holy Sepulchre, and probably modeled after its pattern. The various altars bear witness to the divisions of Christendom, and its joint occupation by the various countries contributes to perpetuate their miserable feuds; nor does the influence of Gethsemane, which is hard by, seem to allay their animosity or to inculcate Christian charity.

There are other sepulchres in and around Jerusalem which are well worth examining. They are found in astonishing numbers along the south side of Hinnom, and, in-

THE MOUNT OF OLIVES.

Church of the Virgin.

deed, almost every where within and without the city, where the accumulated rubbish is removed, these tombs are met with, generally hewn into the perpendicular faces of the rocks, made in quarrying for building stone. They are of all sizes and shapes. Some are merely single rock-graves; others are small rooms, entered by a door in front, and having two, three, or more niches for the bodies; others, again, are much more extensive—a sort of catacomb, room within and beyond room, each having several niches. The best examples of these are the tombs of the kings and those of the judges. Those of the kings are in the olive grove about

TOMBS OF THE KINGS.

half a mile north of the Damascus Gate, and a few rods east of the great road to Nablûs. A court is sunk in the solid rock about ninety feet square and twenty deep. On the west side of this court is a sort of portico, thirty-nine feet long, seventeen deep, and fifteen high. It was originally ornamented with grapes, garlands, and festoons, beautifully wrought on the cornice; and the columns in the centre, and the pilasters at the corners, appear to have resembled the Corinthian order. A *very low* door in the south end of the portico opens into the ante-chamber—nineteen feet square, and seven or eight high. From this three passages conduct into other rooms, two of them, to the south, having five or six crypts. A passage also leads from the west room down several steps into a large vault running north, where are crypts parallel to the sides. These rooms are all cut in rock intensely hard, and the entrances were originally closed with stone doors, wrought with panels and hung on stone hinges, which are now all broken. The whole series of tombs indicates the hand of royalty and the leisure of years, but by whom and for whom they were made is a mere matter of conjecture. I know no good reason for ascribing them to Helena of Adiabene. Most travelers and writers are inclined to make them the sepulchres of the Asmonean kings.

The tombs of the judges are about a mile northwest of those of the kings. The vestibule in front of them is highly ornamented, but after an entirely different pattern from those of the kings. It faces the west, and from it a door leads into a room about twenty feet square and eight feet high. On the north side are seven *loculi*, seven feet deep, perpendicular to the side of the room. Above these are three arched recesses, two feet and a half deep, probably for the reception of sarcophagi. Perpendicular to these recesses, two long loculi penetrate the rock from the back part. Doors on the south and east conduct to small rooms, which have three long niches perpendicular to their three sides, the doors occupying the fourth. There is also an arched recess over the loculi in these rooms. From the northeast corner of the ante-room a flight of steps goes down into a small vestibule, neatly cut, and ornamented by recesses and a slightly-arched roof like a dome. A passage leads into another chamber farther east, nine feet square and six high, each of whose three sides has an arched recess parallel to it, from the back of which perpendicular loculi enter into the

TOMBS OF THE JUDGES—FRONT VIEW.[1]

rock. In some respects this is a more remarkable catacomb than that of the kings, and the arrangement is more varied and complicated. Why the name Tomb of the Judges is given, no one can assign any plausible explanation. In all directions from this locality, but especially toward the city, the strata of the mountain have been cut and carved into perpendicular faces by ancient quarriers, and in them are innumerable tombs of every variety of pattern. Indeed, the prodigious extent of these quarries and tombs is one of the most striking indications of a great city, and of a long succession of prosperous ages, which the environs of Jerusalem furnish.

The tombs of the prophets are here near the southern summit of Olivet. I have never examined them with much care,

[1] For interior view, see vol. i. p. 158.

but they are regarded as very mysterious excavations by antiquarians. Mr. Williams thus describes them. Through a long gallery, first serpentine and then direct, but winding as you advance, one passes into a circular hall, rising into a conical dome about twenty-four feet in diameter. From this hall run three passages, communicating with two semicircular galleries connective with the hall, the outer one of which contains in its back wall numerous recesses for the corpses, radiating toward the centre hall. No inscriptions or remains of any kind have been discovered to elucidate the mysteries of these mansions for the dead.

The so-called Grotto of Jeremiah is beneath the high tell of Ez Zahera, about forty rods to the northeast of Damascus Gate. This tell, no doubt, once formed the termination of the ridge (of Acra?), and the rock between it and the wall of the city has been quarried away. Nor will the magnitude of this work stumble any one who examines the vast subterranean quarries within and beneath the city, the opening to which is nearly south of Jeremiah's cave. The high perpendicular cuttings which sustain the wall are directly opposite to similar cuttings over the cave, and each is about fifty feet high. The yawning cavern of Jeremiah extends under the cliff about one hundred feet, and there are various buildings, graves, and sacred spots arranged irregularly about it, walled off, plastered, and whitewashed. Under the floor of the cavern are vast cisterns. Lighting our tapers, we descended about forty feet into the deepest one. The roof is supported by huge square columns, and the whole, neatly plastered, is now used as a cistern. The water was pure, cold, and sweet. This place is in Moslem hands, but the keepers allowed us to explore every part of it at our leisure. In any other part of the world it would be considered a remarkable work, but here, in the vicinity of such excavations as undermine the whole ridge within the city, it dwindles into insignificance. There is no evidence to connect it in any way with Jeremiah, and no modern theory has sufficient probability to claim attention.

The excavations under the ridge which extends from the

northwest corner of the Temple area to the north wall of the city are most extraordinary. I spent a large part of this forenoon examining them with a company of friends from the city. Passing out at the Damascus Gate, we ascended the hill of rubbish east of it, and just under the high precipice over which the wall is carried, we crept, or rather *backed* through a narrow opening, and, letting ourselves down some five feet on the inside, we stood within the cavern. Lighting our candles, we began to explore. For some distance the descent southward was rapid, down a vast bed of soft earth. Pausing to take breath and look about, I was surprised at the immense dimensions of the room. The roof of rock is about thirty feet high, even above these huge heaps of rubbish, and is sustained by large, shapeless columns of the original rock, left for that purpose by the quarriers, I suppose. On we went, down, down, from one depth to a lower, wandering now this, now that way, and ever in danger of getting lost, or of falling over some of the many precipices into the yawning darkness beneath. In some places we climbed with difficulty over large masses of rock, which appear to have been shaken down from the roof, and suggest to the nervous the possibility of being ground to powder by similar masses which hang overhead. In other parts our progress was arrested by pyramids of rubbish which had fallen from above, through apertures in the vault, either natural or artificial. We found water trickling down in several places, and in one there was a small natural pool full to the brim. This trickling water has covered many parts with crystalline incrustations, pure and white—in others, stalactites hang from the roof, and stalagmites have grown up from the floor. The entire rock is remarkably white, and, though not very hard, will take a polish quite sufficient for architectural beauty.

The general direction of these excavations is southeast, and about parallel with the valley which descends from the Damascus Gate. I suspect that they extend down to the Temple area, and also that it was into these caverns that many of the Jews retired when Titus took the Temple, as we read in Josephus. The whole city might be stowed away in them; and it is my opinion that a great part of the very white stone of the Temple must have been taken from these subterranean quarries.

TOMBS OF SIMON THE JUST AND OF THE SANHEDRIM.

These curious sepulchres are rarely visited. They are in the valley of the Kidron, a short distance northeast of the tombs of the kings, and under the cliffs on the north side of the wady. They are frequented exclusively by the Jews, and mostly on their festival days. I once entered them on the thirty-third day after the Passover—a day consecrated to the honor of Simon. Many Jews were there with their children. Like all other sects in the East, they make vows in reference to shaving off the hair from their own and their children's heads in honor of some saint or shrine. A number had that day been clipped, the hair weighed, and a sum distributed to the poor in proportion to the weight. The surrounding fields and olive orchards were crowded with gayly-dressed and merry Hebrews. I never saw so many pretty Jewesses together on any other occasion. The tombs seemed to me to have been cut in what were originally natural caves. The entrance to all of them was *very low*, and without ornament. The interior was spacious and gloomy in the extreme, especially that which was said to contain the Sanhedrim. There were between sixty and seventy niches where bodies may have been placed, and from this number, perhaps, the idea originated that they were the crypts of the seventy men of the great synagogue. Dr. Wilson seems to have heard of these tombs, but he confounds them with those of the judges, which are a mile or more to the northwest.

On the general subject of *willies* and sacred tombs, have you ever thought of the interpretation put upon them by our Lord? In Luke we read, Wo unto you! for ye build the sepulchres of the prophets, and your fathers killed them. Truly ye bear witness that ye allow the deeds of your fathers, for they indeed killed them, and ye build their sepulchres.[1] *How? why?* Might not the Pharisees have replied that, by honoring their remains and their memory, they condemned their murderers?

The greatest sin of Israel and of the world *was* and *is* apostasy from the true God and his worship by idolatry, and the most popular mode of this apostasy is sacrilegious reverence for dead men's tombs and bones. This is the most prevalent superstition in the great empire of China, and in Western Asia, Jews, Moslems, Metāwelies, Druses, Nesairiyeh, Ismailîyeh, Kurds, Yezedy, Gipsies, and all sects of Christians, are addicted to it. Every village has its saints' tombs—every hill-top is crowned with the white dome of some neby or prophet. Thither all resort to garnish the sepulchres, burn incense and consecrated candles, fulfill vows, make offerings, and pray. So fanatical are they in their zeal, that they would tear any man to pieces who should put dishonor upon these sacred shrines. Enter that at Hebron, for example, and they would instantly sacrifice you to their fury. Now it was for rebuking this and other kinds of idolatry that "the fathers killed the prophets," and those who built their tombs would, in like manner, kill any one who condemned *their* idolatrous reverence for these very sepulchres. Thus the Pharisees, by the very act of building these tombs of the prophets, and honoring them as they did, showed plainly that they were actuated by the same spirit that led their fathers to kill them; and, to make this matter self-evident, they very soon proceeded to crucify the *Lord* of the prophets because of his faithful rebukes. Nor has this spirit changed in the least during the subsequent eighteen hundred years. *Now, here* in Jerusalem, should the Saviour reappear, and condemn with the same severity our modern Pharisees, *they would kill him upon his own reputed tomb.* I say this not with a faltering *perhaps,* but with a painful certainty. Alas! how many thousands of God's people have been slaughtered because of their earnest and steadfast protest against pilgrimages, idolatrous worship of saints, tombs, bones, images, and pictures! And whenever I see people

[1] Luke xi. 47, 48.

particularly zealous in building, repairing, or serving these shrines, I know them to be the ones who allow the deeds of those who killed the prophets, and who would do the same under like circumstances. If you doubt, and are willing to become a martyr, make the experiment to-morrow in this very city. You may blaspheme the Godhead, through all the divine persons, offices, and attributes, in safety, but insult these dead men's shrines, and woe be to you.

It was probably that he might render apostasy into this insane idolatry impossible to a faithful Jew that Moses made the mere touching of a grave, or even of a bone, contamination. The person thus polluted could not enter his tent, or unite in any religious services. He was unclean seven days, and was obliged to go through a tedious and expensive process of purification. And, still more, if the person would not purify himself, he was to be cut off from the congregation and destroyed. Strange, that even this stern law was not sufficient to restrain the Jews from worshiping dead men's graves.

VALLEY OF HINNOM AND GIHON.

This valley commences northwest of Jaffa Gate, above the upper pool of Gihon. Descending eastward to the immediate vicinity of the gate, it turns south, and the bed of it is occupied by the lower pool of Gihon. Below this it bends round to the east, having the cliffs of Zion on the north, and the Hill of Evil Council on the south. It is here that Hinnom properly begins, and it terminates at Beer 'Ayub, where it joins the valley of Jehoshaphat. The cliffs on the south side especially abound in ancient tombs, and it was this part that was called Tophet. Here the dead carcasses of beasts, and every offal and abomination, were cast, and left to be either devoured by that worm that never died, or consumed by that fire that was never quenched. Hinnom was condemned to this infamous service perhaps because in it, when Israel fell into idolatry, they offered their children in sacrifice to Baal. Jeremiah has an extended reference to this place and its horrid sacrifices. Because they have forsaken

LOWER POOL OF GIHON.

me, and have estranged this place, and have burned incense in it unto other gods whom neither they nor their fathers have known, nor the kings of Judah, and have filled this place with the blood of innocents. They have built also the high places of Baal to burn their sons in the fire—burnt-offerings unto Baal which I commanded not, nor spoke it, neither came it into my mind. Therefore, behold, the days come, saith the Lord, that this place shall no more be called Tophet, nor the valley of the son of Hinnom, but the valley of slaughter.[1] This denunciation was doubtless fulfilled when Nebuchadnezzar sacked and destroyed Jerusalem; and more emphatically by Titus and "his men of war." Josephus says that when Titus saw, from a distance, these valleys below Jerusalem heaped full of dead bodies, he was so horrified at the sight that he raised his hands, and called Heaven to witness, that he was not responsible for this terrific slaughter.

Jeremiah was commanded to *break* the potter's "*bottle*" or *jar* in the presence of the ancients of the people and the priests, after he had denounced these terrible judgments upon them in the valley of Tophet.[2] The people of this country have the same custom of breaking a jar when they wish to express their utmost detestation of any one. They come behind or near him, and smash the jar to atoms, thus imprecating upon him and his a like hopeless ruin.

The cruel sacrifices of children in this valley are frequently referred to by Jeremiah. They were made to pass through the fire unto Moloch,[3] from which it appears that Baal and Moloch were names for one and the same deity. The victims were placed on the red-hot hands of the idol, and their agonizing shrieks were drowned by cymbals and the shouts of the phrensied worshipers. Milton thus sing indignant at these "abominations:"

"Moloch, horrid king, besmeared with blood
Of human sacrifice, and parents' tears,
Though for the noise of drums and timbrels loud
Their childrens' cries unheard, that passed through fire
To his grim idol—in the pleasant vale of Hinnom, Tophet thence,
And black Gehenna called, the type of Hell."

[1] Jer. xix. 1-12. [2] Ib. xix. 10. [3] Ib. vii. 31; xix. 5; and xxxii. 35.

The place seems to have become infamous for idolatry at an early age. Isaiah speaks of it metonymically by the name Tophet, for the place where Sennacherib's army was to be consumed by the breath of the Lord. For Tophet is ordained of old, yea, for the king it is prepared. He hath made it deep and large, the pile thereof is fire and much wood. The breath of the Lord, like a stream of brimstone, doth kindle it.[1] Under its original name of Hinnom, Grecized into Gehenna, it is used in the New Testament as synonymous with, or as a type of hell. The idea seems to be borrowed from the above passages, and from the scenes which were witnessed in this valley. The language of our Saviour, as given by Mark,[2] is copied almost verbatim from Isaiah.[3]

As I move about among these sacred localities, an inquiry of this sort is constantly arising, With what amount of reverence should a pious mind regard them?

I prefer to use the word *respect*. There is nothing now in or about Jerusalem that can justly claim from me any religious reverence whatever. This subject is one of much importance, and needs to be placed in a clear light and upon a proper basis, for the number of visitors of all ages who resort hither is rapidly multiplying, and I notice an increasing disposition among many Protestants to glide into the same sort of reverential deportment in presence of these localities that Roman Catholics and Orientals generally manifest. This should be arrested, not by treating with profane levity such places and scenes, but by acquiring correct views in regard to them, and the manner in which we may derive both pleasure and profit from visiting them, while at the same time we escape this dangerous bias toward idolatrous reverence.

There are two or three *distinctions* to be made, fundamental and broad enough to reach every case of the kind that can come before the pious mind. The first is, that in the Mosaic economy, which multiplied holy places and instruments, it was not the place or the thing itself that was regarded and treated as holy. Moses, for example, was com-

---
[1] Is. xxx. 33. [2] Mark ix. 44–48. [3] Is. lxvi. 24.

manded to put off his shoes before the burning bush, not that it was any more holy than any other bush in the desert of Sinai. The reverence was simply and solely to the infinite and uncreated Being who for the moment dwelt in it in a peculiar manner. So the ark, with the mercy-seat and the apartments in the tabernacle and temple where it was placed, were holy, for no other reason than that God, who is ever to be approached with fear and reverence, there made his special abode. The "bush," without the Presence, differed in nothing from any other; and so of the Holy of Holies in the temple, and of every other place on this earth. When Divine presence is withdrawn, all religious reverence before the place or thing must cease of course. There is nothing, therefore, about the Temple area, or the so-called sepulchre of Christ Jesus, that can now receive any other worship than that which is purely idolatrous. The prophets and apostles always acted upon this principle. To mention but one of a hundred instances, the disciples of our Lord, when they hurried to ascertain the truth of the report about the resurrection, manifested not the slightest reverence for the tomb. Peter ran right into it without stopping to take off his shoes, as you must now do before the fictitious sepulchre in the church, and this, too, though he knew with absolute certainty that his Lord had been there, and had but just left the place. The same is true in the case of the women; none of them seem to have dreamed that the rock-tomb merited any reverence when the Lord himself was gone. Nor do we again hear a whisper about this tomb throughout the entire New Testament history. There is no evidence that any one of them ever revisited it.

The second great principle in regard to these shrines is, that no religious reverence to *human beings* or to *angelic spirits* was ever tolerated, nor to any place or thing that represented them. We can not, therefore, participate in any such rites or ceremonies without enacting a piece of naked idolatry every way, and in all ages and places, extremely offensive to God. This sweeps into one general and undistinguished category of condemnation the entire catalogue of shrines, and tombs, and caverns sacred to dead men.

The third grand fact bearing upon this subject is, that God, in his providence, has so ordered matters that not one of all these shrines can show any just title to the honors claimed for them. The bush is gone, the tabernacle has vanished, not one stone of the Holy of Holies remains, and doubt and uncertainty absolutely impenetrable rests on every sacred locality, and upon every thing connected with them. And in view of the sad and ruinous perversions to which their very shadows give rise, I am thankful that there is not a single tomb of saints, nor instrument employed in manifesting miraculous power, nor a sacred shrine, whose identity can be ascertained.

You have given only a negative answer to my inquiry, and, after all, I feel that the whole truth has not been stated.

Certainly not. To discuss the matter of sacred sites and scenes in detail would require a volume, and I have no disposition to enter the arena of such earnest controversy. The proper use to be made of these things can be laid down in a few words. We should so conduct our visits as to confirm faith and deepen the impressions which the Bible narratives of what here took place in former ages are intended to produce, and for this the materials are abundant and satisfactory.

BETHLEHEM.

May 10*th.* Well, how have you enjoyed your excursion to the City of David?

It was perfectly delightful. Having sent our horses to the Jaffa Gate, we looked in upon the ceremonies which were being enacted in the Church of the Holy Sepulchre. Wearying very soon with what we could not understand, we mounted and set off for Bethlehem. Rising out of the valley of Gihon at the point, I presume, where the boundary-line between Judah and Benjamin passed from the valley of Hinnom into the plain of Rephaim, we stopped a while to allow our guide time to point out the precise spot where

RACHEL'S SEPULCHRE—RAMAH. 501

the Philistines had their camp when David fetched a compass, and came upon them over against the mulberry-trees.[1] The plain itself is stony and uneven, and declines rapidly toward the west. In an hour from the gate of the city we reached the convent of Elijah. Of course, the tradition that the prophet rested at that place in his flight from the wicked Jezebel has no foundation in authentic history, and in itself the establishment merits no particular attention. From there we passed round to the southwest, and came in fifteen minutes to the tomb of Rachel. This is a plain Saracenic mausoleum, having no claims to antiquity in its present form, but deeply interesting in sacred associations, for, by the singular consent of all authorities in such questions, it marks the actual site of her grave. Such a spot must ever be regarded with that sort of respect and tender emotion which are accorded to deep sorrow. The first mention of it occurs in the 35th chapter of Genesis, where Rachel, as her soul was departing, for she died, named her new-born babe Ben-oni, son of sorrow. And Jacob set a pillar upon her grave, that is the pillar of Rachel's grave unto this day.[2] He again refers to this matter in the 48th chapter. As for me, when I came from Padan, Rachel died by me in the land of Canaan, in the way, when yet there was but a little way to come unto Ephrath; and I buried her there in the way of Ephrath: the same is Bethlehem.[3] This is the narrative; but it is more than mere history, for the event occurred, and the record was made, to symbolize a greater sorrow that was to occur at Ephrath nearly two thousand years after, in connection with the birth at Bethlehem of that Man of Sorrows in whom every important event in Hebrew history received its final and complete significance.

Not four hundred yards from Rachel's tomb the guide showed us a heap of old rubbish which he said was called Ramah. This appeared to me like a modern invention, originating in a desire of these very accommodating people to gratify the solicitude of Biblical antiquarians. One thing, however, is certain, that *if* there was such a name attached

---
[1] 2 Sam. v. 22-25. [2] Gen. xxxv. 18-20. [3] Gen. xlviii. 7.

RACHEL'S TOMB.

to any site in that vicinity, all obscurity would at once vanish in regard to that much controverted reference to *a* Ramah in the second chapter of Matthew.[1] In Ramah was there a voice heard, lamentation, and weeping, and great mourning;

[1] Matt. ii. 18.

Rachel weeping for her children, and would not be comforted, because they are not.

Whether this locality is in fact the one that existed in the time of Herod is, of course, highly problematical, but not, as I think, the fact that there was such a place in that vicinity when Herod slew the infants in and about Bethlehem. I can not believe that either of the present well-known Ramahs could be meant. They were too far off, and separated from Bethlehem and from Rachel's tomb by other villages, and intervening mountains and wadies. The place in question must have been contiguous to Bethlehem, was subject to the same calamity, and, being near Rachel's tomb, the poetic accommodation of Jeremiah was natural and beautiful.[1] Of course it *is* accommodation. The prophet himself had no thought of Herod and the slaughter of the infants. That such a small hamlet, a dependence of Bethlehem (and all important towns have now such dependent *mezr'ahs*), should have perished, is not strange. The name Ramah, in some of its forms, is applied to *any* place seated on a hill. There are scores of Rams, Ramahs, Ram-allahs, etc., all over the country, and here there may have been one of them, somewhere near Rachel's tomb.

Bethlehem itself shows to great advantage across the valley from Mar Elias. We, of course, looked at the sacred localities pointed out, but without much satisfaction. The so-called Cave of the Nativity is quite as much transformed and mystified as the Holy Sepulchre. This is to be the more regretted, just in proportion to the greater probability that it may really have some connection with the advent of our Lord.[2]

It is not impossible, to say the least, but that the apartment in which our Saviour was born was in fact a cave. I have seen many such, consisting of one or more rooms, in front of, and including a cavern, where the cattle were kept. It is my impression that the birth actually took place in an ordinary house of some common peasant, and that the babe was laid in one of the mangers, such as are still found in the dwellings of the farmers in this region. That

[1] Jer. xxxi. 15.   [2] Matt. ii. 5-6.

VIEW OF BETHLEHEM.

house may have stood where the convent does now, and some sort of cave, either natural, or made by digging the earth away for building and for the roofs of houses, *may* have been directly below, or even included within its court. Thus all the demands of the tradition would be met, without resorting to the suspicious circumstance of a cave. This locating of so many Biblical scenes and transactions in caves has stumbled the faith of thinking and impartial men, and it is to be regretted that we can not separate this tradition

CAVE OF THE NATIVITY.

concerning the birth-place of Jesus from such doubtful associations. The tradition itself can be traced almost up to the death of the Apostle John, and it appears never to have been entirely lost. Justin Martyr, who was born in Nablûs, and educated in this country, though he suffered martyrdom in Rome, says expressly that Jesus was born in a grotto at Bethlehem. He, of course, did not invent, but merely referred to a tradition already established. This carries up the matter very high indeed, nor is there any thing to contradict his testimony in subsequent ages. It must be confessed, however, that Matthew does not much favor the idea of a grotto. He says of the magi that "when they came into the *house*, they saw the young child, with Mary his mother, and fell down and worshiped him." But a truce to dry criticism. The point in dispute is too insignificant to rob us of the delightful reflections and hallowed emotions which the sight of Bethlehem is calculated to awaken. The glorious Redeemer of our lost world was truly born there, according to prophecy and promise. On the neighboring plain were the "shepherds abiding in the fields, and keeping watch over their flocks by night, when lo! the angel of the Lord came upon them, and the glory of the Lord shone round about them, and they were sore afraid. And the angel said unto them, Fear not, for, behold, I bring you good tidings of great joy, which shall be to all people; for unto you is born this day, in the city of David, a Saviour, which is Christ the Lord. And suddenly there was with the angel a multitude of the heavenly host, praising God and saying, Glory to God in the highest, and on earth peace, good-will toward men!"[1] Thus was announced and celebrated the most astonishing event that ever occurred in the universe—and it took place at Bethlehem.

We need not follow minutely the history of Bethlehem. Though mentioned by Jacob, it remained for many ages small and unimportant, as I suppose, for the name does not appear in the list of villages assigned to Judah by Joshua, nor do we meet with it again until the 17th chapter of

[1] Luke ii. 8–14.

Judges, where it is stated that the young Levite, who subsequently became the first idolatrous priest in Micah's house of gods, and afterward the head of that grand religious apostasy which had its seat in Dan, was of Bethlehem-Judah. This is not much to the honor of the place; and the next event in her story is even less creditable, for the terrible catastrophe which befell the tribe of Benjamin was directly connected with a woman of bad character from Bethlehem, as we read in the 19th chapter of Judges. In these narratives *Judah* is added to the name, to distinguish it from another Bethlehem in Zebulon, west of Nazareth. It is not until the time of Boaz and Ruth that any thing pleasant occurs in the history of Bethlehem, but after that it rose to great celebrity as the birth-place of David, and, finally, it was rendered forever illustrious by the advent there of David's greater son and Lord. Still, it never became large, and never will, for there is a fatal lack of water, and of certain other natural advantages, necessary to create and sustain a great city. The present number of inhabitants is not far from four thousand, and nearly all of them belong to the Greek Church. There was formerly a Moslem quarter, which Ibrahim Pasha destroyed after the great rebellion in 1834; but even this terrible vengeance failed to quell the turbulent spirit of the people. They are ever distinguished in the great feasts at Jerusalem by their fierce and lawless manners, and if any row occurs they are sure to have a hand in it. It is asserted in this country that there is something in the water of certain places which renders the people sturdy, hard, and fearless, and it is curious enough that people of this character have ever been connected with Bethlehem. David and his family, his mightiest captains, Joab and others, came from it, and they were fierce, terrible men. Had the water which David so longed for[1] any influence in compacting such bones and sinews, and hardening such spirits? Perhaps we can find another influence. They were noted shepherds, even to the time when the angels announced the birth of the Saviour. This occupation, in such a region,

[1] 2 Sam. xxiii. 15-16.

contributes greatly to educate just that sort of men. The position of Bethlehem is admirably adapted to call out those elements of character and train them to the utmost perfection. Seated on the summit-level of the hill-country of Judah, with deep gorges descending east to the Dead Sea, and west to the plains of Philistia, the shepherds of Bethlehem had to contend not only with bears and lions, whose dens were in those wild wadies, but also with human enemies— the Philistines on the west, and Arab robbers on the east. They would, therefore, from childhood, be accustomed to bear fatigue, hunger, heat, and cold, both by night and by day, and also to brave every kind of danger, and fight with every kind of antagonist. Thus the youthful David learned to sling stones when he led his father's flocks over the hills, and thus was he prepared to conquer Goliath;[1] and so, too, by defending his charge against bears and lions,[2] he learned to face lion-like men in war, and to conquer them.

I saw many flocks of sheep and goats on these same hills to-day, and was vividly reminded of those passages in Bible history in which the flocks and the shepherds of Bethlehem figure with so much interest, as in David's youth and at the birth of Jesus. I was struck by and equally delighted with another sight on the plains of Bethlehem. The reapers were in the fields cutting barley, and after every company were women and children gleaning, just as Ruth did when Boaz came to look at his laborers.[3]

Yes; and in the evening you might see some poor woman or maiden, that had been permitted to glean on her own account, sitting by the road-side, and beating out with a stick or a stone what she had gathered, as Ruth did.[4] I have often watched this process in various parts of the country. That entire scene of Boaz and Ruth might be enacted at the present day by the dwellers in Bethlehem with but trifling omissions and variations. The salutations that passed between the proprietor and the laborers[5] are no exaggeration of modern politeness. "The Lord be with you" is

[1] 1 Sam. xvii. 49. [2] 1 Sam. xvii. 34. [3] Ruth ii. 5-7.
[4] Ruth ii. 17. [5] Ruth ii. 4

merely the "Allah m'akum" of ordinary parlance; and so, too, the response, "The Lord bless thee." Again, it is implied that there was a considerable company of reapers, and that the reaping season was prolonged for a considerable time; for it is added that Ruth continued to glean until the end of barley-harvest and of wheat-harvest,[1] which are quite distinct, occur in the order here stated, and are protracted through several weeks. It is farther intimated by the tenor of the story that the reapers were apt to be rude in their deportment toward defenseless females,.and hence Boaz commanded them to behave respectfully to Ruth; and he told her, also, not to fear, for he had taken care that she should not be insulted. Such precautions are not out of place at this day. The reapers are gathered from all parts of the country, and largely from the ruder class, and, living far from home, throw off all restraint, and give free license to their tongues, if nothing more. The meals, too, are quite in keeping—the *dipping* her morsel in the vinegar, and the parched corn.[2] Harvest is the time for parched corn—not what we lads in Ohio meant by the words. It is made thus: a quantity of the best ears, not too ripe, are plucked with the stalks attached. These are tied into small parcels, a blazing fire is kindled with dry grass and thorn bushes, and the corn-heads are held in it until the chaff is mostly burned off. The grain is thus sufficiently roasted to be eaten, and it is a favorite article all over the country. When traveling in harvest-time, my muleteers have very often thus prepared parched corn in the evenings after the tent has been pitched. Nor is the gathering of these green ears for parching ever regarded as stealing. After it has been roasted, it is rubbed out in the hand and eaten as there is occasion. This parched corn is often referred to in the Bible. So, also, I have often seen my muleteers, as we passed along the wheat-fields, pluck off ears, rub them in their hands, and eat the grains, unroasted, just as the apostles are said to have done.[3] This also is allowable. The Pharisees did not ob-

[1] Ruth ii. 23.   [2] Ruth ii. 14.
[3] Matt. xii. 1, 2; Mark ii. 23; Luke vi. 1, 2.

ject to the thing itself, only to the time when it was done. They said it was not lawful to do this on the Sabbath day. It was work forbidden by those who, through their traditions, had made man for the Sabbath, not the Sabbath for man.

We have on various occasions seen the summer threshing-floors in the open country, and the owners sleeping at them to prevent stealing, just as the wealthy Boaz did when Ruth came unto him.[1] Though it is not allowable that women in general should sleep at these floors, and to do so would produce the same unfavorable impression which Boaz apprehended, yet it is not unusual for husband, wife, and all the family to encamp at the *baiders* (threshing-floors), and remain until the harvest is over. These family groups, however, do not render it proper for single females to be found there at night, and it is a fact that doubtful characters do actually come about them sufficiently often to keep suspicion alive, and there was doubtless the very same occasion for watchfulness three thousand years ago here at Bethlehem.

Boaz measured six measures of barley and put it into Ruth's *veil*.[2] It would appear from this that barley was used for bread in those days, and also that the veil must have been very different from the light article now used by the women.

Barley is, in fact, very often eaten by the poor in Palestine; and as to the veil, you have only to look at those still worn by the fellahin to understand what kind of article is referred to in this story. It is merely a square piece of cotton cloth, and I have often seen it used for just such service as that to which Ruth applied hers.

In view of the impropriety of women resorting to the *baiders* at night, how did Boaz reach the conclusion expressed by him: "All the city of my people doth know that thou art a virtuous woman?"

Boaz, no doubt, knew her general character, and knew also that in the present instance she acted in accordance

[1] Ruth iii. 2–7. [2] Ruth iii. 15.

with the advice of her mother-in-law, who had taught her that she not only had a right to claim Boaz for her husband, but that she was precluded by the law of God from forming any other reputable connection. Boaz also remembered that he was old, and she young and attractive, and, though from the heathen Moabites, yet she preferred to walk in the sober path of honest married life rather than to associate with the young and the gay, by whom, it is intimated, she had been tempted. He was therefore fully justified in ascribing to this very act an honorable and virtuous principle, notwithstanding the *apparent* violation of modesty and propriety; and in this he judged correctly, for such was the fact. Ruth manifested true modesty and virtue, therefore, by claiming that to which she was entitled, and to which, in truth, she was bound by the law of God. That she applied to the wrong person was through the mistake of her mother-in-law.

Is there any thing in modern customs among the Arabs to illustrate the singular act of pulling off the man's shoe who refused to marry his brother's widow?

This matter is passed over very mildly here in Ruth, for it appears now to have become common to omit the harsher features of the law as laid down in Deut. xxv. 7–10, where the details are rough enough certainly. When a man publicly refuses, "in the gate of the city," to take his brother's wife, "then she shall come to him in the presence of the elders, and loose his shoe from off his foot, and spit in his face, and shall answer and say, So shall it be done unto that man that will not build up his brother's house. And his name shall be called in Israel the house of him that hath his shoe loosed." Perhaps, in the case of Ruth, all these offensive actions were omitted, possibly in consideration of the facts that the man in question was not Ruth's husband's brother; that she was an alien and a foreigner; that he could not fulfill the law without injuring his own family; that there was another, the next in kin, who was more than willing to take his place, and also that Ruth wished to avoid any unnecessary publicity in the transaction. So much of

INTERIOR OF THE CHURCH OF THE NATIVITY

the law, therefore, only was observed as was necessary to confirm the transfer of the rights to Boaz.

In regard to modern customs, there is a proverb among the Arabs which may possibly owe its origin to this law of Moses. When an Arab divorces his wife, he says of her, She was my *babûj* (slipper), and I cast her off. In both the law and the proverb the *babûj* represents the woman and her matrimonial rights and claims. It is one thing, however, for a man to kick off his slipper in disgust, and quite another to have it plucked off in scorn and contempt by the insulted lady, especially if she should spit in his face, and fasten upon him in Israel the nickname Beit Khabûtz hanaal, the house of him whose shoe is loosed. In any event, the comparing of woman to a slipper is not very complimentary to the sex, but it is eminently Arabic, and it is a deplorable fact that all her matrimonial rights can be kicked off, like a worn-out *babûj*, at the caprice of her heartless lord and tyrant.

But you must allow me to complete my visit and return home. I examined with much interest the great church, which is certainly ancient and is really worth seeing, and the paintings in various parts of it, which *are not*.

But did you not enter the tomb of Jerome, and his study, where he spent so many years in translating the Bible?

Most certainly I did, and was deeply impressed by the visit. I suppose that these may be genuine, as also the last resting-place of the two ladies, his companions and patrons. These are all beneath the premises which belong to the Latin monks, and it is no more than justice to add that they manifested more decorum and solemnity in their deportment than do the Greeks and Armenians. After completing the circuit of *Holy Places*, and refreshing the inner man at the restaurant, kept by a talkative Greek, we took a long circuit eastward to see the surrounding country, and then returned hither across those plains where the shepherds watched their flocks on that night when the Redeemer of the world was born.

11*th*. In my walks about Zion to-day I was taken to see

the village or quarter assigned to the lepers, lying along the wall directly east of Zion Gate. I was unprepared for the visit, and was made positively sick by the loathsome spectacle.

You could not be more surprised and startled than I was on my first introduction to this awful disease. Sauntering down the Jaffa road, on my approach to the Holy City, in a kind of dreamy maze, with, as I remember, scarcely one distinct idea in my head, I was startled out of my reverie by the sudden apparition of a crowd of beggars, "sans eyes, sans nose, sans hair, sans every thing." They held up toward me their handless arms, unearthly sounds gurgled through throats without palates—in a word, I was horrified. Having never seen a leper, nor had my attention turned to the subject (for a quarter of a century ago Jerusalem and its marvels were not so well understood as they are now), I at first knew not what to make of it. I subsequently visited their habitations, as you have done to-day, and have made many inquiries into their history. It appears that these unfortunate beings have been perpetuated about Jerusalem from the remotest antiquity. One of my first thoughts on visiting their dens of corruption and death was, that the government should separate them, and thus, in a few years, extinguish the race and the plague together; and I still think that a wise, steady, and vigilant sanitary system might eventually eradicate this fearful malady. But it will not be so easily or expeditiously accomplished as I then thought. It is not confined to Jerusalem, for I have met with it in different and distant parts of the country. And what is particularly discouraging is, that fresh cases appear from time to time, in which it *seems* to arise spontaneously, without hereditary or any other possible connection with those previously diseased. This fact, however, has not yet been fully established.

It is evident that Moses, in his very stringent regulations respecting this plague and its unhappy victims, had in view its extinction, or at least restriction within the narrowest possible limits. Those who were merely suspected were shut up, and if the disease declared itself the individual was immediately removed out of the camp, and not only he, but every thing he touched, was declared unclean. For all practical purposes, the same laws prevail to this day. The lepers, when not obliged to live outside the city, have got a separate abode assigned to them, and they are shunned as unclean and dangerous. No healthy person will touch them, eat with them, or use any of their clothes or utensils, and with good reason. The leper was required by Moses to stand apart, and give warning by crying unclean! unclean! Thus the ten men that met our Saviour stood afar off, and lifted up their voice of entreaty. They still do the same substantially, and, even in their begging, never attempt to touch you. Among tent-dwelling Arabs the leper is literally put out of the camp.

Tacitus has some strange stories about the leprosy and the Jews. When he comes to speak of the Jewish war in the time of Vespasian, he takes occasion to give an account of the origin of this people, in which there are almost as many fables as sentences. He then goes on to say that "one thing is certain. The Jews, when in Egypt, were all afflicted with leprosy, and from them it spread to the Egyptians. When the king, Bochorus, inquired of Jupiter Ammon how his kingdom could be freed from this calamity, he was informed that it could be effected only by expelling the whole multitude of the Jews, as they were a race detested by the gods. He accordingly drove them all forth into the desert, where one Moses met them, and succeeded in bringing them all into obedience to himself," with a great deal more of such nonsense. He accounts for the rejection of swine's flesh among the Jews by the fable that the leprosy was caught from swine.[1] This much, I think, can be safely inferred from a careful study of the 13th and 14th chapters of Leviticus, that the Hebrews were actually afflicted with the awful curse of leprosy beyond all modern example—leprosy of many kinds: in their persons; "leprosy in garments"—in the warp and in the woof—leprosy in

[1] Tacitus, Ann., book v.

the skins of animals; leprosy in the mortar, and even in the stones of their houses—phenomena not only unknown, but utterly unintelligible at this day. It is probable that some obscure traditions of these things, which were afloat in the world, furnished the materials out of which the fancy of the historian worked up his malignant libel on the Hebrew nation.

Have you any explanation of this very obscure subject, and especially in reference to leprosy in garments and walls of houses? This is one of many inquiries I wished to have answered during my visit to this country.

I have no light to shed upon it. For many years I have sought in every possible way to get at the mystery, but neither learned critics nor physicians, foreign or native, nor books, ancient or modern, have thrown any light upon it. I have suspected that this disease, which, like the anthropophagous ghouls of the Arabs, leisurely eats up its victims in one long remorseless meal, is, or is caused by, living and self-propagating animalculæ; and thus I can conceive it possible that those animalculæ might fasten on a wall, especially if the cement were mixed with sizing, as is now done, or other gelatinous or animal glues. Still, the most cursory reference to the best of our recent medical works suffices to show how little is known about the whole subject of contagion, and its propagation by fomites. One finds in them abundant and incontestible instances of the propagation of more than one terrible constitutional malady, in the most inexplicable manner, by garments, leather, wood, and other things, the *materies morbi* meantime eluding the most persevering and vigilant search, aided by every appliance of modern science, chemical or optical. This much, however, about leprosy is certain, that there are different kinds of it, and that fresh cases are constantly occurring in this country. What originates it, and how it is propagated, are points enveloped in profound darkness.

But, though we can not comprehend the leprosy nor cleanse the leper, there are many things to be learned from this mysterious disease. It has ever been regarded as a direct punishment from God, and absolutely incurable, except by the same divine power that sent it. God alone could cure the leprosy. It was so understood by Naaman the Syrian, who came from Damascus to Samaria to be cured by Elisha; and when his flesh came again as the flesh of a little child, he said, Behold, now I know that there is no God in all the earth but in Israel.[1] It is a curious fact that this hideous disease still cleaves to Damascus, the city of Naaman, for there is a mild kind there which is sometimes cured, or apparently cured, even at this day. I have met with cases, however, where the cure was only temporary and perhaps it is so in every instance.

There is nothing in the entire range of human phenomena which illustrates so impressively the divine power of the Redeemer, and the nature and extent of his work of mercy on man's behalf, as this leprosy. There are many most striking analogies between it and that more deadly leprosy of sin which has involved our whole race in one common ruin. It is feared as contagious; it is certainly and inevitably hereditary; it is loathsome and polluting; its victim is shunned by all as unclean; it is most deceitful in its action. New-born children of leprous parents are often as pretty and as healthy in appearance as any, but by-and-by its presence and workings become visible in some of the signs described in the 13th chapter of Leviticus. The "scab" comes on by degrees in different parts of the body; the hair falls from the head and eyebrows; the nails loosen, decay, and drop off; joint after joint of the fingers and toes shrink up, and slowly fall away. The gums are absorbed, and the teeth disappear. The nose, the eyes, the tongue, and the palate are slowly consumed, and finally the wretched victim sinks into the earth and disappears, while medicine has no powers to stay the ravages of this fell disease, or even to mitigate sensibly its tortures.

Who can fail to find in all this a most affecting type of man's moral leprosy? Like it, this too is hereditary, with an awfully infallible certainty. As surely as we have in-

[1] 2 Kings v. 14, 15.

herited it from our fathers do we transmit it to our children. None escape. The infant so lively, with its cherub smile and innocent prattle, has imbibed the fatal poison. There are those, I know, who, as they gaze on the soft, clear heaven of infancy's laughing eye, reject with horror the thought that even here "the leprosy lies deep within." So any one might think and say who looked upon a beautiful babe in the arms of its leprous mother, in that little community near Zion's Gate. But alas! give but time enough, and the physical malady manifests its presence, and does its work of death. And so in the antitype. If left unchecked by power divine, the leprosy of sin will eat into the very texture of the soul, and consume every thing lovely and pure in human character, until the smiling babe becomes a Nero, a Cæsar Borgia, a bloody Robespierre, or the traitor Iscariot. These were all once smiling babes.

Again, leprosy of the body none but God can cure, as is implied in the strong protestation of the King of Israel when Naaman came to him: *Am I God, to kill and make alive,* that this man doth send unto me to recover a man of his leprosy? So, also, there is only one physician in the universe who can cleanse the soul from the leprosy of sin. Again, medicines of man's device are of no avail, but with Him none are needed. He said to the ten who stood afar off, and lifted up their voices and cried, Jesus, Master, have mercy on us, "Go show yourselves to the priests, and as they went they were cleansed." And with the same divine power he says to many a moral leper, Go in peace, thy sins be forgiven thee; and it happens unto them according to their faith. To my mind there is no conceivable manifestation of divine power more triumphantly confirmatory of Christ's divinity than the cleansing of a leper with a word. When looking at these handless, eyeless, tongueless wrecks of humanity, the unbelieving question starts unbidden, Is it possible that they can be restored? Yes, it is more than possible. It has been accomplished again and again by the mere volition of Him who spake and it was done. And He who can cleanse the leper can raise the

POOL OF HEZEKIAH.

dead, and can also forgive sins and save the soul. I ask no other evidence of the fact.

I devoted this day to the pools and fountains of Jerusalem. The first one examined was that of Hezekiah, within the city, and just south of the great Greek convent. It is nearly two hundred and fifty feet long, and one hundred and fifty wide: an immense reservoir, capable of holding water sufficient for half the city. My guide called it Birket Hammam, and said that the water was used chiefly for baths. From a terrace near the northwest corner there is a beautiful view of the city—the domes of the Holy Sepulchre—the Mosque of Omar—and of the Church of the Ascension on the top of Olivet. After looking at this as much as its importance merits, I went out at the Jaffa Gate, and to the Upper Gihon as I choose to call it, though its name is Birket Mammilla among the Arabs. The water is brought from it by a small aqueduct into the city, and supplies the Pool of Hezekiah. This Upper Gihon is about one hundred and fifty rods west of the city, near the head of the shallow valley, and is about three hundred feet long, two hundred wide, and twenty deep. From its situation and appearance, it may be of any age which our peculiar theories of the topography of the city demand. There is now no water in it. The lower pool—Birket es Sultan—is in the same valley, south of Jaffa Gate. It is about six hundred feet long, two hundred and fifty broad, and forty deep—a cistern of prodigious capacity. The aqueduct from the Pools of Solomon passed along west of it, round the north end, then down the east side, and so round Zion to the Temple. At some former time a pipe led the water from the aqueduct to an artificial fountain on the top of the south wall of the pool, where it emptied into troughs made of old sarcophagi. From this pool the Valley of Hinnom descends rapidly eastward to Beer 'Ayub—Well of Job (or of Nehemiah)—below the junction of Hinnom and Jehoshaphat. I also examined with much interest the Pool of Siloam and the Fountain of the Virgin, and looked into the tunnel which connects them, but my antiquarian zeal would require to be largely stimulated before I could repeat

POOL OF SILOAM.

the exploit of Robinson and Smith. There are several other pools which I merely looked at in passing round the city, but as the identity of all of them with pools mentioned in the Bible is controverted, I could not get up any great amount of enthusiasm in regard to them. That of Siloam seems to be about fifty feet long, twenty deep, and as many in width, though the sides are so broken down that it is not easy to take correct measurements. It lies in the mouth of the Tyropean, and the water runs from it, under a rock precipice, across the road to some gardens in the Valley of Jehoshaphat. It is a small rill which is soon exhausted among beds of radishes and cucumbers.

The Fountain of the Virgin is about four hundred paces up the valley from Siloam, and I descended to it by twenty-seven steps. I made no new discoveries, however, and have nothing to add to the elaborate discussions in regard to it, and to all the other pools and fountains of the city, which I have been reading in Robinson and Williams. I looked in upon the vast chasm or fosse on the north side of the Temple area, which I hear called Birket Israîl, and see on the maps written Bethesda. There is a considerable pool also outside St. Stephen's Gate, which my guide called Birket sitti Myriam. By this time I was thoroughly tired, and returned home to rest, and to enjoy this delightful view of the Holy City.

I fully sympathize with your lack of interest, but still the questions about the waters of Jerusalem are of considerable importance. The main dependence for a constant and convenient supply is, and always has been, I suppose, the domestic cisterns. Every house has one or more; so has every church, mosque, convent, castle, and bath. Many of these are well kept, and the water is cool, sweet, and free from worms. The house I first rented in Jerusalem had three cisterns; that of Mr. Lanneau, my missionary associate, had four, and two of his were very large.

No fact in relation to this country is better attested than the extreme antiquity of cisterns, and nothing about old sites has so much surprised me as the immense number of them. Often, where every trace of buildings has disappeared, the whole site is perforated with these underground reservoirs. Neither Beer 'Ayub, nor the Fountain of Mary, nor any of these vast pools, nor the aqueduct from beyond Bethlehem, would be much needed except for the Temple service, and during the grand convocation of the tribes in their annual festivals. Jerusalem was so abundantly supplied with water that no inconvenience from this source was experienced even during the many and long sieges which the city sustained. The people perished from famine, not from thirst. It is surprising, and not a little perplexing to a visitor who is obliged to carry a "bottle" of water with him in his excursions round the environs, to learn that there was once such an abundance of water *outside* that King Hezekiah had to summon all the strength of Israel to aid in stopping the *fountains:* So there was gathered much people together, who stopped all the fountains, and *the brook that ran,* or overflowed, *through the midst of the land,* saying, Why should the King of Assyria come and find much water?[1] After suffering from intolerable thirst in many rambles

[1] 2 Chron. xxxii. 3, 4.

around the Holy City, I read with wonder of "much water!" "many fountains!" "brooks overflowing through the midst!" Strange expressions, these, when applied to this topography. Hezekiah and his "much people" stopped them up so effectually that they could never be found again, even by the Jews themselves. This will not appear extravagant if we take into account the calamities by which Jerusalem was utterly overthrown and lay in ruins for seventy years; and also that when the remnant returned from distant Babylon, few and feeble, they were in no condition to search for these fountains, and, in fact, had no particular need of them.

In regard to these pools, whether immediately around the city or those beyond Bethlehem, there is no difficulty in assigning to them any age which history requires. Cisterns that can sustain a thousand years of comparative neglect would last many thousand when in use and properly repaired. So far, therefore, as the works themselves are concerned, they may date back to the age of Solomon; and, if speculation and inference were of avail in such questions, we might suppose that, when Solomon was building his magnificent Temple, and adapting his capital to be the centre of the whole Hebrew race, he would not fail to make ample provision for the indispensable article of water. He therefore may have constructed the pools beyond Bethlehem, and built the aqueduct which brought a supply to the Temple sufficient for the ablutions and other services of that great sanctuary. And as the prodigious assemblies at the national feasts would require a large amount of water, in different quarters and of easy access, he made those pools on the west, and others of smaller size, distributed in and about the city, for the greater convenience of the pilgrims. We find in these conditions an adequate emergency and a suitable occasion for the construction of these reservoirs—a great want, a king wealthy, and wise, and given to building, and a time of peace. It must be remembered that we are speaking of works quite unique and extraordinary. No other city in this part of the world had any thing like these cisterns, and the supposition that most of them were made by Solomon and his immediate successors is not extravagant. The only serious objection that occurs to me is found in the passage already quoted. If there were "many fountains, a brook running through the midst of the land, and *much* water," there would have been no occasion, up to the time of Hezekiah, to resort to such expensive contrivances as these pools. After these fountains had been stopped up, however, and the supply outside the city thus cut off, artificial means would become indispensable. It is quite possible, therefore, that most of these "pools" have been constructed since the return from Babylon. And if those beyond Bethlehem were made by Solomon, and are referred to in Ecclesiastes,[1] yet the *aqueduct* connecting them with the Temple may have been built after the "captivity." Solomon himself intimates that his pools were not designed to supply Jerusalem, but to irrigate his gardens and forests.

These pools about Jerusalem are now empty, and as thirsty as the disappointed pilgrim who resorts to them. How do you account for this?

Certainly not by the assumption that less water falls now than formerly. These mountains are deluged with rains in winter, such as we rarely experience in America, and yet I never saw water running into any of the pools, or down any of those valleys, except just while it was literally pouring from the clouds. On occasions of this kind muddy streams rush down Jehoshaphat and Hinnom with great violence. The water, however, quickly sinks beneath the accumulated rubbish, and finds its way to the Dead Sea without reappearing on the surface. No doubt a far greater quantity of the winter rains was made to flow into the cisterns anciently than now, and they may have been filled in part by streams from living fountains which are now lost. Traditions of such streams are still kept alive among the inhabitants, and they seem to be countenanced by the passage from 2d Chronicles. The main cause of the present deficiency is that the cisterns are not now kept in good condition. It would be quite possible to fill them all during winter if they

---
[1] Eccles. ii. 6.

were made water-tight, and suitable care was taken to conduct into them the rain-water from the rocks and fields above. This whole subject is one of much interest, but there must be more exploration and excavation than has hitherto been possible before all the problems connected with it can be solved. What did you make out of Beer 'Ayub?

I found it in the bed of the Kidron, just below the junction of Hinnom and Jehoshaphat, and five hundred and fifty feet below the top of Zion by the aneroid. Do you suppose that this is the En Rogel of Joshua?[1]

There is no reason to doubt it. In the 18th chapter and 16th verse, where the south line of Benjamin's lot is drawn, the situation of En Rogel at the bottom of Hinnom, south of Jebusi, or Jerusalem, is clearly indicated. It was near this well that Jonathan and Ahimaaz lay hid during the rebellion of Absalom, in order to collect and send news to David, and afterward Adonijah slew sheep, and oxen, and fat cattle by En Rogel, when he conspired to seize the kingdom. The celebrated Joab was with him, and by this act forfeited his life; and if the well was called Beer Yoab instead of 'Ayub, as some have maintained, we might find the origin of the name possibly in this last act of Joab's political career. As matters stand, we can not discover why, or on what occasion the name En Rogel was changed into 'Ayub, or into Nehemiah, or into that of the Well of Fire, by all which titles it has been distinguished. The patriarch Job could have no connection with it, and that Nehemiah recovered the sacred fire from this well after his return from Babylon is a mere fable. In itself it is a singular work of ancient enterprise. The shaft, sunk through the solid rock in the bed of the Kidron, is one hundred and twenty-five feet deep. The idea of digging such a well at that precise spot may have been suggested by the fact that after very great rains water sometimes rises nearly to the top, and then flows out into the valley below, a strong brook capable of driving a mill. This, however, soon ceases, and the water

[1] Josh. xv. 7.

EN ROGEL—SILOAM—GIHON.

in the well subsides to less than half its depth. From that point a stream seems to run constantly across it, and pass down the valley under the rock. This appearance of the water below may have first suggested the plan of sinking a shaft higher up and near the city wall, that there might be access to it in times of invasion. The water is pure and entirely sweet, quite different from that of Siloam, which proves that there is no connection between them. I have seen the water gushing out like a mill-stream, some fifteen rods south of the well, and then the whole valley was alive with people bathing in it, and indulging in every species of hilarity. Thus it was in the time of David, and most likely the quantity and duration of the flow were much greater then than now. "The stone of Zohelath, which is by En Rogel," was therefore a most suitable spot for Adonijah, at which to slay sheep, and oxen, and fat cattle—make a great feast, and complete his conspiracy; for the people were accustomed to assemble there on festive occasions, and multitudes might find themselves entrapped into the rebellion ere they were aware of it. In this connection, it may be remarked that Gihon, *down* to which Solomon was immediately conducted, by order of David, to be anointed king, was probably on the other side of the city. David would certainly not send him into the midst of the conspiracy. It is evident, however, from 1 Kings i. 41, 42, that Gihon was so near En Rogel that Adonijah and his company could hear the rejoicing of the people that were with Solomon, and this incidentally confirms the correctness of the sites of Gihon as now received, on the west and northwest of the city.

The whole vicinity of En Rogel, and of Siloam too, including the slopes of Zion and Ophel, are now the very last resort for any muse, either heavenly or earthly. Milton's famous invocation,

> "If Sion's hill
> Delight thee more, and Siloa's brook, that flowed
> Fast by the oracle of God, I thence
> Invoke thine aid to my adventurous song,"

would never have been written if the poet had encountered

there the sights and scents which disgusted me this morning.

It will do very well for a poet "smit with the love of sacred song" to accommodate Zion with

>"Flowery brooks beneath,
>That wash thy hallowed feet, and warbling flow."

Milton, however, never visited this country, and withal was blind; but I have seen the Kidron in ancient maps expanded into a broad river, and enlivened with boats and *lateen* sails! Where the geographer fables, the poet surely may dream.

Mr. Williams amuses himself with the contradictory accounts of historians and travelers in regard to the taste of this water. Josephus says it is sweet, one calls it bitter, another tasteless. Dr. Robinson makes it sweetish and slightly brackish, and he is right, according to my experience. I never could endure it, always thinking that it smelled and tasted of the bath. I have little doubt but that it is mingled, to say the least, with water used for Moslem ablutions and bathings in the great mosques of Omar and El Aksa.

You think, then, that there is a connection between this fountain and the wells, subterranean cisterns, etc., beneath the southern part of the Temple area?

I do not doubt it, and have always suspected that the irregular fluctuations in the quantity of water are occasioned, in part at least, by the draining into the channel at different times the water from these hidden reservoirs. I suppose it was so in ancient days, and this well-known phenomenon may have suggested to Ezekiel that striking allegory of the mystic river whose small beginnings he saw flowing down from under the altar of God.[1] The machinery of some of Ezekiel's visions was strange and complex—"Wheels within wheels, with living creatures wedded." Others again were remarkably simple, and withal rich in beautiful imagery and suggestive drapery. Of this kind is this river, which the man with the line in his hand showed to the prophet.

[1] Ezek. xlvii. 1-12.

There were things very peculiar and significant in its origin, accidents, and attributes. *Its source.*—Behold, waters issued out from under the threshold of the house—came down from under, at the south side of the altar.

Its course.—It flowed toward the east country—into the desert—and entered the east, that is, the Dead Sea. There is no other in that direction, and water issuing from the "south side of the altar" must, by a topographical necessity, flow down the valley of Jehoshaphat, along the bed of the Kidron eastward into the desert, and thus into the Dead Sea by Wady en Nâr.

Its rapid increase.—A mere rill at the beginning, it was to the ankles at the end of the first thousand cubits, to the knees the second, the loins at the third, and at the fourth thousand "it was a river to swim in, that could not be passed over."

Its effects.—Every thing shall live whither the river cometh. On either bank grow all manner of trees for meat, whose leaf shall not fade, neither shall the fruits thereof be consumed. What a contrast to the present banks of the Kidron—a horrid wilderness, blasted by the curse of God, with nothing to relieve its frightful desolation! But where this river from under the sanctuary comes, the desert blossoms, the banks are shaded with trees, and vocal with music of birds. And more wonderful still, "The river being brought forth into the sea, the waters thereof shall be healed." Now this Sea of Sodom is so intolerably bitter that, although the Jordan, the Arnon, and many other streams have been pouring into it their vast contributions of sweet water for thousands of years, it continues as nauseous and deadly as ever. Nothing lives in it; neither fish, nor reptiles, nor even animalculæ can abide its desperate malignity. But these waters from the sanctuary heal it. When they come thither the shores are robed in green, its bosom teems with all manner of fish, and fishermen stand thick on every rock from En-gedi even unto En-eglaim. They shall be to spread forth nets, for the fish shall be as those of the great sea, exceeding many.

This beautiful allegory was doubtless not thrown into the Bible merely to amuse us. What is your explanation?

There are good men, and learned in the Scriptures, who interpret it literally, and maintain that a mighty physical miracle is here predicted. But we find in it only a spiritual allegory, which foreshadows miracles of mercy in store for the whole world far more stupendous. That God will cause such a river of actual water to flow down from Mount Moriah to gladden the desert of Judæa and heal the Sea of Sodom, I do not believe. There is another desert, however, which he will surely heal—the desert of sin, the sea of spiritual death.

I discover in this richest of allegories a most comprehensive and delightful exhibition of the scheme of redemption, from its inception to its final and glorious consummation. There is good gospel, and much sound and even profound theology in it. Every incident is suggestive, every allusion instructs. The waters flowed out from under the *altar*, intimating, not darkly, that the stream of divine mercy—the river of life—has its source in *sacrifice* and *death*. Until justice is satisfied by the atoning sacrifice of the Lamb of God *upon the altar*, the waters of life can not flow forth from beneath it.

There can be little doubt but that the prophet borrowed the drapery of his allegory from the physical features of the Temple area, and that of the country east and southeast of it. Though the waters first appeared issuing *from under the altar*, yet we need not suppose that the fountain-head was there, but farther back, under the Holy of Holies, beneath the ark and mercy-seat, where abode the Shekinah of God's presence, intimating that the true fountain-head of the river of life is in the heart of infinite love, but on its way out and down to ruined man it must pass *under the altar of divine justice*. There is, therefore, no other place in the universe whence these emblematic waters could flow forth so appropriately as under the altar.

Again, this river was small at first, but increased rapidly as it flowed onward, and thus it has been with the river of life. It was a mere rill from Adam to Noah—the waters were to the ankles. From the Deluge to Moses it grew broader and deeper—the waters were unto the knees, and patriarchs with their flocks reposed in green pastures along the verdant banks. From Moses the lawgiver to David the sweet singer, it rolled onward, ever gathering breadth and power, and its shady groves became vocal with psalms and hymns to the God of salvation. And thus it continued to swell, and expand, and deepen, by the addition of many a rill of prophecy and promise, until He who is the true fountain came, sending forth a mighty river of unfathomable depth, which can not be passed over; a river to swim in; all the world may bathe in it and be cleansed—may drink of it and thirst no more; and ever since the Advent, it has rolled onward farther and farther into the desert, and thus it will continue until its most distant borders shall blossom, and the great dead sea of sin shall be swallowed up of life. The divine allegory foreshadows the millennium in its amplest acceptation.

From the physical topography of the allegory the waters could only descend into the vale of the Kidron and run eastward toward the Dead Sea, a region of hopeless desolation. What it was twenty-five centuries ago to the eye of the prophet it is now to the weary traveler. But when Ezekiel's river came thither, there was life—luxurious, joyous life. Delightful transformation! Now there is another desert whose sterility is more stern and stubborn than this of Judæa, and nothing lives in all that dreary land until it is healed and vivified by the waters which issue out of the sanctuary of God. But wherever these salutary streams come, there spring up the plants of righteousness blooming like Eden, and loaded with the fruits of Paradise. A thousand such deserts have already blossomed, and other thousands are beginning to bloom; and, though these deserts are wide as the world, this river, by its very constitution, is adapted to reach and heal them all. The natural streams from the mountains of Arabia and Africa dwindle and fade away in their thirsty Saharas, but this grows broader and deeper the farther it penetrates the desert. Thank God, it will reach earth's remotest wilderness, and enter at length and vivify the great sea of death itself.

This sea figures largely in the allegory, and well it may. The whole world affords no other type of human apostasy so appropriate, so significant. Think of it. There it lies in its sulphurous sepulchre, thirteen hundred feet below the ocean, steaming up like a huge caldron of smouldering bitumen and brimstone. Neither rain from heaven, nor mountain torrents, nor Jordan's flood, nor all combined, can change its character of utter death. Fit symbol of that great dead sea of depravity and corruption which nothing human can heal. Science and art, education and philosophy, legislation and superstition, may pour their combined contributions into it forever, but they can not heal, can not even dilute its malignity; but the *supernatural* streams of divine mercy from the sanctuary can and will. Let the world-wide desert rejoice. These waters are rolling onward, will surely reach its utmost borders, and clothe its sterile wastes with beauty and life.

Where are those miry and marshy places, mentioned in the 11th verse, which could not be healed, and what may they signify?

They are along the southern shore of the lake, at the base of Usdum and the thick strata of rock salt which there bound the plain. It is interesting to notice how accurate the prophet is in all his topographical allusions. The existence of these salt marshes has but recently been revealed to the world by modern exploration, but Ezekiel was acquainted with them twenty-three centuries ago. If you wish to attach significance to every item in the drapery of the allegory, these strata of rock salt, with their incurable marshes, may represent that fundamental corruption of man's nature which will remain even in millennial peace and purity. The waters from the sanctuary do not heal these marshes, *because they do not come to them.* Wherever the waters come there is life, but they were never intended to reach up to these rock-salt sources of bitterness and death. And so in the spiritual antitype, the river of divine mercy is not designed to reach to and remove the corrupt nature of man. In the full splendor of millennial glory the *fountains* will still be impure, and the ever-descending streams would quickly flood the world with death, did not these waters from the sanctuary continue evermore to flow over and renew them to spiritual life. With the prophet's marvelous telescope I delight to look down the verdant vista of this mystic river, and out upon our world's glorious future. No other glass discloses such enchanting prospects, nor are they mere "dissolving views," fair but fading. More than meets the eye lies deep concealed, and brighter days than fancy paints shall surely dawn on earth's long and dismal night.

In our ride to-day we passed up Wady Gihon, west of the city, crossed over a rocky ridge, and descended into a valley which comes down south from the Jaffa road, our first object being a visit to the Convent of the Cross. This is a large establishment, pleasantly situated, and with surroundings which suggest the idea that its finances must be in a flourishing condition. The monks were very polite, and one of them showed us the place where the tree grew from which the cross was made. Whether true or not, let others discuss; but one thing is certain: this great convent, with all its revenues, has grown up out of that hole in the ground in which the tree is said to have stood.

The good Padre Francesco expresses doubts about this tradition, perhaps because the place is in the hands of the Greeks, for whom he cherishes the utmost abhorrence. He, however, says that, if the belief in the fact serves to awaken devout thoughts, it is not to be condemned. Maundrell sums up its title to our reverence somewhat after the manner of the famous house that Jack built. "It is because here is the earth that nourished the root, that bore the tree, that yielded the timber, that made the cross;" and he adds, rather profanely, "Under the high altar you are shown a hole in the ground where the stump of the tree stood, and it meets with not a few visitants, so much verier stocks than itself as to fall down and worship it."

Leaving this convent, which the natives call El Mûsŭllabeh, we went on nearly an hour farther to 'Ain Karîm, the village of Zacharias and Elizabeth, and of course the birthplace of John the Baptist and Forerunner. In the convent they point out the precise spot where the babe was born. It is beneath the chapel, which is a handsome and neatly-arranged affair of its kind. Our padre labors hard to explain how it could possibly come to pass that the Baptist should be *born in two places*—beneath the rich altar within the convent, and in the grotto at least a quarter of a mile from it, where a convent was also erected over the house of Elizabeth. It is not very important how we dispose of this difficulty. Elizabeth may possibly have divided the time of that important occasion between the two, in order to multiply the number of sacred places, and thereby increase the piety of future generations!

Did you see the Fountain of the Virgin, for which name our padre is again puzzled to find a plausible reason? He thinks it scarcely probable that the Virgin would have been allowed to go to such a distance from Elizabeth's house to fetch water. She might have occasionally frequented it, however, and from that circumstance her name came to be applied to it; but it required a very resolute and robust faith to tear out by the roots the sycamore-trees of skepticism which kept springing up in this gentleman's heart during his excursion to "St. John's in the mountains." He toiled up the rocky hills southwest of 'Ain Karîm for more than an hour to visit the grotto where John dwelt in the wilderness, and practiced those austerities which we read of in the third chapter of Matthew. The whole thing, wilderness, grotto, and all, did not correspond to his preconceived notions, but these, as in duty bound, he magnanimously surrendered to gray-haired tradition. Did you go out into that desert?

Time did not permit. My programme included Kuriet el 'Aineb, and I therefore made the stay at the Convent of St. John very brief. But, before leaving it, let me ask seriously whether there is any good reason to doubt or to disturb this ancient tradition as to the main fact. Why may not this be the village of Zacharias, to which Mary came in haste to salute her cousin Elizabeth?

I know no decisive reason against it. 'Ain Karîm is certainly in the hill-country of Judæa,[1] though not perhaps exactly in that part of it in which, a priori, we should expect to find Elizabeth. When I visited it many years ago, I had no doubt as to the tradition, nor is there any obvious reason why the home of the Baptist should be lost, any more than the site of Bethlehem, or Bethany, or Nazareth, or Cana. The village was probably small, as *no* name is mentioned; perhaps it was not a village at all. But John became very celebrated in his day. Our Lord himself testifies of him that there had not risen a greater prophet than he. It is, however, not likely that he was born in either of the grottoes which tradition selected as suitable sites for convents, but in some humble habitation which has long since disappeared. Thither came Mary with that salutation which made the unborn Baptist leap for joy, and Elizabeth herself, filled with the Holy Ghost, spoke out with a loud voice and said, Blessed art thou among women, and blessed is the fruit of thy womb. And Mary responded in that noble *magnificat*, My soul doth magnify the Lord, and my spirit hath rejoiced in God my Saviour.[2] Who can doubt but that these two inspired cousins—the highly favored among women—spent the three subsequent months of Mary's visit in holy and elevated devotion and communion of spirit, speaking of the instant performance of those wonderful things which had been told them from the Lord. Truly these sacred associations must ever clothe with richest interest the vale and hill-sides of 'Ain Karîm.

Do you suppose that the ordinary food of the Baptist was really locusts and wild honey?[3]

After he had retired to the wilderness to seek preparation for his divine mission, no doubt it was. Nor is there any great difficulty about it, for we know from Leviticus xi. 22 that it was lawful for Jews to eat this insect. I do

[1] Luke i. 39.   [2] Luke i. 46.   [3] Matt. iii. 4.

not suppose, however, that the desert was that rocky hill southwest of 'Ain Karîm, covered with corn, vines, and olive-trees, as Maundrell says. John probably retired much farther from the busy haunts of men, into those barren parts which produce none of these luxuries, and where the wandering Arabs to this day feed on locusts. The monks during the dark ages perhaps thought this incredible, and therefore planted *locust-trees* near John's grotto in the desert, as Maundrell informs us. The kharûb is also found in the same region, and the name of St. John's bread has been given to the gelatinous pods of this tree by pious pilgrims, anxious to rescue the Baptist from the imputation of feeding on locusts.

There are two or three other places of interest in this region, at least to pilgrims and antiquarians. The *well* (?) at which Philip baptized the eunuch tradition has located in the wady south of 'Ain Karîm. This is doubtless a mistake. Again, Mr. Williams believes that he has found the ancient Bether in Wady Beitîr, which comes down from the south, and unites with Wady el Werd. The position will agree well enough with all that is known about the situation of this last stronghold of the Jews. Eusebius says that it was an impregnable fortress not far from Jerusalem.

There the rebel Messiah Barchochobas, in the reign of Hadrian, held out for a long time against the furious assaults of the Roman army. The place, however, was at last stormed, and the slaughter was so dreadful that the brook below it ran blood all the way to the sea, according to the tradition of the rabbis. No calamity, except the destruction of Jerusalem by Titus, was so fatal to the Jews as the sacking of Bether. Eighty thousand of this devoted race fell by the sword in battle, besides a vast number who perished by famine, pestilence, and other calamities.

The only place in the canonical books where the mountains of Bether are mentioned is in the Song of Songs: Turn, my beloved, and be thou as a roe or young hart upon the mountains of Bether.[1] The allusion is natural enough,

[1] Song ii. 17.

for I myself have seen beautiful roes leaping upon those mountains, skipping upon the hills.[1]

They are certainly better adapted to them than to horses, as I can testify. That whole region is rough and rocky in the extreme, especially along the path from 'Ain Karîm to Soba, and thence to Kuriet el 'Aineb. Soba is in ruins, destroyed by order of Ibrahim Pasha in 1834, but its position is naturally very strong, and the whole conical summit was surrounded by a wall. It was long the stronghold of the robber family of Abu Goosh, as I was informed by my companions.

When I first came to Jerusalem it was occupied by one of that famous family, to the no small terror of the pilgrims. You are aware that erring tradition located Modin, the city and cemetery of the Maccabean family, at Soba; but this can not be correct, as that place was at or near the foot of the mountains, not far from Lydd. Dr. Robinson identifies Soba with Ramathaim-Zophim, and his elaborate argument makes the idea at least plausible. The same remark may be made in regard to Kirjath Jearim, or Kirjath Baal or Baalath, for all these names belong to the same place. Kuriet el 'Aineb may represent that city, but the evidence is not perfectly conclusive. The frequent mention of this point in defining the borders of Judah and Benjamin render it certain that it must have been in this neighborhood. Monkish, or rather ecclesiastical tradition, makes it the birth-place of Jeremiah, and many writers only mention it under this name; and it is certainly possible that the prophet may have resided there, though he was born at Anathoth. Convents and churches were early erected at this St. Jeremiah, and I suppose the traces of them are to be found on the hills north and northwest of the present village, where are many tombs in the live rock. The only ancient edifice in it is the ruined church, which strikes one with surprise. Its age and origin are uncertain, though it was probably built by the Crusaders.

If this was Kirjath Jearim, the ark must have had a rough

[1] Song ii. 8.

road from there to the city. The house of Abinadab appears not to have been in Yarim itself, but on the hill northwest of it. In 1 Samuel vii. 1, our version has it *hill,* but in 2 Samuel vi. 3, 4, the Hebrew word Gibeah is retained, as if it were a separate village. It is not likely, however, that there was a town adjoining Yarim, with the identical name of another place not far off to the north, and I suppose that the house of Abinadab, where the ark abode, was on the *hill* above, not at a village called Gibeah. Such an arrangement would be the most convenient and satisfactory to the congregation which assembled from all parts to worship before the ark. The hill was probably called *Gibeah,* by way of eminence, after the ark had been brought there, and thus our translators may have indicated the exact truth by translating it *hill* when it is first mentioned, and *Gibeah* twenty years afterward, when David and all Israel went to remove the ark to Jerusalem. There is no obvious reason at present why it should be called *Yarim — rocky forests.* There are *waars,* however, on every side almost, and some very impracticable ones north and southwest of it.

The first long descent from the village toward Jerusalem is not steep, and a good road could easily be made. Indeed, the traces of an ancient way are visible in several places, and an arch belonging to a Roman bridge below Deir Yesîn is still quite perfect. The names Kŭstŭl and Kulonia along this line suggest the idea of Roman colonies, and somewhere in their neighborhood, I have little doubt, we are to find or fix the locality of that Emmaus to which the two disciples were proceeding when the Lord joined them.[1] Kuriet el 'Aineb itself would be the proper distance from Jerusalem, and being on the road to Jaffa, and on the dividing ridge between the plain and the mountains, the Roman emperor might have deemed it an advantageous post for a colony made up of his disbanded soldiers, who could keep in check the surrounding country. Certain it is that in these later ages the occupants of this place have controlled the whole adjacent region, and for many a generation exercised their lawless tyranny upon helpless pilgrims.

[1] Luke xxiv. 13.

It took just three hours' moderate riding from Kuriet el 'Aineb to Jerusalem: first, a long descent into Wady Hanîna, which passes between it and Soba; then a similar ascent, succeeded by a very steep pass, and a very slippery path down to Kulonia. At this place are some heavy foundations of church, convent, or castle by the road side, which may be of almost any age, and also gardens of fruit-trees, irrigated by a fountain of excellent water. Kulonia is on a hill north of the road, and appears in a fair way to become a ruin itself before long. The path then winds up a valley, and stretches over a dreary waste of bare rocks until within a mile of the city, when the view opens upon its naked ramparts and the mysterious regions toward the Dead Sea.

These rides about Jerusalem reveal to the weary traveler the extreme ruggedness of this territory. It could never have been a corn-growing region, but is admirably adapted to the olive, the fig, the vine, the pomegranate, and other fruit-trees. Such a country, in a high state of cultivation, is incomparably more beautiful and picturesque than those tame, flat plains where grain is the crop. The neighborhood of Jerusalem, when thus clothed with orchards and vineyards, must have shown one of the most agreeable panoramas the eye of man ever beheld. Nor are we to imagine that, because it did not grow wheat, its productions were of little importance. The olive is a more valuable crop, acre for acre, than any kind of grain, more so even than silk. Josephus, therefore, was not mistaken when he represented the country about Jerusalem as more fruitful than other parts of Palestine. Restore to it the proper cultivation, and it would again hold the same relative superiority.

In what sense can the mountains about Jerusalem be regarded as her defense, according to the allusion in the Psalm: As the mountains are round about Jerusalem, so is the Lord round about his people?[1]

Certainly not by their height. None of the surrounding hills, not even Olivet, has any relative elevation above the northwestern corner of the city itself. But Jerusalem is sit-

[1] Ps. cxxv. 2.

uated in the centre of a mountainous region, whose valleys have drawn around it in all directions a perfect net-work of deep ravines, the perpendicular walls of which constitute a very efficient system of defense. The *ravines* on three sides of the Holy City might be made a very important protection, and doubtless were in the days of the Psalmist; but the *mountains* whose rugged ramparts and impracticable passes secured the tranquillity of Zion were at a distance.

NEBY SAMWIL—GIBEON.

This has been a very exciting and instructive excursion, including Neby Samwîl, and the territory of the Gibeonites, who so cleverly outwitted Joshua and the elders, and negotiated a treaty of peace with them. I was forcibly reminded of one item in the sentence of condemnation pronounced upon them for their cunning deception—that they should be hewers of wood,[1] by long files of women and children carrying on their heads heavy bundles of wood. It seemed to be hard work, especially to the young girls.

It is the severest kind of drudgery, and my compassion has often been enlisted in behalf of the poor women and children, who daily bring loads of wood to Jerusalem from these very mountains of the Gibeonites. To carry water, also, is very laborious and fatiguing. The fountains are far off, in deep wadies with steep banks, and a thousand times have I seen the feeble and the young staggering up long and weary ways with large jars of water on their heads. It is the work of slaves and of the very poor, whose condition is still worse. Among the pathetic lamentations of Jeremiah there is nothing more affecting than this: They took the young men to grind, and the children fell under the wood.[2] Grinding at the hand-mill is a low, menial work assigned to *female slaves*, and therefore utterly humiliating to the young men of Israel. And the delicate children of Zion falling under loads of hard, rough wood, along the mountain paths! Alas! for these things I weep; mine eye, mine eye runneth down with water because the comforter that should relieve

---
[1] Josh. ix. 21.   [2] Lam. v. 13.

GIBEON, FROM MIZPEH.

my soul is far from me; my children are desolate because the enemy prevailed.[1]

But to our excursion. Passing into Wady Beit Hanina, west of the tombs of the judges, by a very rocky path, we climbed the long mountain to Neby Samwîl, making this distance in little over two hours. The prospect from the neby is very extensive and grand. Dr. Robinson identifies it with Mizpeh, but an old tradition makes it the Ramah of Samuel, and hence its present name. I shall not attempt to decide, and my companions from Jerusalem are equally in doubt. No better place certainly could be selected for a mizpeh, or watch-tower, but then no place would be more naturally called *Ram*, or *Ramah*, or some other compound of that favorite title of high hills.

After looking at the prospect from the top of the mosque (once a Christian church), we descended northward into the deep valley which lies between Neby Samwîl and El Jîb, the Gibeon of the Bible. This village is situated on an isolated and rocky hill of moderate elevation, with plains, valleys, and higher mountains all around it. Remains of ancient buildings, tombs, and quarries indicate a large and important city, though it is now a miserable hamlet, occupied by a few hundred sour and stupid Moslem peasants. We of course drank of the famous fountain, deep under the perpendicular rock in the vale to the southeast of the village.

Those old Gibeonites did indeed "work wilily" with Joshua. Nothing could be better calculated to deceive than their devices. I have often thought that their embassadors, as described in the narrative, furnish one of the finest groups imaginable for a painter, with their old sacks on their poor asses; their wine-bottles of goat-skin, patched and shriveled up in the sun, old, rent, and bound up; old shoes and clouted upon their feet; old garments, ragged and bedraggled, with bread dry and mouldy—the very picture of an over-traveled and wearied caravan from a great distance. It is impossible to transfer to paper the ludicrous appearance of such a

[1] Lam. i. 16.

company. No wonder that, having tasted their mouldy victuals, and looked upon their soiled and travel-worn costume, Joshua and the elders were deceived, especially as they did not wait to ask counsel at the mouth of the Lord.[1]

This El Jîb was a great city; as one of the royal cities, greater than Ai, and all the men thereof were mighty. Their treaty, therefore, with Israel very naturally struck terror into their neighbors, and hence that combination of kings against them which brought up Joshua in all haste to their relief. It must have been somewhere in those open plains east of Jîb that the great battle took place, and the memorable rout and flight of the Canaanitish host down Wady Yalo (Ajalon), when Joshua said, in the sight of Israel, Sun, stand thou still upon Gibeon, and thou, moon, in the valley of Ajalon,[2] an event to immortalize any site on earth!

Jîb is well supplied with water, not only by the fountain you mentioned, but in the wet season there is also a considerable pond in the plain below the village. It was probably on this account, in part at least, that the Tabernacle was established there for many years, and in part, I suppose, because the plains around Jîb afforded suitable camping-ground for the vast multitudes who came thither to keep the great feasts of the Lord.

The existence of this little lake, I suppose, is referred to in Joshua xviii. 14, in drawing the northwest border of Benjamin from near Beth-horon to Kirjath-Jearim. Thus it reads: And the border was drawn from thence, and compassed the *corner of the sea southward*, from the hill that lieth before Beth-horon southward. It has always appeared to me impossible that the line should have made a grand sweep from Beth-horon, without an intervening point, clear down to the sea, and back again to Kirjath-Jearim. But if we suppose that this little lake near El Jîb is the *yam*, or sea, in this passage, all difficulty vanishes. This explanation is confirmed, as I think, by two other passages. In Jeremiah xli. 12 we read, Then they took all the men, and went to fight with Ishmael, the son of Nethaniah, and found him by

[1] Josh. ix. 3-15.   [2] Josh. x. 12.

the *great waters* that are in Gibeon. And in 2 Sam. ii. 13 it is stated that Joab, the son of Zeruiah, and the servants of David, went out and met together (with Abner's army) by the pool of Gibeon, and they sat down, the one on the one side of the pool, and the other on the other side of the pool. It is clear that this *pool*, which separated the two companies, must have been a pond or small lake. The Hebrew sometimes has that meaning, and the identical word in Arabic is now applied to Lakes Hûleh and Tiberias, and even to the Dead Sea. I suppose, therefore, that this was actually the *sea* at the corner of which the border of Benjamin passed, and thus a curious obscurity is cleared away from the face of our good old Bible.

From El Jîb the road to Beth-horon, now called Beit Ur, winds round the head of the great Wady Yalo, the Ajalon where the moon stood still. The village of Beit Ur occupies a conical hill just at the top of the ascent from Beth-horon the lower, which is one hour below it toward the northwest. Both these places abound in marks of antiquity, and were celebrated, particularly in the wars of the Maccabees. The ascent between them is very rocky, and along it were fought by those leaders of Israel some of their bloody battles with the great armies of the kings of Antioch.

The profound Wady Sûleyman, which passes on the north of Gibeon, may have derived its name from the fact that Solomon was in the habit of going to Gibeon to sacrifice before the Tabernacle, which was there until after he had completed the Temple. That was the great high place: a thousand burnt-offerings did Solomon offer upon that altar.[1] There the Lord appeared unto him in a dream by night, and God said, Ask what I shall give thee. His petition was for wisdom. And the speech pleased the Lord, that Solomon had asked this thing; and because he neither asked for long life, nor for riches, nor for the life of his enemies, therefore he gave him not only a wise and understanding heart, so that there was none like him, neither before nor after, but also added what he had not asked, both

[1] 1 Kings iii. 4.

riches and honor. Alas! that such a glorious beginning should have ended in foul disgrace and apostasy! Solomon loved many strange women, and when he was old his wives turned away his heart after other gods, Molech, the abomination of the children of Ammon, and Chemosh, the abomination of Moab,[1] whose temples he reared

> "On that opprobrious hill
> Right against the temple of God—
> Audacious neighborhood."

After lunching at the Fountain of Gibeon, we took over the country to the east, sometimes without any road, and always along most rocky paths, leaving Ramah on our left, and also Jîb'a, the ancient *Gibeah*, which we could see from different points, and descended to "poor Anathoth," the city of Jeremiah. There is no reason to question the identity, and I am always pleased to find certainty when I am groping about among these ancient ruins. The prospect east and southeast toward the Dead Sea and the lower Jordan is one of the most dreary that my eye ever rested on, and again and again it reminded me of the author of "Lamentations," who gazed upon it with tearful eyes two thousand five hundred years ago. 'Anātā is a small, half-ruined hamlet, but was once much larger, and appears to have had a wall around it, a few fragments of which are still to be seen. It took us just one hour to reach our cottage from the hill above the village. Several wadies along the path run down to the valley of the Jordan, and the road sometimes keeps round the head of them, and at others passes through them. I did not note their names.

All those places which you passed without visiting are mentioned in the 10th chapter of Isaiah, with several others to the north of them. The prophet is describing the approach of Sennacherib's army. He is come to Aiath, he has passed to Migron; at Michmash he has laid up his carriages. They have gone over the passage, they have taken up their lodging at Geba. Ramah is afraid, Gibeah of Saul is fled. Lift up the voice, O daughter of Gallim, cause it

---

[1] 1 Kings xi. 1–7.

ANATHOTH (ANATA).

to be heard unto Laish, O poor Anathoth.[1] Thus one can follow, step by step, the invading host of Assyria, until they reach "poor Anathoth," and shake their hand against the mount of the daughter of Zion, from Nob, which was at the north end of this Mount of Olives.

No neighborhood in Palestine is more crowded with interesting Biblical associations than this over which you have passed so hastily. I should like to spend a day wandering over the rough hills between Er Ram, Gibeah, Michmash, Rimmon, Bethel, and Beer. Perhaps we might stumble upon the site of Ai, which Joshua's curse has hidden from all the world, for he burned Ai, and made it a heap forever, even a desolation unto this day.[2] It must be somewhere between Michmash and Rimmon, a region greatly cut up with gorges and ravines; and as I passed from Beit-în toward Michmash, I could easily understand how Joshua's ambush of five thousand men could lie hid between Ai and Bethel.[3] Some of our Jerusalem friends identify Ai with a conspicuous mound which I saw from a distance. It bears now no other name than tell, which you may translate "heap," and as for "desolation," it remains complete unto this day. No doubt traces still remain, could we but find them, of that great heap of stones which Joshua raised over the carcass of Ai's hapless king.[4]

May 14th. Is it not remarkable that there is no allusion to the common barn-door fowl in the Old Testament, and that in the New they are only mentioned in connection with Jerusalem? In Matthew Christ thus addresses this wicked city: O Jerusalem, Jerusalem, thou that killest the prophets, and stonest them which are sent unto thee, how often would I have gathered thy children together, even as a hen gathereth her chickens under her wings, and ye would not![5] Matthew,[6] Mark,[7] and Luke[8] refer to the crowing of the cock when Peter denied his Lord, and Mark mentions cock-crowing as one of the watches of the night in connection

---

[1] Isa. x. 28–32. [2] Josh. viii. 8. [3] Josh. viii. 12.
[4] Josh. viii. 29. [5] Matt. xxiii. 37. [6] Matt. xxvi. 34.
[7] Mark xiv. 30. [8] Luke xxii. 34.

with Christ's prophecy concerning the destruction of Jerusalem[1].

I have often thought of this remarkable silence in regard to one of man's most common associates and greatest comforts, especially in this country. The peasants, not to say citizens in general, would scarcely know how to live without fowls. Their eggs, and they themselves, answer the place of meat for most of their meals. They swarm round every door, share in the food of their possessors, are at home among the children in every room, roost over head at night, and, with their ceaseless crowing, are the town-clock and the morning bell to call up the sleepers at early dawn. If they were thus common among the ancient Hebrews, it seems strange that they should never have been mentioned.

Is not the cock-crowing a very indefinite division of time? I have noticed throughout our wanderings that they seem to crow all night long.

That is true, particularly in bright warm nights; and what is curious too, I have heard a single cock crow so often and continue so long that I gave over counting from mere weariness. It is, however, while the dawn is struggling into day that the whole band of chanticleers blow their *shrill* clarions with the greatest energy and emulation. It seems to be an objection to the sign given to Peter that a thousand cocks in Jerusalem might crow at any hour. For him, however, it was sufficient that in the house of Caiaphas there was but one which gave forth its significant note in immediate response to his cruel and cowardly denial of his Lord, and it answered the purpose intended perfectly. Peter heard, and then went out and wept bitterly. We must not be very severe upon the Armenians for attempting to preserve the identical spot where this incident occurred, since the Evangelists record the fact with so much particularity.

CHURCH OF THE HOLY SEPULCHRE.

When you were laying down rules for visiting these sacred localities with safety and advantage, I felt and remark-

[1] Mark xiii. 35.

ed that the whole truth had not been stated, and I now resume the subject in connection with my visit to the Holy Sepulchre, and inquire whether it is not possible that we carry our disgust at what is doubtful or puerile much farther than is necessary or profitable. For example, do not the purest and best feelings of our nature prompt us to preserve and protect from desecration such sites as this of the Holy Sepulchre? And then, again, look at another aspect of the matter. Suppose that on our arrival here we inquired for the tombs of prophets and kings who rendered this place so illustrious, and were answered by the people that they knew nothing about them; that they had never heard of such men as David and Solomon; that there was neither tradition nor memento of their ever having lived and reigned in this city. "Strangers from a distance, like you, come to us with these stories, but neither we nor our fathers ever heard of them, nor is there any locality in our vicinity that has now or ever had any such associations connected with it."

And if our most diligent inquiries proved fruitless—there really was no Calvary at Jerusalem, no Garden of Gethsemane, no Bethlehem, no Olivet, no Bethany—would we not, upon opening our New Testaments, look into each other's face with perplexity and blank dismay? On the other hand, what is it now that gives such supreme gratification to our visit at Jerusalem? Is it not these very names, clinging to these sacred sites and scenes with invincible tenacity, through wars and destructions absolutely without parallel, and repeated down long centuries of most dismal darkness and confusion worse confounded? And because, in the death-struggle to hold fast these sacred landmarks, ignorant men or crafty priests have perverted them to selfish purposes, or pushed becoming reverence and love over into sinful superstition, are we therefore to scout the whole thing, and scowl upon these cherished sites, and upon those who have cherished them, as though they were guilty of the sin of witchcraft? I more than admit that nothing can justify idolatry; but is even a little too much reverence in such a

Vol. II.—A a

case as odious to Him in whose honor it is manifested as cold contempt or proud neglect?

One more of my many thoughts and reflections to-day. If these sacred sites were to be preserved at all, how was this to be done? Leave the stable and the manger just as they were on the night of the advent, you reply; and so Calvary, and the garden, and the sepulchre. Certainly this would have been more satisfactory, but then it would have required a succession of the most stupendous miracles from that day to this. War, earthquake, fire, and fierce fanaticism have driven by turns their plowshares of destruction through all these scenes, and to preserve them exactly *where* and *as* they were became impossible; and when kings and princes sought to restore and preserve them, they did it in accordance with the sentiments of the age. Hence arose over and around these sites the splendid basilica and the spacious convent. We may regret their bad taste, we condemn their superstitions, we must abhor their frauds, but we can not wisely refuse the confirmation of our faith and hope which their faulty zeal has furnished.

This train of reflection has, as I said, been suggested by a visit to the Holy Sepulchre. I have come to regard that as by far the most interesting half acre on the face of the earth. Nor is this appreciation materially affected by the doubts which hang over the questions of identity and genuineness. Around that spot, whether it be or be not the real tomb, have clustered the hopes and affections of the great Christian world for sixteen centuries at least, and with all but a few learned men it is still the accepted representative and *locale* of events of such transcendent magnitude as cast all others into the category of mere vanities. The reputed sepulchre of the Son of God is no place for soulless criticism, calm, cold, and hard as the rock itself.

Your imagination, I perceive, has been quite captivated, and yet I do not believe you have explored half the wonders of that wondrous temple. Did you see the altar of Melchisedec? No! Nor that on which Isaac was sacrificed—nor the chapel of St. John—nor of the angels—nor the marble chair on which St. Helena sat—nor the chapel of the division of garments—nor the sweating pillar—nor the *navel* of the world—nor the place where Mary Magdalene stood—nor the chapel of Adam—nor the rent in the rock whence his skull leaped out—nor the altar of the penitent thief—nor—

You may cut short your categories; I saw none of these things, probably because I asked not for them.

Possibly the "scourge" of modern skepticism has whipped them all out of this temple; no very wonderful achievement, for, as credulity brought them in, unbelief can cast them out. But you should not have undertaken to go the round of these "pilgrim stations" without some courageous champion for their integrity by your side. Here, for example, are three smart volumes of Padre Francesco Cassini, an Italian monk of the Minori Riformati. They are the very latest thing of the kind, hot from the press at Genoa this very year, and dedicated to Ferdinand Second of Naples, better known by the sobriquet of Bomba, a real curiosity in their way, lively, full of *wit*, *Metastasio*, and the *Bible*, three things remarkable in a brother of the Riformati. His countless quotations from the Bible are, however, all in good old canonical Latin, and therefore harmless to the general reader. It is refreshing to follow a gentleman and a scholar who treads fearlessly among all these crumbling traditions of the Dark Ages. He would have been an admirable guide for you.

I prefer my own way, and my own thoughts were my best companions. There were but few people present, and but little noise, and the impression produced was solemn and very sad. Though there may not be one thing there that had any actual connection with the passion of our Saviour, yet they have long represented the various scenes of that mysterious and awful, yet joyful transaction, and I gave myself up to reverent, devout meditation and humble prayer.

You have been fortunate. My introduction to this church was totally different, and the first impressions most unhappy. It was on the 6th of April, 1833. I arrived from Ramleh much fatigued, but, as an important ceremony was going forward in the church, I hastened thither at once. The whole vast edifice was crowded with pilgrims from all parts of the world, and it was with difficulty that I followed my companion into the rotunda. There a priest who knew us came up, and, after inquiring about the news of the day, asked if we would be conducted into the interior of the Greek chapel, where the religious services were going on, and then, summoning a Turkish *cawass*, we began to move in that direction. To my amazement and alarm, the cawass began to beat the crowd over the head, when down they crouched to the floor, and we *walked over their prostrate bodies*. There was no help for it; those behind, rising up, thrust us forward. After proceeding some distance, we paused to take breath where the crowd was more dense and obstinate than usual, and I was seriously informed that this was the exact *navel* of the earth, and these obstinate pilgrims were bowing and kissing it. Finally we reached the altar at the east end without any serious injury to the living causeway which we had traversed, and I had time to look about me. The scene throughout had all the interest of entire novelty. I was young, and fresh from America, and was seized with an almost irrepressible propensity to laugh. The noise was deafening, and there was not the slightest approximation to devotion visible, or even possible, so far as I could judge; while the attitudes, costumes, gestures, and sounds which met the eye and stunned the ear were infinitely strange and ludicrous. Such splendor, too, I had never seen. By the aid of numerous lamps, the whole church seemed to flash and blaze in burning gold. I stood near the altar, which was covered with gold cloth, and decorated with censers, golden candlesticks, and splendid crucifixes. A bench of bishops and priests filled the entire space within the railing, and two monks were waving, or, more accurately, swinging their censers before them. The "cloud of incense" rose wreathing and circling to the upper dome, diffusing on all sides a strong aromatic odor.

CHURCH OF THE HOLY SEPULCHRE—FRONT VIEW.

After some delay, the whole priesthood of those denominations which then united in this ceremony were assembled, properly robed and fumigated, and, with lighted candle in either hand, stood ready for the grand feat of the day. In single file, seventy priests and bishops, in long robes of gold and silver texture, marched out into the body of the church with solemn pomp. Turkish officers went before, beating the heads of the crowd, who bowed down as they had done for us. Slowly the gorgeous procession worked its way along the north side, singing, with nasal twang and stentorian lungs, harsh harmony in barbarous Greek. In a few minutes they returned, laid aside their robes, extinguished their tapers, and the multitude dispersed, greatly enlightened by—a vast number of wax candles, and edified by a devout manifestation of splendid canonicals. Our friend in his robes, and with candles lighted, inquired in the careless tones of ordinary conversation concerning our journey, the roads, Ibrahim Pasha, and the war that was then going on with the sultan, while the people in the body of the church were laughing, talking, praying, shouting, or quarreling, as suited their convenience. The noise was perfectly astounding to American ears. I would have taken the whole affair for a city auction, or the exhibition of a traveling show, rather than an assembly engaged in the worship of God. Such was *my* introduction to the Holy Sepulchre, and I have never been able to banish from my mind the first unhappy impressions, nor can I visit the church with either pleasure or profit.

I am thankful that I have no such associations to disturb and disgust. I entered the open court from Palmer Street, which there runs east and west. This court is paved with the common flag-stone of Jerusalem, and I judged it to be about ninety feet long and seventy wide. Certain parts of the church seem to be ancient, that is, of the Greek empire anterior to the Crusades. The two ample doorways are elaborately ornamented with the architectural devices common on all temples and churches of that era. The whole, however, is much dilapidated, and disfigured with additions and patchwork of every conceivable degree of barbarism. The campanile on the west of the court must have been an imposing tower when perfect.

It is said to have been five stories high, and richly ornamented, but there remain now only the two lower, with the ruins of the third. The under story is the chapel of St. John, south of it is that of Mary Magdalene, and adjoining this is the chapel of St. James. These are now ordinary churches.

Having entered by the great door, only one of whose large leaves was open, I came upon the Stone of Unction, with its colossal wax candles. Turning westward along the aisle, and then north, I entered the grand rotunda between two huge square columns. This is striking and impressive. I estimated the height of the dome to be about one hundred feet, and the circular opening at the top, for light, to be about fifteen feet in diameter. This dome is sadly out of repair, and the rain must descend in torrents over the whole southwestern part of the rotunda.

Its covering of lead has been torn off by the winds, and a contest between the rival races of monks for the privilege of making the repairs keeps it in this ruinous condition.

Of course, "the Sepulchre" was the object which most attracted my attention, and I had as good an opportunity to examine it as could be desired. Externally it looks very much like a small marble house. All the world knows that it is twenty-six feet long and about eighteen broad, and, I should think, something more than twenty feet high. It stands quite alone, directly under the aperture in the centre of the dome. I went into the Chapel of the Angel by its low door, saw the stone on which the angel sat, crept into the proper sepulchre room, and looked at the raised, altar-like recess on the north side, whose fine *marble* slab is said to cover the real rock couch where the body of our Lord was laid. I did not measure these rooms, nor count the silver lamps which crowd the little apartment overhead. A thousand pilgrims have counted and measured, and given very various results.

THE HOLY SEPULCHRE.

As to the lamps, they seem really to vary in number from time to time. There are at least forty of them now, and I do not well see how there can be any more suspended from the roof. The Chapel of the Angel is admitted to be artificial, but it is stoutly maintained by all who venerate the place that the small interior room is a genuine rock tomb, merely *cased* in marble. The ecclesiastical tradition is, that Constantine's architect caused the rock to be cut away all round this tomb, so as to leave it standing alone, beneath the church raised over it. This is certainly possible, and if it could be proved it would settle nothing as to the identity of this sepulchre with that of Joseph of Arimathea. I could not tell whether it were native rock or artificial masonry, nor do I care which it is, or whether it is partly natural and partly artificial.

After standing a long time in front of this affecting tomb, I sauntered off into the Greek church. It is a gorgeous affair, blazing with gold quite up to the dome. It is a sort of cruciform structure, with the high altar at the east end, and broad transepts at the west. I judged it to be about one hundred feet from west to east, and nearly the same from north to south. The only other places that I cared to visit were the Chapel of St. Helena, to which I descended eastward from the grand circular aisle by thirty steps. It is a half-subterranean church, nearly fifty feet square. There are various altars and sacred places in it connected with the "invention" of the cross, which, however, actually took place in a real cave, to which one descends still farther eastward by twelve steps. In this cave the pious Helena, so the Church tells us, was rewarded for her long travail and labor by finding the *three* crosses, the *nails*, the crown of thorns, etc. After examining the place sufficiently, I returned along the southeastern aisle, and ascended *Calvary* by a flight of eighteen steps; there looked at the three holes in which the crosses are said to have stood; but this seems to me the most bungling arrangement in the whole "invention." The three holes are too close together, and there is an air of desperate improbability about the entire contrivance that can not be overcome. Besides, it is notorious that a large part of this Golgotha is an *artificial vault*, with rooms underneath.

I see you are yet less than half a pilgrim. Your faith is not sufficiently robust to cast into the sea the dark mountains of skepticism over which it stumbles. You must summon to your aid the courageous maxim of Padre Francesco, "that it is better to believe too much than too little." With this brave maxim he valiantly assaults all impertinent improbabilities, and steadfastly stares them out of countenance. I myself have been a much more persevering *pilligrino* than you. Why, there are some seventy "stations" within and connected with this vast and confused mass of buildings, all of which I have had the resolution to visit, and most of them many times. It is no light achievement, to be done up in an hour. The whole pile of edifices connected together is three hundred and fifty feet long, from Joseph's sepulchre, within the aisle on the west of the rotunda, down to the extremity of the chapel of the "Invention" on the east; and *it* is not less than two hundred and eighty feet from the south wall of St. James's Chapel to the north side of the apartments belonging to the Latins. Within this vast inclosure there seems to be no end to aisles, windows, stairways, vaults, tombs, dark recesses, chapels, oratories, altars, concealed relics, and other holy "inventions." Verily, nothing is too hard for stout-hearted credulity. She has not only removed mountains, but wrought *impossibilities* of transposition and aggregation. At her bidding, rocks, and caves, and distant localities gathered from all quarters into this temple, as the wild beasts came to the ark, and, having got them in, it is very difficult to get them safely out, however offensive their presence may be to the eye of modern research.

I have very little of this wonder-working credulity in my composition, but your raillery (scarcely becoming on such a subject) can not rob the place of all its sacred titles and honors. It is not *certain* that the main claims to respect and affection are mere "inventions." Though some may fancy that they have completely exploded the whole series of traditions which have clustered around the spot for so many centuries, they are egregiously mistaken. That battle is not over yet. Many, perhaps most of even Protestant critics, either maintain the reality of the sepulchre, or, at least, are doubtful; while all the rest of the Christian world, with one voice and one heart, as stoutly and earnestly defend it now against the assaults of skeptics as the knights and militant monks of yore did against the Saracens. The difficulty of the defense is immeasurably augmented by this herd of impertinent and intolerable intruders, that have no right to be there, but still victory is not yet declared in favor of the assailants.

After leaving the church and examining some curious old buildings a little to the southwest of the court, I returned by the Via Dolorosa, stopping for a moment at each of the "stations" along its crooked line. This whole street, with all its sacred points and places, I give up at once. The buildings are modern, and no plausible evidence can be produced for the identity of any one of the "stations."

You should have had our friend P. Cassini with you, who would have stoutly contended for the integrity of the whole *fourteen*. According to him, however, this street is intolerably long. He says that the Via Dolorosa for the human race began in Eden when Adam was condemned to eat his bread in the sweat of his brow, and all men traveling along it from that day to this have had their "stations" of sorrow and of suffering!

To return now to your original inquiries. I am free to confess that it is utterly impossible for me to regard the church of the Holy Sepulchre, and its incredible congregation of sacred sites, with complacency, nor could you, if you had been a spectator of the scenes which I have witnessed there, not once, but often. I will not shock your sensibilities with details of the buffoonery and the profane orgies performed by the Greeks around the tomb on the day of the Holy Fire. I doubt whether there is any thing more disgraceful to be witnessed in any heathen temple. Nor are the ceremonies of the Latin monks on the night of the Crucifixion a whit less distressing and offensive. The whole scene, in all its parts, is enacted before a strong guard of Turkish troops, stationed all around to keep the actors in this dismal tragedy from being assaulted by the rival players in the Greek *comedia*—a precaution absolutely necessary and not always successful. Furious and bloody riots have occurred several times since I have been in the country, and many travelers mention similar battles between the monks in former years. I was here in 1834, when several hundred pilgrims were crushed to death on the day of the Holy Fire.

Now I am devoutly thankful that no amount of learning or research can establish the remotest connection between any act of our Saviour and any one of these so-called holy places. And I seem to find, in this uncertainty which hangs over every sacred locality, the indications of a watchful Providence in beautiful accordance with many similar interpositions to save God's people from idolatry. The grave of Melchisedec, the typical priest—of Joseph, the rejected of his brethren and sold—of Moses, the lawgiver and deliverer—of Joshua, the captain and leader into the land of promise—of David, the shepherd and king—of John the Baptist and forerunner—and of Mary, the mother whom all nations shall call blessed—the tombs of all these have been irrecoverably concealed, and the same watchful care has hid forever the instruments of the Saviour's passion, the exact spot where he was crucified, buried, and whence he rose again to life, and also the place from which he ascended into heaven. I would have it thus. And certainly, since God has concealed the *realities*, we have no need of these fictitious sites to confirm our faith. We are surrounded by witnesses, in these mountains, and valleys, and ruins, that can not be effaced or corrupted. They are now spread out before our eyes. *There* was the Temple, type of the Saviour. *Beyond* it was Zion, symbol of the Church of God. *Here* lies the whole scene of our Lord's last actions, teaching, and passion. *There* he instituted the Supper. *Below* us is the garden of agony and betrayal. The

HOUSE OF A CHRISTIAN FAMILY IN JERUSALEM.

palace of Pilate was on that hill above it, where He was examined, was scourged, buffeted, robed in mock purple, and crowned with thorns. Along that rocky way he bore his cross; there he was nailed to it, was lifted up, was reviled, was given gall and vinegar to drink, and when all was finished he bowed his head and died. Then the sun refused to shine, and darkness fell on all the land; the earth quaked, the rocks rent, and the graves were opened. There was the new tomb in the garden of Joseph of Arimathea. Thither the angels came down and rolled the stone from the door, while the Lord of life burst the bars of death, and rose triumphant o'er the grave. All those things

"Which kings and prophets waited for,
But died without the sight,"

did actually take place here. These eyes gaze up to the same heaven which opened to receive him ascending to his Father's right hand. The great atoning sacrifice of the Lamb of God, and every item of it, was offered up here on this unquestioned platform of the Holy City. This is all I care for, all that mere topography can offer. If sure, to the fraction of a foot, in regard to the sepulchre, I could no more worship it than I could worship the boat in which he sailed over Gennesaret, or the ass upon which he rode into Jerusalem, and hence I have no need of any of these "inventions;" and since they are perverted to an idolatry worse than the burning of incense to the brazen serpent, I would have them all removed out of sight, that He who is a spirit may be worshiped, even at Jerusalem, in spirit and in truth.

My cicerone took me to his house this morning, and I was pleased to be introduced to the interior of a native Christian family on Mount Zion. There was an ease and a cordiality in the reception which surprised as much as it delighted me, and a grace displayed by the ladies in presenting sherbet, sweetmeats, coffee, and argelehs, which would have attracted the admiration of any society in the world. They showed me over their house, and explained the various contrivances which excited my curiosity. Nothing can be farther from our notions in regard to the fixtures necessary for the comfort of a family; yet some things are pretty, and all are adapted, I suppose, to the country, and the actual state of civilization. The reception-hall, with its heavy vault above, matted pavement, and low divan ranged round three sides of the apartment, was cheerful and inviting; and the floor of an inner room was beautiful, with its

PATTERNS OF TESSELATED PAVEMENT.

WOOD PANEL-WORK—TESSELATED PAVEMENTS. 571

tesselated pavement of various-colored marble drawn in many elegant and complicated patterns. The Arab artists exhibit great skill in this kind of work, and, indeed, one rarely sees prettier pavements in any country.

One reason of their success in mosaics of both stone and wood is that this art has always been in demand in the East.

PATTERNS OF WOOD PANEL-WORK.

Tesselated pavements are found beneath the rubbish of all ancient cities, and, beyond a doubt, our Lord and his apostles often reclined upon them at meat. The "large upper room" where he celebrated his last Passover and instituted the "Supper" may have been finished in this style.

Tesselated pavement is seen in greatest abundance and highest perfection in Damascus, around their delightful fountains and in their magnificent *lewans*. The Damascenes also take great pride in having their window-shutters made after patterns even more intricate than those of the pavement. Having no glass, their ambition is to show window-blinds as elaborate and attractive as possible. I have counted more than two hundred bits of polished walnut wood in the shutter of a small window.

I saw a woman sitting at the door of her hut on Zion, spinning woolen yarn with a spindle, while another near her was twirling nimbly the ancient distaff, and I felt some curiosity to know whether in other things they resembled King Lemuel's good wife, according to the "prophecy that his mother taught him."

There are such even now in this country, and in this city, where the prophecy was uttered. They are scarce, however, and their price is above rubies.[1] The very first item in the catalogue of good qualities is the rarest of all: The heart of her husband doth safely trust in her.[2] The husband, in nine cases out of every ten, does not feel very confident that "she will do him good and not evil," and therefore he sets a jealous watch over her, and places every valuable article under lock and key. His heart trusts more in hired guards and iron locks than in his wife. This is mainly owing to two things, bad education and the want of love, both grievous sins against her, and committed by her lord and tyrant. She is kept in ignorance, and is married off without regard to the affections of her heart, and how can it be expected that the husband can safely trust in a wife thus trained and thus obtained?

There are numerous allusions to the domestic habits of

[1] Prov. xxxi. 10.   [2] Prov. xxxi. 11.

Orientals in this "prophecy" of Lemuel's mother which are worth noticing: She seeketh wool and flax, and worketh diligently with her hands.[1] In Sidon, at this day, a majority of the women are thus working in raw silk and cotton instead of wool and flax. Many of them actually support the family in this way, and by selling the produce of their labor to the merchants, bring their food from afar. A leading Moslem told me that nearly every family in Sidon was thus carried through the past scarce and very dear winter.

"She riseth while it is yet night," and "her candle goeth not out by night."[2] The industrious of this country are very early risers. Long before day they are up and about their work; but, what is especially remarked, they never allow their lamp to go out by night. This, however, is not always a sign of industry. The very poorest keep a light burning all night, more from timidity or from habit than from any thing else.

"She girdeth her loins with strength, and delivereth girdles to the merchants."[3] The use of the girdle is universal, under the impression that it greatly contributes to the strength of the loins, around which it is twisted tightly in many a circling fold. Being always in demand, it is an important article of domestic manufacture. And again, scarlet, and purple, and tapestry, and embroidery, mentioned in verses 21, 22, are still the favorite colors and patterns of Oriental taste. The husband of such a faithful and industrious wife is known in the *gates*, where he sitteth among the *elders* of the land. What the *Bourse* is in Paris and the Exchange in London, the open spaces about the gates of the city were to the Orientals, and still are in many parts of the East. There the elders congregate to talk over the news of the day, the state of the market, and the affairs of their particular community. The husband of such a wife is distinguished among his compeers by a costume clean, whole, and handsome, and a countenance contented and happy. Her children, also, call her blessed, and her husband he praiseth her[4]

[1] Prov. xxxi. 13.
[2] Prov. xxxi. 15, 18.
[3] Prov. xxxi. 17, 24.
[4] Prov. xxxi. 28.

—a most happy exception; for children in this country too often treat their mother with contempt, and the haughty husband says "ajellak"—my *woman*—when he has occasion to speak of his wife.

Isaiah says that because God had brought it to pass that Sennacherib should lay waste defensed cities, therefore the inhabitants were dismayed, * * * and became as grass on the house-tops, * * * blasted before it be grown up;[1] and this morning I saw a striking illustration of this most expressive figure. To obtain a good view of the Tyropean, my guide took me to the top of a house on the brow of Zion, and the grass which had grown over the roof during the rainy season was now entirely withered and perfectly dry.

When I first came to reside in Jerusalem in 1834, my house was connected with an ancient church, the roof of which was covered with a thick growth of grass. This being in the way of a man employed to repair my house, he actually set fire to it and burned it off, and I have seen others do the same thing without the slightest hesitation. Nor is there any danger; for it would require a large expense for fuel sufficient to burn the present city of Jerusalem. Our translators have unnecessarily supplied the word *corn*, and thus confused the idea and diluted the force of this passage from Isaiah. Corn does frequently wither away; but the reference here, I suppose, is to that grass on the house-tops which David says withereth afore it groweth up, wherewith the mower filleth not his hand, nor he that bindeth sheaves his bosom. Neither do they which go by say, The blessing of the Lord be upon you; we bless you in the name of the Lord.[2] The latter expressions are most refreshingly Arabic. Nothing is more natural than for them, when passing by a fruit-tree or corn-field loaded with a rich crop, to exclaim, "*Barak Allah!*"—God bless you! we bless you in the name of the Lord!

Expressing a desire to visit a synagogue, my obliging cicerone took me to a large one which was crowded with worshipers. The room had nothing in or about it like any other

[1] Isaiah xxxvii. 26, 27.   [2] Ps. cxxix. 6–8.

place of worship I ever entered, and the congregation was in character and keeping with the place. I never saw such an assemblage of old, pale, and woe-begone countenances. There is something inexpressibly sad in the features, deportment, and costume of these children of Abraham, as they grope about the ruins of their once joyous city.

This is partly owing to the fact that many of them have been great sinners elsewhere, and have come up here from all countries whither the Lord hath driven them, to purge away their guilt by abstinence, mortification, and devotion; then to die, and be buried as near the Holy City as possible. This also accounts for the ever-increasing multitude of their graves, which are gradually covering the side of Olivet. The Jews come to Jerusalem to die, and a community gathered for that specific purpose will not be particularly gay, nor very careful about appearances.

The behavior of the worshipers was very peculiar and somewhat ridiculous. The men, with broad-brimmed hats, or whatever other head-dress they possessed, were reading or muttering prayers, and while doing so they twisted, and jerked, and wriggled about incessantly, and at times with great vehemence, that "all their bones should praise the Lord," as one of them explained the matter to me. When they began what was understood to be singing, it was the most outrageous concert of harsh nasal sounds I ever heard. It was Hebrew, too; but if David thus "praised the Lord," I should never have thought of calling him the *sweet* singer of Israel.

And yet, I presume, it was very much after this style that he and all his band of trained musicians did actually celebrate the praises of the Most High. You hear the same nasal twang and grating gutturals in the singing of every denomination throughout the East. The Orientals know nothing of harmony, and can not appreciate it when heard, but they are often spell-bound, or wrought up to transports of ecstasy, by this very music which has tortured your nerves. It is useless to quarrel about tastes in this matter. I have never known song more truly effective than among these

576 THE LAND AND THE BOOK.

Orientals; and no doubt the Temple service, performed by those trained for it, stirred the deepest fountains of feeling in the vast assemblies of Israel gathered at Jerusalem on their great feasts. They had also instrumental music, which

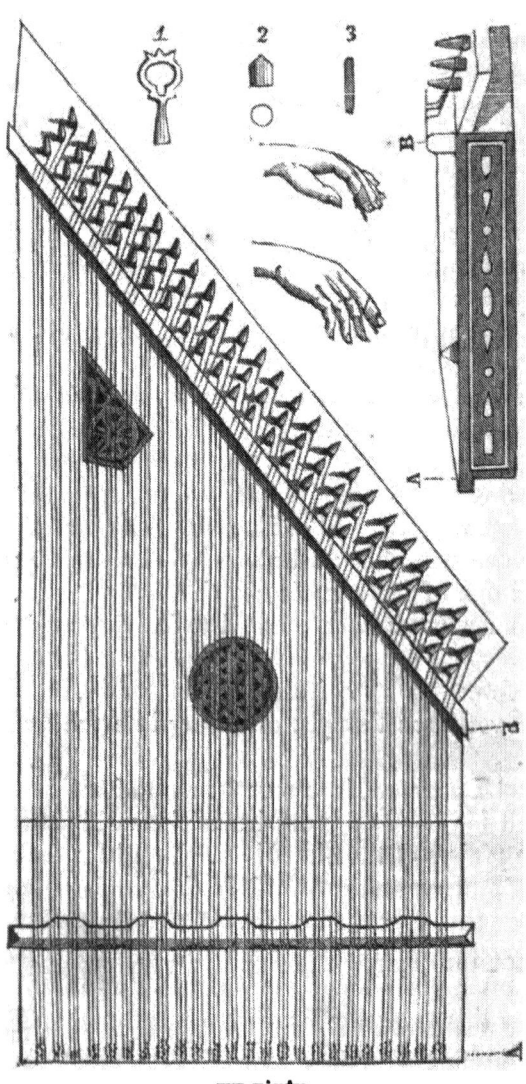

THE KÁNÛN.

these have not, and David himself was a most skillful performer.

I made that remark to my guide, and he immediately offered to take me to a coffee-shop where I should hear a grand concert of instrumental musicians. Thinking it would be a pleasant remembrance to carry away from the Holy City, I went, and was not disappointed. Seated on a raised platform at one end of the room were half a dozen performers, discoursing strange music from curious instruments, interspersed occasionally with wild bursts of song, which seemed to electrify the smoking, coffee-sipping congregation. They had a violin, two or three kinds of flutes, and a tambourine. One man sat by himself, and played a large harp lying upon his lap.

That is called a kânûn; and an expert performer, with a

KÂNÛN, AND MODE OF PLAYING IT.

voice not too sharp, often makes very respectable music with it.

There was one with a droll but merry countenance, who told stories and perpetrated jokes, to the infinite amusement of the audience, and now and then he played with spasmodic jerks and ludicrous grimaces upon an instrument called kamanjeh. There were also players on the guitar, and one

KAMANJEH, AND PERFORMER ON IT.

MODE OF PLAYING THE 'OOD.

of them had a very large instrument of this kind, over whose chords his nimble fingers swept, at times, like magic. The notes are much louder than those of an Italian guitar.

The Greeks, and especially the Albanians, manage this 'ood with the greatest skill. They have a small kind, which they take with them in their extemporaneous pic-nics, and on the shady bank of some murmuring brook they will sit by the hour, and sing to its soft and silvery note.

But the most popular of all music in this country are the derbekkeh, the tambourine, or deff, and the nŭkkairat, or kettle-drum, with cymbals, castanets, and the clapping of hands. At weddings, birth-days, and all other festal gatherings, this is their chief entertainment; and they will beat the derbekkeh, thrum the deff, rattle the castanets, and clap their hands in concert, without weariness or intermission, until long after midnight.

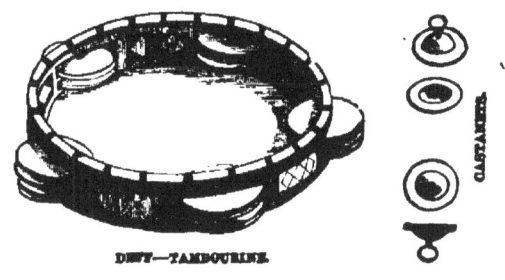

I attempted to look into the Temple area this morning at the pool inside of St. Stephen's Gate, but was rudely ordered away by some loungers within. This is the only instance in which I have been insulted during my walks about Jerusalem.

The Moslems have become suddenly very fanatical in regard to this holy harem, owing in part to the injudicious behavior of travelers. In company with a large party I was taken in by the British consul, and the old sheikh of the harem treated us with great respect, showing every thing about the mosque without reserve, and allowing us afterward to ramble as we pleased in the vaults below, and over the area above, without any surveillance whatever.

DERBEKKEH.   DERBEKKEH.

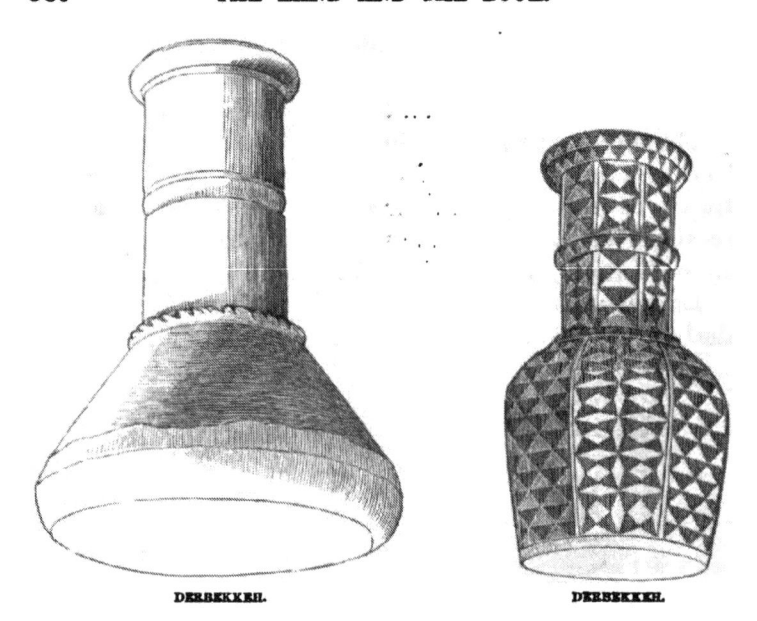

We entered by a small rude door near the northwest corner of the area, and walked in our ordinary shoes to the raised *stoa* upon which the Mosque of Omar stands. Here we put on red morocco shoes purchased from the bazars for the purpose, and kept them on until we left the Mosque of El Aksa.

The first thing that struck me within the inclosure of the harem was its great size. It contains about thirty-five acres more or less; for, owing to irregularities in its outline and boundaries, it is not possible to arrive at entire accuracy. It is about 1500 feet on the east side, 1600 on the west, 1000 on the north, and 900 on the south end. This large inclosure undoubtedly takes in, on the north, the whole area of the castle of Antonia. I noticed that the rock on the northwest corner had been cut away, leaving a perpendicular face, in some parts at least twenty feet high.

The surface is not a perfect level, but declines in various directions. From the entrance we walked over smooth bare rock, descending rapidly toward the southeast, then rose over greensward to the foot of the stoa, which may be ele-

MOSQUE OF OMAR—TEMPLE AREA.

vated about twelve feet at the north end. There is also a large descent southward from the Mosque of Omar to El Aksa, and on the east side there is quite a depression at the Golden Gate.

The stoa is not paved with marble, as has been often stated, but with slabs of the ordinary flagging-stone of this country. We have admirable drawings of the Mosque of Omar and its surroundings, and from them one obtains a good idea of the whole affair. The pen-pictures are immensely overdrawn, and the colored views are glaring exaggerations. Externally, at the base, the edifice is an octagon of about one hundred and seventy feet diameter, each of the eight sides being sixty-seven feet long. There are four doors at the opposite cardinal points. The dome is sustained by four great piers, and has twelve arches which rest on columns. There are also many other columns with arches which mark off the inner aisles. But you can study the details of this curious edifice in the works of Williams, Catherwood, Bartlett, Fergusson, and many others, if you have a desire to do so. Dr. Richardson's account of what he saw within the harem is also worth reading. We found nearly every thing mentioned by him, and very much as he describes them.

The beauty of the interior of the mosque is greatly marred by numberless contrivances for illuminating the edifice, and by railings and galleries which seem to answer no particular end that I could discover. The greatest curiosity is certainly the immense stone from which the name, Es Sakhrah (the Rock), is derived. It is a mass of native rock, the sole remnant of the top of the ridge of Moriah, some sixty feet long by fifty-five wide, and ten or twelve feet high on the lower side. All the rest of the ridge was cut away when leveling off the platform for the Temple and its courts. No tool of iron has left its mark upon this sakhrah, and I please myself with the idea that it was the basis on which the altar of sacrifice was arranged. Nor am I convinced by the reasoning of those who hold that the Temple was a small edifice erected farther to the south. It is not yet *proved* that the substructions by which the area in that direction has been extended are not of an age long posterior to Solomon, and therefore, on any scale of measurement, it must remain a matter of uncertainty just how far northward the Temple stood. Hence I do not quarrel with the tradition that the Mosque of Omar is on the site of that sacred sanctuary, and if this be so, the *sakhrah* may well mark the exact spot of the altar. Beneath the southeast end of it is a cavern, the bottom of which is covered with the usual flooring of the country. Stamp upon it, and you discover that there is a well or shaft below, and the sheikh of the harem told me that this shaft terminated in a horizontal passage, leading southward from some place farther back under the edifice, and that water descended along it. May not the blood and the ashes from the altar have originally been cast into this pit, and thence washed down into the valley of the Tyropean or of the Kidron, quite beyond the precincts of the holy house? Those who now speak of *fountains* in the inclosure must mean merely places where water is obtained from cisterns below the stoa. The curb-stones of these openings are deeply worn by the ropes of those who have drawn from these enormous reservoirs during many hundred years.

El Aksa was undoubtedly a Christian church, and probably the one built by Justinian. In converting it into a mosque, but little alteration was necessary, and hence we have the columns very much as they were in the original building. There is a close resemblance to the interior of the church at Bethlehem. The vaults beneath are very remarkable, but whether any of the huge limestone columns, with their architectural peculiarities, were of Solomonic times, I will not attempt to decide. It is my opinion, however, that there is nothing absurd in ascribing arches and columns to that age, for they were both employed in architecture long anterior to it.

Instead of attempting to describe these vaults, columns, gateways, and mysterious passages, I must direct you to the works of others, and to the numerous drawings of artists. I ran about, half wild with excitement, until I was quite ex-

VAULTS UNDER EL AKSA.

hausted. The main vaults now accessible are beneath the southeastern corner of the area. The piers which sustain the most eastern group are arranged in lines running from south to north, parallel to the outside wall of the harem. There are fifteen rows, at very unequal distances, ranging from about six to twenty-three feet apart. And so also the length of the lines is very different. Those which extend farthest northward may reach two hundred feet, while the shortest terminate at the solid rock in less than forty feet. The piers are built of blocks about four feet square more or less, rudely *beveled*, and laid up somewhat carelessly. This group of piers and vaults is succeeded by another farther west similar to it, but less every way, and they extend to the substructions beneath El Aksa. No one can examine them for an hour without being convinced that the pillars are made out of older ruins, and that the vaults spread over them are comparatively modern. There are many remains, however, extremely ancient, particularly near the southeast corner. The roof has fallen through in several places, and we descended to the vaults from one of these openings. The time will come when these interesting remains, in a most remarkable locality, will be fully cleared of rubbish, and thoroughly explored by scientific architects, and then we shall know what revelations they have to disclose. The description of these will take volumes, and, moreover, they will be very dry to all but artists and minute critics. I looked at the various traditional sites, Moslem and Christian, sat down on Solomon's throne and Mohammed's judgment-seat, and stood on the top of the Golden Gate for an hour, looking at this most suggestive spot and its surroundings. Olivet is beautiful, even in its present desolation, and the area itself, with its mosques, minarets, oratories, columns, cypress, kharûb, olive, and other trees, forms a tableau which will never be forgotten.

Nehemiah speaks of bringing *sheaves* into Jerusalem:[1] is it not singular that the people should carry their grain into the city to thresh it?

It would be strange with us, because our citizens are not husbandmen. In the East, however, the farmers all live in villages and towns, and *go forth* to cultivate the surrounding country. It is not unusual, therefore, for them to bring their harvest home to thresh it, and thus we find that Araunah, the Jebusite, had his threshing-floor on the present site of the Temple in the days of David.[2] The farmers brought their grain within the walls of Jerusalem at the time of Nehemiah to secure it against robbers, for the country was then in an unsettled and unsafe condition; and I do not suppose that he rebuked them for adopting this precaution, but because they did the work on the *Sabbath*. They made the disturbed state of the country an excuse for violating the law of God, which was clear and emphatic on this very point. In earing time and harvest thou shalt rest.[3] These people, as thousands still do, set aside this command, and maintained that during harvest and the vintage they must work on the Sabbath-day—so they treaded their wine-presses, gathered grapes and figs, and brought in sheaves on that day. If Nehemiah were here now, he would be grieved with precisely the same violations, and might also find men of Tyre who *bring fish*, and all manner of ware, to sell on the

[1] Neh. xiii. 15. [2] 2 Sam. xxiv. 16, 18. [3] Ex. xxxiv. 21.

JEWS LAMENTING THE DESOLATION OF THEIR TEMPLE. 587

Sabbath;[1] nor would he be able to break up these practices, and free Jerusalem from that sin on account of which God brought all this evil upon this city.[2]

No traveler thinks of leaving Jerusalem without paying a visit to the Wailing-place of the Jews in the Tyropean,

JEWS' WAILING-PLACE.

at the base of the wall which supports the west side of the Temple area. Those stones, no doubt, formed part of the

[1] Neh. xiii. 16.   [2] Neh. xiii. 18.

foundations of the holy house, placed there certainly not later than the time of Herod, perhaps long before. They are, however, not very large, and here, as every where else about Jerusalem, either the stones have been broken and *ensmalled*, or the measure used by Josephus was much shorter than has been assumed, or he greatly exaggerated. The latter is true, at any rate. There is not a specimen in any part of the Temple area, or about the castle of David, which even approaches the size of those which he repeatedly affirms were placed in these towers and walls. Still, those at the place of wailing are large enough for all the purposes of strength and durability.

No sight meets the eye in Jerusalem more sadly suggestive than this wailing of the Jews over the ruins of their Temple. It is a very old custom, and in past ages they have paid immense sums to their oppressors for the miserable satisfaction of kissing the stones and pouring out lamentations at the foot of their ancient sanctuary. With trembling lips and tearful eyes, they sing, Be not wroth very sore, O Lord, neither remember iniquity forever: behold, see, we beseech Thee, we are all Thy people. Thy holy cities are a wilderness, Zion is a wilderness, Jerusalem a desolation. Our holy and beautiful house, where our fathers praised Thee, is burned up with fire, and all our pleasant things are laid waste.[1]

South of this wailing-place are the great stones of the arch which Dr. Robinson identified as part of the bridge on which Titus stood in order to hold a parley with the Jews in the Temple. One of these stones is twenty-five feet long, another a little more than twenty, and the whole width of the bridge was about fifty-one feet, while its length across the Tyropean to the perpendicular face of Zion could not have been less than three hundred and fifty. Of course there must have been several piers and arches. The whole causeway is supposed to have formed a magnificent passage from Zion to the south porch of the Temple. The identification, history, and object of this gigantic work have in our day furnished an arena of debate and strife almost as noisy

[1] Is. lxiv. 9-11.

SPRING OF THE GREAT ARCH.

and earnest as when the Temple was sacked and burned by the Romans. It is subsiding now, and we shall do nothing to renew it. In consequence of a vast growth of cactus in that neighborhood, and the closing of the blind paths which formerly led to it, one can not reach the spot without much trouble, and few travelers now visit it.

Looking down upon the city this morning, and comparing the area with that of other great capitals, the question how Jerusalem could have accommodated the vast multitudes that resided in or resorted to her continually occurred to my mind with unwonted emphasis.

It has perplexed many before you, but the problem has been embarrassed by extreme assumptions. We are not required to find room for more than 200,000 *regular* inhabitants at Jerusalem in her highest prosperity and largest expansion. As to the 2,565,000 assembled at the Passover in the time when Cestius was governor, or the 1,200,000 shut in by Titus and his army, they were not citizens, but strangers. Josephus has given us an elaborate and minute topographical description of the city, from which, if no mistake has crept into his numbers, it is certain that the area within the walls did not much exceed one mile square. Other statements give larger dimensions, but we shall adhere to the thirty-three furlongs of Josephus for the entire circuit of the walls. Allowing for the Temple, there could not have remained more than the above superficies for dwellings, markets, offices, shops, streets, pools, and all other purposes and demands of a great city. Reasoning from these data, and from the statistics of *modern European* cities, Mr. Fergusson, in his ingenious but reckless critique, reduces the population to a very low figure indeed, and scouts the numbers of Josephus with utter contempt. But there are many circumstances overlooked or overleaped by Mr. Fergusson which must be carefully considered and allowed for if we would arrive at even an approximation to the truth. I do not believe his basis of calculation, that no modern European city has more than 25,000 inhabitants to the square mile. But, admitting this extreme statement, it does not follow, because modern cities have only this number, that therefore Oriental cities in olden times had no more! We must remember that these ancient cities were built within walls; that gardens, parks, and open spaces were excluded, and the entire area occupied with buildings; that the streets were narrow, and covered over with houses; that stores, shops, markets, etc., were small, and had dwellings in the rear and above them; that the houses were several stories high; that Orientals have even now but little furniture, and can and do crowd into very small apartments—an entire family in one room—many families in a single house; that the topography of Jerusalem, broken into valleys, is favorable to the erection of houses having many stories, as in certain parts of Edinburgh, for example; and, finally, that the pressure of a constant necessity would lead both the government and the people to make provision to receive within the walls the largest possible number. These things considered, it will not appear unreasonable to allow for ancient Jerusalem twice as many rooms on the *ground floor* as can be found in a mile square of any modern European city, and *double* the number of people, on an average, to each room. This would give 100,000 inhabitants upon Mr. Fergusson's own data. But there were doubtless two, if not three stories to the houses, and upper stories have more rooms and larger available space than the lower, and so always accommodate much the greater number of people. This at once furnishes accommodation for at least 200,000 inhabitants, and no impartial person who has opportunity to examine modern Oriental cities, or to observe how densely the poor Jews can and do pack themselves away in the most wretched hovels, will deem these calculations extravagant. But we are prepared to lay aside all speculations and theories, and take Jerusalem *as she now is* for the basis of calculation. I have seen *more than twenty-five thousand people in the present city*, nor was it overcrowded. Then it must be remembered that the whole of Bezetha, and a large part of Acra, is uninhabited; the space taken up by the Mosque of Omar is much larger than was that of the Temple; the parts about Bab el Mugharabeh and the southeast end of Zion are either plowed fields or overrun with cactus; the entire western face of Zion is occupied by the gardens of the Armenian convent; the space south of Calvary is vacant; convents, churches, and mosques take up much room; and, finally, that even in those parts occupied by dwellings, the houses are low, small, badly contrived, and many of them in ruins. All these things taken into account, we can readily admit that, if the whole area was covered over with high houses, economically built, a hundred thousand inhabitants could find homes within *the present walls*. It only remains to state that the southern half of Zion, all of Ophel, and the broad expansion of the lower Tyropean, is *without* the walls on the south; and so, also, on the north, is the entire space inclosed by the *third* wall, about which Josephus speaks in such glowing terms. Take in the whole, cover it with habitations as it once was, and I hesitate not to say that two hundred thousand inhabitants could dwell comfortably "within thy walls, O Jerusalem." Should any one think differently, I will not argue the point with him. We are not obliged to assume so high a figure, for neither the Bible, nor Josephus, nor any other old author gives such a number for the actual resident population of the Holy City.

How the vast multitudes at the great feasts could be accommodated may easily be explained. Let us take even the astounding statistics of Josephus himself, and suppose that the two millions and a half who partook of the Passover at the time of Cestius was neither an exaggeration nor an exception, it is by no means certain that one fifth of this multitude sat down to the Paschal Supper within the walls. The Jews originally were dwellers in tents. It is certain that in some parts of the country they did not abandon this custom, at least not until after many generations. The proverb, "To your tents, O Israel!" was not a mere Oriental metaphor; and the tribes, when they assembled at small places, such as Gilgal and Shiloh, *must* have come up with their tents, or, at least, prepared to sleep out-doors. Nor is even this last supposition absurd. The feasts occurred in the warm, non-rainy months, and throughout all the southern part of Palestine the people at this season do not hesitate to sleep in the open air, under trees, vines, or even in open gardens. Now not only two, but half a dozen millions of people could find room to eat and sleep on the mountains which are "round about Jerusalem." At such times, no doubt, every garden was thrown open, and every available spot occupied. We may gather this much from two incidents in the history of our Lord. When he drew near the city, and sent two disciples to prepare the Passover, they were to say to the man whom they should meet bearing a pitcher, *Where is the guest-chamber?*[1] implying the existence of such apartments, and the custom of allowing the use of them as a matter of course. Again, after supper our Lord

[1] Mark xiv. 12-17.

went out into a garden in Olivet.[1] Neither he nor his disciples owned a garden there, but the matter thus mentioned clearly implies that such gardens were on these occasions left open for all who needed them.

I have often tried to realize the appearance of these profound valleys and high hills around Jerusalem during the great feasts. Covered with olive-groves, fruit-orchards, and vineyards, beneath whose friendly bowers many a happy family and neighborhood group assembled, rising rank over rank to the very top of the mountains, I marvel that no artist has thought of reproducing this scene. Innumerable thousands gathered to the Passover, with happy children, busy servants, festooned victims, and all the joyful host, in picturesque costumes, hastening hither and thither, as business, or pleasure, or worship prompted, furnishing all the elements for the most magnificent and impressive panorama the world has ever beheld. It might require the life-time of the artist, but he who should realize the idea would need to execute no other work.

These hills, and valleys, and mounts lie all around the Holy City, as if on purpose for such convocations. The artist might arrange the tribes, with their ensigns and standards, round about Jerusalem, as they were commanded to pitch their tents about the Tabernacle in the wilderness. Judah would then occupy this Mount of Olives; for that tribe, with Issachar and Zebulon, encamped on the east side, toward the rising of the sun. Reuben, Simeon, and Gad, with their standards, pitched on the south. On the west were Ephraim, Manasseh, and Benjamin; and on the north, Dan, and Asher, and Naphtali.[2] Thus they continued to pitch and march for forty years. Now it is not improbable that when the Tabernacle was in Gilgal and in Shiloh this same order was preserved, and, as far as circumstances permitted, it might have been kept up even after the Temple at Jerusalem took the place of the Tabernacle. Without some well-arranged system, there would be endless confusion in such vast assemblies. Each tribe, therefore, had its proper station

[1] John xviii. 1.   [2] Numbers ii.

on these noble hills. Every important city may also have had its appropriate quarter, every village its terrace, every family its shady tree or sheltered arbor. Fancy now if you can this great city, thus surrounded by all Israel, assembled here to worship; the glorious Temple towering up on Moriah like a pyramid of snow; the smoke of victims and the clouds of incense ascending up to heaven from morning to night, while Temple, court, hall, street, valley, and hill-side echo and re-echo with the songs of Zion from millions of devout and joyful worshipers of the living God. Who would not join the sons of Korah in their triumphal psalm: Great is the Lord, and greatly to be praised in the city of our God, in the mountain of his holiness. Beautiful for situation, the joy of the whole earth, is Mount Zion, the city of the great King. God is known in her palaces for a refuge. Walk about Zion, and go round about her; tell the towers thereof; mark ye well her bulwarks; consider her palaces, that ye may tell it to the generation following. Let Zion rejoice; let the daughters of Israel be glad; for this God is our God forever and ever; he will be our guide even unto death.[1]

Josephus, near the close of his Wars, gives the following rapid sketch of the history of Jerusalem.[2] He who first built it was a potent man among the Canaanites, and is in our tongue called the Righteous King, for such he really was; on which account he was the first priest of God, and first built a temple, and called the city Jerusalem, which was formerly called Salem. However, David, the King of the Jews, ejected the Canaanites, and settled his own people therein. It was demolished entirely by the Babylonians four hundred and seventy-seven years and six months after him; and from King David, who was the first king of the Jews who reigned therein, to this destruction, were two thousand one hundred and seventy-nine years. It had been many times besieged and taken—first by David, then by Shishak, King of Egypt, afterward by Nebuchadnezzar, then by Antiochus, after him by Pompey, then by Sosius, then

[1] Ps. xlviii.   [2] Wars, vi. 10.

by Herod, and finally by Titus, in the second year of the reign of Vespasian, on the eighth day of the month Gorpieus —September. He closes the sad story with this affecting remark: yet hath not its great antiquity, nor its vast riches, nor the diffusion of its nation over all the habitable earth, nor the greatness of the veneration paid to it on a religious account, been sufficient to preserve it from being destroyed.

How much importance do you attach to the statement of Jerome, that the Salem of Melchisedek was near Beisan?

Not enough to disturb my settled belief that he was mistaken. I follow Josephus, and am convinced that his account coincides with the Bible; but the old tradition that Melchisedek was no other than Shem is a vast improvement on the Jewish historian. Such an origin for the city of the great king is so gratifying that one is reluctant to carry research into the cold region of critical skepticism. Let us therefore believe, if we can, that here the son of Noah founded the City of Peace, reigned in righteousness, and was priest of the most high God. Perhaps it was near his very altar that Abraham, in a figure, offered up Isaac— type of that other sacrifice, when an infinitely greater Father offered his only-begotten son on this same mountain.

From Abraham's sacrificial visit to the conquest under Joshua there is nothing said about Jerusalem. At that time it bore the name of Jebus, and appears to have been already a very strong place. Though the king of it was slain in the great battle of Gibeon,[1] the city did not fall into the conqueror's hands, nor was it until the reign of David that the Jebusites were finally subdued. Having taken the stronghold, he transferred the seat of government at once from Hebron to Zion, and ever afterward Jerusalem appears as the capital of the Jewish commonwealth, and the centre of the Hebrew faith and worship.

The siege of Jerusalem occupied Titus four months and twenty-five days—from April 11th, A.D. 70, to the 7th of September. After this destruction we hear but little of Jerusalem until the reign of Hadrian. No doubt it was

[1] Josh. x.

speedily occupied by both Jews and Christians, and I am disposed to credit Eusebius, who supposes that the city was not wholly destroyed by Titus. Indeed, such a thing is scarcely to be imagined. There were, doubtless, multitudes of the lower vaulted rooms uninjured, and in these, when slightly repaired, a considerable population could reside, and no doubt did. Indeed, it soon acquired somewhat the proportion of a city and the character of a fortress, for when the Jews rebelled against Hadrian, about A.D. 132, it was able to make a prolonged resistance. Having destroyed it, Hadrian built a new town, which he called Ælia, and for several generations afterward Jerusalem was only spoken of under this heathen name. Constantine restored its ancient name, and greatly enriched and adorned it with splendid churches and other edifices. Henceforward it became the grand centre of pilgrimages from all parts of the Christian world, and such it has continued to be down to the present hour.

Jerusalem during the last fourteen centuries has suffered terrible calamities and undergone many important changes. It was taken by the Persians under Chosroes II., with vast slaughter. The Basilica of the Holy Sepulchre was burned, and the city sacked and pillaged, about the year 614; and in 636 it was permanently wrested from the Christians by the Khalif Omar. From this event to the appearance of the Crusaders before her walls, about the first of June, 1099, the history of the city is almost a blank. There were, however, frequent contests between the Moslem rulers of Egypt and of Syria for its possession, and it suffered many calamities from its peculiar position and character, being sacred to Mohammedan, Christian, and Jew.

The Franks kept possession of it less than one hundred years, for it was given up to Saladin in 1187, and from that day to this it has remained in the hands of the Mohammedans. Saracen and Osmanly in succession have held it, and the flag of the Turk still floats over the Tower of David. Such is a rapid survey of the long history of Jerusalem. If it had existed 2177 years when overthrown by Titus, its

RYDAL.

whole age is now about 3964 years. Spreading over almost the entire historic period of the human race, it has shared largely in that history—*and the end is not yet!*

It took half an hour to walk over Olivet to Bethany this morning, and the distance from the city, therefore, must be about two miles. This agrees with what John says. Now Bethany was nigh unto Jerusalem, about fifteen furlongs off.[1] The village is small, and appears never to have been large, but it is pleasantly situated near the southeastern base of the mount, and has many fine trees about and above it. We, of course, looked at the remains of those old edifices which may have been built in the age of Constantine, and repaired or changed to a convent in the time of the Crusades. By the dim light of a taper we also descended very cautiously, by twenty-five slippery steps, to the reputed sepulchre of Lazarus, or El Azariyeh, as both tomb and village are now called. But I have no description of it to give, and no questions about it to ask. It is a wretched cavern, every way unsatisfactory, and almost disgusting.

I have never been so painfully impressed as to day with the importance of the advice not to allow mere topographical controversies to rob one of the delightful and precious influences which these sacred scenes ought to afford. We not only disputed about the tomb of Lazarus, but fell into an earnest discussion in regard to other matters equally indifferent—as whether Bethpage (of which no one now knows any thing) was east or west of Bethany, according to the directions of our Lord to the two disciples in reference to the ass, or whether it might not have been on the north or south of the village. Then came the grand question about the true site of the "Ascension," whether in this church at Et Tûr, or on the spur of Olivet, which lies over against Bethany to the north; and thus we walked through scenes suggestive of the most glorious anticipations to the Christian, with scarcely a single profitable reflection. Indeed, we came out of the Church of the Ascension with feelings of utter disgust.

[1] John xi. 18.

You have certainly fallen into a serious mistake. Olivet, including Gethsemane on the west, and Bethany on the east of it, has witnessed the most affecting and the most stupendous scenes in the history of our blessed Redeemer. It was in connection with this mount that the God-man—the divine Logos—chose to reveal more of his *human* nature than any where else on the earth. How often, after the fatigues and temptations of the day in this wicked and captious city, did he retire in the evening to Bethany to enjoy the hospitality and affectionate sympathy of Lazarus and his pious family. There he laid aside the awful character of prophet and teacher divine, to rest his hard-tried energies in the gentle amenities of social life; and such was the freedom of intercourse between these chosen friends, that Martha could even come to him with her little domestic troubles. Alas! how many Marthas there are, careful and troubled about many things, and how few Marys, anxious to sit at Jesus' feet and hear his word! As excuse for this Martha, we should remember that she was the responsible housekeeper, and that they belonged to the class of society in which the women of the family performed the household work with their own hands, and hence it was perfectly natural that she should claim the assistance of her younger sister. What a touching exhibition of lowliness and divine condescension does this reveal! He who was Lord of the universe selects, of choice, the humble poor for his dearest friends and most intimate associates. "He whom thou lovest is sick," was the only message sent by the sorrowing sisters. Most honorable distinction! He whom angels adored, and from heaven to earth hastened to serve, lavishes his richest love upon a poor man called Lazarus. The Son of God groaned in spirit at the sorrow of Mary and Martha. He *wept* over the grave of his friend. He did more. He asked of the Eternal Father, and received power to raise him from the grave, and, standing at the head of that dark cave, he cried with a loud voice, "Lazarus, come forth!" Wonderful voice! It startled the dull ear of death, and the inexorable grave heard, and gave up his prey. Here on Olivet the Christian learns to sing the song of victory over the king of terrors: "O grave, where is thy victory? O death, where is thy sting?" No wonder that much people of the Jews came six days after, not for Jesus' sake only, but that they might see Lazarus also, whom he had raised from the dead; nor that on the next day they should take branches of palm-trees and go forth to meet Jesus, crying, Hosanna! Blessed is the King of Israel that cometh in the name of the Lord!¹

Again: it was on this mount, with the city and Temple in view, that our Lord sat down, and in private answered those three pregnant inquiries of the anxious disciples: *When shall it come to pass that there shall not be left one stone of the Temple upon another? What shall be the sign of thy coming?* and the sign *of the end of the world?*² And in response there fell from his sacred lips those wonderful revelations recorded in the 24th and 25th chapters of Matthew. It was from this same mount, also, that the compassionate Jesus beheld the city and wept over it, saying, If thou hadst known, even thou, at least in this thy day, the things which belong unto thy peace! but now they are hid from thy eyes.³

It was also unto Olivet that he retired to pray on that doleful night when his sweat became as it were great drops of blood falling down to the ground.⁴ Here he was betrayed with a kiss; was surrounded by soldiers with lanterns, and torches, and swords; was rudely seized, bound with cords as a malefactor, and led away to Caiaphas.

And, finally, this favored mount witnessed the glorious out-come and consummation of this mystery of sorrow and suffering. It had been watered by his tears, had drunk his bloody sweat, and it must also behold his triumphant and glorious ascension to the right hand of the Majesty on high. Olivet first heard the grand commission to the Church: GO YE INTO ALL THE WORLD, AND PREACH THE GOSPEL TO EVERY CREATURE. He had led out his disciples as far as to Bethany, and, having thus spoken, he lifted up his hands

[1] John xii. 1, 9, 12, 13.   [2] Matt. xxiv. 3.
[3] Luke xix. 42.   [4] Luke xxii. 44.

and blessed them; and it came to pass that while he blessed them he was parted from them and carried up into heaven.[1] Men of Galilee, favored of God above all the race, I would, oh! I would have been of your company on that triumphant morning, with you to look steadfastly toward heaven as he went up, and with you to worship; or, better still, I would have been among the heavenly host that

> "thronged his chariot-wheels,
> And bore him to his throne;
> Then swept their golden harps, and sung,
> 'The glorious work is done.'"

[1] Luke xxiv. 50, 51.

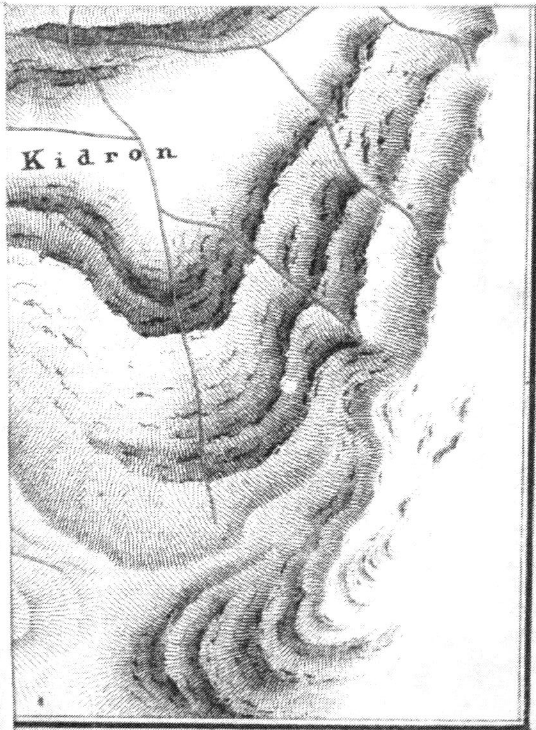
Kidron

INDEX OF NAMES AND SUBJECTS FOR VOL. II.

EXPLANATION OF TERMS AND CONTRACTIONS USED.

'Ain, Hebrew En, Fountain.
Beit, Hebrew Beth, House.
Deir, Convent.
Jebel, Mountain.
Jisr, Bridge.
Khan, Caravansary.
Kul'aet, Castle.
Mazar, Shrine.

Merj, Plain.
Nahr, River.
Neb'a, large Fountain.
Neby, Prophet.
Scr. all., Scripture allusions to.
Tell, Mound, Hill.
Vill., Village.
Wady or *W.*, Valley and Brook.

Abadiyeh, vill., 64.
'*Abd el Hâdy*, feudal family in Belad Nablûs, war of, 190–191.
Abel-Mitzraim, site of, 385.
Abimelech and Phicol, official titles, 352.
Abraham offering up Isaac, Samaritan tradition of, site, 210–213.
Abraham's mourning for Sarah, 381; oak of, and house of, 414–415.
Absalom caught in an oak; heap of stones on grave of, 284; tomb of, 481–482.
Abu Gúsh, robber of Kuriet el 'Aineb, 309.
Abu Zabúra, River (Kanah?), 259.
Achor, valley of, Hosea's prophecy concerning, 185.
Adullam, cave of, 424–427.
'*Ain el Fuliyeh*, not 'Ain Barideh, tepid fountains near Tiberias, ruins at, 99.
'*Ain es Sultan*, fountain of Elisha, 439–440, 444–457.
'*Ain Karim*, birth-place of John Baptist, 536; Fountain of Virgin at, 536; identification of site, 537; food of the Baptist, 537–538.
Ajalon, valley of, Wady Yalo, 304, 546.
'*Akil Aga*, visit to encampment of; adventure with a hunting leopard at, 156–157.
'*Akir*, vill., Ekron, 309.
'*Akkûb*, wild artichoke (Heb. gülgâl?), 357–358.
Amwas, vill., not script. Emmaus, history of, 307–308.
Ana's discovery of mules doubtful, 70.
Anathoth, birth-place of Jeremiah, 548–551.
Ancient population of Jerusalem, Mr. Fergusson's theory concerning, 589–592.

Antipatris, Kefr Saba, 259.
Ants laying up store, great robbers, 286.
'*Aolom*, vill. (Ulama), 156.
Aphek. See Fik.
Apples at Askelon, scr. all. to, 328–329.
Aqueduct in Wady Fedjas, 65; from Sübbarîn to Cæsarea, 238.
Arbela. See Kul. Ibn M'ân.
Arch of Titus, spring of, etc., 588–589.
Argob, country, not city, 54–55.
Arimathea, possibly present Renthieh, 290.
Arrâby, vill. in Jebel Nablûs, 192.
Arsûf, vill., possibly Apollonia, 268.
Ascension, church of, 599.
Ashdod, *Usdúd*, absence of ruins at, historical notices of, 320.
Askelon, approach to, 327; ruins of, described, 328–30; apples of, 328–329; sycamore figs of, 329; worship of Venus at, 330.
Athlît, Castellum Peregrinorum, Phœnician ruins at, not noticed in history, 246-48.
'*Aujeh* River, not Kanah, 259; mouth of, 265.

Baal, worship of, 497.
Balm of Gilead, 193–194; manufactured from seed of zükûm, 457.
Barak, battle of, with Sisera, 141–144.
Barchochobas, false Messiah destroyed, 538.
Barley bread, scr. all. to, 166; eaten by the poor, 511.
Basalt, rocks of, 5, 8; formations of, 89.
Bear, Syrian, 373–374.
Bedawin robbers, 22–23; adventure with, 40; bad character of, 45, 46; suspect travelers of seeking for lost treasure in ruins, 52, 53; resemble ancient

INDEX TO SUBJECTS.

Midianites, 163; attack before break of day, 167.
Beer Lahai-roi, site of, 350.
Beersheba, site of, 349, 352.
Bees in lion's carcass, 362.
Beisan, advantageous situation of, 175–176.
Beisan. See Bethshan.
Beit Jibrin, identification of, with Eleutheropolis, 358; with Gath, 360; ruins and excavations at, 360; character of inhabitants, 371; caverns, and idols, and inscriptions at, 375.
Beit Kod, vill., 186.
Beit 'Ur et Tahta, Lower Beth-Horon, 304.
Benhadad, defeat of, at Aphek, 54, 55.
Bethany, El Azariyeh, described, sepulchre of Lazarus, 599.
Bether, mountains of, 538–539.
Beth-Hoglah, 'Ain Hajla, 489.
Beth-horon, Upper and Lower, 547.
Bethlehem, visit to, 500–515; appearance of, 503; cave of nativity at, 504–507; birth of Jesus not in a grotto, 507; history of Bethlehem, 508; present inhabitants of, 508; reapers, gleaning, 509.
Bethpage, site of, 599.
Bethsaida, site of, discussed, 9, 29–32; not two Bethsaidas, 31, 32.
Bethshemesh, 'Ain es Shems, ark taken to, from Ekron, 309, 359.
Bethshan, Gr. Scythopolis, Arabic Beisan, 171; ghor of, 173; ruins and theatre of, 173–175; bodies of Saul and Jonathan taken from wall of, 174.
Birthright, Jacob's purchase of, 377–379.
Blessings and curses published from Mount Ebal and Gerizim, 204.
Bride of a Bedawy, 22.
Buffaloes, love of bathing, 9.
Butaiha, plain of, early vegetables on, 10.
Buttauf, plain of, identity with plain of Zebulon, 122–123.
Butter, not given by Jael to Sisera, 149.

Cæsarea Palestina, town there before Herod, 239; artificial harbor of, 239; scene of scriptural events, 239–240; ruins of, described, 240–242; causes of its desertion, 243; aqueducts of, 243; Cæsarea interesting to a missionary, 250–251; road from, to Jaffa, 252.
Caimon Tell, 219; probably ancient Sycamenon, 248
Cana of Galilee. *See* Kana.
Capernaum, reference to, by Josephus, 9; not in plain of Gennesaret, 31.
Carmel, Elijah's sacrifice upon, 220–226;
Vespasian's sacrifice upon, 228; description of Carmel and scr. all. to, 229–230.
Centipede described, 96, 97.
Chinneroth, site of, discussed, 69, 76.
Chorazin, Khorazy, site of, 8.
Christ, character of, wholly different from other Jews, 86–90; freedom from mercenary traits, 87–93.
Christian family on Zion, visit to, 569–570.
Circumcision, ceremony of, at Hebron, antiquity of the rite, 402; extensive spread of practice, 402, 403.
Cisterns used as granaries, scr. all. to, 262–264.
Cliffs, remarkable, on sea-shore, 260.
Cock-crowing, division of time, 552.
Colocynth, not cause "of death in pot," 179.
Columns, antiquity of, 348.
Contracts, Oriental, manner of negotiating them, 382–384.
Convent of the Cross, 535.
Cooking meat soon as butchered, scr. all. to, 162.
Covenant of bread and salt among Bedawin, 41; resemblance to the Eucharistic Supper, 42.
Covenants mentioned in Bible, 42.
Crib, Isaiah, chapt. i., a manger, 97–98.
Crocodiles in N. Zerka, 244.
Crocodiles, city of, 248.
Crusaders, imperfect histories of, 395.
Cucumbers of the Butaiha, 10; lodge in a garden of, 11.
Cyprus, salt marshes of, 43, 44.

Dalhamia or *Dalmamia*, ruin, possibly scriptural Dalmanutha, 60, 61.
Dancing-girls, Oriental, dancing, 345–346.
David, night's adventure with Saul, 21; battle with Goliath, 363; not recognized by Saul, 365–366; deceives King Achish, 367; his control over his followers, 369; contests with wild beasts, 373; his presence in Carmel, 416; tomb of, 477; tower of, 475.
Dead Sea, peculiarities of, 449 and 462–463; analysis of its water, 462–463.
Deborah, ode of, 148–150.
Deburieh, vill. at Tabor, 150 and 158.
Deceitful brooks, scr. all. to, 231.
Deir Senad, vill. near Gaza, wady and bridge at, 331.
Dew, heavy, at Sindiany, 235.
Dibs, grape molasses, 41.
Donkey, pugnacity of, 98; Egyptian, 407.
Dor, Tantura, city, 248.
Dorcas, grave of, near Jaffa, 281.
Dothan, Tell Dothaim, 193; miracle of Elisha at, 194.

INDEX TO SUBJECTS.

Doves' dung, probably a kind of bean, 200.

Ebal, Mount, 204.
Ed Diab, Bedawîn tribe, visit to, 40–41.
Eglon, *'Aglan*, site of, 856.
Egyptian perishing on plain of Askelon, 868.
Ekron, *'Akir*, 809.
El Aksa (mosque of), former church of Justinian, vaults beneath, 584–585.
El Hamany, vill., 819.
El Haram, ruin, precipice, and view at, 265.
El Mansûrah, vill. and ruin, 218.
Elah, Wady Sumpt, site of David's battle with Goliath, 368.
Eleutheropolis. See Beit Jibrin.
Eliezer, embassy of for Rebekah, 403–406.
Elijah at the Mukhrakah, 220–222; running before Ahab's chariot, 227; meeting Ahab, 228; convent of Elijah, 501.
Elisha raising to life the Shunamite's son, 177–178; miracle of in Dothan, 194.
Em el Fahm, vill., 192.
Emeer Hassein el Fudle, visit to his camp, 14–17; servants "born in his house," 14–15; evening scene at the camp, 15.
Emeers, Bedawîn, manners of, 899.
Em Khalıd, vill., watermelons of, 261.
Emmaus on Lake Tiberias, possibly Hamath, hot baths at, described, 66–70.
Emmaus, near Jerusalem, site of, 807–308; possibly Kuriet el 'Aineb, 540.
Endor, *'Ain Dûr*, description of, 161.
Engedi, *'Ain Jidy*, vineyards of, cluster of camphire, 419; David's adventure with Saul in caves of, 420; wild goats on cliffs of, 420–421.
En Haud, vill., possibly En Hadda, 248.
En Rogel, *Beer 'Aiyub*, described, 528.
Es Sakhrah (rock of), possible site of altar of the temple, cavern below it, 583–584.
Esdraelon, battle-field of nations, 191; character of the plain, 215; desolation of, 217 and 219.
Esdraelon, plain of, view of from Tabor, 137.
Etam, *Urtas*, vill., 423–424.
Evangelical narratives accordant with state of the country around Tiberias, 83–86.
Ezekiel's allegorical river explained, 580–585.
Ez Zoar, marsh near Cæsarea Palestina, 238.

Fairs, Oriental, description of, 151–155.
Falej, River, also called N. Arsûf, 268; babeer cane at, 268.

Famine in time of Elijah, extent of, 228.
Feasts of the Jews, numbers attending them at Jerusalem according to Josephus, 590–591.
Feudal families in Jebel Nablûs, wars of, 190.
Fik, vill. (Aphek), destruction of Benhadad's army in, 52–54; plain of, 55.
Fish, sacred, 880.
Fishing, different modes of described, 79–81.
Fleas, scr. all. to, Bedawîn dislike of, 94.
Flying-fish, 257.
Fog on plain of Philistia, 821.
Fountain, sealed, 423.
Francesco Cassini's travels in Palestine, 555.
French canal to unite Red Sea and Mediterranean by the Jordan valley, 216.
Fûleh, vill., scene of Kleber's battle, 216.

Gadara, *Um Keis*, not the scene of the devils in the swine, 84–88; warm baths below, 87 and 59.
Gamala, *Kul. Husn*, described, 49–51.
Gamala, destruction of, by Vespasian, 47–49; granite columns at, 51.
Gath, site of, discussed, 860.
Gaza, *Guzzeh*, population of, original site of, 884; mosque of, 884; commerce of, with Egypt overland, 887; Samson's adventures at, 838–843; wedding at, 848.
Gerar, site of, 848–849.
Gerizim, Mount, 204; Samaritan temple on, and view from, 214.
Gersa, ruin on east shore of Lake Tiberias, identification with Gergesa discussed, 84–88; mountains and tombs near it, 85; nature of the shore at, 86.
Gethsemane, garden of, described, 483–484.
Ghor Beisan, extent and fertility of, 173; scripture rites in, 176.
Giants, scr. all. to, 895; Rabbinical and Arab stories about, 396–897.
Gibeon and Gibeonites, their doom, 542–545; great waters at, and incidents connected with, 546–547.
Gideon threshing in a vineyard, 164; overthrows the Midianites, 165–167.
Gihon, valley of, 494; pools of, 523.
Gilboa, mountain, rain and dew on, 169; range of, 186.
Gilgal, *Jiljûlia*, 290 and 439–440.
Glass manufactured at Hebron, 893–394.
Gnats and fleas at Tiberias, 93.
Goats, wild, 421.
Golden gate, 478.
Goliath's battle with David, 864.
Grass on house-tops, scr. all. to, 574.
Gülgûl, possibly the wild artichoke, 857–858.

Hadathy, vill., 155.
Halhûl, vill., 415.
Hamath, water-wheels of, 279.
Hammath of Naphtali (Emmaus?), 66 and 76.
Hand-mills, women grinding at, scr. all. to, 295.
Harothieh, Harosheth of the Gentiles, identification discussed, 143–145 and 218.
Harvest scene in Philistia, 321.
Hauran, country of, 17.
Heber, the Kenite, on plain of Esdraelon, 144–145.
Hebrews, increase of, in Egypt, 408–409.
Hebron, first view of, 381; houses, population, pools, vineyards of, 388–392; glass factory at, 393–394; antiquity and history of, 394; not visited by our Saviour, 394; lower pool of, 410; houses and watch-towers in vineyards of, 411–412; scripture sites in neighborhood of, 416.
Hens not mentioned in Old Testament, 551–552.
Hermon, seen from Dead Sea, 438.
Herodium, Frank Mountain, Jebel Fureidis, 427–428.
Hinnom, valley of idolatrous worship in, 494–497; sacrifice of children in, 497–498.
Holy fire in Church of the Sepulchre, 565–566.
Holy Sepulchre, church of, 552–565; sacred shrines within it, 554–555; scenes enacted in it, 555–559; description of the edifice, 560–563; of the "Sepulchre," 560; of Calvary, 563–564; not site of the Crucifixion, 565–566; holy fire in, 565–566.
Honey in forest-trees and in carcass of a lion, 362.
Hot springs at Emmaus, 66–70; are hot springs mentioned in the Bible? 70.
House, Arab, construction of the roof described, 6–8.
Houses built with untempered mortar, 56–57.
Hûttîn, vill., horns of, 117; great hedges of cactus at, 117; legends of, 118; Saladin's victory at, 118.

Idolatry, prevalent sin of all Oriental sects, 493.
Imprecations, Biblical, on mountains, sites, etc., significance of, 170.
Irby and Mangles, discovery of mustard-tree by, 111.
Isaac at Gerar, 350–353; digging wells, 251; denying his wife, 352; his character, 353; deceived by Jacob, 354–355.

Jabesh Gilead, men of, rescuing Saul's body, 173–175.
Jackals used by Samson to set fire to the wheat-fields, 340–341.
Jacob with Laban at Mizpeh, 23–26; not returning to his father, 24; his favoritism in his family, 25, 26; meeting with Esau, 27–29; Jacob's well at Nablûs, 209; Jacob deceiving Isaac, 354–355, 398–399; Jacob his own cook, 399; Jacob's funeral, 385; his sons going down to Egypt for corn and their caravans, 407, 408.
Jael's killing Sisera, justification of, 146–148; nail used was a tent-pin, 149.
Jaffa, Joppa, Yafa, port of Judah, 273.
Jaffa history of, recent date of present city, 274; trade of, insecurity of harbors, 275; gardens of, irrigated by Persian wheels 275–276; fruits of, 280; profits of the gardens, 280–281; Dorcas and Simon the tanner, 281; gate of city, 287.
Jalûd, fountain of, 180.
Jarmuth, Yarmuk, 359.
Jaulan, Golan, Golanitis, 12; journey through it, 12–23; elevation of Jaulan, 16; tells of, and nature of country, 16, 17; trees and game of, 18–19.
Jeb'a, Gibeah of Judah, 359.
Jeb'a, vill. in Jebel Nablûs 197.
Jebbûl, salt lake of, 44.
Jebel ed Dûhy, Little Hermon, 158.
Jefat, Jotapata, description of, 105.
Jehoshaphat, valley of, described (Kidron), 478–481; fountains, tombs, and sacred scenes in, 478–484; tomb of, 482–488.
Jenuin, En Gannin, source of the Kishon at, 141.
Jenuin, description of, 139.
Jereed, playing with, 343–344.
Jeremiah, grotto of, described, 490.
Jericho, plain of, 439; present village and inhabitants of, 443; reflections at Jericho, 444, 451; site of the ancient city, 450.
Jermûk River, Sheriat el Mandhour, junction with the Jordan, 60.
Jerome, tomb of, at Bethlehem, 515.
Jerusalem, fountains, pools, and cisterns of, 523–525; age of pools, 526–527; ancient supply of water abundant, 525–526; has the amount of rain diminished? 527–528; fountain of En Rogel, overflow of, 528–529; Siloam, character of its water, 529–530; Ezekiel's allegorical river, 530–535; rocky region about Jerusalem, 541–542; scripture sites north of Jerusalem, Gibeah, Bethel, Michmash, Rimmon, Beer, and Ai, 551.
Jerusalem, first impressions of, writers

INDEX TO SUBJECTS. 607

upon charts and plans of, new discoveries not to be expected, common property of the Christian world, 467-468; conflicting theories concerning the topography of, 468-469; reconstruction of the ancient city impossible, 469; general platform of ancient city clearly defined, 469-470; topographical points admitted by all, 470; lines of all the ancient walls uncertain, 471; modern walls, character, age, and length of, 471-472; gates of ancient and modern, 472-473; streets and castles described, 474-475; excavations beneath the city, 490-492; scenes at Jerusalem during the great feasts, 592-594; history and population of Holy City according to Josephus, 590-595; incidents in history of city, 595-599; siege and destruction of, by Titus, 595-596; taken by Crusaders, 596.

Jews' wailing-place and ceremonies at, 587-588.
Jezebel, death of, 183; painting her eyes, 184.
Jezreel, Zer'in, valley and city of, 171; Hosea's prophecy concerning valley, 185; situation of, 180; approach of Jehu to, 183; wheat of, 188.
Jibbata, mentioned by Josephus, 182, 219.
Jiftah, ruin, possibly Gath-hepher and Jipthahel, 122-123.
Jiljûlia, Gilgal, 290.
Jimzu, Gimzo, 304.
Jisr el Kunatûr, bridge over the Jordan, 60.
Jisr el Mujamia, bridge over the Jordan, 60.
Joaiza, ruins, Bedawîn encampment at, 14; coldness of the night at, 16.
Job like an Arab emeer of the Jaulan, 16.
John the Baptist, birth-place of, 'Ain Karim, 585-588; food of, 587-588.
Jonah, tradition of his birth-place at Jiftah, 122; story of Andromeda derived from his adventure, 278.
Jordan, outlet from L. Tiberias, ruined bridge at, 58; windings and rapids, 63-64; insignificant appearance of, 488; allusions to in hymns, 488-489; banks of, 445-446; crossing of the Israelites, 446; overflow of, explained, 452-456; fountains of, 454-455; harvest time at Jericho, 453-454; fertility of its valley, 456-457; width and depth of the river, 458.
Joseph of Arimathea, city of, 290.
Joseph's tomb at Nablûs, 205.
Josephus, his battle with Sylla, 9.
Jotapata. See Jefat.

Jûb Yusef, well of Joseph and khan at, 6.
Julias, Bethsaida, 9; account of, by Josephus, 11.
Juniper-tree, 486-488; roots of, coals of, 487-488.

Kadesh Barnea, site of, 350.
Kana, Cana of Galilee, described, hunting ground at, 124-125.
Kaukab el Howa, Castle Belvoir, 156.
Keferrût, possibly Cephirah, 304.
Kefr Harib, vill. and castle, 55.
Kefr Kenneh, vill., its claims to Cana of Galilee, 121-122.
Kefr Kûd, vill. Capercotia, 192.
Kefr Nuffakh, ruin in the Jaulan, 18.
Kerak, ruins at, outlet of Jordan from L. Tiberias, possibly Rakkath and Tarichea, 58, 66.
Khalasa, Elusa, possibly Chesil, 349.
Khan et Tejjar, fair at, described, 151-155; Khan el Ahmar, 198.
Khurbet Arbâin, ruin in the Jaulan, 19.
Khurbet Samra, ruin at L. Tiberias, 56.
Khusm en Nusur, precipices above the marsh of Zoar, 237.
Kidron, valley of, 431. See Jehoshaphat.
Kishon, River, Nahr Mukkut'ah, sources of, described, 139-141.
Ksalis, Kesal, 140.
Kubbatiyeh, vill., 192.
Kuliet Ibn M'an, Arbela, fortified caves of, soldiers let down in boxes at, 114.
Kûly, alkali used in the manufacture of soap, 302.
Kunaitera, ancient ruin in the Jaulan, 19.
Kuriet el 'Ainab, Kirjath Jearim, not birth-place of Jeremiah, 589; residence of the ark, 540; Gibeah, 540; possibly Emmaus, 540; road from and distance to Jerusalem, 540-541.
Kusr Bardawîl, Castle of Baldwin, 84.
Kustul and Kulonia, 540-541.

Laban and Jacob at Mizpeh, 28-26.
Lachish, Em Lakis, site of, 856.
Latrone, vill., possibly Maccabean Modin, ruins at, 809.
Law of Moses, writing or engraving of, discussed, 204-206.
Leben, Arabic soured milk, scr. all. to, 149.
Lejjun. See Megiddo.
Lemuel's good wife, 572-573.
Lentils, 'Adis, 409-410.
Leopard hunting, adventure with one at 'Akil Aga's camp, 156-157; scr. all. to, 157.
Lepers, vill. of, 516; appearance of, 516; outside of the city gate, 200.
Leprosy at Damascus, 200; character of the disease, 517-520; Mosaic regula-

tions concerning, 516–517; Tacitus' account of the leprosy among the Jews, 517; various forms of, 517–518; manner of propagation, 518; Naaman the Syrian, 519; typical signification of leprosy, 519–520.
Locusts, visitations of, described, 102–108; young locusts near Tiberias, 102; contest with an army of marching locusts at Abeih, 102–108.
Lodge in a garden of cucumbers, 11.
Lydd, ruins of church of St. George at, 291–292; fine orchards and scenery of, 292–293; former trade of, 293.

Machpelah, Abraham's purchase of, 381–382; mosque over it, 385; age and character of the mosque, 586; Benjamin of Tudela's account of it, 386–387; Monro's description of it, 387–388.
Magdala, Mejdel, 108.
Mallows, food for the poor, 486.
Mandrake, apples of, 380.
Manger, description of, 98.
Manoah, village of, 361; jealousy of his wife, 361.
Mar Saba, convent of, described, 428, 431.
Masada Castle described by Mr. Wolcott, 417.
Masada described by Josephus, 418; massacre of Jews at, 418–419.
M'ather, vill. and beehives at, 155.
Megiddo, city, 142; battles at, 192.
Mejdel, vill. near Askelon, 330.
Melons, scr. all. to, 261.
Merj I'bn Omeir, 304.
Meskina, ruins of, 121.
Miamas, ruins and ruined theatre at, 236–237.
Midianites, overthrow of, by Gideon, 163–167.
Mills on Crocodile River, description of, 244.
Miracle of feeding the five thousand, site of, 29–31.
Miracle of casting out devils into swine, site of, 34–38.
Mirage on plain of Sharon, 287–288.
Mizferah, sulphurous spring, 39.
Modin, city of Maccabees, 309, 589.
Moloch, same as Baal, 497.
Moreshah, site near Gath, 360.
Mufjur, stream, 248.
Mukhrakah, place of Elijah's sacrifice on Carmel, 228–226; sacrifice at, by Vespasian, 223–224.
Mulberry (Damascus), fruit of, 296.
Muruibbah, stream of (Wady Surar), 310.
Music, Oriental, character of, 575–576; instruments used, performers and performances on, described, 576–580.

Mustard, wild, 100; Christ's reference to it, 100–102.
Muzzling the ox, scr. all. to, 316.

Naaman the Syrian cured of leprosy, 199.
Nabal's character, 369.
Nablûs, Shechem, description of, 203.
Naboth, vineyard of, 183.
Nain, tombs at, 158.
Natron, scr. all. to, 303.
Nazareth, original obscurity of, 129; present state of, 130; absence of remains in, 181; Chapel and Fountain of Annunciation, 132–135.
Neby Samwil, Mizpeh, 542–545.
Neby Sha'eb, shrine visited for cure of insanity, 118.
Nezib, Beit Nasib, 359.
N'keib, ancient site near Gamala, 53.
Nüsleh, ruin, 173.

Oak of Abraham, 414.
Og, size of, according to Jewish rabbis, 396–397.
Olive groves on plain of Gaza, 331.
Olivet, mount of, cottage on, view of Dead Sea and Edom from, 464; view of Holy City from, 464–467; sacred sites and scenes in connection with, 599–602.
Omar, mosque of, described, visit to, 579–586; dimensions of area, 580; character of surface, 580–583; Es Sakhrah, 583; sight of ancient temple and altar, 583–584.

Painting the eye, 184.
Parables of our Lord, naturalness of, 85–86.
Parched corn, 510.
Paul before Felix in Cæsarea, 240; as a prisoner in Cæsarea, 251; his route from Jerusalem to Cæsarea, 258.
Pella, city, Tubukat Fahel, 176.
Persian water-wheels, 276–277.
Philip and eunuch, route of, 310.
Philistia, plain of, fertility of, harvest scene on foggy morning, villages of, 321–324; resemblance to American prairies, 348.
Philistines, origin of, 255, 288–289.
Piles of stones on murderers' graves, 284.
Pilgrims' trip to Jordan described, 440–452; bathing of pilgrims, 445; character of pilgrims, 451; accidents of, and night adventures, 445–446, 451.
Pine stone, tree, 265; varieties of pine, cones of, scr. all. to, 266–267.
Pious fraud enacted in Lebanon, 85.
Plucking off the shoe, scr. and Arab all. to, 512, 515.

INDEX TO SUBJECTS.

Pomegranate described, 892; scr. all. to, 892–893.
Pools and fountains of Jerusalem, of Hezekiah, of Upper Gihon, of Lower Gihon, Well of Job, Pool of Siloam, Fountain of the Virgin, Bethesda, Birket sitt Miriam, 523–525.
Pottage, Esau's, 397; Frank children extravagantly fond of it, 397.
Potter and his wheel, 282; scr. all. to, 283.

Quagmires common in Syria and Palestine, 10.
Quarantania, Mountain of Temptation, 450.
Quarries near Cæsarea, 289.

Rachel stealing her father's idols, 24–25; tending sheep, 400; tomb of, 501–502.
Rain, unequal distribution of, 66.
Ramah, site of, 501–503.
Ramleh, tower at, 296–297; view from it, 299–300; vaults at, 298; origin of the name, church of St. John at, 301; soap factories at, 302.
Reapers, gleaners, 509–510.
Rebekah's marriage, history of, illustrated, 403–406.
Rehoboth, site of, 350.
Religion, a mercantile commodity in the East, 88–93; political rights guaranteed by religion, 91.
Renthieh, vill. (Arimathea), 290.
Rephaim, plain of, 500–501.
Rimmon of Zebulon, 128.
Rose of Sharon described, 269.
Rûm, ruin, Ruma of Josephus, 128.
Ruth and Boaz, 509–515.

Sacred shrines, fanaticism concerning, 493–494; their identification not necessary to faith, 566–569.
Saint Saba, 435; his residence in the desert of Judæa, 435–436.
Salt losing its savor, 43–44.
Salt lakes and marshes in Syria, 44.
Samaria, Sebustia, situation of, 197; view from, colonnade of, church of John Baptist at, 198.
Samaria, present inhabitants of, 199.
Samaritans, traditions about Melchisedek and Mount Moriah, 210–213; temple of Samaritans on Gerizim described, 213–214; Pentateuch of, 215.
Samson carrying gates of Gaza, 339; grinding at mill, 339; setting fire to wheat, 340–341; overthrowing temple, 340–342; wedding feast of, in Timnah, 362; character of his wife, 363.
Sand along the sea-coast, 255; effect on mouths of the rivers, 264–265; encroachments on plain of Philistia, 327.
Sanûr, plain and castle of, 197.

Saul visiting Witch of Endor, 168; death of, on Gilboa, 169; government of, a cruel despotism, 370.
Sea-coast of Syria, configuration of, 245–246.
Seely, vill., civil war in, 199.
Sefûrieh, ancient Sephoris, description of, 132.
Sehm Jaulan, probably Golan, 19.
Selûkia, ancient ruin in Jaulan, 18.
Semakh, village on south end of Lake Tiberias, the ancient Hippos, 57–58.
Semmunia, vill., 132, 219.
Sennacherib's approach to Jerusalem, 548–551.
Sepulchres of prophets, idolatrous reverence for, 493–494; of prophets, scr. all. to, 492–493.
Shadûf, Egyptian irrigating machine, 277.
Sharon, plain of, rose of, 269; extent and character of, 287.
Sheaves brought into Jerusalem on Sabbath, scr. all. to, 586, 587.
Shechem, Nablûs, Jotham's speech to people of, 209–211.
Sheikh Fareij, chief of Arab tribe, visit to, 19–22.
Sherd of pottery to take fire in, 284.
Shields and spears, 344–345.
Shochoh, Shuweikeh, town, 359.
Shrines, reverence due them, 498, 500, 553, 554.
Shŭgshab, ruin, probably ancient Sennabris, 65.
Shunamite woman and Elisha, 177; restoration of her land, 178.
Shunem. See Sulam.
Shŭtta, vill., 168.
Silk, gardens of, on the 'Aujeh, 289.
Siloam, non-poetic surroundings of, 529–530.
Simon the tanner, house of, at Jaffa, 281.
Sindiany, vill., camp-ground, 233; oaks and morning scene at, 234–235; insecurity of neighborhood, 236.
Sirocco wind, varieties of, 311–312.
Skaik, ancient ruin, possibly the Saccea of Ptolemy, 12.
Sling used at Hasbeîya, 372.
Slingers, left-handed, Benjamites, 372.
Soap factories at Ramleh, ashes, alkali used in manufacture of soap, 302–303.
Soba, Ramathaim Zophim, destroyed by Ibrahim Pasha, 539.
Sodom, plain of, ancient fertility of, theory concerning, 458–463; overthrow of, explained, 461–462.
Sogana (Sujan), 12.
Solomon's sacrifices and dream at Gibeon, 547–548.
Solomon's Pools described, 421–422; aqueduct from, to Jerusalem, 423.

INDEX TO SUBJECTS.

Sparrows, field, 260.
Spinning with distaff, 572.
Stanley, his adoption of Samaritan traditions, 210-213.
Storms on Lake Tiberias, 82-88; windstorm at Gamala, 51.
Strato's Tower, not original name of Cæsarea, 239, 247-255.
St. James's cave and tomb of, 481.
St. Mary's church and sepulchre of, 484.
St. Saba Convent, region about it, 428-429.
Sübbarin, vill. and fountain on Carmel, 288; aqueduct from, 288.
Succoth, Arabic Sakût, 176.
Sugar-mills near Jericho, 457.
Sujan, Sogana, ancient ruin, situation and view from, 12.
Sulam, Shunem, camp-ground of Philistines, 168.
Summach, ancient ruin in Jaulan, 14.
Swords and daggers, Oriental, 871.
Sychar, identification of, 206.
Synagogue at Jerusalem, visit to, singing and worship in, 575.

Taanach, village, Tiennukh, 42.
Tabor, Mount, height of, appearance of, from different points, 186; ascent of, 187; ruins on, 138; not scene of Transfiguration, 189; watershed between Kishon and the Jordan discussed, 139-141.
Tantûra, Dor, described, 248.
Tares, Arabic zowan, description of, 111-114; not degenerated wheat, 112-114.
Tarichæa at outlet of Jordan, site of, 58; Josephus's fleet at, 59; castle at, 65.
Tekoa, ruined village, 424.
Tell Abu Zabûra, columns on, 255.
Tell Caimon on Esdraelon, 219.
Tell Delwa, 18.
Tell Husn, at Beisan, 171.
Tell Kussîs on the Kishon, 218.
Tell Taalib in the Ghor, 56.
Tell Thora and marshes in Esdraelon, 142.
Tells of Jaulan, 16-17.
Temple area, fountains beneath, 584; vaults under it, 584-586; traditionary sites within it, 558.
Tent life, pleasures of, 163.
Tent-pins (watads), scr. all. to, 149.
Tesselated pavement, 570.
Theatre at Miamas, near Cæsarea, 287.
Thief, penitent, city of, 809.
Threshing-floors and machines, scr. all. to, 814-816.
Thuban, large ruin in Jaulan, 18.
Tiberias, city of, spared by the Romans, not visited by our Saviour, 74-75; ruins near it discussed, 75-76; sacred city of the Jews, 76; walls and buildings of, 76; heat in summer, 77.
Tiberias, lake of, north shore described, varied climate of, 5-6; storms on lake, 82-88; sunrise upon, 71; length and breadth of, 77; geological formation of shores, 77; absence of boats and fishermen upon, 78.
Timnath, Tibneh, place of Samson's wife, 859.
Tombs of kings, 487-488; of the judges, 488-489; of the prophets, 489-490; of Simon the Just and of the Sanhedrim, 492.
Tophet, type of Hell, 494, 498.
Tower of David, 475.
Trees, sacred and remarkable, 151.
Tubukat, Fahel-Pella, 176.
Tur'an, vill. and plain of, 121.

Um ez Zeinat, vill. in Carmel, 229.
Untempered mortar, scr. all. to, 57.
Urtas, vall. of, described, 431-482.
Usdûd, Ashdod, 820.
Usdum, ridge of rock salt, 461-462.

Vaults under Temple area, 584-586.
Via Dolorosa, 565.
Village of Ruth, 511.

Wady Nashif, near Capernaum, 8; Ruzzaniyeh, or W. Sulam, in Jaulan, 18; Tellaiyeh, in Jaulan, 18; Jermiah, in Jaulan, 19; Shukaiyif, night at, Arab encampment in, 20-22; Semak, east of Lake Tiberias, site of Kersa, wild boars in, 88; Fedjas, fountain and aqueduct in, 65; Hamam, fortified caves of Arbela in, Kul. Ibn M'an described, 114-117; Sherrar, 140, 155; Jalûd, 155, 176; Osheh, 178; Mukhurkush, 173; Yabis, 176; Belamy, 192; Küsab, 218, 229; Milhh, 218; Dalia, on Carmel, 282; Zicharíyeh, caves in, 804; 'Aly, 307; Surar, 310; Simsim, 357; Sumpt, battle-field between David and Goliath, 359; Suleiman, 547; Senaber, 876; 'Ain el Küf, 876; en Nar (the Kidron), 486; Kelt (Cherith of Elijah?), 458.
Watchmen on city walls, 412; of vineyards on mountains, 412-414.
Watering with the foot, 279-280.
Water-jars and bottles, 379.
Water-spouts on sea and on land, scr. all. to, 256-257.
Water-wheels of Hamath, 278.
Water-wheels, Persian, described, 276-277.
Wedding, Oriental, 430.
Well of Jacob at Nablûs, 209.
Wells, public, in plain of Philistia, 824.
Wells, digging of, 851; covered with

great stones, 400; typical significa-tion of, 400; washing sheep at, 401.
Wild artichoke, Hebrew gûlgâl, scr. all. to, 357-358.
Wives, Oriental, characteristics of, 363, 572-573.
Women grinding at a mill, scr. all. to, 295.
Women not insulted in Syrian civil wars, 191.
Wood panel-work, 571-572; best specimens of, at Damascus, 572.

Yaffa, vill., Japhia of Zebulon, 132.
Yalo, vill. and valley, Ajalon, 304.
Yebla, vill., possibly Ibleam, 248.
Yebna, ancient Jamnia, large agricultural town, 313; threshing-floors at, 314.

Yidma, ancient ruin, 156.

Zebulon and Naphtali, land of, prophecy of Isaiah concerning, 122-123.
Zechariah, tomb of, 481.
Zephath Horma, probably Sebâta, 349.
Zer'in, Jezreel, 180.
Zerka, Crocodile River, mills at, 241; camp-ground, night-watch at, 250.
Ziklag given to David, 367; taken by Amalekites, 368.
Zikrin, remarkable cisterns at, 376.
Zorah, vill. of Manoah, 359; Samson descends from it to Timnath, 361.
Zion described, plowed as a field, 475-476; sites and buildings on, 477-478; Armenian convent on, house of Caiaphas on, David's tomb on, Cœnaculum, 477; cemeteries on, 478.

INDEX OF SCRIPTURE TEXTS ILLUSTRATED IN VOLUME II.

ARRANGED ACCORDING TO THE BOOKS OF THE BIBLE.

Chapter.	Verse.	Page.
Genesis.		
iii.	14	332
x.	19	338
xiii.	10	461
xvi.	13, 14	350
"	14	351
xvii.	23	401
xxiii.	—	381
xxiv.	—	408
"	63	351
xxv.	11	351
xxvi.	12, 13	349
"	22	350
xxx.	14-16	379
xxxi.	29	23
"	40	16
xxxii.	24	29
"	27, 28	29
xxxv.	4	351
"	18-20	501
xxxvi.	24	70
xxxvii.	14-17	192
xliii.	11	194
xlvi.	26	406
xlviii.	7	501
xlix.	31	384
l.	25	206
Exodus.		
x.	4-14	107
xi.	5	295
xxviii.	34	313
xxxiv.	21	586
Leviticus.		
xi.	22	108, 537
Numbers.		
ii.	—	593
xi.	5	261
xiii.	23	411
"	32, 33	396
xx.	11	351
xxi.	3	350
"	6	333
Deuteronomy.		
iii.	13, 14	54
viii.	8	392
xi.	10	279
xxv.	7-10	512
xxvii.	—	208
"	4-8	204
xxviii.	—	208

Chapter.	Verse.	Page.
Joshua.		
iii.	15	458
viii.	—	208
"	12	551
"	28, 29	551
"	30-32	204
ix.	2-15	546
"	17	304
"	21	542
x.	12	546
"	—	595
xi.	28	338
xii.	23	290
xv.	7	528
"	30	349
"	44	360
"	46, 47	320
"	62	419
xvii.	9, 10	259
"	16	171
xix.	12	158
"	14	122
"	21	189
"	26	245
"	27	122
xxi.	29	141
xxiv.	25-27	352
"	32	209
Judges.		
i.	17	350
iv.	5	150, 352
"	14	142
v.	6, 7	219
"	24-31	148
vi.	2-5	168
"	11	352
"	19	164
vii.	13, 14	165
viii.	10	167
ix.	7-21	209
xiii.	2	361
"	20	361
xv.	19	351
xvi.	21	295
"	27	342
xix.	27	508
xx.	16	373
xxi.	8-12	174
Ruth.		
ii.	4	509
"	5-7	509
"	14	510
"	17	509

Chapter.	Verse.	Page.
ii.	23	510
iii.	2-7	511
"	15	511
1 Samuel.		
v.	6	320
vi.	10-12	309
vii.	1	540
xi.	1-11	175
xiv.	2	325
xvii.	2	363
"	34	509
"	35	373
"	37	364
"	40	352
"	49	509
xxii.	2	369
"	4, 5	424
xxiii.	29	419
xxiv.	1-6	419
"	14	94
xxv.	10	369
"	15, 16	369, 416
"	25	369
xxvi.	1-12	416
"	7	20
"	15, 16	21
"	20	94
xxviii.	11	163
"	13, 14	163
"	24	161
xxx.	3-5	368
2 Samuel.		
i.	17-27	169
"	24	186
ii.	13	547
v.	6	476
"	22-25	501
vi.	34	540
xiv.	—	494
xviii.	7, 8	284
xxiii.	15, 16	508
xxiv.	16, 18	586
1 Kings.		
i.	41, 42	529
iii.	4	547
iv.	13	54
"	33	161
xi.	1-7	548
xvi.	24	199
xvii.	1	220
xviii.	5, 6	220
"	8, 10	220

INDEX OF SCRIPTURE TEXTS ILLUSTRATED. 613

Chapter.	Verse.	Page.	Chapter.	Verse.	Page.	Chapter.	Verse.	Page.
xviii.	15–17	221	xxxi.	15, 18, 28	573	ii.	3, 6, 7	105
"	19, 28	221	"	17, 24	573	"	9	106
"	30	223				"	31, 32	311
xix.	4	436	*Ecclesiastes.*					
"	10	220	ii.	4–6	423	*Amos.*		
xx.	26–30	54	"	6	527	i.	2	231
			x.	13	56	iv.	7, 8	66
2 Kings.			xii.	4	295	ix.	2, 3	230
iii.	19, 25	351						
iv.	8–10	177	*Solomon's Song.*			*Micah.*		
"	19, 26	177	i.	14	419	i.	14	360
"	38, 41	179	ii.	1	269	iii.	12	475
v.	7	199	"	8	537	vii.	14	230
"	14, 15	519	"	17	538			
"	27	200	iv.	12	421	*Nahum.*		
vi.	13–23	194				iii.	17	106
viii.	8	178	*Isaiah.*					
ix.	17	190	i.	24	97	*Zechariah.*		
"	24, 26	183	"	8	11	x.	4	149
"	33, 34, 36	183	x.	28–32	551	xiii.	1	400
			xvii.	13	358			
1 Chronicles.			xviii.	4	322	*Malachi.*		
vi.	77	128	xxii.	22–25	149	iii.	2	303
xvii.	29	209	xxv.	5	312	iv.	2	249
			xxx.	6	333			
2 Chronicles.			"	14	294	*St. Matthew.*		
vii.	13	107	"	33	498	ii.	5, 6	508
xi.	6	431	xxxiii.	9	268	"	18	502
xxvi.	6	312, 320	xxxiv.	11, 13	329	iii.	4	107, 587
"	9	351	xxxv.	2	230	iv.	15	128
"	10	230, 351	"	7	288	v.	13	43
xxviii.	18	304	xxxvii.	26, 27	574	viii.	24	59
xxxii.	4	525	xli.	15–17	315	"	28	34
			xliv.	9–11	588	xii.	1, 2	510
Nehemiah.			xlvii.	2	295	xiii.	29, 30	111
xiii.	23, 24	320	liii.	—	412	"	31, 32	101
"	15	586	"	8	412	"	47, 48	80
"	16, 18	587	lxv.	10	269	xiv.	15–21	29
			lxvi.	24	498	"	39	60
Job.						xvii.	5	139
v.	15–19	231	*Jeremiah.*			xxiii.	37	551
xv.	23	56	ii.	22	303	xxiv.	41	295
xxiv.	16	323	vii.	31	497	"	3	601
xxxvii.	17	312	viii.	22	193, 194	xxvi.	34	551
xli.	24	295	xviii.	4, 6	283			
			xix.	1–12	497	*St. Mark.*		
Psalms.			"	5	497	ii.	1–12	6
x.	9	45	"	10	497	"	23	510
"	10	157	xx.	14	170	iv.	30, 32	101
xlii.	7	257	xxv.	10	295	"	38, 41	33
xlviii.	—	504	xxvi.	18	475	v.	1	34
"	8	477	xxxi.	15	508	vii.	31	60
"	12, 13	476	xxxii.	35	497	ix.	2–9	139
lxii.	8	300	xli.	12	546	"	44–48	498
lxii.	7	300	xlvi.	18	230	xiii.	35	552
lxxvi.	1–12	211				xiv.	12–17	592
lxxxiii.	13	358	*Lamentations.*			"	30	551
xcv.	6, 7	249	i.	16	545	xv.	43	290
cix.	23	106	v.	13	542			
cxx.	4	487				*St. Luke.*		
cxxv.	2	541	*Ezekiel.*			i.	39, 46, 47	587
cxxix.	6–8	574	xii.	5	323	ii.	8–14	507
			xiii.	10–16	57	"	41–49	452
Proverbs.			xlvii.	1–12	590	iv.	27	200
vi.	8	262				"	29	135
xi.	22	58	*Hosea.*			v.	4–9	80
xviii.	16	23, 369	i.	4, 5	185	"	18–26	6
xxv.	20	303	ii.	21, 22	185	vi.	1, 2	510
xxx.	27	107				vii.	11–15	158
xxxi.	10, 11	572	*Joel.*			viii.	26	34–36
"	13	573	i.	7, 15, 18	105	ix.	28–36	139

INDEX OF SCRIPTURE TEXTS ILLUSTRATED.

Chapter.	Verse.	Page.
xi.	47, 48	493
xii.	18, 19	264
xiii.	18, 19	101
xix.	42	601
xxii.	34	551
"	44	601
xxiv.	13	307, 504
"	33	307
"	50, 51	602

St. John.

Chapter.	Verse.	Page.
ii.	1–11	124
iv.	21–24	214
vi.	1	72
"	9	29
"	16, 17	30
"	23	72

Chapter.	Verse.	Page.
vi.	24	30
xi.	18	599
xii.	22	32
"	1, 9, 12, 13	601
xiii.	4–17	477
xviii.	1	593
xxi.	1	72
"	6, 7	81

Acts.

Chapter.	Verse.	Page.
ii.	19, 20	311
viii.	5	310
"	25–27	310
"	40	320
x.	28, 34, 35	240
xxi.	8–11	251
xxvii.	2	252

Romans.

Chapter.	Verse.	Page.
iv.	11	403
ix.	20	183

1 Corinthians.

Chapter.	Verse.	Page.
ix.	10	319

Hebrews.

Chapter.	Verse.	Page.
xii.	14	194

2 Peter.

Chapter.	Verse.	Page.
iii.	16	283

Revelation.

Chapter.	Verse.	Page.
xviii.	22	295

THE END.

By William C. Prime.

Boat Life in Egypt & Nubia.

Boat Life in Egypt and Nubia. By WILLIAM C. PRIME, Author of "The Old House by the River," "Later Years," &c. Illustrations. 12mo, Muslin, $1 25.

Tent Life in the Holy Land.

By WILLIAM C. PRIME, Author of "The Old House by the River," "Later Years," &c. Illustrations. 12mo, Muslin, $1 25.

The Old House by the River.

By WILLIAM C. PRIME, Author of the "Owl Creek Letters." 12mo, Muslin, 75 cents.

Later Years. .

By WILLIAM C. PRIME, Author of "The Old House by the River." 12mo, Muslin, $1 00.

LA PLATA:

THE ARGENTINE CONFEDERATION,

AND

PARAGUAY.

Being a Narrative of the Exploration of the Tributaries of the River La Plata and Adjacent Countries, during the Years 1853, '54, '55, and '56, under the orders of the United States Government.

By THOMAS J. PAGE, U.S.N.,
Commander of the Expedition.

One Volume Large Octavo, with Map and numerous Illustrations. Muslin, Three Dollars.

This Volume contains the Official Narrative of one of the most important expeditions ever sent out by our Government. Early in 1853 the steamer *Water Witch* was placed under the command of Lieutenant PAGE, with instructions to explore the Rivers of La Plata, and report upon their navigability and adaptation to commerce. Lieutenant PAGE executed his commission with rare fidelity and intelligence, and has embodied the results in this volume. The explorations described in the Narrative embrace an extent of 3600 miles of river navigation, and 4400 miles of journey by land in Paraguay and the Argentine Confederation. The River Paraguay alone was found to be navigable, at low water, by a steamer drawing nine feet, for more than two thousand miles from the ocean. The basin of La Plata is almost equal in extent to that of the Mississippi, and not inferior in salubrity of climate and fertility of soil, while the head waters of its rivers penetrate the richest mineral provinces of Brazil and Bolivia. The products of this region must find their outlet through the River La Plata. The population numbers scarcely one person to a square mile, but great inducements to emigration are now offered by the Argentine Confederation. The commerce of the country, already considerable, is capable of immediate and almost indefinite increase.

Lieutenant PAGE's Narrative contains ample information respecting the soil, climate, and productions of the country, and the manners, habits, and customs of the people. A full account is given of the unfortunate rupture with Paraguay, showing conclusively that the attack upon the *Water Witch* was altogether unwarranted, and the allegations by which President Lopez attempted to justify it entirely destitute of truth. An interesting and valuable account of the Jesuit Missions in La Plata is appended to the Narrative.

The Illustrations comprise the accurate Map of the Country prepared by the orders of our Government, Portraits of Urquiza, Lopez, Francia, and Loyola, and numerous Engravings of Scenery, Character, and Incident.

Published by HARPER & BROTHERS,
Franklin Square, New York.

HARPER & BROTHERS will send the above Work by Mail, postage paid, to any part of the United States, on receipt of $3 00.

DR. LIVINGSTONE'S TRAVELS.

Missionary Travels and Researches in South Africa; including a Sketch of Sixteen Years' Residence in the Interior of Africa, and a Journey from the Cape of Good Hope to Loando on the West Coast; thence across the Continent, down the River Zambesi, to the Eastern Ocean. By DAVID LIVINGSTONE, LL.D., D.C.L. Two Maps by ARROWSMITH, a Portrait on Steel, and numerous Illustrations. New Edition, with Copious Index. One Volume, 8vo, Price $3 00.

NOTICE.

Messrs. HARPER & BROTHERS take this opportunity of cautioning the public against several spurious publications, which, by artful advertisements, are made to appear as though emanating from Dr. Livingstone. They are authorised to say that Dr. Livingstone repudiates them entirely, and wishes it to be generally known that the present work is the *only authentic narrative of his Adventures and Travels in Africa.*

A book which, before it has been ten days in the hands of the public, will have been perused by perhaps 80,000 readers—a book second only to Lord Macaulay's History of England in the inordinate extent of its circulation. No wonder—it addresses itself to large and numerous classes—the great religious world, the commercial world, the scientific.—*Literary Gazette.*

The book is one of the most captivating description; in style simple, clear, and graphic, and in matter such as no other living traveler's experience could afford. From the beginning to the end of the volume there is not a page that does not compel the attention, not a page that does not offer something novel. It is a wonder-book all through.—*N. Y. Courier and Enquirer.*

This remarkable narrative, distinguished throughout by the modesty characteristic of true merit. Clear, concise, unaffected, and fluent, it charms the reader, and bears him along irresistibly, securing his attention from first to last.—*N. Y. Commercial Advertiser.*

At once scientific, literary, and religious, it deserves to be read and studied by all classes.—*Boston Post.*

A new chapter in the history of the world.—*Boston Leader.*

Since the days of Mandeville, Marco Polo, and Captain Cooke, no one person has traversed a more extended theatre of travel, or added more to the great discoveries of the world than Dr. Livingstone. The work combines the dignity of scientific research with thrilling narratives of personal adventure.—*Richmond Enquirer.*

The African Columbus has broken the egg, and let the world into his secret. What he has achieved, and endured, and conquered; the witchcraft which, for sixteen years, he has used against a vertical sun and a malign climate—how he has run the gauntlet of carnivores and pachyderms, and ophidia—how he has lived on roots, and locusts, and frogs, and moistened his mouth only with rain or river water—how he has striven with thirst and fever, with the loss of letters and the absence of intelligent companionship—how he has sounded unknown lakes, broken through thorny jungles, navigated unknown rivers, opened to light a world teeming with floral, animal, and mineral wonders—obtaining ingress for science, for commerce, for religion—and leading after him, as the special spoils of his expedition, a throng of colored indigeni, drawn along by no other fetters save of love and admiration. So runs the story of his book—a book not so much of travel and adventure as, in its purport and spacious relation, a veritable poem.—*Athenæum.*

The book will be sought for and read with more eagerness than a romance.—*N. Y. Observer.*

Published by **HARPER & BROTHERS,**
Franklin Square, New York.

⁂ HARPER & BROTHERS will send the above Work by Mail, postage paid (for any distance in the United States under 3000 miles), on receipt of Three Dollars.

"The most magnificent contribution of the present century to the cause of geographical knowledge."

DR. BARTH'S
NORTH AND CENTRAL AFRICA.

Travels and Discoveries in North and Central Africa. Being a Journal of an Expedition undertaken under the Auspices of H.B.M's Government in the Years 1849-1855. By HENRY BARTH, Ph.D., D.C.L., Fellow of the Royal Geographical and Asiatic Societies, &c., &c. Profusely and elegantly illustrated. Complete in 3 vols. 8vo, Muslin, $2 50 a Volume; Half Calf, $10 50 a set.

Dr. Barth's wonderful travels approach the Equator from the North as nearly as Dr. Livingstone's from the South, and thus show to future travelers the field which still remains open for exploration and research.—Vol. III., completing the work, is in the press, and will be published shortly.

The researches of Dr. Barth are of the highest interest. Few men have existed so qualified, both by intellectual ability and a vigorous bodily constitution, for the perilous part of an African discoverer as Dr. Barth.—*London Times, Sept.* 8, 1857.

It richly merits all the commendation bestowed upon it by "the leading journal of Europe."—*Corr. National Intelligencer.*

Every chapter presents matter of more original interest than an ordinary volume of travels.—*London Leader.*

For extent and variety of subjects, the volumes before us greatly surpass every other work on African travel with which it has been our fortune to meet.—*London Athenæum.*

Dr. Barth is the model of an explorer—patient, persevering, and resolute.—*London Spectator.*

No one who wishes to know Africa can afford to dispense with this work.—*Boston Traveler.*

A most wonderful record.—*Poughkeepsie Democrat.*

It is the most magnificent contribution of the present century to the cause of geographical knowledge.—*N. Y. Evangelist.*

The most important contribution to Geographical Science that has been made in our time. Thousands of readers in our country will be anxious to get possession of this treasure of knowledge.—*N. Y. Observer.*

One of the most important works of the kind which has appeared for an age.—*Lutheran Observer.*

It can not fail to find its way into the libraries of most scholars.—*Lynchburg Virginian.*

The personal details give the work great interest.—*Philadelphia Press.*

Dr. Barth's work is a magnificent contribution to geographical and ethnographical science.—*N. Y. Independent.*

Your curiosity is awakened, step by step, as with diminished resources he works his way through fanatical and rapacious tribes, ready in resources and never desponding, and buoyed up by the unconquerable desire to surpass his predecessors in the thoroughness and in the range of his discoveries.—*Albion.*

Among the most wonderful achievements of modern times.—*Western Christian Advocate.*

A most valuable contribution to the standard literature of the world.—*Troy Times.*

Published by **HARPER & BROTHERS**,
Franklin Square, New York.

*** HARPER & BROTHERS will send the above Work by Mail, postage paid (for any distance in the United States under 3000 miles), on receipt of the Money.

☞ Every Number of Harper's Magazine contains from 20 to 50 pages—and from one third to one half more reading—than any other in the country.

HARPER'S MAGAZINE.

THE Publishers believe that the Nineteen Volumes of HARPER'S MAGAZINE now issued contain a larger amount of valuable and attractive reading than will be found in any other periodical of the day. The best Serial Tales of the foremost Novelists of the time: LEVERS' "Maurice Tiernay," BULWER LYTTON'S "My Novel," DICKENS'S "Bleak House" and "Little Dorrit," THACKERAY'S "Newcomes" and "Virginians," have successively appeared in the Magazine simultaneously with their publication in England. The best Tales and Sketches from the Foreign Magazines have been carefully selected, and original contributions have been furnished by CHARLES READE, WILKIE COLLINS, Mrs. GASKELL, Miss MULOCH, and other prominent English writers.

The larger portion of the Magazine has, however, been devoted to articles upon American topics, furnished by American writers. Contributions have been welcomed from every section of the country; and in deciding upon their acceptance the Editors have aimed to be governed solely by the intrinsic merits of the articles, irrespective of their authorship. Care has been taken that the Magazine should never become the organ of any local clique in literature, or of any sectional party in politics.

At no period since the commencement of the Magazine have its literary and artistic resources been more ample and varied; and the Publishers refer to the contents of the Periodical for the past as the best guarantee for its future claims upon the patronage of the American public.

TERMS.—One Copy for One Year, $3 00; Two Copies for One Year, $5 00; Three or more Copies for One Year (each), $2 00; "Harper's Magazine" and "Harper's Weekly," One Year, $4 00. *And an Extra Copy, gratis, for every Club of* TEN SUBSCRIBERS.

Clergymen and Teachers supplied at Two DOLLARS a year. The Semi-Annual Volumes bound in Cloth, $2 50 each. Muslin Covers, 25 cents each. The Postage upon HARPER'S MAGAZINE must be paid at the Office *where it is received.* The Postage is *Thirty-six Cents a year.*

HARPER & BROTHERS, Publishers, Franklin Square, New York.

HARPER'S WEEKLY.
A JOURNAL OF CIVILIZATION.

A First-class Illustrated Family Newspaper
PRICE FIVE CENTS.

HARPER'S WEEKLY has now been in existence three years. During that period no effort has been spared to make it the best possible Family Paper for the American People, and it is the belief of the Proprietors that, in the peculiar field which it occupies, no existing Periodical can compare with it.

Every Number of HARPER'S WEEKLY contains all the News of the week, Domestic and Foreign. The completeness of this department is, it is believed, unrivaled in any other weekly publication. Every noteworthy event is profusely and accurately illustrated at the time of its occurrence. And while no expense is spared to procure Original Illustrations, care is taken to lay before the reader every foreign picture which appears to possess general interest. In a word, the Subscriber to HARPER'S WEEKLY may rely upon obtaining a Pictorial History of the times in which we live, compiled and illustrated in the most perfect and complete manner possible. It is believed that the Illustrated Biographies alone—of which about one hundred and fifty have already been published—are worth far more to the reader than the whole cost of his subscription.

The literary matter of HARPER'S WEEKLY is supplied by some of the ablest writers in the English language. Every Number contains an installment of a serial story by a first-class author—BULWER'S "*What will he do with It?*" has appeared entire in its columns; one or more short Stories, the best that can be purchased at home or abroad; the best Poetry of the day; instructive Essays on topics of general interest; Comments on the Events of the time, in the shape of Editorials and the Lounger's philosophic and amusing Gossip; searching but generous Literary Criticisms; a Chess Chronicle; and full and careful reports of the Money, Merchandise, and Produce Markets.

In fixing at so low a price as Five Cents the price of their paper, the Publishers were aware that nothing but an enormous sale could remunerate them. They are happy to say that the receipts have already realized their anticipations, and justify still further efforts to make HARPER'S WEEKLY an indispensable guest in every home throughout the country.

TERMS.—One Copy for Twenty Weeks, $1 00; One Copy for One Year, $2 50; One Copy for Two Years, $4 00; Five Copies for One Year, $9 00; Twelve Copies for One Year, $20 00; Twenty-five Copies for One Year, $40 00. *An Extra Copy will be allowed for every Club of* TWELVE *or* TWENTY-FIVE SUBSCRIBERS.

32101 063698748

Lightning Source UK Ltd.
Milton Keynes UK
UKHW020818020919
348932UK00005B/37/P